BOOK REPORTS

ROBERT
CHRISTGAU

BOOK REPORTS

A Music Critic on His First Love, Which Was Reading

DUKE UNIVERSITY PRESS *Durham and London* 2019

Printed in the United States of America on acid-free paper ∞
Designed by Matthew Tauch
Typeset in Minion Pro by Westchester Publishing Services
Cataloging-in-Publication Data is available from the Library of Congress.

ISBN 9781478000112 (hardcover : alk. paper)
ISBN 9781478000303 (pbk. : alk. paper)
ISBN 9781478002123 (ebook)

"The Pop-Boho Connection, Narrativized: Bernard Gendron's *Between Montmartre and the Mudd Club*" previously published as "The Pop-Boho Connection: History as Discourse, or Is It the Other Way Around?" © Summer 2002, *Bookforum*
Review of David Wondrich's *Stomp and Swerve*, October 9 issue © 2006, *Seattle Weekly*
"The Impenetrable Heroism of Sam Cooke: Peter Guralnick's Dream Boogie," previously published as "In Search of Sam Cooke" © 2005, *The Nation*
"A Darker Shade of Noir: The Indefatigable Walter Mosley," © 2006, *The Nation*
"Biography of a Corporation" published in *Where Did Our Love Go?* © Nelson George
All selections that have appeared in *The New York Times* are reprinted here by permission.
All selections that have appeared in *The Village Voice* are reprinted by permission.

In memory of Marshall Berman

1940–2013

who read more books than anyone I've ever known

except maybe Simon Frith

(and Jonathan Lethem)

Contents

V Fictions

VI Bohemia Meets Hegemony

Acknowledgments

These 80 reviews and essays date back to 1970, so long ago I often can't remember who edited them. But I thank everyone who did. Post 1980, my memory improves, with three enablers earning their own sentences. M. Mark, the onetime copy chief I'd asked to be my *Village Voice* editor even before she conceived the *Voice Literary Supplement*, oversaw selections as evanescent as "15 Minutes of . . ." and as massive as "Living in a Material World," neither of which anyone else would have published. At the *Los Angeles Times*, Steve Wasserman steered me to life-changing books by Dave Hickey and Ned Sublette as well as many merely excellent ones. And in the '10s *Barnes & Noble Review*'s Bill Tipper nurtured my every enthusiasm as he oversaw a quarter of this collection. Nor have I forgotten Michael Anderson welcoming me to the *NYTBR*, Adam Shatz letting me go long at *The Nation*, *Voice* editors Scott Malcomson, Michael Miller, and Joy Press picking up where M. left off, former *Voice* music editors Eric Weisbard and Ann Powers overseeing a pop conference where Henry Pleasants and Charlie Gillett fit right in, or *Voice* editor Ed Park alerting *The Believer* to a minstrelsy overview the journal that convinced me to write it gratis decided was over its readers' heads. Thanks as well to my old friend Greil Marcus for enthusiastically supporting this project and my rabbi without portfolio Joe Levy for ongoing conceptual and promotional suasion as well as last-lap editing. Warmest ongoing thanks to my dear friend and forebearing agent Sarah Lazin and her editorial assistant extraordinaire Margaret Shultz, who pitched in on more details than I have the heart or humility to enumerate. At Duke University Press, Sara Leone and Stephanie Gomez Menzies oversaw production and Laura Sell, Chad Royal, and Jennifer Schaper kept spreading the news. But my deepest thanks there go to Ken Wissoker, who decided that I had not one collection to write for Duke—that would be 2017's *Is Is Still Good to Ya?*—but two.

Have I forgotten anybody? Of course not, just saved her for last. Adoring gratitude to my wife, Carola Dibbell, who improved the manuscript discreetly from "The Informer" to "My Friend Marshall" and kept thinking about it when she had far more urgent matters on her mind. It's my dearest hope that I can return the favor sooner rather than later, and my nagging regret that I didn't scare up the chutzpah to devote a chapter here to her novel, *The Only Ones*, a cult hit I know very well indeed.

Introduction

I learned to read first week of first grade and never looked back. By age seven I was reading everything I could get my eyes on, with a major in baseball journalism and a minor in ladies-magazine fiction. But soon I loved books even more, meaning the youth classics and middlebrow bestsellers a culturally aspirational lower-middle-class family had around the house (plus baseball novels from the holy Queensborough Public Library). In high school, rock and roll slowed me down some, but only some—the Bantam *Grapes of Wrath* I read on the 7 train to my college interview so impressed my designated alumnus it helped get me into Dartmouth. And there I quickly decided that I wanted to be a writer rather than a lawyer and dove into Literature with a capital L: all-lit all-the-time coursework augmented with moderns in the summertime, when I cheated on my parkie hours to lap up *U.S.A.* and try to love *Steppenwolf.* I kept three or four books in my backpack as I hitchhiked the country in 1963—a novel or two, some American studies theory, and my complete Yeats. And in 1964, while somehow managing to spend less than I took home at a Chicago encyclopedia company as I failed to write a decent short story or get through *The Charterhouse of Parma* in French, I discovered the journalism collection, which changed my life as much as English 2.

First came a fifty-cent Pocket Book called *The Best of Red Smith*, a sportswriting generalist whose casual lucidity, calm morality, and unassuming punch lines I'd been drawn to young by my baseball major. But thanks to Hemingway and Mailer, I was also interested in boxing, so I picked up a Grove paperback called *The Sweet Science*, where *New Yorker* press-food-pugilism critic A. J. Liebling quickly surpassed Hemingway and Mailer as a role model. Think about it—why shouldn't the path to rock criticism lead through sportswriting? Sportswriting celebrates popular pleasures and rewards colloquial color; the symbolic events it details gain resonance in a telling that's most telling when it exploits veins of vernacular unavailable to hard-news hardnoses and back-of-the-book art arbiters as well as most litterateurs. And before long journalism collections by Pauline Kael, Tom Wolfe, and Susan Sontag were excavating such notions with more intellectual force than Liebling had the stomach for.

Sontag's *Against Interpretation* explicated thinkers of daunting complexity with humbling clarity and then flipped the switch by climaxing with not only "Notes on Camp," written for the *Partisan Review*, but "One Culture and the New Sensibility," initially published in none other than *Mademoiselle*. Enlightening young women who envied her haircut as well as her IQ, Sontag postulated not only that the "crudely put" C. P. Snow distinction between "literary-artistic" and "scientific" cultures was "plainly unwarranted," and that the "most interesting and creative art of our time is not open to the generally educated" (who I didn't then see might include me), but that "the affection many younger artists felt for the popular arts wasn't a new philistinism," because what Sontag declined to call pop was "a new, more open way of looking at the world"—although never (ever) did she articulate exactly what the name-checked Beatles, Supremes, and Dionne Warwick saw when they looked. Her opposite number was Wolfe, whose *The Kandy-Kolored Tangerine-Flake Streamline Baby* delivered hi-res reports on pop exotica like stock car racing, Phil Spector, and Cassius Clay as well as tonier arcana like a MoMA opening and an ad man visiting his son on Avenue B, all translated into wild-style rhetoric whose excitable pizzazz and overstated punctuation were as inspirational as his content.

The earliest of these three books, however, proved the best and most influential: *I Lost It at the Movies*. Not yet at *The New Yorker* when it was published in 1965, Pauline Kael was deeply into movies for love alone. I met her once at the Algonquin and didn't dig her queen bee act. But her secular intellect and honed prose, her brassy candor and democratic gusto, her nose for the laugh line and love affair with American English, her ideas as juicy as her descriptions, and her enthusiasm for artworks from *The Grand Illusion* to *The Sugarland Express* all rendered her an earthshaking critic. And except for *Raising Kane*, initially a very long *New Yorker* essay, every one of the dozen-plus books she published was a collection. I'm no Kael—nobody is. But I've always figured that if collections were good enough for her, they're good enough for me.

Book Reports is my eighth book, and all but the memoir *Going into the City* compile my journalism one way or another. What distinguishes *Book Reports* is that strictly speaking it isn't about music. Half of it is anyway, of course: I'm a music critic, so editors assign me music books. That acknowledged, however, book reviews work differently. The music history laid end-to-end in the foundational section titled "From Blackface Minstrelsy to Track-and-Hook" expands on passing observations and isolated paragraphs in my music criticism proper. The rock-bio section examines personas more than music proper. And the laurels and brickbats I toss my coworkers in "Critical Practice" I've always kept to a minimum in my music writing except in the big annual essays I devoted to the *Village Voice*'s annual Pazz & Jop Critics' Poll, where criticism criticism was part of the assignment. Hater hogwash that rock critics write for each other notwithstanding, I've always striven, with the occasional irresistible exception, to refer to my co-workers only when a fact or insight merits a credit. But that hardly means I never assessed their work—I've edited hundreds of rock critics and "mentored" dozens I'm proud I passed a few tips. So here I get to stretch out on a bunch who've published books and indeed collections of their own.

By stringing book reviews together, I also get to dive deeper into two themes I'm always returning to in my rock criticism. Regarding one I claim special expertise: bohemia, a realm so amorphous and declasse it's remained obscure as a scholarly byway even though many academics—as well as most of my readers and almost all musicians—have inhabited or at least brushed up against it. So in the "Bohemia Meets Hegemony" section the previously unpublished "Épatant le Bourgeoisie" surveys bohemia theory as of the late 1980s, Christine Stansell's *American Moderns* occasions a 2000 update, and 2010's "Bohemias Lost and Found" tops the story off, with a protoypical bohemian's memoir appended as an envoi and hippie-slash-counterculture variations arrayed in between.

And on the other hand there's politics, let's just call it, which unlike bohemia isn't my turf—thousands of journalists know more about it than I do. But few of these are also rock critics. Sure most of my colleagues lean left, just as most musicians do, but few critics and fewer musicians feel politics is intrinsic to what they do. This is often just as well—preaching to the converted risks message fatigue, preaching to the unconverted instant overkill. But such reticence has never been my way. I believe ignoring pop's tangled ties to capitalism is bad reporting. And since my main job as a critic is telling readers what I like and why I like it, I'm obliged to break down the moments when I'm drawn to a song's conscious compassion or militant outrage, succinct truth-telling or offhand gibes. As a critic as well as a citizen, therefore, I've always felt obliged to educate myself politically, leading some editors to figure I might have wound up with something fresh to say about the kind of books covered in "Culture Meets Capital." From the Marshall Berman review that sparked a lifelong friendship to my forced march through a million-and-a-half words about the banking industry, I've striven to put as much analysis, emotion, and entertainment value into these pieces as into my rockcrit.

Which leaves us with the college sweetheart I never got over: Literature with a capital L. Although roughly a third of the forty or fifty books I read a year are fiction, exactly what fiction has evolved. In my Kael-Wolfe-Sontag '60s, which were also my movement-theory '60s, I stubbornly remained an English Honors guy, catching up with Dickens and Austen and Faulkner and keeping up with Mailer and Burroughs and Barth. Beyond Olympia Press-style porn and less hifalutin smut, genre novels just weren't in my program until in the early '70s I finally heeded my own pop principles and began dipping into the sci-fi and detective novels that for decades now have constituted a major chunk of a fiction intake that in the past year has also included Balzac and Lessing, George Saunders and Yuri Herrera. And thinking about it, I'm struck by how the appetites reading sated when I was seven still sit there with their mouths open today: for language, information, ideas, narrative pull.

Narrative pull is the vaguest and most elusive of these; my wife, a novelist and critic who reads many more novels than I do, believes it's not the pull but the (discrete) world, not the pace but the (imaginary) place. But I read more history, criticism, and biography than she does, and while I acknowledge that momentum is a rarer and less compelling thing in nonfiction, I also insist that it's present by definition in any book you finish of your own free will. That's why I strive to generate forward motion in every sentence I write. Writing, pal, is supposed to *move*.

Information is the grubby one. Although it's obviously the point of any but the most elevated and abstract nonfiction, fiction mavens get miffed at practical seekers who use novels to educate themselves about unfamiliar landscapes, folkways, and historical moments. Tsk-tsk though you may, however, cultural orientation was one of the reasons I downed Raymond Queneau's *Zazie in the Metro* and Romain Gary's *Momo* a/k/a *The Life Before Us* (a/k/a *Madame Rosa*) before I visited Paris last year, and *The Leopard* and Leonardo Sciascia on a 2005 vacation in Sicily. Sciascia, I should mention, writes procedurals, which are excellent for this purpose—check out Archer Mayor if you ever visit Brattleboro, Vermont.

Ideas weren't yet a priority for me when I was seven, but as a brainy kid in a church where biblical inerrancy was bedrock, I was into abstraction early, with memorable impetus from a book in the church library called *The Chaos of Cults*, which helped undermine my faith by holding that Roman Catholicism was no less a cult than Christian Science and thus damned adherents like my mother's parents to hell. So in high school and college, the strictly philosophical passages of *Crime and Punishment*, *The Brothers Karamazov*, and *Notes from Underground* were formative for me even if Hermann Hesse wasn't.

But as I started to clock dollars as a public intellectual, a professional idea generator soaking up abstract speculation from record reviews to Marx, from Hannah Arendt to Fredric Jameson to for a few lost four-page hours even Jacques Lacan, the ideas and information in Literature proper got harder to tell apart. So grant that fiction by its very nature generates ideas in at least two crucial realms: identity and language. I mean identity in the narrow sense of human character formation but also as the p.c. catchall it's become. Not only did I know more about Turks after reading Orhan Pamuk's *Snow*, I knew more about young female publicists, hundreds of whom I'd encountered in real life, after reading Helen Fielding's *Bridget Jones's Diary*. And any white person who gets spiritual sustenance from African-American music (like you, say) should devote time to African-American fiction: Langston Hughes and Zora Neale Hurston, Alice Walker and John Edgar Wideman, Walter Mosley and Iceberg Slim. But as for language, well, that's another paragraph.

When I was seven, language meant vocabulary. Because I loved reading, I loved words, and became competitive about mastering as many as I could. Style I never thought about, not consciously. Looking back at my special favorites *Treasure Island* and *Tom Sawyer*, in fact, I see I was so entranced by their narrative pull that I barely noticed their narrative voices—Stevenson's first-person teenager touched indelibly with the author's Victorian fustian, Twain's third-person vernacular evoking a mischievous Midwestern teenager more than the literary lion who made him up. But as writing became my calling I felt pulled in many stylistic directions—first-person vernacular in my stabs at fiction and declarative clarity in the college papers where I first incubated my discursive strategies, but also Hemingwayesque understatement and Faulknerian fustian and lesser strains, until finally I made my decision for the hyped-up Americanese of Liebling, Kael, and Wolfe—only with partner Ellen Willis edging me toward Sontag's abstraction and then wife-for-life Carola Dibbell prodding me to squeeze out some more juice already.

Yet though by now I've arrived at a style of my own that mixes in all of the above, I still find myself knocked hither and yon by the infinite possibilities of prose exemplified by whatever novel I happen to be reading. Tasked with revisiting *1984* before it was too late, I immersed in Orwell, and observed among other things that "the clarity, candor, and common sense of Orwell's style made a kind of transcendent ideal of ordinary English decency"—a sentence that was written, like the entire review, in the thrall of said style. Or take the modern French classics above—less *Momo*, which merely opens new vistas of intelligent ignorance for its young vernacular narrator, than *Zazie in the Metro*, which even in translation convinced an aged critic besotted with the idiomatic that, done right, besetting your sentences with nonwords like "congener," "forrard," "hormosessual," and "Sanctimontronian" is a dandy way to affiance the roto-reader, meaning me.

The main reason the title I came up with here was *Book Reports* rather than *Book Reviews* is that *Book Reports* has some cheek to it—it's hookier. But it was also to honor that seven-year-old, who grew up to favor a pragmatic, just-the-facts approach when he wrote about books—to always describe and evaluate the work whose title provided the review's header. So in this collection you'll find only three of those exhaustive multi-volume *New York Review of Books*–style disquisitions I envied as a youngblood—on bohemia, blackface minstrelsy, and Raymond Williams, each gestated over years. Moreover, there's not much up-and-down here—while making room for half a dozen polemics and one joke, I avoided pans because who cares anymore. Hence the stylistic pull of these books can be assumed although I expect few readers will find even the supplest and smartest academic musicology as gripping as I do. There aren't many mixed reviews, either—several that were in my original proposal gave way to more consequential stuff.

That "consequential" does give me pause, however. I am the guy, after all, who assembled this book hard upon preparing a rock criticism collection anchored to the premise "Forget good *for* you—art should be good *to* you." That can certainly be said of every novel praised herein, and many of my nonfiction authors are a serious pleasure to read, as I detail in cases that include Marshall Berman and Terry Eagleton, Peter Guralnick and William Finnegan, Lester Bangs and Nick Tosches, Bruce Springsteen and Richard Hell, and at stubborn length the lumpily indefatigable Williams. But the majority just write what is called "well," meaning they know how to make their content *move*. And embarrassingly, the master stylists among them are John Leonard, Jonathan Lethem, and best of all Dave Hickey, authors of the three collections it seemed only natural to begin mine with. Figure these guys are critical essayists like me, only better—like Pauline Kael, say. But that doesn't make their three books my top picks in any up-and-down sense. It's easy and obvious enough, if arguable, to say music should be good to you. Nonfiction is a trickier case. But I loved reading before I loved music without ever believing those two loves felt the same. Music happens foremost to the body, reading to the mind—even if some books do take you for quite the ride.

So in the up-and-down sense and leaving fiction out of the competition, what are my very favorite books here? Oops, one is a collection—Hickey's *Air Guitar*, right at the top with Berman's *All That Is Solid Melts into Air*. Still, if I were grading these things, Ned Sublette's *Cuba and Its Music* and Jerrold Seigel's *Bohemian Paris* and probably Samuel Delany's *The Motion of Light in Water* and conceivably Dylan's *Chronicles: Volume One* or even Springsteen's *Born to Run* would be A plusses too. And with almost every selection my underlying motive is out in the open in the lead piece, which hangs the title "The Informer" on a review of John Leonard's *When the Kissing Had to Stop* and dislocates a sentence of his to sum up his and my task at hand: "I read this stuff so you don't have to."

Ultimately, this is a book about the adventures of an autodidact. I've reprinted these polished, pruned, and occasionally revised reviews and essays because my standard method is to condense, interpret, and contextualize what the book at hand has to tell my readers that they didn't know, which I generally didn't know either. That is, to inform. I want you to know this stuff. And then, if something interests you enough, I want you to read the book in question and not only deepen your knowledge but find out whether you get what I do from it. Because let's face it—you probably won't, not exactly. And then we go on from there.

PART I
COLLECTIBLES

The Informer

John Leonard's *When the Kissing Had to Stop: Cult Studs, Khmer Newts, Langley Spooks, Techno-Geeks, Video Drones, Author Gods, Serial Killers, Vampire Media, Alien Sperm Suckers, Satanic Therapists, and Those of Us Who Hold a Left-Wing Grudge in the Post-Toasties New World Hip-Hop*

Begin by rereading—or reading, because you couldn't be bothered the first time—that gaudy subtitle. Think about it a little. Do those adjective-noun combos interest you? Do they interest you more than the long, defensive final clause puts you off? I ask because, even if it was deceptive of this Serious Fiction maven to bury "Author Gods" in the middle, he's summed up his latest collection pretty well. "I read this stuff so you don't have to," he declares, and although he's referring to the novels of the "Poisoned Twinkies" (Bret Easton Ellis et al.), that could be his credo. In the same essay, Leonard, who is sixty, recalls "the monastic cell in which I read all night" as a teenager. When he's on, he writes like he's still that teenager—inhaling a raft of spy books, or several decades' speculation on Atlantis, or the whole vast oeuvre of Doris Lessing (obliged to review each new one because none of his colleagues had the heart to keep up), then coming downstairs with all-new info. In addition to outlandish noun-adjective combos fueling arcane series, his discourse bristles with weird theories bouncing off each other, with words and names you never heard of. *Paranomasia, sacajou, fatidic, tiger op, parlamente, torii.* Gaviotas, Yuratum, Akroteri, Rawalpindi, Hermapolis, Ascona. Matteo Ricci, Sabbatai Zevi, Aristarchus, Aby Warburg, Christa Winsloe, Johann Valentin Andreae.

Leonard worked for the *New York Times* from 1967 to 1982—reviewing books, profiling culturati, even editing the *Book Review* during the brief period when radical connections had cachet on 43rd Street—and by age forty had published three novels and three essay collections. He's also written TV criticism for *Life*, *Newsweek*, and eventually *New York*, his money gig since 1983, and held down broadcast spots with NPR and CBS; from 1995 to 1998, he ran an excellent book section with his wife, Sue Leonard, at *The Nation*, where most of the gratifyingly full-bodied essays that dominate *When the*

Kissing Had to Stop first appeared. This is a prodigious amount of writing for a guy who watches so much television on top of reading everything in creation. But without both inputs Leonard couldn't have turned himself into a twentieth-century generalist. It's clear from 1996's *Smoke and Mirrors* that TV is his main way of staying in touch with the world beyond books. Far from having no personal life, he's unusually forthcoming with autobiographical marginalia—about his marriages, his friendships, his career, his alcoholism—that put flesh and crotchet on his ideas. But the normal guy in him is hooked on the tube, which he believes has its mitts on some crude version of the American zeitgeist—plus it's good for more info.

Cultural journalists are paid to care mightily about how they write, which leaves a book man like Leonard in a state of ongoing post-partum anxiety—all his tiny babies, interred in microfiche. He's so productive you assume he doesn't sweat blood over every sentence, but he's such a showoff you know he loves his own prose. So he must have suffered in the fourteen-year stretch between his hot youth and his gray eminence, when he published no books. Having read one of his novels once, I'm entitled to hope there'll be no more; he has better uses for his creative juices, like transforming journalism into bound volumes with his name on them. This isn't as easy as is believed. His *Times*-dominated 1973 collection, *This Pen for Hire*, which opened with a longer essay (written for *Cultural Affairs*) dissecting the limitations of the book reviewer's "800-word mind," ended up exemplifying them—however entertaining and insightful, it also seemed arbitrary, undeveloped, a bit herky-jerk. Humbler now, he's edited hard and worked for flow with his three '90s titles—which include the 1993 anthology *The Last Innocent White Man in America* as well as *Smoke and Mirrors*, a full-length polemic that folds plot descriptions and analyses from his *New York* and CBS work into the thesis that TV is our most socially responsible popular medium.

When the Kissing Had to Stop is the best-realized of these, in part because it avoids the left-liberal point-scoring that was right on in the context of *New York* and *New York Newsday* but seems too predictable from the nonprofit New Press (although it's nice to imagine high school students happening upon his class warfare stats in the library, a possibility that would be enhanced were the books indexed). Freed of any obligation to preach to the heathens, Leonard reserves *The Nation* for more recondite projects. There's the Atlantis essay, which climaxes in two utopian communities, the fictional Botswanan one of the glorious Norman Rush novel *Mating* and the actually existing Colombian one of Gaviotas. There's a measured appreciation of Edward Said opening onto the surprising vista of the obscure Ahmadou

Kourouma masterwork *Monnew*. There's a mordant overview of the moral lives of the philosophers—against the mean-spirited likes of Hypatia, Wittgenstein, Simone Weil, Foucault, and other more curtly dismissed notables, he'll take the "boozehound, pillhead, and womanizer" Jean-Paul Sartre and his twenty pages a day. There's an invidious Willie Morris-Paul Krassner comparison, a surreal history of the CIA, a defense of Luddism, a piece that calls complaints about public television's "Byzantine complexity" "unfair to Constantinople." There's more.

For any partisan of intellectual journalism, Leonard is a small treasure. Combined with his sheer fecundity, his double specialty in television and literature leaves such fellow progs as Barbara Ehrenreich and Ellen Willis (although not the Alexander Cockburn of the wild and woolly *The Golden Age Is in Us*) looking rather austere. But while his intimacy with Serious Fiction—the subject of nearly half the book—adds flair and texture to his arguments, which break into literally novelistic detail at the oddest moments, it's also his weakness. Like many left-wing aesthetes before him, Leonard wants to believe that his pet pleasure is the key to human progress. But if indeed "good writers are better citizens than most of the rest of us," constituting "a parliament of hungry dreamers," then they're trickle-down legislators at best. When television's feel-good humanity fails to dent America's real-life social brutality, how are mandarins writing for other mandarins supposed to make themselves felt?

Though Leonard is no snob, he's enough of a climber to forgive elitism in the unforgiving likes of William Gass and Joan Didion (about whom he at least has the perspective to cite Randall Jarrell on T. S. Eliot: "He'd have written *The Waste Land* about the Garden of Eden"). As a corollary, he's a brazen old fart. Novel lovers of every birthdate share his disdain for the Poisoned Twinkies. But when his essay on the cyberpunks, whom he's sci-fi enough to enjoy, ends by suggesting they read Toni Morrison, fight Viacom, and help the homeless, the burnt-rubber smell of '60s self-righteousness spinning its wheels leaves one to conclude that his sniping at sitcoms in general and *Seinfeld* in particular has nothing to do with art. And hey, he's not to be trusted on popular music either. But without him I would never have discovered *Mating*, gotten the dirt on James Jesus Angleton, or had the chance to opine that *Monnew* is twice the formal achievement *Beloved* is. Really, who has the time? Somehow John Leonard does. Then he comes downstairs and tells us about it.

Village Voice, 1999

Advertisements for Everybody Else

Jonathan Lethem's *The Ecstasy of Influence: Nonfictions, Etc.*

This hefty and remarkable miscellany is Jonathan Lethem's fifth book since his bestselling breakthrough of 2003, the hefty and remarkable bildungsroman *Fortress of Solitude*. It follows the fanciful story collection *Men and Cartoons* (2004), the memoiristic criticism collection *The Disappointment Artist* (2005), the rock novel *You Don't Love Me Yet* (2007), and the hefty, well, Manhattan novel *Chronic City* (2009). Plus *They Live*, about the John Carpenter film, and a pseudonymous one about the 2005 Mets. Plus the five '90s novels (and two story collections, one a collaboration, and a 2000 novella). The man writes a lot.

The Ecstasy of Influence reminds us that he also reads a lot. As those movie and baseball projects indicate (and by the way, a Talking Heads monograph is due shortly), Lethem is not strictly a literary man. Even when he sticks to literature he's not strictly a literary man. He helped spearhead the canonization of Philip K. Dick, and is given to mixing genre fiction, particularly science fiction, into putatively belletristic projects. His extra-literary enthusiasms are all over *The Ecstasy of Influence*, named after a notorious defense of open sourcing that he constructed from other people's work and published in *Harper's*. The new book includes sections headed "Film and Comics," "The Mad Brooklynite," "Wall Art" (his father's calling), and "Dylan, Brown, and Punk" (mine). Published just months before James Brown's death in 2006, his *Rolling Stone* profile stands as the best writing ever about the greatest musician of the post–World War II era.

These byways, all of which make room for eccentric flights as well as proper essays, augment the charm and impact of what Lethem prefers to call an "autobiographical collage," a phrase he lifts from Vonnegut. This influence seems only natural, for dominating all is Lethem's prime concern always: the novel. In the preface Lethem discloses that he'd proposed the subtitle "Advertisements for Norman Mailer," and an essay of that title describes how Mailer's brawling 1959 miscellany *Advertisements for Myself* enthralled Lethem as a teenager and impresses him as an adult. Mailer's definition of and claim to greatness as a novelist is a model here. But as a fellow fan of Mailer's disreputable manifesto, let me point out that Lethem knows more fiction than Mailer did, and pumps his own prowess less.

At forty-seven, Lethem is eleven years older than Mailer was in 1959, so he's had time to get more reading in. But that's hardly the biggest advantage of an omnivore who devoured a book a day on the subway in high school and has spent twelve years working in bookstores. While watching *The Searchers* twelve times and immersing in Dylan bootlegs, he's read thousands upon thousands of volumes with but one thing in common, which is that eventually they'll go out of print. Where Mailer aims to be, if not "President" or some Hemingwayesque "champion," then at least "a major writer," Lethem concludes: "I began writing in order to arrive into the company of those whose company meant more to me than any other: the world of the books I'd found on shelves and begun to assemble on my own, and the people who'd written them, and the readers who cared as much as I did, if those existed."

Lethem reports that *The Ecstasy of Influence* comprises a quarter of his uncollected work, with enough literary reviews and introductions left over to make another volume. A good hunk of it has never seen print, and not just the Mailer-style italicized interstitials—crucial stuff like "Advertisements for Norman Mailer" itself; "Zelig of Neutrality," about his Bennington classmates Bret Easton Ellis and Donna Tartt; "My Disappointment Critic," his argument with James Wood; and best of all "Rushmore Versus Abundance," his argument with novelists who want to be president. This argument Lethem frames by extending rhetorical aid to noncanonical writers inside and outside the belletristic drawing room as well as to the likes of Ernie Kovacs, Stan Lee, Rick James, and Drew Barrymore.

He also frames it by conceiving rhetoric itself so permissively. A critical foray as accomplished as any of the straighter essays, for instance, is "The Drew Barrymore Stories," a two-page trifle knocked off for a glossy semiannual in what Lethem designates "a mode I'd call 'ecstatic,'" where Barrymore's saucy mischief and fondness for chocolate deflect the ill spirits of Alfred Hitchcock, Miles Davis, Howard Hawks, Dustin Hoffman, and a hot tub full of bitchy novelists. Equally post-essayistic is the tandem of "Top-Five Depressed Superheroes" (Ragman, Deadman, and others I knew naught of) and a *Playboy* piece about Lethem's own imaginary comic-book protagonist, the Epiphany, whose archenemy is named Le Petit Mort and whose acolytes are Eureka!, Tour De Force, and Non Sequitur. Lethem believes that any deviser of nonfictions is ipso facto a fictional creation. In these two pieces, that creation reads like Robert Benchley's favorite grandson giving art snobs what for.

Finally, however, the deviser of these nonfictions is a novelist. Although novelists do carp about each other, Lethem's inclusiveness extends to his own clan—he even defends *American Psycho*. Its parameters are established in a rich new essay called "Postmodernism as Liberty Valance," where Lethem sides with the postmodernists he links metaphorically to John Ford's chaos-sowing gunman without belittling designated upholders of the old order like Alice Munro, Cormac McCarthy, and Jonathan Franzen. Lethem believes that like all novelists, such traditionalists are just following their druthers, "whether consciously or in merry obliviousness to the range of options available." How well they succeed can only be decided on a case-by-case basis. Tie goes to the runner.

The fiction section begins with Lethem's evangelistic (and convincing) review of Roberto Bolano's *2666* before moving on to advocacy proper, reprinting introductions to novels by Paula Fox, Thomas Berger, Shirley Jackson, G. K. Chesterton, and Nathanael West. As is Lethem's generous habit, all six pieces honor writers who, except for the then-ascendant Bolaño and of course West ("the great precursor to Heller, Pynchon, Philip K. Dick, Colson Whitehead, and so much else"), have been underpraised. As "Rushmore Versus Abundance" puts it, "How on earth can abundance damage anything for anyone, unless what's damaged is some critic's pining to control what shouldn't be controlled, or to circumscribe boundlessness?"

But poking around among his fiction choices, three of whom I'd never read a whole book by, I was struck by how fabulistic all save Fox tended to be—even Chesterton in *The Man Who Was Thursday*, which is subtitled *A Nightmare*. Although Lethem is always discreet and perhaps even genuinely humble about pumping his own prowess, he thus manages to valorize his fictional practices by comparison. He's pro-genre, absolutely. But he clearly prefers J. G. Ballard to Walter Mosley, say, and within science fiction is drawn to the fanciful and quasi-surrealist as opposed to covertly realist cyberpunks like William Gibson and Bruce Sterling. This penchant pertains in his own novels right through *Chronic City*. Probably that's why I—as a detective guy and a full-time critic as well as a Queens-born East Villager for whom Lethem's Brooklyn-bohemian biography resonates—find both *The Disappointment Artist* and *The Ecstasy of Influence* more exciting than any of his interesting-to-terrific fiction except his most realistic novel, *Fortress of Solitude*. But it could just be that he's such a hell of a critic himself.

New York Times Book Review, 2011

Democratic Vistas

Dave Hickey's *Air Guitar: Essays on Art & Democracy*

It is a humbling thing to come upon writing by a contemporary you distantly respect and realize that, pretty much hidden from sight, he's been doing work that leaves your own flopping around on the deck. But it is also a thrilling thing. Two decades ago, I edited a dozen of Dave Hickey's record reviews—I particularly recall one in which a fictional skateboarder named Martin extolled Aerosmith's *Rocks*. Although these somehow failed to attract much attention over at the American Academy of Arts and Sciences, adepts of the form quickly recognized their audacious smarts. Yet good as they were, they didn't come near to preparing me for the "essays on art & democracy"—most of them written for the Los Angeles–based *Art issues*—that constitute the "memoir without tears" Hickey calls *Air Guitar*.

What's more, neither does Hickey's prize-winning 1993 minicollection, *The Invisible Dragon*, which to my taste turns a mite obsessive after driving home the welcome, essential, and mysteriously less-than-obvious point that Robert Mapplethorpe's *X Portfolio* achieves its power by *advocating* the unusual sexual acts it depicts. Having sought asylum as an art professor at the University of Nevada after a garishly checkered freelance career in trades that included Nashville songsmith, gallery owner, and worse, Hickey has a tendency to hector when addressing the museum system and its attendant "therapeutic institutions"—institutions that, after all, pay his health insurance (such as it is). Over a mere sixty-four well-argued pages, you start thinking, Enough already. Indeed, something similar happens two-thirds into this book, only at a much higher level—here you find yourself thinking, Hey, he *is* mortal after all. Finally obliged to theorize his impolite tastes, judgments, and ideas, Hickey lays his prejudices a little barer than altogether becomes them.

Even caught in that old trap, however, he's as good as it gets, starting with his prose. Although his diction is often hifalutin (he was doing a doctoral thesis about Foucault and Derrida way back in 1967), his rhythms aren't, and he's more than fluent in colloquial English—I mean, the guy can flat-out write. "Between the Jews and the Blues," he has Hank Williams say, "the only redneck thing about my songs was me singing them through my nose." Stuck in the middle of "A Rhinestone as Big as the Ritz," a discourse on Liberace that looks like a light-hearted tribute from one Las Vegan to another and instead establishes the keyboard-stroking closet king as a pivotal actor in the battle for gay liberation, is an epigram every critic should write on the blackboard till the chalk breaks: "Good taste is the residue of someone else's privilege." Then there's the freelancer's epitaph: "If This Dude Wasn't Dead, He Could Still Get Work." And the title essay lays out the plain truth of our shared calling with startling eloquence and wit: "Colleagues of mine will tell you that people despise critics because they fear our power. But I know better. People despise critics because people despise weakness, and criticism is the weakest thing you can do in writing. It is the written equivalent of air guitar—flurries of silent, sympathetic gestures with nothing at their heart but the memory of the music."

I should immediately add that although Hickey means every word of this disclaimer, he also means to sandbag us—the essay in question ends up situating criticism on the barricades of democratic militance. Hickey is a master of this kind of setup. "My Weimar" moves from a hilarious nightmare in which Marx and Montesquieu beat him for the check to an expatriate professor's analysis of how "Aryan muscle-boys" returned from World War II to take over the American avant-garde and its therapeutic institutions. "The Birth of the Big, Beautiful Art Market" celebrates planned obsolescence in automobile design, which it traces to Chicano low riders. "The Delicacy of Rock-and-Roll" (delicacy? what?—well, it's a "comic delicacy," as opposed to jazz's "tragic theater") is in substance a memoir of the underground film society at the University of Texas. "Shining Hours/Forgiving Rhyme" starts as an indelible sketch of a jam session his jazzman dad took him to and ends as a no-holds-barred defense of Norman Rockwell.

As should be obvious by now, this book's chosen objects of critical scrutiny are rarely highbrow. Cézanne gets most of one piece (and gets slammed, too), and there's a lovely essay up front on Flaubert's "A Simple Heart." But in case you've forgotten, that story turns on "an obnoxious parrot named Loulou," who is transfigured into a gaudy simulacrum of the Holy Spirit by the devotion of its doggedly uncomprehending protagonist, the servant Felicité. Hickey believes Felicité's *simplicité* was conceived by Flaubert as a reproach to the *sensibilité* of his friend George Sand, and the parrot as an argument for replacing Sand's "aristocracy of feeling" with a democracy of desire: "a society of the imperfect and incomplete, whose citizens routinely discuss, disdain, hire, vote for, and invest in a wide variety of parrots to represent their desires in various fields of discourse."

No aristocrat he, at least not so's he'd tell us about it, Hickey identifies with Felicité, and devotes *Air Guitar* to his own parrot collection, which in addition to the specimens already noted includes Perry Mason, Chet Baker, and LSD; the illusionists Siegfried and Roy, the wrestler Lady Godiva, old color Hollywood cartoons, and basketball; his dead Texas journalist pal Grover Lewis; the provincial bohemias of his peripatetic childhood; talking art with the postman, the paperboy, and anybody who might buy some from him; and the slot machines, gaming tables, dress code, and neon architecture of his adopted home, Las Vegas. My list mixes up Hickey's autobiographical sequence; *Air Guitar* certainly does "work as a book," as publishers who won't publish collections are always complaining they don't. It defines a present, then flashes back to childhood and works through school and freelance years whose "church," Hickey tells us, was Perry Mason reruns on daytime TV. And immediately after explaining how that could be so—*Mission Impossible*, by contrast, is "The Church of the Small Business Guy"—he launches the final third of his book with a thematic overview.

In essence, "Romancing the Looky-Loos" is a defense of participatory connoisseurship against the idle curiosity of leisure-consuming spectators. Among devotees of popular culture, no issue is more fraught with complexity, but when it comes down to cases almost all such devotees—who are also, let me point out, connoisseurs—go along with Hickey: "In the world I grew up in . . . you used the word 'spectator' as a term of derision—not as bad as 'folksinger,' of course, but still a serious insult." Hickey is alert enough to groupthink that you'd think this consensus would make him suspicious, but it doesn't, in part because the evidence is so strong. Just as he claims, most worthwhile arts of any "level"—W. B. Yeats or Bugs Bunny, disco or abstract expressionism—are initially supported by like-minded communities. And just as he claims, reaching an audience of undifferentiated consumers is always intensely alienating for the artist and certain to subject the work to distortions of perception it was not designed to withstand. So Hickey is right—we need "undergrounds." Perhaps, however, his art-world orientation renders him overly defensive about them, leading him to ignore or deny something else: sometimes connoisseurs are one-upping status addicts, and sometimes spectators add dimension to a work that no comfy little community can approximate.

In the like-minded community I live in, fans who move on when spectators move in, a process Hickey regards as perfectly natural, earn their own terms of derision: "contrarian," "hipper-than-thou," even "trendy," an insult Hickey reserves for first-wave spectators. And as a Perry Mason fan who boasts in this very essay that he helped convince Warner Bros. to sign Funkadelic, he must understand that strange and wondrous things sometimes happen to the hugely successful. Designed for mass consumption, *Roots* and *Roseanne*, *E.T.* and *Superman III* would feel altogether more commonplace if they weren't. Megasales didn't normalize Prince, whom he seems to like, and cutting their teeth in three-thousand-seaters defined Led Zeppelin's music, which he probably considers inferior to Aerosmith's. Well, too bad for him.

But all this is simply to afford myself the opportunity of arguing with a rather large kindred spirit, which Hickey rightly identifies as one of the signal pleasures of democracy. His book survives this divagation, and indeed takes up a variant on the looky-loo argument in a more convincing finale called "Frivolity and Unction" before embarking upon an obscure envoi about a fictional Spaniard with whom Hickey discusses bean counting while attempting to collect a gambling debt. I wish I believed the American Academy of Arts and Sciences is quaking in its boots—it ought to be. Given how he feels about therapeutic institutions, do you think Hickey would turn down a National Book Award? My guess is that this old freelancer would cash the check. Here's hoping we get the chance to find out.

Los Angeles Times Book Review, 1997

PART II

FROM BLACKFACE MINSTRELSY TO TRACK-AND-HOOK

In Search of Jim Crow

Why Postmodern Minstrelsy Studies Matter

In 1828 or 1829, so the story is told, in free Cincinnati or down the river in slave Louisville, or maybe in Pittsburgh (or was it Baltimore?), an obscure actor named Thomas Dartmouth "Daddy" Rice came across a crippled black stablehand doing a grotesquely gimpy dance. "Every time I turn about I jump Jim Crow," the stablehand would sing, illustrating his words with an almost literally syncopated dance ("syncope": "a partial or complete temporary suspension of respiration and circulation due to cerebral ischemia"). The effect was comical, all accounts agree; it was also rhythmically compelling or exciting, though how this effect is achieved through a discontinuity in which one half of the body is acrobatic and the other immobilized is apparently too self-evident to be addressed. Rice was so impressed that he bought the black man's clothes and made off with his song and dance. "Jump Jim Crow" became a major smash—in Gilbert Chase's words, "the first big international song hit of American popular music."

Like many European-American entertainers in the 1820s and a few going back some fifty years, Rice was already appearing regularly in blackface. Not until 1843 would the Virginia Minstrels, the first (professional) (white) ("white") fiddle-banjo-tambourine-bones music group, kick off a craze that would soon accommodate interlocutors and endmen and skits and variety acts and pianos and what-have-you. In expansive mutations of fluctuating grotesquery and brilliance, the craze would dominate American show business until the end of the nineteenth century. And after a long period of shame-faced obscurity cemented by the civil rights movement, its daunting tangle of race and class and pop culture and American music would render it a hot topic of historical debate at the end of the twentieth century. Nevertheless, Rice's strange cultural appropriation continues to stand at the headwaters of what we now call minstrelsy—its foundation myth. As a myth, the incident retains explanatory and illustrative power even though there's no way we can ascertain whether any version of it occurred.

Since the kind of reporter who would go hunting for the stablehand is rare enough in these racially sensitive times, we might expect that the sole witness on record would be Rice himself—building a colorful reputation in interviews with the press, most likely. Yet in the dozens of retellings I've checked, Rice isn't cited either; the commonest source by far—and also, remarkably, just about the earliest—is "Stephen C. Foster and Negro Minstrelsy," an article by Robert P. Nevin that appeared in *The Atlantic Monthly* in 1867, nearly forty years after the "fact," and several years as well after a by-then crippled Rice (and Foster too) had died in poverty. Even so the appropriation could have taken place—although one would like to know more about Robert P. Nevin (whose other published writings focus on Pittsburgh, Foster's hometown), the story was apparently an uncontroversial commonplace by the time it got to the *Atlantic*, and it has a ring, doesn't it? In fact, it's such a hell of a metaphor that one understands why few historians of minstrelsy have resisted it, and why it shows up frequently in less specialized accounts of race relations and popular music. All one would expect, especially of modern scholars attuned to the ideological baggage concealed beneath the surface of such undocumented tales, is a touch of skepticism. It's kind of amazing how rarely one gets it.

OK, it figures that old-time pop historians David Ewen and Sigmund Spaeth (for whom minstrelsy was "a black snowball which kept on rolling") would swallow the story whole. But one appreciates Gilbert Chase's simple "tradition has it" and Eileen Southern's relaxed "as the story goes," and wishes recent chroniclers Christopher Small, Russell Sanjek, and Donald Clarke had exercised more caution. One knows better than to seek scholarly decorum in Carl Wittke's chatty (and useful) 1930 *Tambo and Bones*. One admires Hans Nathan's 1962 *Dan Emmett and the Rise of Early Negro Minstrelsy* for analyzing the artistic content of Rice's song-and-dance and appending its supposed origin as an "it is reported" afterthought. And one is rather shocked the tale is bought so unquestioningly by Robert Toll, whose 1974 *Blacking Up* kicked off modern minstrelsy studies; Robert Cantwell, whose 1984 *Bluegrass Breakdown* linked Bill Monroe to minstrelsy and jazz when such lineages were all but unthinkable; and Roger Abrahams, whose 1994 *Singing the Master* traces the minstrel-show walk-around to plantation corn-shucking festivities.

Then there's Lawrence Levine, whose seminal 1977 *Black Culture and Black Consciousness* repeats the story, unfootnoted, to launch the argument that white minstrels often served as conduits from one African-American (the stablehand, "an old Louisville Negro, Jim Crow") to another (the "North Carolina Negroes shucking corn" whose virtually identical 1915 song was recorded in Newman I. White's 1928 *American Negro Folk-Songs*). One wonders what Levine would make of musicologist Charles Hamm, who in 1979 reprinted most of Nevin's *Atlantic* version in *Yesterdays: Popular Song in America*, the most thorough and thoughtful history of American pop we have. After noting the racist relish of Nevin's "colorful" style (which upon reflection evokes a minstrel stump speech), Hamm acknowledges that Rice "may have been telling the truth" before making what ought to be an obvious point: "It is equally likely that the story of the tune's origin was invented to give authenticity to a white man's portrayal of a black." Hamm believes Rice needed the help. He can discern no African elements in "Jim Crow," which suggested "both an Irish folk tune and an English stage song," had small success as sheet music, and failed to enter oral tradition (unlike its counterpart, George Washington Dixon's "Zip Coon," transformed by Dan Emmett into "Turkey in the Straw"). Hamm conjectures that if Rice did indeed copy it from a black man, the black man might well have copied it earlier from a white. Conduits have a way of connecting to other conduits.

This is a reassuringly sane take on the legend. But one reason it's so sane is that it recognizes the legend's power. By quoting Nevin in all his condescending glory, Hamm implicitly recognizes why Eric Lott, whose obsessively researched 1993 *Love and Theft* kicked off postmodern minstrelsy studies, calls the *Atlantic* article, which he also quotes at length, "probably the least trustworthy and most accurate account of American minstrelsy's appropriation of black cultural practices." "According to legend—the closest we are going to get to truth in the matter—" is how Lott sources the Rice story. Never mind that in her own contribution to the 1996 essay collection *Inside the Minstrel Mask*, co-editor Annemarie Bean attributes a considerably more credulous version of the story to Lott himself, because facts, likely or unlikely, have nothing on the inexorable, poetic, legendary truth. And so, completing his sentence by summing up without comment the *Atlantic* article he reproduced thirty pages before—"T. D. Rice used an old black stableman's song and dance in his first 'Jim Crow' act"—Lott launches one of his more tendentious disquisitions on, to cite jargon that has dated revealingly, "the production of the minstrel show out of gendered commodity exchange," replete with permissive definitions of bohemia, imaginative inferences of the homoerotic, century-hopping cultural generalizations, and shards of evidence that don't nearly prove what he claims they do.

Now, *Love and Theft* is a remarkable book, the most purely brilliant in minstrelsy studies. Its insistence on respecting and understanding the much-disparaged white working-class minstrel audience was long overdue. But it's too bad brilliance is the closest Lott can get to truth in the matter. I know it's only a fantasy, but let me say right here that I personally would love to know whether Rice ever actually met such a stablehand, and—if he did, which by now I doubt—exactly what cultural commodities he borrowed, arrogated, or stole.

The reason the myth remains so redolent, after all, is that it tells a story about the white-from-black "appropriation" of not just minstrelsy but all American popular music. Afro-America makes, Euro-America takes—seldom is it put so baldly, but at some level that's what many of us feel. In one line of thought, it follows that the stablehand's "Jump Jim Crow" was intrinsically irresistible, so much so that a straight imitation made Rice a star; it follows that all that stood between the stablehand and a career in show business was the refusal of middlemen like Rice to help a black originator overcome troublesome initial audience resistance, with all projections through the next two centuries self-evident. There's an alternate possibility, however. What if Rice's "Jump Jim Crow" was a syncretic creation, sparked by components of one or more individual black performances that might even include the song itself, but incorporating as well stray elements of other songs and dances black and/or white—and also, crucially, skills, mannerisms, attitudes, and values Rice was born with, or absorbed during his long stage and idiosyncratic life experience?

This is not only what Hamm suspects, it's probably what Lott thinks too; the syncretic is as much a cultural studies trope as the trope itself. Once when discussing Rice, in fact, Lott identifies and counterposes the two models. Imitation, which he calls "theft," he links credibly to anxiety about slavery, while syncretism, "expropriation," he links dubiously to anxiety about miscegenation. Lott's reluctance to choose explicitly between them reflects not so much his scholarly modesty as his scholarly method—he'd rather explore metaphors than establish facts. But for sure the theft model dominates the other accounts I've described, and that's because Lott is surely right to align it with slavery. In whites who resist racism, the anxiety slavery provokes is rarely distinguishable anymore from guilt, in part because the rage slavery provokes in blacks is rarely masked anymore in let-bygones-be-bygones noblesse oblige. This compels whites to either share that rage or defend themselves against it. And even more than the Confederate flag (although perhaps not the burnt cross or the KKK hood), nothing symbolizes the outrageous dehumanization of slavery as vividly for most African-Americans as "the big-lipped, bug-eyed, broad-nosed buffoons" of blackface stereotype.

The quote is from "a 26-year-old African-American who just finished reading Ted Gioia's" 2000 *New York Times* defense of Al Jolson, which was illustrated with a poster from *The Jazz Singer*. Fumed another letter writer: "Does it matter to me that [Jolson] opted for blackface to enhance the theatrical qualities of his performance and not to degrade blacks? No. What matters to me as an African-American woman is how it makes African-American people feel." Both voice an indignation that dates in print to Frederick Douglass, who in 1848, Lott reminds us early on, branded blackface minstrels "the filthy scum of white society, who have stolen from us a complexion denied to them by nature." For uplifters of the race like Douglass, minstrelsy's burnt cork has always seemed nothing less than a theft of identity all too precisely analogous to slavery's theft of freedom. So ever since black pride became a formula for self-actualization in the 1960s, ex-minstrel W. C. Handy's assertion that minstrelsy engendered black show business has been swept under the rug. The pleasure much of the Negro audience once took in, to choose the obvious example, *Amos 'n' Andy*—in 1930, for instance, Duke Ellington's orchestra played its theme song at a *Chicago Defender* parade—is recalled as a tragic anomaly of benighted times when it's acknowledged at all.

In this context, the slavery model of minstrel appropriation obviously has an insuperable advantage among African-Americans. Even when they strain to be fair, as Mel Watkins does in *On the Real Side: A History of African American Comedy*, black critics and historians are so appalled by blackface they find it hard to work up any respect or sympathy for the white men who exploited it. The sole exception I'm aware of is Wesley Brown's 1994 novel *Darktown Strutters*, which begins with a fictionalization of the Jim Crow legend. Brown's protagonist is Jim Too, the adopted son of the crippled stablehand Jim Crow. Jim Too remakes himself as a professional dancer who also calls himself Jim Crow, but he performs without makeup, initially in Daddy Rice's troupe. Renowned and sometimes imperiled for his refusal to don the blackface that is the coin of American entertainment, he pursues a nineteenth-century African-American picaresque that makes no pretense of chronological or historical precision. Brown depicts Rice as a tortured grotesque and compulsive performer, incapable of living inside his own skin, yet "several cuts above most men I've known who do a lotta damage tryin too hard to be white."

The quote is from another white blackface artist in the historical record, dancer Jack Diamond, in Brown's story a staunch antiracist who's literally cut off at the waist at the Battle of Chancellorsville (I think—typically, Brown muddles the year). His name is found pinned to the pants that clothe his known remains, an image that soon feeds "the legend of the greatest jig dancer ever to heist his legs! And every time Jim heard another version of the story, the loss of Jack Diamond didn't weigh on him so heavily." When Afro-America makes and Euro-America takes, Brown wants us to know, sympathy is a luxury for any black person set on getting some back.

> The story I propose here veers awry from the usual accounts of the origin of Jim Crow. That usual story, reiterated from the earliest middle-class articles on working-class performance right up through the latest scholarly accounts of minstrelsy, has it that Rice nicked 'Jump Jim Crow' from a real man, usually specified as a crippled black hostler named Jim Crow. A corollary story, equally dubious, specifies a source in an individual named Cuff, who it is supposed wrestled luggage along the Pittsburgh levee.
>
> These stories are false in fact and spirit. There was no such hostler, no such baggage man. What's more, the way these stories tell it is simply not the way cultural gestures come into being.
>
> —W. T. LHAMON JR., *Raising Cain*

So much for legend being the closest we are going to get to truth in the matter, at least as far as W. T. Lhamon Jr. is concerned. Lhamon is the author of two of the four major pieces of minstrelsy scholarship to follow *Love and Theft*, all almost as obsessive as Lott about secondary sources and, in the standard history-versus-theory pattern, rather more obsessive about primary sources. William J. Mahar's *Behind the Burnt Cork Mask: Early Blackface Minstrelsy and Antebellum American Popular Culture* (1999) enlists a profusion of playbills, plays, and songs to bolster a solid if flat-footed argument that minstrelsy is better understood as birthplace of showbiz than engine of racism. Dale Cockrell's *Demons of Disorder: Early Blackface Minstrels and Their World* (1997) mines court records and newspapers to connect minstrelsy to the carnivalesque class hostility of charivari and callithumpianism. Lhamon's new *Jump Jim Crow: Lost Plays, Lyrics, and Street Prose of the First Atlantic Popular Culture* (2003) is a monumental labor of textual reconstruction matched by a long and extraordinary introduction. His earlier entry, *Raising Cain: Blackface Performance from Jim Crow to Hip Hop* (1998), is more fanciful and theory-happy. Lhamon centers its well-documented vision of New York's Catherine Street Market as mixed-race cultural exchange on an 1820 folk drawing depicting three black performers "Dancing for Eels," and somewhat shakily credits George Christy with staging the first true minstrel show in Buffalo in 1842, well before the Manhattan debut of Dan Emmett's

Virginia Minstrels cited by everyone else. *Raising Cain* also revealed the existence of a pamphlet called *The Life of Jim Crow* that's reprinted in *Jump Jim Crow*. Rice probably didn't write it, but he sold it at shows. It makes no mention of hostlers or baggage men.

Scornful of speculation, the text-based Mahar is one of the few historians of minstrelsy to ignore the Jim Crow legend. Cockrell assumes the legend is true because no one bothered to deny it at the time, although he wishes he could prove the stablehand was actually a performer at one of the black festivals he's studied. He finds its "outlines" in an 1837 Rice profile by *New York Herald* editor James Gordon Bennett, convincingly dates the song itself to 1830 rather than 1828, and refutes the truism that it was an instant hit.

Like Cockrell, Lhamon means to begin where Lott leaves off by celebrating rather than just respecting minstrelsy's audience—the counter-nobility Lhamon, following Thomas Pynchon, dubs "the mobility." But the two scholars have different agendas, and these correspond to their distinct versions of the legend. In an autobiographical epilogue, Cockrell identifies himself as a white working-class Southerner who resents Northerners' assumptions about his racism; Lhamon is cagier about personal details, putting his cultural capital on the table with stray references to Eliot, Wittgenstein, Ginsberg, Dylan, etc. Cockrell the good old boy takes for granted the kind of "borrowing" the Jim Crow legend is about and doesn't think that ends the story, citing as proof Southern musicians from Jimmie Rodgers to the Everly Brothers and "on and on, up to many of the current crop of stars." Lhamon the postmodernist emphasizes how the legend served the ideological needs of those positioned to construct and promulgate it—rival actors jealous of the popularity of this cheap craze and privileged pundits fearful of the cross-racial class solidarity he demonstrates coexisted with white racism, especially before the minstrel show proper.

As noted, the minstrel show proper, whether in the form of Dan Emmett's Virginia Minstrels or George Christy's much longer-lived troupe, begins in 1843, perhaps 1842. That's also the starting point for Mahar, who defines his subject as antebellum minstrelsy. In contrast, both Lhamon and Cockrell focus on the pre-1843 period; both, in fact, devote considerable attention to pre-1828 intimations. The first section of Lhamon's book teases out the 1820 drawing, while Cockrell outlines the history of "Lord of Misrule festivities." These include mumming plays, Morris dancing, slave Christmases, West Indian John Canoe celebrations, the black elections that were quickly banned in eighteenth-century New England, Pinkster days, the German belsnickel wassails imported to Mobile by a Pennsylvania Dutch cotton broker, and callithumpian bands—soot-faced working-class youths who would roam the streets of Philadelphia, New York, and Boston around New Year's, banging drums and anything else that would make a noise until they were bought off with food and drink.

Cockrell downplays the racial significance of preminstrel blackface. Well before Rabelais, he tells us, black makeup was a way of announcing disguise and signifying Otherness, and it retained those meanings even when its overt content became racial, which onstage has been dated to 1769. He seeks out black Lord of Misrule action, and finds evidence of its influence on whites (and vice versa). But with the separate-but-equal exception of the New Orleans carnival, the actors in (as opposed to spectators at) black festivals were all black, while charivari and such excluded blacks—the belsnickels were all white, as were the callithumpians, who picked fights with black freemen as well as the ruling-class whites they were out to harass. In contrast, the Manhattan of early minstrelsy (and early Jacksonian democracy) was a hotbed of miscegenation. According to health records Lhamon unearths, the Five Points environs of Catherine Street Market were twenty-five percent black, with intermarriage common, and many other blacks visited the market as workers, slaves, servants, vendors, and/or, in a few cases, entertainers; Cockrell quotes heartrending court records in which cross-racial couples of the lower classes were separated by the state's Amalgamation Law.

Lhamon also connects Manhattan to George Christy's Buffalo via the Erie Canal, in whose construction he discerns a "mudsill mutuality" of black and white workers—slave, indentured, contracted, or just deeply oppressed—who constitute a key element of the lumpenproletariat Marx would conceive so contemptuously in *The 18th Brumaire*, well after the rationalization of blackface on the burgeoning minstrel circuit was getting this ruffian ragtag under control. What did Jim Crow's syncope signify? Among other things, Lhamon says, stoop labor—not the upright autonomy of Sean Wilentz's artisans, but the forced contortions of Lionel Wyld's "hoggees": "The whole stooped posture of the hoggee, permanently bent by the shovel and the barrow, and still evident in laborers today, is caught in Jim Crow's gimp."

We can't know how deeply romanticism and wishful projection distort Lhamon's and Cockrell's histories any more than we can know who really wrote "Jim Crow." Cockrell himself is careful to stress the coexistence of integration and racism. Mahar, who shares the middle-class positivism associated with the Institute of Popular Culture Studies at Bowling Green (he notes with a straight face the lack of "gentlemanly refinement or common decency" in minstrel scripts) but whose main agenda is downplaying minstrelsy's racism, assumes its patrons disliked blacks and the rich "equally" and is more troubled by their offenses against women. This is wrongheaded. Nonetheless, when Lhamon observes that the "racism and vulgarity" of wealthier whites was even more pernicious, "if only because these people had far greater power to elaborate their inclinations," his argument resonates. Which racism does more harm today, after all? The working-class racism of exacerbated competition for limited resources—a competition that according to *Raising Cain* grows directly out of the bourgeois response to early minstrelsy's cross-racial threat? Or is the big hurt the ruling-class racism that still denies so many African-Americans jobs, education, housing, health care, and anything else they need?

Both Lhamon and Cockrell, moreover, take their celebration of minstrelsy's white audience a step further—they extend it to minstrelsy's white artists. Nathan's Dan Emmett book excepted, earlier minstrelsy studies can lull the most alert reader into the retrograde condescension of classic mass culture theory, in which individual producers are assumed to be hacks, schemers, cogs in a machine—and which traces back to the same class-bound notions of respectability discernible in Douglass's talented-tenth talk of "the filthy scum of white society." Lott is especially prone to this fallacy, which dovetails with cultural studies' emphasis on the social and consequent reluctance to valorize the art hero. So much else is at stake that it's easy to forget that every minstrel song and skit was created by men whose need for display and self-expression drew them to the theater, which isn't many people's idea of a rational career choice. Not only does Lhamon's work on Rice's plays counteract such lazy thinking, so does Cockrell's long biographical sketch of George Washington Dixon. Both make a special point of the artists' creative personal connection to the new urban culture of rootless, single young men who have been a prime pop market ever since.

The Dixon Cockrell describes was "one of the most complex, eccentric, and enigmatic men ever to have crossed the American musical stage": a skilled singer and proven songwriter, a scandal-sheet proprietor who was in jail occasionally and in court often, a hypnotist and clairvoyant and distance walker, a sometime proponent of labor abolitionism who wasn't above using music "to remold himself into an idol of the white middle class." Before he last performed in early 1843, just when the Virginia Minstrels were creating their sensation, his Ethiopian delineations had inspired many, most prominently Rice himself. In *Raising Cain*, Lhamon asserts the enduring literary value of Rice's raucous lumpen burlesques, particularly *Bone Squash Diavolo*, which the ship rigger's son who jumped Jim Crow first mounted in 1835. *Jump Jim Crow* pursues the argument by exhuming prompt manuscripts of nine plays written by or for Rice (four of each, with a ninth in doubt). Rice was obviously no Melville or Dickinson, no Whitman or Twain, no Douglass, and Lhamon avoids grand claims. But *Jump Jim Crow* opens the possibility that a blackface minstrel may yet be remembered as the most original nineteenth-century playwright of a nation whose first major dramatist was Eugene O'Neill. That would be a good joke.

Tickled though the pop advocate in me is by any transformation of hack into auteur, this one weakens a pet theory of mine. So do Mahar's dogged readings of the printed record, which establish that both cornball comedy and skirmishes in an undeclared class war are as endemic to minstrel wordplay as racist stereotypes. The theory is that logocentrism does the story of minstrelsy even less justice than it does most history—that we must somehow make the imaginative leap from the published scripts and songs to the performed music, dance, and slapstick, but especially music, that dominated most playbills. Because African-derived usages are barely hinted by notation, minstrel music is even further beyond our ken than the rest of pre-gramophone pop. And few historians of minstrelsy are inclined to help much—Toll, Lott, Cockrell, and Lhamon are word men all, explicators of culture and ideology without much to say about how minstrel music altered the surrounding soundscape.

A welcome corrective is David Wondrich's *Stomp and Swerve: American Music Gets Hot, 1843–1924* (2003), which puts minstrelsy first in an argument that the special heat of US music, as opposed in particular to the Afro-Latin music from further south, derives from its fusion of Celtic stomp and African swerve—a perfect account of "Jump Jim Crow." After the appropriate apologies, however, Wondrich relies on Nathan for descriptive detail. The dance focus of *Raising Cain* adds something new, and in *Jump Jim Crow* Lhamon unveils a revealing Irish description of Rice's hit: "The song from which he derives his name and celebrity is paltry and vulgar—the air brief and pretty; but it has a feature that belongs to few songs—it is mostly made up of dancing. Half of each verse is chorus, and then all the chorus motion—so that it is of compound and really complex character." Lott's abstruse discussion of European versus African canons of repetition also bears pondering. In minstrel songs, he says, poetic refrain meets catch-phrase beat, ego reinforcement meets ego loss, *plaisir* meets *jouissance*, and then everyone changes partners, so complexly that the talent and vision of individual creators inevitably inflect how particular interactions play out and what they mean.

There's more meat in music prof Mahar, who interlards many useful points through his lengthy demonstrations that—gloriosky!—sexist stereotypes pervaded a theatrical form directed at young, unmarried, working-class urban males. Although most of these were known or inferred—and despite Mahar's reluctance to attribute distinction to Africa's rhythmic heritage or, for that matter, chattel slavery's economic one—it's still good to have them substantiated. He rides the sheet music hard, never once addressing the great unnotatables grain and groove and barely mentioning tempo. But he is aware of the "vocal inflections or gestures" sheet music misses. In explicit contradistinction to Charles Hamm, he believes (correctly, the evidence suggests) that certain minstrels—he names Joel Sweeney, Dan Emmett, and Cool White—learned a lot from black musicians, distinguishing sharply between Emmett's "limited melodic compass, modal pitch structure when performed with the banjo-fiddle instrumentation, and frequent interruption of the vocal line by instrumental breaks" and the ornately quasiclassical British product of the time. And he points out that the structure in which a single singer was accompanied by a single instrumentalist whose brief interludes accompanied dancing was "unique to blackface entertainment and the slave behavior on which it may have been based."

Nevertheless, our most searching investigation of minstrel music remains a few late '70s and early '80s articles by banjo-playing ethnomusicologist Robert B. Winans, the most important of which, "Early Minstrel-Show Music, 1843–1852," is collected in *Inside the Minstrel Mask*. To my knowledge, Winans was first to suggest the debt owed minstrelsy by white-identified styles like bluegrass and its predecessors. But Winans resists equating minstrel music with the old-timey string bands recorded in the 1920s. For one thing, he points out, the instruments were different. The drumlike minstrel tambourine made a much louder and deeper sound than the flapjack-sized versions we know today, and the bones were far less delicate than the castanets that are their closest modern equivalent. Crucially, the banjo was bigger and deeper too, and not yet played in the chordal, "classical" style developed to accommodate the rise of the guitar in the late nineteenth century. Instead it was "frailed," struck rather than plucked, with a rhythmic emphasis that can be traced back to Africa and forward to Appalachia, where Winans believes the new beat was transported (along with many pop songs) by both traveling minstrel shows and prodigal sons who brought their city lore on home (to which Robert Cantwell would add local blacks, since no part of the South was totally white). Like Mahar, Winans—who has criticized Lott's habit of extrapolating theory from isolated songs of minimal currency in actually performed minstrelsy—cares about what songs were popular. Surviving programs reveal that at the dawn of minstrelsy proper, between 1843 and 1847, comic songs greatly predominate, only to recede between 1848 and 1852, when the standard-issue heart-tuggers of nineteenth-century pop reasserted themselves, with operatic parody accounting for much of the new comic material and nonsense songs like "Old Dan Tucker" and the passé "Jump Jim Crow" a vanishing fad.

Imagine an America in which stage singing was accompanied, if at all, by piano (the English-born songwriter Henry Russell), chamber trio (the protest-singing, abolitionist Hutchinson Family, a favorite blackface butt), or small opera orchestra (the run of matinee idols). Tempos and sonics suit a restless but slow-moving world in which machines are rarely heard. In the 1830s appear performers like Rice and Dixon, Joel Sweeney and Dan Emmett—sometimes solo, sometimes alongside or in front of traditional orchestras. Cutting impolite lyrics with fancy steps, showing off on the fiddle or banjo, all are perceived as a welcome affront to the prevailing gentility by an emergent audience of rowdy young men with a few coins to throw away. But they don't break out until Emmett constructs a laff-a-minute show around a bunch of them, at which point they change everything. As Winans sums up: "They were new and different, earthy and 'exotic' at the same time, and comic and antisentimental." Toll's tribute to the Virginia Minstrels fleshes out this basic and too easily lost point: "Once on stage, they could not sit still for an instant. . . . Whether singing, dancing, or joking, whether in a featured role, accompanying a comrade, or just listening, their wild hollering and their bobbing, seemingly compulsive movements charged their entire performance with excitement. . . . From beginning to end, their shows provided an emotional outlet. Most of all, the performers seemed to have fun and succeeded in involving the foot-stomping, shouting, whistling audiences in the festivities."

Rhythmic and angular where the genteel competition was harmonic and mellifluous, hyperactive and uproarious in rhetoric and principle, minstrel music was only one part of the class drama postmodern minstrelsy studies can't get enough of. But it was the most momentous part, and the most honorable. The democratization of culture identified with the minstrel show would have happened sooner or later—P. T. Barnum didn't need minstrelsy, and neither did Hollywood (which did, however, make the most of it). But although minstrel music may have been inevitable too, putting it together required something like genius. "Jump Jim Crow" and the thousands of songs that followed established an African tendency in American pop that has waxed and waned and waxed some more ever since, with worldwide repercussions. It's hard to grasp this music's reality, as in Winans's underwhelming attempt to re-create it on an album called *The Early Minstrel Show*—the ensemble precision recalls the neat simulacra of jazz repertory, and you can hear the singers wince whenever they pronounce the word "nigger." But for all we can really know, Winans's band of ethnomusicologists on a spree may have every inflection just right. It's impossible to be sure from this side of the divide that minstrel music opened up—impossible to adjust our ears back to before blue notes, gospel melismas, ragtime, bebop, railroad trains, gramophone records, saxophones, electric guitars, Chick Webb, James Brown, punk, hip-hop, the sandpaper musicality of uncounted rough baritones, and the omnipresence of more noise than can be comprehended by a Monday morning or a Saturday night.

What we can know is this: the rise of minstrelsy in the 1840s (or maybe, following Lhamon, we should say the 1830s *and* 1840s, privileging neither) constituted a cultural upheaval remarkably similar to the rise of rock and roll in the 1950s. Right—minstrel music was only a part of the minstrel show, which proved the foundation of the entire American entertainment industry. Right—rock and roll was only one in a series of modern musical mongrelizations, from coon song to jazz age to swing era. Nevertheless, both were benchmarks. Minstrelsy transformed blackface from a theatrical to a musical trope. It established that in a Euro-America obsessed with African retentions (the violence of the blood, the puissance of the penis, the docility of the grin), music was the star attraction, especially for the young riffraff who gave American cities their bustle. Like minstrelsy, rock and roll posed not just a racial danger, but a class danger. Although it arted itself up soon enough, a good thing as often as a bad one, it delivered pop music from status anxieties and polite facades. It made a role model of the unkempt rebel. And by finding simple tunes in the three-chord storehouse of folk modality, it cleared a space for unencumbered beat. Got it? Now ask yourself how much of the rock and roll description can be applied to minstrelsy and vice versa. Most of each for sure.

This is one reason minstrelsy's various historicizations are fascinating, and amusing, for anyone who has read many histories of rock and roll. The patterning is so similar, with specifics that go well beyond cultural reminiscence's usual golden-ageism. In both we find parallel visions of unspoiled, unpretentious white youth transcending racism in simple musical expressions soon bedizened by crass impresarios and under assistant promo men. Rock and roll has generated many golden ages—the halcyon '60s, punk in its CBGB and/or Sex Pistols clothes, and "real hip-hop," to name just three. But absent romanticizations of sweet Stax music, only its original '50s version has the proper cross-racial charge, which always seems to fade. Nor is this, initially, a scholarly construction: Nick Tosches's 2001 biography of twentieth-century minstrel Emmett Miller, *Where Dead Voices Gather*, unearths the wondrous 1854 headline "Obituary, Not Eulogistic: Negro Minstrelsy Is Dead" and tells how in 1858 *George Christy's Ethiopian Joke Book, No. 3* "bemoan[ed] the departures from genuine negrisimilitude that had begun to degrade minstrelsy." By 1930, when Duke published *Tambo and Bones*, Carl Wittke's regrets over the increasing paucity of "genuine Negro characterizations" were standard among the few who still gave thought to minstrelsy—which Tosches shows survived as a residual entertainment, especially in the South, well past its presumed death at the turn of the century and in fact past World War II.

Where Dead Voices Gather is typical Tosches cup-half-empty: killer prose and genius archive-digging stunk up with dull contempt for academics more soulful than he is and the racial philosophy of Joe Colombo. But give it credit for insisting, early and often, that no concept is as corrupt as purity: "Blackface, white face, false face. 'Originality is but high-born stealth.' These may be the only words written by Edward Dahlberg that are worth remembering; and who knows where he got them." Originality, purity, their toney cousin authenticity—as rhetorical tools, all are made to order for a conservative agenda. If, as Charles Hamm says, the Jim Crow legend meant "to give authenticity to a white man's portrayal of a black," was the intention to fend off objections from Afro-American intellectuals? Of course not. As Lhamon argues, powerful Americans feared the race-defying underclass impulses minstrelsy's aesthetic made manifest. Whether those impulses were genuinely African-American matters less than that they scared gatekeepers, who often responded with the belittling claim, a shrewd fusion of cooptation and condemnation, that they were inauthentic—and still do, sometimes.

In *Jump Jim Crow*, Lhamon shows how supposedly sympathetic middle-class observers attacked Rice's credibility with invidious comparisons—to "the veritable James" discovered by actress-diarist Fanny Kemble among the slaves on her husband's Georgia Sea Islands plantation, or to black New Orleans songster and acknowledged Rice influence Old Corn Meal. Inevitably, incongruent details were ignored. How veritable did Kemble find her black servants when she censured their "transparent plagiarism" of "Scotch or Irish airs"? Was Old Corn Meal still the real thing when he performed Rice's "Sich a Gittin' Up Stairs"? Certainly some impresario could have made a few bucks putting Old Corn Meal on tour, as soon happened with free-born black tap pioneer William Henry "Juba" Lane, the toast of London in the 1840s who died there broke before he reached thirty. As with millions of other racist injustices, that it didn't happen is a disgrace—it should have happened a hundred times over. But don't therefore assume that, if it had happened a hundred times over, the flood of pure African-American art would have been the undoing of Daddy Rice and all his kind. Somewhere in that cross-racial nexus lurked a uniquely American sensibility whose decisive attraction was that it was no respecter of propriety. And though it proved far less dangerous than the powers feared, they fear it still.

It's misguided to overload this sensibility with political meaning, or declare it irrelevant after that potential plays itself out. Inconsequentiality was one of its attractions. The signal term is an elusive one: "fun," which starts picking up *O.E.D.* citations just as minstrelsy gets going in the 1830s. The Christy Minstrels invited audiences "to see the fun, to hear the songs, and help to right the 'niggers' wrongs"; circus press agent Charles H. Day published an 1874 history of minstrelsy called *Fun in Black*. By Emmett Miller's time, the trades and dailies were using "fun-makers" and "the fun contingent" as ready synonyms for blackface performers. Struck by "the regularity with which observers resorted to the word 'fun' to describe their enjoyment of blacks and of blackface," Lott calls a whole chapter "Genuine Negro Fun"—and turns out to care at least as much about the "Fun" part, which is hard to parse, as the "Genuine Negro" part, too patent to merit unpacking.

To his credit, Lott emphasizes that what he takes for minstrelsy's attempts to "tame the 'black' threat" always risk leaving something untoward in the woodpile. But he executes his analysis from on high. All this fun, he is certain, has the function of mitigating a "roiling jumble of need, guilt, and disgust." The less said the better about his Freudian readings of blackface usage—although I'm certain he overdoes them, I'm probably too skeptical. Let me merely cite his tendency to assume the worst about the minstrel audience of the 1840s, when he believes working-class consciousness, disemboldened by the Panic of 1837, was fleeing politics at every turn and with no exception. Of more moment is his disapproval of the Christy-style minstrel show's presumably parallel flight into spectacle from narrative, meaning plays like Rice's. And crucial is his search for the meaning of fun in jokes, costumes, and business, ignoring the music that was foregrounded during precisely the same period. We've been here before, but let's ratchet up our objections by emphasizing that—where Rice, for instance, worked solo-with-backup—the Virginia Minstrels and their progeny were *bands*. Rock and rollers know the difference, which is usually fun in a way that barely suggests race or class while saying much that's otherwise inexpressible about human interaction.

And now for Freud. At a crucial juncture, Lott cites the patriarch himself, unmasking fun as "lost moments of childish pleasure evoked by the antics of children, or of 'inferior' people who resemble them": "constant repetition," "supreme disorderly conduct," "oversized clothes," "performative irruption," "the gorging and mucus-mongering of early life." Perhaps Lott would be less discomfited by this structure of feeling if he tried harder to distinguish between children and infants, but either way it can be explicated sans Freud. The idealization of childhood is a well-known tenet of romanticism and hence our era, throughout which it has been disparaged to no avail by pundits and cynics of every political orientation. And admittedly, returning to childhood is a lousy way to pass laws or get the laundry done, a journey that's always doomed in the end. But in a system where the same can be said of many other things worth doing in themselves, an idealized youth is a hell of a good place for low-level ungovernables with dirty drawers to spend Saturday night, a site of worldly transcendence in which egoisms needn't always get in the way of other egoisms. It's a satisfaction, a recourse, damn right an escape—a feat of imagination. We should be grateful that it no longer involves big-lipped buffoons with their feets too big. But we should be proud that it's been a special destination of American popular music since more or less the time of "Jump Jim Crow."

Jump Jim Crow's collected narratives are unlikely to leave Rice our first important playwright. Literary arbiters are literary arbiters, after all, and anyway, the plays aren't good enough. Not only are several by English actors with ties to drawing-room farce who'd rather Jim were a prince from the Congo than a ne'er-do-well from the Five Points, but only two of Rice's much impress. The stunner is *Bone Squash Diavolo*, a dizzying one-act "burletta" full of nonsense, deviltry, and love sweet love that ends with the Jim figure ascending heavenward in a balloon—an image of orgasm, Lhamon ventures more convincingly than Lott finding phallic symbols whenever he turns over a lithograph. Yet equally remarkable is Rice's burlesque *Otello*, first mounted in 1844, perhaps as a rebuke to the mobility after the Christys bigged up his act. Lhamon relates much worth reading about Othello in pre–Civil War culture, with two of Rice's strokes crying out for special mention. First, Othello and Desdemona have a baby—not one of the high yallers blackface poked fearful fun at, but a chiaroscuro pied piper in potentia, his face half black and half white. Before too long, you just know, he'll be strumming on the old banjo. Second, Othello isn't reassuringly tragic. He doesn't die. At the end of the play he and his issue are triumphantly alive.

But rather than exit on that encouraging note, let me cite another idea Lhamon lets slip. Unlike the transparently racist construction Sambo, Lhamon argues proudly, Jim Crow is not docile: "His lyrics show him fighting 'white dandies,' Jersey blacks, and Philadelphia Sambos." Lhamon goes on: "This transgressive power of Jim Crow is what the political regime of Jim Crow laws in the South projected on all African Americans, of every class, and then used to contain them as a category after the North's betrayal of Reconstruction."

What he doesn't add is this: To hell with art. To hell with Saturday night. Why shouldn't African-Americans hate Jim Crow?

This is a damning indictment. If "Jump Jim Crow" lay behind the machinery of state-mandated racial segregation, what can mitigate that? But if segregation was inevitable anyway, then perhaps its naming only represents a setback for a people's culture we must struggle to reclaim. So permit me one final story.

Abraham Lincoln loved a joke, loved music, and loved minstrel music. He was an instant fan of the infernally catchy "Dixie," composed by Dan Emmett in 1859—although it has also been attributed to the black Snowden family, sometime professional musicians from Ohio who shared music with Emmett—and soon expropriated as the Confederate anthem. Right after Appomattox, Lincoln asked an attendant band to strike up "one of the best tunes I ever heard." "Dixie" was our "lawful property" now, he joshed. Would it were that simple.

By then Lincoln's musical tastes had gotten him in trouble. Two weeks after the battle of Antietam—twenty-three thousand dead and wounded on September 17, 1862, the bloodiest day in American history—Lincoln met nearby with General George McClellan, soon to be relieved of his command for excessive caution. In the president's party was his former law partner Ward Lamon, who served as a bodyguard and wielded a mean hand on the banjo. Dispirited by the shadow of death and his distrust of McClellan, Lincoln asked Lamon for a lost weeper by one W. Willing called "Twenty Years Ago," but that just made him bluer. So Lamon tried the cheerful minstrel standard "Picayune Butler," named for a black New Orleans colleague of Old Corn Meal. When Lincoln remained despondent, Lamon gave up. At no point did McClellan object.

Within months the story was out in the opposition press. Lincoln, always archly characterized as a clown or jester, had insulted the dead of Antietam "before the corpses had been buried" by calling for "a negro melody"—identified first as "Jim Along Josey," then "Picayune Butler," and eventually, what else, "Jump Jim Crow." During the 1864 presidential campaign, with McClellan his opponent, the lies and vilification intensified. Always at issue was the crass, low, common, unserious vulgarity that disqualified this smut-monger turned abolitionist from pursuing the peace as sixteenth magistrate of the United States. Always the proof was not just his insensitive choice of occasion, but his attraction to what was always called a "negro" song—not "nigger," thank you very much, but never "minstrel" either. This at a time when the blackface brethren of the Northern stage were pumping McClellan for all they were worth, which by then, Lhamon and the others have it right, wasn't much—not culturally, anyway.

We may feel that Lincoln was also too cautious—that he should have freed the slaves sooner, that as with almost every white American of the nineteenth century, his racial attitudes were lamentable. We may also feel that minstrel music did the freed slaves more harm than good. But this incident suggests a kinder interpretation. Full-bore racists of the gatekeeping classes didn't care how authentic "Picayune Butler" was. It was close enough to colored to alarm them just because it evoked a world in which bastard spawn like Abraham Lincoln could get past the gatekeepers. Not only that, some voters thought such songs fun, and fun worth pursuing. That alarmed them too. Daddy Rice and Dan Emmett must have been doing something right.

The Believer, 2004

The Old Ethiopians at Home

Ken Emerson's *Doo-Dah! Stephen Foster and the Rise of American Popular Culture*

Stephen Collins Foster was the world's first professional songwriter—first to earn his living by composing popular songs he did not perform, first to be paid in royalties rather than flat fees. He was also the most gifted pop songwriter of the nineteenth century. Is there even a hymnodist who can claim a body of tunes as well remembered as "Oh! Susanna," "Camptown Races," "The Old Folks at Home," "My Old Kentucky Home," "Jeanie with the Light Brown Hair," and "Beautiful Dreamer," to name only absolute classics? Not until George M. Cohan and Irving Berlin in the twentieth century did such durability begin to seem a realistic possibility. Such successors as Henry Clay Work ("Marching Through Georgia," "My Grandfather's Clock") and Charles Harris (the self-published "After the Ball") fell well short.

The story of Foster's brief life remains obscure primarily because his survivors wanted it that way. As Ken Emerson notes in *Doo-Dah!*, the first true biography of Foster in over sixty years and the only good one (although William Austin's 1975 *"Susanna," "Jeanie," and "The Old Folks at Home"* is superb musicology), a mere thirty of Foster's letters have come down to us; most of the others were destroyed by Morrison Foster, the only one of four brothers to live to old age, who thoughtfully compensated with an 1896 memoir. But as Emerson suggests, Foster's story also remains obscure because the culture he represents isn't considered worthy of the scholarly digging that can cast light into the corners of history. Working with a commercial publishing house, Emerson deserves thanks for meticulously researching a project unlikely to garner him many professional perks.

In a way, the paucity of materials was a blessing. Additional facts about this shy young man's struggles with composition and his contact with African-Americans and their music would be immensely valuable, and it would be nice to know more about the inner life and external transgressions of his intermittently estranged wife, Jane (with the light brown hair). But at least Emerson wasn't tempted to write one of those month-by-month play-by-plays that turn biography into brickmaking. Instead, he breaches scholarly decorum by finding parallels in the lives of Foster's contemporaries: pioneering Afrocentrist Martin Delany, who came to Pittsburgh as a teenager in 1827, a year after the composer was born; the slightly later Pittsburgh success story Andrew Carnegie; Harriet Beecher Stowe, who wrote the novel that would insure Foster's fame in Cincinnati, the most important of his homes away from home; Edgar Allan Poe, caught in a comparable cycle of success and failure; and Louis Moreau Gottschalk, the New Orleans–born classical composer-pianist whose celebrity outstripped Foster's, although he was such a troublemaker he didn't outlive him by much. As a result, Emerson's biography doubles as a cultural history—for its first hundred pages, as balanced and authoritative a summary of early American popular music as anyone has devised.

In the definitive tension of Foster's art, the parlor ballad fended off blackface minstrelsy. The parlor embodied middle-class comfort with the express purpose of putting a polite face on domestic life, blackface a "freedom from bourgeois conventions and expectations" for the predominantly male audience that felt the call of its rough humor and jumpy music. But both were recent developments that fed off innovations in piano manufacture, piano transport, printing, communications, and travel. And although minstrelsy proved the wave of the future, its victory was hardly unequivocal. Emerson lays out this complex story with grace, originality, dispatch, and a level of insight that owes much to his experience as a rock critic.

Because writers gravitate toward verbal texts, most accounts of blackface concentrate on its scripts, and Emerson emphasizes that racism also infected the music. But his critical orientation helps him understand that the stolen, emulated, aped, fabricated, and faked "blackness" of minstrel songs announced a change in the way Americans would make music far more fundamental than anything portended by the class animosities of minstrel theater. Moreover, he knows his pop well enough to find relevant recent comparisons—between nineteenth-century English singer and songwriter Henry Russell and Elton John, or Foster's confusion over the Civil War and Brian Wilson's over Vietnam.

Although Foster's family is often described as educated and well-to-do, Emerson establishes that it was only genteel and prominent; renowned relatives all the way up to President James Buchanan couldn't save his father from bankruptcy while he was mayor of the Pittsburgh suburb of Allegheny City. His family's many moves and ingrained sense of dashed opportunity lent extra savor to the longing for home that Foster shared with a century whose signature song was "Home Sweet Home"—a nostalgia that obviously infused "Old Folks at Home" and "My Old Kentucky Home" if not "Oh! Susanna" or "Camptown Races." The latter two songs represent a peak for Foster—bright, energetic, apparently meaningless divertissements with no parlor in them, both treated to convincing lyrical analyses of the sort resented by philistines who believe a ditty is a ditty is a ditty. But there's no denying that the composer was informed and animated by the ideal of an all-nurturing home even when he was escaping it. So it's striking that both the great "Home" songs were also "Ethiopian" songs (as opposed to elevated fare like "Jeanie" and "Beautiful Dreamer"), although the title phrase in the one about the Swanee River was changed from "old blacks at home," and although "My Old Kentucky Home" rejected the gratuitous dentals and other demeaning cliches of blackface dialect convention.

Like his father, Stephen Foster had big ideas and no head for business. The decent money he made in the early and mid 1850s was never on a par with his fame, which was spread not just by minstrel troupes but by countless musical productions of *Uncle Tom's Cabin* where "Old Folks at Home" and "My Old Kentucky Home" were staples. Emerson believes he was drinking heavily as early as 1852, and by the time he settled in New York in 1860 he was a half-forgotten alcoholic who wrote for cash on the barrelhead. This was his most prolific period, and his worst—great pop songs aren't cranked out by formula any more than any other kind of art. Although his racial attitudes were suffused with a sympathy that touched millions, not all of them white, his family ties to the anti-abolitionist Democratic Party ill prepared him for the Emancipation Proclamation, and Emerson doubts he could have adjusted to post–Civil War America. But we'll never know if he had any "Beautiful Dreamer"'s left. He died at thirty-seven in the same low-rent Manhattan hotel where the Virginia Minstrels had first rehearsed a little over two decades before.

Los Angeles Times Book Review, 1996

Before the Blues

David Wondrich's *Stomp and Swerve: American Music Gets Hot, 1843–1924*

A man with a taste for the wild side, David Wondrich has wagered the accrued status of his published oeuvre—namely, *Esquire Drinks: An Opinionated and Irreverent Guide to Drinking with 250 Drink Recipes*—on a hot book about hot music: a book that honors the art of, to choose some modern examples he throws out for clarity's sake before his antiquarian passions take over, Merle Haggard, Nirvana, and hip-hop (as opposed to Alabama, Pink Floyd, and ambient techno) by translating their tone into written English. The topic is fine in an era when the reluctant pedagogues Wondrich breezily brands "the thought gang" will write 250 pages about any cultural byway. But the manner marks him as a troublemaker. Although Wondrich's discographical researches render him a scholar of sorts, he's slangy, irreverent, nontechnical, given to gratuitous wisecracks, and scornful of any jargon not his own. For all these reasons he has produced a book with a rare ear for its subject, but also a book that risks neglect from the thought gang. I would have appreciated footnotes myself—there are leads worth exploring, and once in a while a generalization that cries out for double-checking. A bibliography to augment the pungent essay on sources would be nice, as would record-buying advice beyond "Google it." But Wondrich rejects such academic apparatuses as spiritually incongruent with the art he loves, and for that he deserves the respect he won't get.

Wondrich defines his I-know-it-when-I-hear-it subject as elegantly and unpretentiously as it's ever been defined. Come on, he declares, poking millions of fellow hot music lovers in the ribs. You know and I know that two kinds of musical motion move us. One propels and the other wiggles. Either can be hot; put them together and they combust. It's that simple. Why did the fire leap so high in the U.S.A.? Because "something happened to African music in Anglo-Saxon North America that didn't happen to it anywhere else"—namely, it became *less* African. Not only were there proportionally fewer Africans here, but they were counterbalanced by another outcast group, the Celts. Admirably, Wondrich never infers musical or political parity from this familiar construct, nor adduces the crude formula in which Africans add rhythm to Scotch-Irish tunes. He just believes American music fuses two species of drive, Celtic stomp and the swervier African kind.

With 80 percent of the 250-odd pages devoted to 1890 and after, the timespan promised by the subtitle is misleading. If Wondrich had dug deeper into such thought gangsters as Charles Hamm and W. T. Lhamon, he might have found more to say about post–Civil War stage music—Henry Clay Work's emancipation ditty "Kingdom Coming" was pretty hot. But since hotness is better heard than notated or described, his decision to concentrate on recordings makes sense. His 1924 cutoff date is the year before Louis Armstrong first recorded as a leader and electrical recording replaced acoustic, which Wondrich likens to "two condensed-orange-juice cans and a string" (hardly his most fanciful approximation of how cruddy old cylinders and 78s now sound). But the cutoff guarantees that he'll write about lots of music by white people.

With a handful of very significant exceptions, no African-Americans were recorded before Valentine's Day 1920, when headstrong hustler Perry Bradford, his ad hoc Harlem band the Jazz Hounds, and beauteous black vaudevillian Mamie Smith cut "Crazy Blues," judged by Wondrich "the most riveting recording of American music the record business had yet produced." It scared the little Okeh label so much that it wasn't released until July, when it proved an instant hit, supposedly selling seventy-five thousand in Harlem alone. Just by demonstrating that African-Americans bought records, it opened the gates to Ethel Waters, Bessie Smith, King Oliver, Ma Rainey, Blind Lemon Jefferson, and countless other black performers. It changed music forever, and Wondrich knows it. But he also believes that the changes it manifested were already well under way.

In a turn of events both curious and just, black pop between 1890 and World War I now receives far more detailed attention than white. Pantheon songwriters like Berlin and Kern enjoy ceaseless adulation, and not even Wondrich wants to waste thought on the bestsellers of the acoustic-recording era—say the Peerless Quartet, which produced both Arthur Collins and Henry Burr (and thus also produced over four hundred hit records). But in many other white musicians of the period, still remembered but seldom scrutinized, Wondrich finds evidence of heat.

There were the Virginia Minstrels transforming blackface into showbiz in 1843: "The first truly American band, playing American music." There were the 20,000 brass bands active between 1890 and 1910, most prominently the Marines led by second-generation Portuguese-American John Philip Sousa, especially as brought to the studio by cakewalking trombonist extraordinaire Arthur Pryor. There were white musicians ripping off unrecorded pianists Scott Joplin and Ben Turpin and red hot mamas ripping off St. Louis cathouse singer Mama Lou. There were banjo kings Vess Ossman from Hudson, New York, and his less funky acolyte Fred Van Eps from Somerville, New Jersey. There was the most prestigious pop star of the acoustic era, Enrico Caruso, who for eighteen seconds of "Vesti la giubba" gave posterity "one of the hottest things ever recorded."

Most decisively, there were turn-of-the-century white singers specializing in pseudo-black "coon songs," which whether indefensible racist propaganda or arguably subversive "tales of violent love and lost poultry"—many of the best written by such non-Caucasian pioneers as self-billed "Unbleached American" Ernest Hogan and Bert Williams, who Wondrich presumptuously nominates "the first black man in America"—relegated "ee-nun-see-yating parlor singers" to the dustbin of gentility. And in 1917 there was the Original (they claimed) Dixieland Jazz Band, who in preparing the way for King Oliver also inspired legions of better-mannered white imitators playing what Wondrich likes to call "Synco-Pep," the politeness of which, he believes, "fronted for a smooth drive and a carefully disguised swerve that could and sometimes did break out into a raw excitement."

But that excitement couldn't bust altogether loose until the African-American rhythmic-harmonic complex Wondrich dubs "the Senegambian mode" achieved full emancipation. The scandalously underrecorded Williams, the durable blues popularizer W. C. Handy, and the paradigm-shifting Harlem/Army/society orchestra leader James Reese Europe are conscious, heroic rebels in a book where white guys just do what comes naturally, which is fall under the Senegambian sway. What tipped the balance is something the author of *Esquire Drinks* is well prepared to notice: prohibition. In a nation that systematically crushed blacks into a de facto Underworld (upper case Wondrich's), the illegalization of alcohol handed nightlife to the actually existing criminal classes. Public drinking turned into risky business, tony boites turned into roughneck joints, and before anyone knew what hit them it was the Jazz Age. American music had gotten hot, and the best hooch ever was on the house.

Seattle Weekly, 2006

Rhythms of the Universe

Ned Sublette's *Cuba and Its Music: From the First Drums to the Mambo*

"This is a history of music from a Cuban point of view," Ned Sublette explains right off in *Cuba and Its Music*, sounding a little nervous about his unconventional project. This isn't exactly true. Sublette's subject isn't music, it's Cuban music, although if you were to get him drunk he might tell you that in the twentieth century the two concepts were nearly identical. Nor is the music described from a Cuban point of view, and that's not because Sublette is a New York–based Texan.

The vantage is Afro-Cuban—this book is one of the few general music histories to give African usages, values, and materials more weight than European ones. As Sublette notes, even Alejo Carpentier, the Paris-educated Europhile whose 1946 *La musica en Cuba* insisted prophetically on granting black Cubans something approaching musical parity, reserves a separate chapter for the African-tinged music of white avant-gardists Amadeo Roldan and Alejandro Garcia Caturla while barely discussing twentieth-century Cuban popular music. Similarly, in Helio Orovio's *Cuban Music from A to Z*, recommended by Sublette as "a basic reference tool," Roldan and Caturla get four or five times as many lines as band-leading songwriter-virtuoso Arsenio Rodriguez and seminal bassist Israel "Cachao" Lopez.

That's not how Sublette parcels out the kudos. A schooled musician, he gives Roldan and Caturla their remarkable-to-heroic due. (Caturla, also a corruption-fighting judge, was assassinated.) But he leaves little doubt that Cachao, "arguably the most important bassist in twentieth-century popular music," stands as a more original and momentous artist. And Rodriguez, the blind grandson of a Congo-born slave, is for Sublette the wellspring. As a leader he invented the modern trumpet-conga-cowbell conjunto; as a player he established the guitar-like tres as a decisive influence on the rhythmic ostinatos that now anchor Latin music; as a lyricist he articulated the Cuban version of pan-Africanism. Also, he writes, "Arsenio played a decisive role in the new clave consciousness." "Clave" is Spanish for key, and claves are the hardwood ship pegs with which Havana musicians beat out Latin music's characteristic three-and-two rhythm, familiar to Yankees in the form of the African-American "soul clap." In Sublette's conception, clave is a "rhythmic key," and Rodriguez, steeped in African retentions and Matanzas rumba, is a fundamental genius.

Not that Sublette subscribes to what kindred spirit Robert Palmer dismissed as great-man theories of African-based music. This is not merely a history of musicians, or even of music. Assuming correctly that few English speakers know anything about Cuba before, say, 1952, which happens to be when this fascinating six-hundred-page first volume ends, Sublette also hones in on straight history: Cuba's early prominence as a Caribbean nexus, its conversion to a sugar economy, its relatively late and extremely brutal dependence on the slave trade, its troubled relationship with its royalist proprietors in Spain and its democratic exploiters in the US.

And Sublette doesn't start there. Before he even gets to Cuba, he has devoted sixty pages to a prehistory that may be the most remarkable thing about the book. For if Cuban music is to prove as crucial as he believes, there had better be more to its Spanish heritage than is generally understood by musicologists such as *Music in Western Civilization*'s Paul Henry Lang, who called Spain "indescribable." So Sublette limns an untold pre-Columbian history in which Spain, with helpful input from Muslim invaders, is a more cultured and happening place than Rome, France, Britain, or Germany. Although he concentrates on Spain's Moorish phase, detailing competing strains of Islam and the different Africans who participated in the faith's bitter and myriad sectarian disputes, he goes all the way back to first-century Cadiz, described fancifully but plausibly as a seafaring hot spot whose night life was already "informed by centuries of direct and indirect contact with black Africa." His story moves through Cordoba, where in the ninth century Baghdad-born "Black Songbird" Ziryab had the lineaments of a rock star, then to the "cosmopolitan boomtown" of Seville, a center of the slave and gold trades from which spread the sixteenth-century craze for the saraband, a dance Sublette traces linguistically to Bantu tongues. Seville was rife with guitars and drums, the latter barely known in the rest of Europe. And Havana, he tells us, was the New World Seville.

Even before sugar fully Africanized Cuba, music was a black trade in Havana, where the substantial free population had limited career options. Havana was one of the largest cities in the Western hemisphere, surpassed by New York only in 1810, and in the 1840s boasted one of America's two resident Italian opera companies, owned by a major slave trader. Havana's black musicians mastered European forms and instruments but found audiences for their more rhythmic music in bars and brothels and within the four distinct Afro-Cuban religions Sublette lays out, santeria being the polite one. Sublette also gets specific about which Africans lived where in Cuba and floats the convincing theory that Cuba's jungle Congos and Yorubas established a very different rhythmic tradition from that of the US's desert and savanna Wolofs—one that renders Cuban-US musical fusions clumsier than is usually admitted. Through the nineteenth century, most African Cuban music fermented in the baracones where plantation slaves resided. But constant commerce between Cuba's isolated Oriente province and hyperactive Havana, as well as between Congo Havana and Wolof New Orleans across the sea, assured that none of these demarcations would hold firm.

Racism was always potent in Cuba, but after the US ousted Spain in 1898 it got worse—an early governor was Robert E. Lee's nephew Fitzhugh Lee, "only one of a cast of American characters who knew well the heartbreak of people who had lost their slaves." Democracy brought the de facto colony a disgraceful succession of kleptocratic presidents who minimized services even in the up phases of sugar's boom-or-bust. Drums had been no big deal in the baracones, but in an urbanizing Cuba where it was government policy to encourage white immigration they were suppressed. Yet the music itself was unstoppable. It flourished in the country and the city, in cultic secrecy and bustling public spaces, on recordings in the early days and the radio later. It flourished in low-life dives, equal-opportunity dens of iniquity, and clubs, hotels, theaters, and concert halls designed for an arrogant elite and their moneyed foreign guests. The crucial innovations were rhythmic and usually came from the dark-skinned poor, often those with a conscious connection to Africa. But their countless mulatto and white admirers certainly influenced harmony and presentation, strictly Spanish retentions exerted their own formal logic, and North American musics bounced back to Cuba, where "jazzband" long designated a distinct genre.

Sublette has his evangelistic side, which occasions leaps he should be called on, from his assumption that African rhythm was fully developed at the time of Christ to his tendency to attribute so much African-American musical innovation to Cuban influence. He's got a right to surmise that Scott Joplin, that fulcrum of rhythmic change, knew the Cubanized compositions of Louis Moreau Gottschalk, and that "Louie Louie" is in some fundamental sense a habanera (hey, maybe it was about Gottschalk), but there could be more to those stories.

For all its polemical thrust, however, *Cuba and Its Music* is exceptionally evenhanded. Sublette's research is monumental. Even in Spanish, there is nothing nearly so thorough. Although he has worked mostly as a musician and radio producer, he proves a readable stylist with a knack for popular history. His writing is as vivid and fast-moving as the music he loves—its tone passionate but never purple, its intelligence and rigor completely compatible with sardonic wisecracks and irrepressible bursts of informal verve. The book's sole formal flaw is that it doesn't so much end as stop, presumably at the insistence of a publisher who convinced Sublette to save his ammo for a sequel. Even so, he has added a major work to the tiny canon of social histories of music—perhaps even the grandest of them all.

Los Angeles Times Book Review, 2004

Black Melting Pot

David B. Coplan's *In Township Tonight! South Africa's Black City Music and Theatre*

There is no more fascinating test case in the politics of culture than apartheid South Africa. Torn but not yet destroyed by an internationally disparaged system, South Africa tolerates considerable freedom of expression for a police state. To convince local liberals they live in a democracy and prevent harsh words from turning into meaningful action among civil liberties fetishists the world over, the regime customarily (although not consistently, since a dose of governmental caprice keeps troublemakers looking over their shoulders) averts its gaze from Marxist scholarship, underground perodicals, experimental drama, and the like. Why ban works outright if you control work permits, travel permits, assembly permits, and the airwaves? When selecting circuses to go with the black majority's bread, however, Pretoria is less devil-may-care—anything deemed likely to reach a large black audience inspires paranoid scrutiny. Forbidden is any piece of pop culture that might stir up the natives' unfortunate propensity for sex and violence, or focus their attention on African politics, or plant the seed of animosity against those who happen to have white skin. At the same time, Pretoria encourages art that fosters the right kind of black pride—especially tribal pride, which by definition accentuates the differences between Africans and reinforces their suspicion that cities are the white man's foolishness.

Has Pretoria hit upon an effective compromise between a repression it can't afford politically or economically and the freedom its lip service insults? Is its censorship policy another half-measure under duress that can only delay the inevitable? Are such musings all superstructure, pretty much irrelevant to the substance of the apartheid struggle? The unavoidability of such questions compels anyone who writes about South African culture to take sides—not merely to oppose apartheid, but to try and understand the historical shape of this battle of form, content, style, and syncretic innovation, and to make tactical judgments about its future.

This is a big responsibility for a white American scholar who arrived at his speciality almost by accident. In 1975, David B. Coplan was studying West African drumming while acquiring a master's in anthropology from the University of Ghana when an acquaintance asked him to research a film on South African music. Soon he was hooked, pursuing his graduate work at the University of Witwatersrand in Johannesburg and also appearing part-time with the black-consciousness band Malombo. Waiting to drive some musicians home to Soweto without the proper permit one night, he was stopped by police and detained, as they say, for three weeks; although he was eventually permitted to return to school, his residence permit wasn't renewed. So he spent the next year in the border states (and with exiles in London) continuing to research his PhD thesis, which he rewrote as *In Township Tonight!*, a "history of South Africa's black city music and theatre."

Trained as an anthropologist, Coplan works with real historiographical sophistication, adding to extensive interviews such primary sources as police blotters and colonial records as well as the published reports of anyone who's been there, from black newspapermen to European memoirists. He owes his grounding in these methods to such South African labor specialists as Charles van Onselen and Shula Marks rather than any school of journalistic narrative or cultural history. Yet he writes with lively detail, and he's mastered the journalist's trick of recapitulating received facts in a way that will neither confuse the ignorant nor bore the knowledgeable, couched as it is in the fresh, clear contextual framework of black cultural history. And he writes as a musician who's disinclined to reduce the significance of a performance to its ostensible ideology. He thinks good art is good for those who love it, and while he worries that apartheid's hegemony will cut into black South Africans' creative capacity, his instinct is to trust the people. For fifty years Pretoria's foes have found in this mongrel-to-hybrid world of postfolk performance very much what the oppressors found: inferiority feelings, imitation, frivolity, decadence, escape. Coplan finds Africans thrust into a new situation and defining their own prerogatives within it.

As a result, the chief fascination of *In Township Tonight!* isn't political—it's artistic, or rather cultural. By filling in just enough economic and political background, Coplan helps the novice see what an amazing place South Africa is. With its temperate climate, long colonization, extensive development, and complex juxtaposition of tribes and immigrant groups, it's unique in sub-Saharan Africa, as much like the US as it is like Ghana. Demographically, it's a basically biracial melting pot, with blacks having the numbers but never the power of America's whites, while "coloureds" and Indians assume minority roles like Hispanics and Asians here. Despite the Dutch influence, its Anglo-African mix recalls both the British West Indies and the American South—with continuous, immediate African input. On top of this, South Africa is a living challenge to elitist aesthetics. Even at their most well-meaning, the colonizers' efforts to civilize blacks with respectable European culture only serve to emphasize the depth and necessity of the popular syntheses forever welling up in the locations and townships—syntheses that seized upon Afrikaner folk music dismissed by Boer-baiting English do-gooders and imperialists, or discerned the higher civilization of American Negro spirituals and jazz, or put into practice a spontaneous pan-Africanism.

Coplan's story avoids knee-jerk populism: even though some of its most exciting moments are devoted to convivial working-class institutions like the *stokfel* and the shebeen, genteel mission-school Africans with arty pretensions play almost as heroic a role as rude proletarians. What's more,

Coplan reports that many of the prime movers of South African city music fit neither social category. As in so many other places, they're drifters and hustlers of marginally criminal tendency, their tribal identity muddled by some admixture of racist exploitation and personal quirk. Coplan certainly doesn't evade issues of class—he's exceptionally sensitive to them. But he's convinced that everything else in South Africa is swallowed up by race—and that thus the black middle class is betrayed into something very much like poverty by whites who groom uppity kaffirs as a buffer against the hordes below only to cut them loose when a particular crisis stabilizes. He's also enough of an aesthete to understand that unmitigated class analysis rarely does justice to the vagaries of form and style that define particular musical or theatrical pieces, much less the vagaries of context, motive, use, and insight that inform particular acts of appreciation.

Ever since the first Dutch colonists reached Cape Town in 1652, a nonwhite underclass has performed and adapted the masters' music. Though Xhosa, Zulu, Tswana, and Sotho migrants as well as West African slaves have long been part of Cape life, the natives of the region were nomadic, brown-skinned Khoi-khoi, and most of the imported slaves were Malays who added their own melismatic cadences to the Euro-Khoi music that inevitably evolved. As the Boers trekked north and east after the British seized the Cape in the early nineteenth century, Bantu-speaking blacks were introduced to this music on hybrid instruments. By the time diamonds were found inland in 1867, the styles of coloured entertainers were ripe for further Africanization by musicians among the black "dressed people" or *abaphakathi* (Zulu: "those in the middle"), who rejected both middle-class Christianity and tribal traditions. The discovery of gold in the Witwatersrand in 1886 assured South Africa's wealth and urbanization, and after the Boer War ended in 1902 black dispersion from rural areas and mission settlements went into full swing.

By then such trade-store instruments as guitar, concertina, harmonica, and violin were so thoroughly integrated into tribal music that they were shunned by urban African Christians. American blackface minstrels had inspired the coloured Cape Coon Carnival, which still exists, as well as a middle-class African Native Choir milked for local and international profits by white impresarios. Zulu clan rivalries were spurring men without women to unprecedented heights in institutionalized miners' dance competitions previously dominated by Mozambicans. The Durban parades of a secret society of urban Zulus called the Ninevites made prominent use of harmonica, which never caught on like the pennywhistle favored by the Ninevites' successors, the young Johannesburg outlaws known as the *amalaita*. And none of this is even to mention the influx of European folk and popular styles, or the missionary-taught tonic sol-fa notation mastered most conspicuously by the Xhosas, or the Afrikaner usages toward which uneducated African musicians gravitated. South Africa was already host to a musical culture of unchartable complexity.

What Coplan posits as the underlying theme or goal of this culture is an old favorite of writers with a weakness for dance music, race mixing, and the great narrative of human progress: urbanization. The complication is that South Africa is a society which for almost four decades has been organized to keep blacks away from its cities. By stifling community life in the townships and making it onerous if not illegal for blacks to travel to and within urban areas, Pretoria deliberately exacerbates the apprehension city life always arouses in recent arrivals, and by segregating not only races but, when possible, tribes, it stanches the diversity that is the city's fundamental educational opportunity. It's hard to say just what urbanization means in such a place. Is the "homeland" black who schemes for a Jo'burg work permit truly rural? Is an mbaqanga show satirizing the pretensions of neourban blacks legitimate expression or tribalist propaganda? Do black playwrights' unflattering depictions of the black underworld serve the state or help define black pride? All that's certain is that apartheid's victims have been impelled to forge rural-urban syntheses that could have unanticipated uses in a world where the conflicts of urbanization are rarely resolved to the satisfaction of all parties. And though these syntheses are often cultural in the anthropological rather than aesthetic sense, the African integration of art and everyday life soon comes to bear on them.

An example is the speakeasies that the Irish cops of Cape Town christened with the Gaelic word "shebeen." Since "in traditional Southern African societies, beer is an economic and social currency as well as a nourishing food," the African women of Cape Town and Johannesburg were quick to transform their slumyard quarters into bars for municipal and domestic workers, joined on weekends by miners in for a blowout. By the '20s, amateur music making in these illegal drinking houses had given way to the wedding, courting, and walking songs of semiprofessional Zulu *abaqhafi* musicians, who frequently dressed in cowboy garb copied from movies, and Mozambican Shangaans playing Portuguese guitar music. A somewhat more respectable variant was the *stokfel*, in which five or six women banded together in mutual assistance associations inspired by both the Southern African pastoral tradition of beer-drinking cooperative work parties and, it would appear, the rotating English "stock-fairs" of the Eastern Cape. In these credit rings, which began with the Cape Town Xhosas and were developed in Johannesburg mostly by northern Tswanas, women would take turns collecting payments and then use the capital to finance what amounted to rent parties. "If a woman contributed liberally to the club and her husband spent freely at parties, they became popular and did well when she held her own party. Such participation built prestige and a reputation for generosity, reliability, and community-mindedness. Club hostesses added music, making it more profitable and entertaining through the bidding custom."

During the '20s, all of this activity coalesced into marabi. Marabi was a musical style—which went almost unrecorded, Coplan believes, more out of ignorance than snobbery—that offered something for every Johannesburg black: *tyickey draai*, a coloured Afrikaner ricky-tick guitar style; *tula n'divile*, Xhosa music converted to Western keyboards; Zulu melodies; pan-tribal polyphony; a ceaseless rhythm derived from ragtime and Nguni wedding celebrations. But as with rock and roll, its musical boundaries were far-flung, and it wasn't just music, it was a subculture—the dances and parties where it was played were also called marabi, as were the dancers, and how can you tell the marabi from the marabi? The white elements in the synthesis signified no interest in white notions of respectability or moral uplift—on the contrary, marabi articulated a defiantly African cultural outlook determined to adapt old ways to the hard options of city life, and middle-class Africans, Coplan tells us, "did what they could to stifle" it. One response was the attempt to cultivate a "Bantu National Music" at annual festivals called Eisteddfodaus (as it happens, the term is Welsh rather than Afrikaans), where educated blacks made personal and organizational contacts and developed political strategy. Another was black music criticism as lively, committed, and insightful as any of its white counterparts in England or America. Despite dissenters typified by one such critic, Musicus—who decried the "perversion" of "the remarkable syncopating rhythms to be found in the Native music of many races"—the African middle class gradually focused its musical attention on jazz, first imitative but then more and more distinctly South African in its accents.

Although he maintains a distance from *makwaya*, a hybrid of African hymnody and European artsong, Coplan recounts all this with fannish critical enthusiasm. Arguing that politically effective black consciousness must attune itself to both daily need and geopolitical reality—that it must combine the nitty-grit practicality of the *stokfel* with the theoretical reach of *makwaya*—he's unfazed by apparent cultural contradictions. Middle-class minstrelsy evolves into full-scale musical comedy with a large white audience, which in turn influences a style of black radical theater that puts tribal ritual in a township context. Though tsotsi (from "zoot suit") thugs come under regular attack in urban performance arts, they're major music patrons whose Afrikaans-based Euro-African dialect turns into the lingua franca of working-class Africans. Jazz musicians' retreat into bebop alienation is accelerated by the fast-rand cynicism of white record entrepreneurs and their black factotums, which nevertheless induces some of them to make crucial contributions to such r&b-compatible pop styles as tsaba-tsaba, kwela, and mbaqanga.

It's no insult to Coplan's analysis to say that what's most welcome about *In Township Tonight!* is its descriptions of music and theater scarcely available to Americans in any other form. For just that reason, my objections must be conjectural, but toward the end the book does seem to fall victim to the myopic despondency and special pleading that often afflict popular culture histories as they near the present. Coplan sees that marabi was a turning point in South Africa's black consciousness even though it appalled progressive Africans at the time; he sees how piggish white impresarios gave individual blacks opportunities that eventually benefited the black majority as a whole. But the spectacle of authentic black expressions co-opted into a culture industry controlled by white capitalists, their racism ever more ingrained as apartheid rationalizes its state of siege, is too much for him. Although he seems to respect and enjoy the music, he can't abide the anti-urban lyrics of working-class mbaqanga or the slick Americanism preferred by those who cherish fantasies of upward mobility—enforced in each case by record executives and acceded to by artists whose sense of what they can't say is no less oppressive for its accuracy.

As a result, he doesn't give the pop of the past thirty years the space it deserves in a study of this length. And for all we can know, he may be right—maybe at this point in the struggle only explicit political messages are of any political usefulness. Yet neither my own ears nor Coplan's descriptions altogether convince me that the cross-tribal style and reach of contemporary mbaqanga can't (and don't) transcend its ostensible ideology, or that for all its racism and tacit support of Pretoria the US doesn't remain a progressive model in the South African context, or that the fusion and black-consciousness bands he praises are of much international appeal—which isn't to say that in South Africa they don't serve a function even more crucial than that of earlier hybridizers whose interest is now historical.

Even if I'm right, however, the error is more of tone and shape than of substance, and although it lapses briefly into academic abstraction at the end, I know of few more compelling investigations of popular culture: it has scope, color, a sense of pace, loads of information, and an intellectual organization that does well to center around that elusive notion, urbanization. In Coplan's view, the key to any definition is choice—a luxury almost as hard to come by in tribal life (not to mention the "homelands") as it is in townships hemmed in by pass laws, police violence, and structural unemployment. Black South Africans want more choices, and black South African culture proves it. For all their depredations, the European conquerors opened up a world of new possibilities, and the evidence of Coplan's study suggests that those possibilities are now coming back to haunt them. I hope I won't offend orthodox cynics if I call *In Township Tonight!* a credible celebration of the human spirit—of men and women's indomitable need to find expressive outlet in any life situation short of total privation. The masters have to tolerate that need because they can't repress it, and sooner or later it will do them in.

Village Voice, 1986

Bwana-Acolyte in the Favor Bank

Banning Eyre's *In Griot Time: An American Guitarist in Mali*

To read about Afropop is to put oneself at the mercy of folks for whom tourism means vocation rather than vacation: the intrepid obsessives who set out from Europe and America to experience the stuff in situ. Academic or journalistic, good or bad, the most putatively objective overviews begin with some wanderer's adventurism, a/k/a fieldwork. *In Griot Time*, Banning Eyre's tale of seven months he spent studying guitar in Mali, falls into a more candid subsubgenre: the first-person narrative in which the white bwana-acolyte turns his or her quest into travel literature. This has proven an engaging gambit elsewhere. Helen Q. Kivnick's earnest *Where Is the Way* gains so much readability from its subjective POV that you don't mind the way it glosses over the internal contradictions that have glared since apartheid fell. A similar benefit befalls even Lewis Sarno's embarrassing *Song from the Forest*, in which the author goes so native that he's tricked into marrying a Pygmy who doesn't like him any more than you will.

Intellectually, Eyre doesn't resemble Kivnick or Sarno so much as his chief academic predecessor, John Miller Chernoff, whose 1979 account of his long drumming studies in Ghana, *African Music and African Sensibility*, found the warp and woof of the axiom that African music is woven into the fabric of African life. Chernoff's insistence that Westerners who want to understand Africa make a personal investment in its culture, rather than maintaining their polite scholarly perspective, shifted paradigms in African studies as surely as Robert Farris Thompson's dance- and music-saturated art histories. *In Griot Time*'s narrative skill, however, sets it apart. In the *Boston Phoenix*, on NPR, and for many more specialized venues, Eyre has covered Afropop more prolifically than anyone in America, but nothing in his criticism or reporting promised this level of writerliness. There's truly a story here; you want to know what will happen next.

The setup is simple. In 1995, Eyre quit his comfy Boston computer job to take guitar lessons in Mali from Djelimady Tounkara, leader of the government-supported Rail Band, where international stars Salif Keita and Mory Kante once wailed. Eyre embraces the move, suggested casually by Tounkara after the American visitor shows aptitude on a few riffs during a 1993 visit to Bamako, with intrepid obsessiveness. Nearly forty, he uproots himself to one of the poorest nations on earth, where his teacher is a big man who supports a large extended family and drives a Nissan so decrepit that it expires before the book is over.

Living in the new house Tounkara is slowly building and hanging out at the present Tounkara compound, Eyre is thrust into an alien social nexus where he is at once Hapless Interloper and Mr. Moneybags. Characters emerge: the generous, irascible, elusive Tounkara; his strong-willed wife and kindly brother; his irreligious bass player; the family griot whose function is mediation, not entertainment. Numerous dramas unfold, especially after another brother and his griot wife return home, soon followed by the real Mr. Moneybags, a fabulously wealthy and extravagantly disruptive Malian named Babani Sissoko. But the drama that drives the book takes place between all these people and Eyre, who conducts himself with impressive grace and tact, partaking fully of this incomprehensible world without losing hold of his own needs and values—without going native.

Mali definitely has a money economy, as Sissoko proves by throwing African francs around. But much of the money changes hands in a barter system akin to the "favor bank" of Tom Wolfe's *Bonfire of the Vanities*—every kindness anticipates some sort of reciprocation sooner or later. Expected to pay for taxis and beer or advance loans and underwrite equipment repair,

Eyre is hit on constantly: "Over and over in Bamako, I felt forced to choose between being a sap and having friends or standing firm and remaining at a distance." Often he resists, but in musical settings he's usually a sap—for Africans you feel really are his friends even as they scheme over his possessions while he departs. The financial boons he spreads around seem to him only a proper return of the Malians' trust. But he can't help noticing (as did Christopher A. Waterman in his study of juju) that the much-praised social relevance of Africa's praise-singing tradition comes down to fawning over the rich and powerful. Lyrics are often elaborate, cleverly rationalized lies; centuries-old chestnuts are played past their breaking points as flattery is heaped on to elicit a bigger payout. Soon Eyre finds himself dissenting hesitantly from Chernoff's first dictum: "Having come all this way to learn the music in context, I found I preferred the music *stripped* of its context." With the arrival of the famously music-mad Sissoko, everyone Eyre knows goes into a tizzy—rehearsals and a trip to Cuba are scotched as men and women as big as Tounkara himself polish up their begging bowls. Back in the States, in fact, Sissoko lays some largesse on Eyre himself—to help him finish this book.

If none of this leaves Eyre—or me—disillusioned with Mali, thank the music, which testifies eloquently for its context even when stripped of it. Not that there isn't plenty of context. Portraits of womanist diva Oumou Sangare, kora virtuoso Toumani Diabate, and Grammy-winning guitar god Ali Farka Touré provide both star power and thematic elaboration. Toure's oft-parroted theory that the blues were invented in northern Mali is dispassionately examined and discarded, although Eyre wonders whether the hunter music of the Wassoulou region down south mightn't support a similar claim. There are enticing descriptions of a Bamako bar scene no tourist could find without a guide. But equally enticing are Eyre's descriptions of the music itself, whether they ride a musician's detailed technical insights or an acolyte's one-of-a-kind epiphanies. They're so vivid, in fact, that they bear out what anyone who's ever loved an African CD without visiting Africa is free to discover—that the music motivates and signifies merely as an organization of sounds no matter how incomprehensible Mali may be, even to Malians themselves.

As has never been clearer, there isn't a single Malian music. Mali is home to many distinct peoples, and for both long-standing cultural reasons and short-term (we wish) economic ones produces an abundance of full- and part-time musicians, the most gifted of whom spend their lives inventing, syncretizing, cross-fertilizing, reaching out and back and around. Eyre is a touch propagandistic about his home away from home—although Mali is the hot Afropop ticket right now, similar riches can be found in South Africa, Senegal, Nigeria, Congo. But he knows that big pictures usually comprise small details. He doesn't flinch from inequities or inconsistencies. And he never pretends to an objective authority he doesn't have.

Salon, 2000

In the Crucible of the Party

Charles and Angeliki Keil's *Bright Balkan Morning: Romani Lives and the Power of Music in Greek Macedonia*

"The power of music lies in its participatory discrepancies, and these are basically of two kinds: processual and textural." So declared Charles Keil in his previous book, *Music Grooves*, an essay collection he co-wrote with ethnomusicologist Steven Feld. Since you're wondering what this jargoneering academic is spouting about, let him continue: "Music, to be personally involving and socially valuable, must be 'out of time' and 'out of tune.'" Now perhaps you're getting Keil's gist, grinning or just as likely grimacing. He's saying that any music worth a damn forswears foursquare rhythms and pure note values. But let him go on: "For *participatory discrepancy* one could substitute 'inflection,' 'articulation,' 'creative tension,' 'relaxed dynamism,' or 'semiconscious or unconscious slightly out of syncness.' For *process* one could say 'groove,' 'beat,' 'vital drive,' 'swing,' 'pulse,' or 'push,' and for *texture*, 'timbre,' 'sound,' 'tone qualities,' 'as arranged by,' and so forth." And so on. You know.

Keil surfaced in 1966 with a repurposed master's thesis based on club interviews focused on two blues stars with no profile beyond Afro-America: B. B. King and Bobby Bland. Titled *Urban Blues*, this serious study of *currently popular entertainers who earned good livings with electric guitars* was a radical departure that heartened a generation of like-minded listeners back when rock criticism and popular music studies were gleams in a nerd's eye—when it still took chutzpah to admire James Joyce and James Brown in the same lifetime, never mind the same sentence. Specifying scholarly debts, pinpointing the moldy-fig fallacies of the gullible blues buff Samuel Charters and the sacrosanct amateur culture theorist LeRoi Jones, offering a credible phylogeny of blues and a knowledgeable account of the then uncodified concept of soul, and paying detailed, enthusiastic attention to both artists and fans, Keil not only broke academic ground but wrote more eloquently about it than all but a handful of the thousands who followed.

Then he vanished. It took him a dozen years to force out 1979's *Tiv Song* after traumatizing research in the teeth of Nigeria's Biafran war, and thirteen more to resurface with a bang via a string of three collaborative books. In 1992 came *Polka Happiness*, a university-press coffee-table job that scandalized Keil's African-humanist admirers by positing an equivalence between Polonian happiness and Afro-musical spiritual release while arguing convincingly that what we call polka isn't Polish but Polish-American, descendant of an urban, working-class, obscurely eastern European dance that swept western Europe circa 1844 on its way to becoming indigenous from Mexico to Indonesia. In 1993 followed the deeply collective *My Music*, where Keil, doctoral candidates Susan D. Crafts and Daniel Cavicchi, three graduate seminars, and two undergraduate classes winnowed 150 interviews with Buffalo-area music users into a lively whole comprising forty-one, none pigeonholing into one of those neat taste subcultures beloved of marketers, programmers, sociologists, and rock critics. Spontaneously and unpretentiously, one respondent likes rap and Elvis, another rock and roll and "vernacular music," another Broadway shows and Polish village styles and Chopin, another Neil Diamond and Willie Nelson and Neil Diamond and Liza Minnelli and Neil Diamond. What unites them is how uncontrollably each bends music to his or her own semiconscious needs or well-conceived purposes.

Published in 1994, the Feld collaboration *Music Grooves* won the 1995 University of Chicago Folklore Prize even though it's about far more than music or folklore—that's why Feld's broadly suggestive scholarship won him a MacArthur. In contrast, Keil's sui generis anarcho-humanist thinking cuts too wide a swath and too many corners to achieve much academic acceptability outside the tiny discipline of ethnomusicology. Accommodating some two hundred illustrations shot and collected by Dick Blau, with a Feld soundscape CD situating the archaic music of the Macedonian Roma in a modern ambience of Stevie Wonder and Christmas carols, *Bright Balkan Morning* is his finest work so far—a beautiful and important work recommended to anyone who cares about how ordinary outsiders get by and get over in a world economy of rampaging corporations and embattled nation-states.

Keil's notion of participatory discrepancy was seeded by his experience of black musics in America and Africa. But it was formulated after prolonged contact with the white ethnics who inspired *Polka Happiness*, and now in the crucible of northern Greece, where his wife and co-author Angeliki grew up. Fundamentally a musical concept, participatory discrepancy serves too as metaphor and model for both universalist humanism and radical pluralism. Africans meet Polish-Americans meet "Gypsies"; the groove of the process meets the roughness of the texture meets the tense-yet-relaxed dynamism of the slightly out-of-sync.

Rather than equating the serious with the somber, the painful, the long-suffering, the tragic, Keil valorizes the urge to party: "Today we let it all go—release, discharge, breaking, spilling, spraying—we give of ourselves, our substance, to each other, and it feels very good." And balancing his flights is his wife's detailed attention to human context. Not that her husband doesn't see such things; he's a sensitive reporter who scrupulously follows the money that passes to these professional musicians. But he leaves full description to Angeliki, a sociologist who fills in some history and contributes nine oral autobiographies and three roundtables. And first, Roma scholar Ian Hancock lays out origins.

Gypsies, as the Roma are still often known, began as soldiers or camp followers in armies raised in India to repel Islamic invaders shortly after 1000 A.D. Their language is a patois inflected by all the many tongues with which it's coexisted, especially Byzantine Greek, and while their musical vocation goes back to their army days, "gypsy music" per se is a chimera. The Roma have no music of their own—Spanish flamenco and Hungarian verbunkos, both also considered Gypsy genres, sound nothing like the zurna-and-dauli trios chronicled by Keil, who had no luck locating the "authentic" music he was told Greek-Macedonian Roma played for themselves. They are entertainers who are prouder of their technique than their culture and who call themselves "instrumentalists" rather than the artier "musicians." Keil dwells on this distinction; he likes the idea of artists being merely "instrumental," servants of some larger force. In Macedonia, two such forces are prominent.

First is the ancient sound of the zurnas (imagine a cross between a clarinet and an alto sax with wavery pitch), and the dauli (a double-headed bass drum thumped with a big stick on one side and rattled with a little one on the other). Second is the modern culture clash of Greek Macedonia, where Keil breaks down influences into "Vlach, Sarakatsan, Slavic, Pontic, Thracian, Romani—and so many more local variants"—not least the "ethnic Greeks" from Asia Minor who were forcibly repatriated circa 1923, after the Greco-Turkish War. The zurnas, which are fighting a rear-guard battle against clarinets, bouzoukis, and DJ sound systems, link Macedonian revelers to both immemorial ritual and the party ideal of *kefi*, a borrowed Turkish term whose meaning Keil teases out in an eloquent endnote. But the zurnas achieve this link to the deep past only by encompassing the heterogeneous impurity of the region where they happen to survive.

Given the ethnic warfare that triggered World War I and has beset the Balkans post-Tito, we may think of Greece as a paragon of democratic stability. But into the bitterly fought Communist insurgency of the late '40s, its twentieth-century history was every bit as Balkanized, with the Roma a visible dark-skinned minority. Identified with none of the region's supposedly indigenous groups, they mediate among them all. Weddings typically bring together families of inconveniently mixed ethnic loyalties as well as a stew of bosses, clients, employees, co-workers, neighbors, and fellow students. As a result, Roma musicians pride themselves on their knowledge of multiple song traditions, all filtered through instruments that predate those traditions and played with technical skill, crafty showmanship, and expressive flair—in strict request order.

Bright Balkan Morning celebrates the interactive energy of this process—the participatory discrepancies that animate the relationship of an instrumentalist to his audience and his fellow players. Moreover, its form embodies the values of collaboration—Blau and Feld contribute illuminating essays, and in the end Angeliki gets more pages than Charles. This is a plus—her prose has loosened up since *Polka Happiness*, and her vivid description of the war-ravaged Greece of her childhood helps establish a tone the interviews flesh out.

The slant here could be branded anti-modern; after thirty years pursuing an instrument that could be disappearing from the face of the earth, no anarcho-humanist is likely to be down with disco sound systems or, more broadly, capitalist development and homogenization. But the Keils never allow their devotion to music to compromise their deeper devotion to human society. Angeliki's documentation of the Romas' material struggles make it seem not just natural but admirable for the instrumentalists to count their money, move up the class ladder, and put music aside when a more remunerative line of work presents itself. And far from dismissing self-consciously "cultural," often government-supported attempts to prop up old musics as unnatural, they welcome them as the progressive historical developments they are.

In the end, however, it's the music itself that inspires Charles Keil—music he describes with a vigor and affection rare in any species of writing: "With my back to a wall, I immediately feel the throbbing overtones. Sometimes I feel them as an identifiable higher-pitched tone inside my head, but more often they register as a sensation of blurring, static, dust on the needle of a record player, a buzz like the one that sometimes comes from being too close to the speakers of a loud rock band." Mere sensationalism, sniff the canon-keepers of "classical"'s rival European tradition. Keil, who has been combatting this tradition all his life, begs to differ. The party goal of *kefi*, he observes, is a conscious spiritual mechanism, different from *duende* or *Gemutlichkeit* or even ecstasy—it's more a "contemplative 'emotional engrossment'" that shouldn't be romanticized or sensationalized. "There is in Greek parties an element of 'fake it until you make it,' as when African-American gospel shouters pretend to be filled with the holy spirit until in fact they are. But as Greek partyers shout out 'Oh!' or 'Aman!' or people at tables burst into song, they may be in their kefi or inducing it in themselves and others, but they are not out of their minds or having an 'out-of-body' experience."

This is what Charles Keil envisions—nothing less than a reconciliation, as opposed to obliteration, of the mind-body dualism that causes so much pain in the world. He's too realistic to believe that this reconciliation will be accomplished in history with zurnas; he'll be pleased if the horns he loves hang on at all. But he's never going to stop promulgating it. *Bright Balkan Morning* is his strongest argument yet for what in *Music Grooves* he also breaks down as a conflict between "culture" and "civilization." Italics in original.

Civilization is the crap that culture leaves behind.
Civilization, as a whole, piles up; culture gets smothered.
Being more civilized means having more museums and libraries; culture is giving yourself to prime and present time.
Conversation is culture; writing is civilized.
Culture is yeasty, fermenting, a single germ or seed generating a growth process; civilization is the wine bottled, labeled, and corked.
Improvising is cultural; following the letter of the law or the law of the letter is civilized.
Civilization is all grasp; culture is reach.

Los Angeles Times Book Review, 2002 · Revised and expanded

Defining the Folk

Benjamin Filene's *Romancing the Folk: Public Memory and American Roots Music*

Benjamin Filene's premise—that the realities of artistic practice "call into question . . . rigid definitions of 'pure' folk music"—is by now so widely accepted that even purists have to live with it. His conclusion "that the backward glance can be more than nostalgic—that memory can create American culture anew" never discusses the American present in the detail it deserves. But between these two rhetorical disappointments, *Romancing the Folk* proves a fascinating history of an idea and a shape-shifting body of song.

Filene, a public historian at the Minnesota Historical Society, declares himself unconcerned with who the proper creators of "folk music" might be, and never gets very specific about what forces in modern life rendered their presumably unspoiled isolation so enticing to those bent on redefining America's past. What interests him is how the concept of "folk" was adjusted according to the tastes, needs, and ambitions of those who dedicated their lives to it, and how many different kinds of music such reconceptualizations brought to the surface. Filene traces the way changing notions of the "pure" and the slightly less exclusionary "authentic"—always counterposed to a vaguely defined "commercial"—inflected what "folk music" genres were disseminated and how they were performed, and the profound effect these ideas exerted on all of American *pop* music and its overlapping audiences. The folklorists, academics, bureaucrats, and entrepreneurs who dominate his story are colorful characters, and they are joined by artists who inspire Filene to critical heights few historians approach.

Filene begins at the unavoidable beginning: with Francis James Child, the Harvard Shakespeare scholar whose name lives on in the "Child ballads" he canonized in 1882's *The English and Scottish Popular Ballad*, and then with the English folklorist Cecil Sharp, who after years of scouring his homeland crossed the ocean in 1916 to certify a great motherlode of "authentic" Child ballads transcribed in an Appalachia he idealized as a simulacrum of England past. In keeping with the reflexively racist nativism of the time, this pseudoscientific research marginalized black American song, which had been attracting white chroniclers since the Civil War. It also denied that Sharp's Appalachian subjects exercised any legitimate aesthetic prerogatives in choosing or (heaven forfend) changing the songs he elected to preserve—and ignored the pop and black music they also performed, which he dismissed as irrelevant.

It was commercial exploiters like the traveling talent scout and soon-to-be publishing mogul Ralph Peer who first secured phonograph records of the breakdowns, ballads, and blues that dominate what we now think of as folk music. But another wayward Harvard professor with a passion for authenticity forever changed how such recordings were understood. Where Child and Sharp condescended to "folk music"'s creators as passive conduits of a static, immemorial tradition, John Lomax and his doubly influential son, Alan, honored them as active producers of an evolving one. The Lomaxes sought out both new variants of old material and contemporary topical songs as long as they were convinced their subjects had generated the music without input from the increasingly inescapable mass media. Lugging a 350-pound recording machine through the South on a 1933 song-hunting expedition that eventually gained them entree to the Library of Congress, the Lomaxes came upon Huddie Ledbetter, who as Lead Belly became the first folk "primitive" sold as such. Imposing their own standards of authenticity, the Lomaxes urged their discovery ("a nigger to the core of his being," John Lomax once remarked) to remain "raw"—as Filene puts it, "premodern, unrestrainedly emotive, and noncommercial"; they even put him onstage in convict's stripes. Yet at the same time they encouraged him to insert spoken explanations and political messages into songs that had never required them before. Moreover, as Filene's diligent analysis of successive recordings of "Mr. Tom Hughes' Town" makes clear, Lead Belly himself deliberately sentimentalized, desexualized, sweetened, and slowed his music to cater to listeners who preferred their authenticity tamer.

For Filene, no career better epitomizes the professional quandary of the putative folk musician than that of another Lomax discovery, Muddy Waters. Spurred first by Mississippi-born Chicagoans nostalgic for home and later by folkies and rock and rollers with related but distinct notions of what authenticity might entail, this paragon of the true Delta never stopped adjusting to fashion. Quickly abandoning a sophistication tailored to the pop blues of the day, first freeing and then simplifying his beat, deploying a broad spectrum of electric and acoustic timbres, putting his all into Willie Dixon lyrics that stylized and commodified the macho voodoo of the "hoochie coochie man,"

Waters made some awkward records. But at his frequent best he bent his overwhelming physical presence to recombinant interpretive genius, adapting usages he had absorbed in one place and time to the social and aural realities of another.

Alan Lomax and New Deal allies like the Federal Writers Project popularizer B. A. Botkin were more open-minded about who qualified as folk than John Lomax, much less Child and Sharp—Anglo-Saxon heritage, white skin, and even rural isolation were no longer a priori requirements. But even though this folk establishment had built its own economic infrastucture—dominated by genteel, progressively inclined outsiders, with considerable support in government and academia—not until the 1960s, if then, was it equipped to appreciate the hitmaking likes of Waters, whose crucial patron was the highly unidealistic label owner Leonard Chess. That establishment's direct legacy was the line running from Woody Guthrie and Pete Seeger, himself the son of a left-wing classical composer turned folklore honcho. Filene is plainly inspired by Seeger, whose music and persona he describes with a nuanced complexity that could beguile one into pulling out records whose bug-eyed earnestness has not worn well with casual fans. And he is obviously right to identify the apostate Bob Dylan, who so enraged Seeger by playing electric instruments at the Newport Folk Festival in 1965, as the last half-century's most original explorer of the folk idea.

But Dylan is so protean and prolix that you can use him to explore any number of things, and parsing his songs is a favorite ploy of intellectuals set on demonstrating their intimacy with popular culture. So given Filene's interest in the remade past, he should have gone easier on Dylan's '60s output, concentrating instead on the '90s, which he stuffs in at the very end. Over the past decade, a new vision of America's musical and spiritual past has been half-articulated by two Dylan albums reprising little-remembered canonical material combined with his folk-sounding, Grammy-winning *Time Out of Mind* (1997) and the rerelease of Harry Smith's 1952 *Anthology of American Folk Music*. Rooted in the recordings of Ralph Peer and his contemporaries, and in the Lomaxes' collecting as well, this work spins a vision of pre–World War I America as Bizarroworld Lost—a site of magic, myth, and mystery, a place where honest men told their desperate truths and vanished into the dust. This vision has risen up alongside a wide-ranging and inchoate folkie culture that is busy being born right now—a culture that stretches from black blues neotraditionalists to the punky faux honky tonkers of the alt-country movement.

There is no reason to believe that the new vision is any more factual than those that preceded it. It is merely the richest and most recent story certain seekers after the real and the beautiful have devised for themselves. In an era when increasingly interconnected and information-laden media have rendered both reality and beauty harder to grasp, and to live for, such stories play the vital function of sparking new kinds of musical creation—the products of which, at their best, transcend their theoretical underpinnings as the best art always does. Benjamin Filene has set himself the task of telling the stories' story. If he has failed to bring them into the present, that's because he too finds more comfort and inspiration in the past.

New York Times Book Review, 2000

Folking Around

David Hajdu's *Positively 4th Street: The Lives and Times of Joan Baez, Bob Dylan, Mimi Baez Fariña, and Richard Fariña*

One of the signal perversities of celebrity culture is the way it induces ordinary Janes and Joes to identify with the love lives of men and women who by the nature of their calling are no good at loving. Celebrities are extraordinary performers, and as extraordinary performers share two attributes: self-centeredness and fame. Self-centeredness isn't egotism, but it's close enough, and bad enough when it comes to empathy (as opposed to pushing people's buttons, which is what extraordinary performers do for a living). And fame is the cure for alienation that's worse than the disease, alleviating anonymity in a world of big cities and bigger media while making it impossible to know who your friends are.

Hence the pathology of *People*-style examinations of pop musicians, movie stars, athletes, politicians, etc. But what about more literary endeavors—namely, biographies, which beyond fanbook cash-ins are presumably devoted to folks who have changed history, and thus justify intelligent curiosity about what made them tick? Well, especially outside academia, that's presuming a lot. David Hajdu's 1996 *Lush Life* qualifies by delving into the life and work of Billy Strayhorn, a heroic composer who happened to be black and gay, and whose contribution to the Duke Ellington canon—as Hajdu argues rather too strenuously, but grant a fella his thesis—deserves more attention than it gets. *Positively 4th Street* smells a little different.

Commercially, this story of four romantically linked folksingers—Bob Dylan and Joan Baez stellar, Richard Fariña and Joan's little sister Mimi Fariña merely mythic—posits the same untapped nostalgia market courted by Rhino's three-CD *Washington Square Memoirs: The Great Urban Folk Boom, 1950–1970*. Farrar, Strauss would be overjoyed to rope in half the college students who made the pilgrimage to Newport in the '60s, and knows that even back then this literate, middle-class target audience had a weakness for the past, romantic please if possible. A lucid stylist and diligent interviewer, Hajdu performs the narrative chore of contextualizing and limning the Fariñas' tragic marriage and Joan and Bobby's doomed affair with considerable grace and enough insight to get to the next quote. But in order to afford his story the patina of respectability he and the audience require, he feels he needs a bigger thesis. And the one he comes up with should give Billy Strayhorn partisans pause.

For what Hajdu implies is that, just as Duke Ellington gets credit that Billy Strayhorn deserves, Bob Dylan gets credit that *Richard Fariña* deserves. The analogy isn't explicit; *Positively 4th Street* never mentions Strayhorn. But as I read *Lush Life* in the new book's wake—much preferring it, in part because Strayhorn was such an admirable human being—it became inescapable. For somebody treading ground already pounded into dust by legions of Ellington and Dylan adepts, the expediency of such theories is self-evident. Hajdu doesn't overdo it—because Fariña died in 1966, his must be a tale of cheated potential rather than neglected achievement. But he does report that Fariña inspired Dylan to take up with Baez. He does adjudge Fariña's literary endeavors a spur to Dylan's, which even if true means Fariña distracted Dylan from a verbal genius that dispenses with the page. And most remarkably, he does credit Fariña with inventing folk-rock by adding electric guitar to a song called "Reno, Nevada," *even though Dylan had recorded "Mixed Up Confusion" with a rock band ten months before*—quickly explaining that Dylan "would later dismiss" (what Hajdu doesn't mention was) his first single, as if Dylan is to be taken literally about anything, especially his own work. Sheesh. "Mixed Up Confusion" is no masterpiece, but at least it has some bite to it, while anyone who believes Fariña "snarls" "Reno, Nevada" has listened to too much Billy Strayhorn.

Not that Hajdu is utterly clueless about this music. I'd say he's excellent on Baez, although maybe that's just because I share the disdain informing such stinted praise as "gifted with exceptional intonation, especially by the forgiving standards of vernacular music" (well, not *that* disdain, but disdain in general). When he cites Dylan's "illusion of artlessness," he's hit the nub even if he's incapable of understanding how difficult, world-historic, and postliterary it might be to sustain that illusion, as Dylan miraculously does thirty-five years past the expiration date of Hajdu's period piece. But you'd never know from this book that the Fariñas couldn't sing even by the forgiving standards of vernacular music, where mildness rarely cuts it, and that like most folkies they were too polite (and "literary") by half. Physically gorgeous, synergistic, interested in rhythm, they were great in theory. But like Fariña's preciously word-drunk Ivy League Ivy League novel *Been Down So Long It Looks Like Up to Me*, whose sole surviving virtue is as an early case study in hip male chauvinism, their compilation CD has only documentary value. A thesis can be a worrisome thing.

The Fariñas' love story, on the other hand, had promise. True, when Mimi assayed her engagement ring sometime after her dead husband got on one too many motorcycles, she found out the "ruby" was glass. Richard was a charming rogue, and rogues stray; Hajdu faithfully tracks his flirtations with his sister-in-law, which given Joan's self-centeredness could conceivably have gotten very ugly. But Fariña also seemed to be learning something about conjugal interaction, as sometimes happens to rogues as they push thirty, and it's unlikely he would ever have achieved the pitch of celebrity that makes love so impossible. Bob and Joan were different. Because Baez was much warmer and funnier as a person than as an artist, Hajdu's belief that Dylan brought out her maternal side rings true, and his tender description of the hugs and giggles they shared is convincing. But so is a jealous jape by MacDougal Street godfather Izzy Young: "They would get married, if only they could agree on whose last name to use." And you have to wince when folk promoter Dick Waterman describes the pain he saw on Baez's face the first time she heard "Don't Think Twice, It's All Right": "Goodbye's too good a word, babe/So I'll just say fare-thee-well."

Politicians, athletes, and even movie stars have it easier—their public lives don't depend on their love lives. Pop musicians are expected to make art out of their romantic ups and downs. We need them to feed our own emotions. But a biography like this one demonstrates unequivocally that we take them literally at our peril. And that's a thesis Hajdu doesn't have it in him to explore.

Village Voice, 2001

Punk Lives

Legs McNeil and Gillian McCain's *Please Kill Me: The Uncensored Oral History of Punk*

Punk was a musical movement that reacted against the pastoral sentimentality, expressionistic excess, and superstar bloat of '60s rock with short, fast, hard, acerbic songs. It was also a subculture that scornfully rejected the political idealism and Californian flower-power silliness of hippie myth. Both strands first surfaced not in Great Britain, where punk became a cause celebre as of late 1976, but in the lower Manhattan of the early '70s. *Please Kill Me* concentrates on the second. Constructed entirely of excerpted interviews with several hundred principals, this is an immensely entertaining portrait of a bohemia. It bills itself as "uncensored" because it never stints on dish, cheerfully laying out what the nosy want to know—including, by my rough count, a hundred sexual liaisons and thirty individually identified heroin users, with cameos for a panoply of alcoholic beverages and just about every mind-altering substance then known. Sex and drugs and rock and roll—always a potent combo.

If this description makes you sniff, skip *Please Kill Me*, as well as the dozen or two excellent-to-epochal albums that are the direct legacy of a scene whose influence is now ascendant. All are probably too cheap for your blood. As a devotee of these musical works who got married and gave up pot before the punk era even began, I didn't find the sleazy connections the authors hammer home altogether comforting myself. And I was fascinated nonetheless. In part the book's appeal is sheer voyeurism. But having witnessed Dee Dee Ramone pounding his bass at dozens of shows, cried out at Richard Lloyd's string-punishing solos with Television, and learned to hear Richard Hell's zigzagging *Blank Generation* as a triumph of the life-force, I found these tales of unholy madness and drug-fueled abandon all too thought-provoking.

Scene-sucking photographer-manager Leee Black Childers can sum up an early Iggy Pop sighting easily enough: "It was so sexual, so outrageous, it was so un-allowed! To me, that's what rock and roll should always come down to—the un-allowed." But if you believe rock and roll is bigger than this humongous cliche, you have to wonder how such rich music can proceed from such mean and messy lives. You have to wonder how it came to be that three of your favorite musicians were notorious heroin addicts expert at trading their small-time celebrity and personal charm for a quick fix.

Basically, McNeil and McCain go along with Childers. I attribute their know-nothing bias to McNeil, who has been pumping some version of it since his tour of duty as "Resident Punk" at the short-lived but justly influential *Punk* magazine, which he named. What he didn't name but would like us to think he did was punk rock, a term that had long been floating around rock criticism—especially at the Detroit-based *Creem*, one of many non-*Punk* publications whose impact on the scene *Please Kill Me* minimizes by omission.

Even more than most oral histories, *Please Kill Me* imposes arguments on its materials. McNeil hates the idea that his bohemia was homophobic, and on this he is fairly convincing—gay men were clearly numerous and taken for granted in bands and behind the scenes, and a famous brawl involving the transvestite rocker Wayne County ends up looking like his fault. The defense of punk's flirtation with Nazi imagery is also plausible. More difficult to credit is the suggestion that this almost entirely white scene wasn't at least as racist as any other, especially after *Punk* magazine's founding genius, John Holmstrom, climaxes the presentation with a pronunciamento worthy of David Duke: "I always thought, if you're black and you want to be hip you're a Black Panther. . . . And you carry a gun. That's what I thought was cool. And if you're white, you're like us. You don't try to be black."

Probably because *Please Kill Me* has no use for artistic transcendence, certain visionaries—including Television's self-consciously poetic Tom Verlaine, drummer-theoretician Tommy Ramone, and David Byrne of Talking Heads, whose "yuppie whine" McNeil slags—are virtually absent, while the members of the Dead Boys, who have devoted their lives to the pathetic illusion that they were unsuccessful only because they were unallowed, mouth on for pages. But most of the interviewees are engaging talkers, as the likes of the late drummer Jerry Nolan and the irrepressible poet-rocker-mystic-comedian Patti Smith proved long ago in material skillfully recycled here. And quite a few in-crowd obscurities finally get their due as masters of improvised narrative and analysis, including hyperintelligent guitarist Bob Quine, unjudgmental participant-observer Mary Harron, mistress to the stars Bebe Buell, and urbane scenemaster Danny Fields, the Warhol Factory hand and teenmag editor who ended up managing the Stooges and the Ramones and getting this gossipfest dedicated to him.

As *Please Kill Me* would have it, punk's dissolute utopia wasn't killed solely by substance abuse, about which it grows properly grave by the close, or by the quest for fame among dull suburban teens and other people Legs McNeil doesn't like. There were also those English posers convincing the world that *they* had invented punk rock. I agree that punk crystallized in New York, but it's myopic boosterism to imply that the Sex Pistols, the Clash, and their progeny weren't as momentous and valid as our bands. Moreover, Fields's reasonable complaint that the instant onslaught of the Pistols "had nothing to do with anything musical" leaves open the question of just exactly what kind of music punk rock was. But for an answer you'll have to resort to Clinton Heylin's stodgier and stupider but more serious *From the Velvets to the Voidoids*, which quotes the principals on very little else. *Please Kill Me*'s lowbrow narrative strategy can only offer fatuous assertions to the effect that punk "was just rock & roll. We weren't taking the music anywhere new."

In fact, punk was so new that its formal ideas remain fruitful to this day. It distilled from the heedless drive and abrasive electric guitars of "just rock & roll" a bravely imagined popular response—angry, hilarious, incisive, any two, all three, and more—to post-industrial desperation. That desperation was enough to drive some of its creators to self-destruction. Others merely bulled or romped or joked or muddled or suffered through. But every one was possessed by a musical intuition. And the product of that intuition was and remains an antidote to desperation for all of us with ears to hear it.

New York Times Book Review, 1996

Biography of a Corporation

Nelson George's *Where Did Our Love Go?: The Rise and Fall of the Motown Sound*

Ideally, biographies are written from primary sources. The writer interviews subject, family, and close associates, examines documents and correspondence, and then fans the research outwards, gathering testimony from friends and fans and neutral experts. The result is expected to at least aim for impartiality, and sometimes disinterested observers will agree that it has hit the target.

That's how it's supposed to work. But even when most of these guidelines are respected, one is customarily ignored: the writer doesn't interview the subject because the subject is dead. Living human beings who are famous or important enough to merit biographies rarely encourage an objective assessment of their achievements. Their firsthand biographers are handpicked toadies or dazed admirers; often the biographees will only trade access to his or her exalted presence for the opportunity to "check the manuscript for accuracy"—that is, censor it. So the life stories of living persons are either "authorized," a polite way to say biased, or gathered from sources who are willing to talk because they aren't especially close to or have something against the principal. This syndrome has been responsible for a vast sea of stupid-to-mediocre writing. In popular music, such writing is rendered doubly dubious by the widespread assumption that the mean age of its target audience is fourteen.

Strictly speaking, Nelson George's *Where Did Our Love Go?* isn't a biography. It's the history of a corporation, Motown Records, beginning well before its inception in Detroit in 1959 and following its legend closely until 1971, when the label's move to Los Angeles signaled that its legendary days were over. But while Motown became the largest black-owned corporation in America by selling the creations of other black Americans, all lovingly and searchingly described here, the corporation itself was the creation of one man, Berry Gordy, which is why George's story must be Gordy's story. Authorized it isn't. In the grandest and most arrogant tradition of early Hollywood, Motown has always fed the press pap and expected unmitigated subservience in return. That's not how George does things, and as a result he didn't get to talk to Gordy (which doesn't distinguish him from countless more slavish but equally frustrated journalists) or to the (mostly white) men who run the company with him.

Unfortunately for Motown, I suppose, this noncooperation proved nowhere near as disabling as the company's flacks and protectors hoped. First of all, as he's already proved in his masterful quickie bio of Michael Jackson, George knows how to use secondary sources. He doesn't just go for the obvious, but finds obscure stuff—local newspaper stories both in and out of Detroit, court cases, old kinescopes. Then too, as America's foremost journalist of black music, black music editor of first *Record World* and then *Billboard*, as well as a respected critic whose reviews have appeared in a wide range of journals respected and otherwise, George enjoys considerable access to the artists who are the other half (or 90 percent) of the story. Some are disaffected now, of course, although quite a few have returned to the fold or never ventured away—unlike the behind-the-scenes personnel who dropped out as Gordy's reluctance to share the wealth became evident. Over the years George has talked to every one he could get to.

I'm sure Motown won't like the outcome of his research, but that's just vanity if it isn't paranoia. Not only is George's account evenhanded, it's by any reasonable criterion account warmly complimentary as well, which for Motown ought to be the ideal combination, because it guarantees credibility. While George deserves credit for resisting the bitterness of the ex-Motowners who provided their version of the story, it's clear that one reason he still admires Berry Gordy is that even Gordy's nominal enemies retain not just regard but affection for the man. Of course, one reason for that is the unvanquishable vitality of the music Gordy made happen. The Motown hits (and quite a few of the misses) of the '60s may stand as the most impressive and enduring body of pure pop for now people that rock and roll will ever produce. Individual artists as remarkable as Smokey Robinson and Marvin Gaye and the Temptations and Diana Ross and Stevie Wonder—not to mention composers like Holland-Dozier-Holland and Ashford & Simpson and the glorious backup band the Funk Brothers—all put their stamp on the music. But it was Gordy's quality controls, organizational flair, and unflagging desire to sell millions upon millions of records that shaped it.

George's narrative moves with grace, dispatch, and attention to detail. Because he's both a reporter and a critic, he doesn't shortchange history and he doesn't shortchange art—he keeps his eye on the money and his ear on the music and explains how they fit together. When he focuses on one portion of his tale, be it the Gordy family saga or the sad defeat of Florence Ballard, it's because he wants to exploit its illustrative value. There is, after all, an underlying theme here.

For finally, *Where Did Our Love Go?* is a book about black capitalism. George is no left-winger—he's sympathetic to black capitalism. But he sees how the paradoxes of power for black people in America undermines their temporary triumphs. People of any color can build an enterprise from a good idea and then move away from what they know best, with consequences that are disastrous spiritually if not economically. But in Gordy's case that familiar tragedy of success has an inescapably racial dimension. He made great music by tailoring black rhythm-and-blues to the tastes of a notably openminded generation of white American teenagers, but he knew that if this was to be a true American success story it couldn't stop there. So not only did he act like any boss and treat the talented people around him like peons, but he ended up where the American entertainment business always ends up—in Hollywood. As a result, Motown is now like any other record company, only a little smaller. Maybe none of this could have been avoided in any case. But Gordy's response to his American dilemma certainly accelerated the process.

In the end, Gordy's stonewall does leave a big question unanswered. George tells us where Gordy came from and what he did, but he can't make us feel exactly why he did it. His character, as opposed to his situation, remains frustratingly enigmatic. Given what George does tell us, though, we can be fairly sure that even those who know him best have a lot of trouble getting inside the man. When somebody is as driven as the prime mover of *Where Did Our Love Go?*, ultimate motivation is always a mystery. Just the facts will have to do. And they're here.

Introduction, *Where Did Our Love Go?*, 1985

Hip-Hop Faces the World

Steven Hager's *Hip Hop: The Illustrated History of Break Dancing, Rap Music, and Graffiti* | David Toop's *The Rap Attack: African Jive to New York Hip Hop* | Nelson George, Sally Banes, Susan Flinker, and Patty Romanowski's *Fresh: Hip Hop Don't Stop*

Although each of these books makes a brief fuss about the exploitation of the hip-hop subculture, only one—*Fresh*, conceived after it had established itself as a hot subject—is candid or reflexive enough to acknowledge its own inevitable complicity in the process whereby rude forms are tamed and brought to market. Not that they're obliged. Especially as rockbooks go, these are honest, loving, knowledgeable, and (except for *The Rap Attack*) written with commendable grace. And except for the introduction to *The Rap Attack*—appended, ain't socialism grand, by the left-wing house which published this eccentric musicological treatise in the US—all avoid the moralistic posturing that might put a guy in a debunking mood. But just because they're so well-meaning and well-executed, their problematic relationships to the dissemination, distortion, deracination, and ultimate destruction of the simple thing they care about are worth examining more closely.

Resistance to commercial cooptation generally begins with either a prior commitment to what's being coopted or a prior opposition to commerce. On the one hand, a possessive/protective identification with something that's been yours for generations (as in bluegrass) or at least months (skinny ties, say, or blackened redfish); on the other, the militant leftism and sentimental/conservationist reaction that are often hard to tell apart in cultural commentary. On the one hand, *Fresh*'s Nelson George (who shaped the book with Patty Romanowski, although the credits simply list them among the authors of its four essays on rapping, graffiti, fashion, and breaking), a rap fan since he was a teenager at St. John's and *The Amsterdam News*, or *Hip Hop*'s Steven Hager, who got interested in graffiti early in 1980 and rap later that year; on the other, *The Rap Attack*'s David Toop, a left-wing British musicologist and co-editor of the much-missed *Collusion*, who didn't catch on to rap until his *Collusion* colleague Sue Steward brought the news (and the records) back from a trip to New York in 1981.

Although George and Hager have followed (and spread) the story for years and enthuse fondly over its good old days uptown, neither trucks with any myth of the golden age. Having seen hip-hop survive more than one greatly exaggerated report of its demise, they have confidence in what George calls "its independent, determined spirit," a spirit both are certain will enable rap and its related forms to "continue to evolve despite the mass media's discovery of them." Too certain, perhaps—no form continues to evolve forever, after all, and in pop music most subgenres transmute pretty thoroughly within ten or fifteen years. Toop's view is wryer, more noncommittal and probably more realistic. Anything but a purist, he takes a gleeful pleasure in rap's cannibalization of competing musics, and while his analysis of recent developments isn't exactly oracular—writing in 1984, he seems to place more stock in Warp 9 than in Run-D.M.C.—he clearly expects things to keep on breaking. But though Toop's tone twists like a postmodernist's, his style plods like a cultural worker's. He betrays a typical lefty credulousness about just how easy hip-hop has been to package, and gets a little tight-lipped when he mentions such putatively inauthentic phenomena as punk, Chic, and *Beat Street*. Thus he leaves me wondering why he closes his text with the title of I.R.T.'s "Watch the Closing Doors." Is it too late for anybody else to get on the train? The implication is more ominous than he probably intended.

The more ominous the better, thinks Tony Van Der Meer, who takes it upon himself to squeeze Toop's uneven and unorthodox text into some semblance of left correctness. Van Der Meer's three-page introduction is so clumsily written and loosely argued that coherent summary does it an injustice, but you can probably figure his drift. Hip-hop, he tells us, is a "cultural expression . . . nurtured by a long heritage of slavery and resistance to racial, economic, political, social, and cultural oppression." Yet somehow it also strikes a chord within "poor and alienated white youth," at which point "white entrepreneurs" try to make money off it "by stripping it bare of feeling and content, leaving only the packaging." So, comrades, what is to be done? "Can hip hop be regained, or is it long gone?" Watch the closing doors indeed.

In case it isn't evident how inaccurate and baldly oversimplified this account is, let me run it down for you. Hip-hop does resist consumer capitalism's economic/social/cultural oppression, but it also accepts and even affirms it (and not always dialectically, as they say); like all Afro-Americana, it's rooted in slavery, but it owes much of its spirit to the real if brutally partial social/cultural/political freedom American capitalism affords. Hip-hop's white audience isn't notably "impoverished" and may not even be "alienated," whatever exactly that slippery catchall means in this context. Many of the entrepreneurs who've crossed hip-hop over have been black and Latin, and their most significant incursions—moving graffiti into the gallery, translating rap to disc—have been formal, though every such change inevitably alters "feeling," another catchall.

Admittedly, Van Der Meer is a straw man; his kind of demonistic hyperbole is dying out even among leftists, Toop among them. Yet the sad fact is that none of these books provides any more useful a dissection of hip-hop's cooptation, commercialization, popularization, historic triumph, whatever you want to call it. Toop doesn't even try. His history is musicological and mostly discographical (although he did get some good interviews when he finally came to New York), distinguishing casually if at all between seminal and marginal records and quite expeditious about how rap "packaged itself." Hager offers a good helping of relevant data, bringing us through the two phases of graffiti's art-world acceptance, pinpointing crucial journalistic moments (although not his own *Voice* profile of Afrika Bambaataa, which is where *Beat Street* began), and devoting an epilogue to the fallout from the biggest of all hip-hop's breakthroughs—the crassly out-of-context appearance of the Rock Steady breakers in the crassly pop-populist *Flashdance*. But Hager is an ace reporter, not a critic or social historian. He doesn't have the theoretical chops to stipulate the aesthetic failures of what he calls "overly commercialized" hip-hop, or to analyze the potential (and limitations) of its mass appeal. And though all the essays in *Fresh* begin in the streets and end in the media, only Sally Banes fleshes out historicist assumptions with linked examples.

Banes's account of the changes in break dancing post–"media hype" (her term) is impressive and somewhat depressing: *Soul Train* locking and other acrobatic borrowings help inflect the style toward "theatrical legibility," streetwise fourteen-year-olds give way to young-adult careerists, obscene gestures disappear, and the supremely expressive moment of the final freeze atrophies into part of the exit. But she offers virtually no description of the hype itself, and although she's forthright enough to indicate that it began with her own 1981 *Voice* cover story, she brushes by what is generally agreed elsewhere: that by the time she found out about the style it was dead as a street phenomenon, preserved mainly in the neoclassicist proselytizing of the late-breaking Ritchie Colon a/k/a Crazy Legs, one of her primary sources. Pretty mind-boggling: a folk form revitalized by a basically nonexploitative piece of criticism. Kept alive, that is, by the hint of a promise that it needn't remain a folk form—that there might be some rich-and-famous in it. This promise was of course fulfilled. But without Sally Banes—and her art-world informants Martha Cooper and Henry Chalfant, who have since published their own long-planned graffiti book—there'd be no *Breakin'*, no *Beat Street*, no ghetto kids diving for dollars outside Gimbel's. Certainly no *Fresh*, probably no *Hip Hop*, possibly no *Rap Attack*.

In case you think I'm trying to blow my newspaper's horn, that's not my intention. (For the record, I had no prior knowledge of Banes's piece—or of break dancing—and served only as a contact between Hager and his editor, Thulani Davis.) While Hager is kind enough to credit the *Times*'s Robert Palmer and the *Voice*'s Robert Christgau with furthering "the growing acceptance of hip hop" in 1981 and 1982, and while I'm proud I caught on to rap sooner than most critics, I'm all too aware in retrospect that the *Voice* should have been on the story in the late '70s, when I came across DJ Hollywood at the Apollo without realizing that he wasn't just strange but fucking incredible. In my analysis, no critic except Banes had more than an ancillary effect on the commercial fate of rap, which had already been fed into the music machine when we arrived. By 1981 Blondie had released "Rapture," Tom Tom Club was recording, and Blue's hip-hop nights were on their way to the Roxy; soon thereafter Sylvia Robinson and then Russell Simmons would make street hits out of two watershed records, "The Message" and "It's Like That"/"Sucker M.C.'s." Journalists helped disseminate, of course, but not as primary "tastemakers." It was a friendly alliance of bohemian rock and rollers and black bizzers which assured that in 1985 Run-D.M.C. would have fans in North Dakota, and if Palmer and I hadn't been around other writers would have noticed soon enough.

Because critics pack clout in the visual arts, they've had more effect on the salability and formal development of graffiti, although not as much as the *Times* reporter who found Taki 183, various middlemen/entrepreneurs, the Transit Authority, or our white-and-proud mayor. Unfortunately, while graffiti has been salutary for the art world (viz. Keith Haring and allied street people), the art world hasn't been so great for graffiti, diminishing its physical and social scale. Perhaps folk forms fare better when thrown straight into the maw of the culture industry. I wouldn't get too absolute with that one, though, and in any case it's a side point dwarfed by the central truth that all these writers either take for granted or studiously ignore: hip-hop's originators have never resisted the blandishments of the outside world. Art, commerce, whatever—as long as you weren't the law and seemed ready to give them money or publicity, they'd deal.

In this, hip-hop is just like any other classbound—that is, nonbohemian—urban subculture. There have been exceptions in its past, and there are probably more now. But for the most part, graffiti writers want to be artists, breakers want to be dancers, and rappers want to be pop stars—all vocations that beat working, not to mention unemployment. Sharing such broad general ambitions, some are more subversive than others: Rahiem of the Furious Five plays the crooner not just to reach a wider and less discriminating audience but also because a record company is letting him, while Afrika Bambaataa tries to coopt back, bending Kraftwerk and Billy Squier and even James Brown to his own funky purposes. But all have tended to interpret their continuing mainstream nonrecognition as a matter of time, of failed communication, of insufficient influence, at worst of racism—*not* of the recalcitrant authenticity of their styles.

In short, to fuss about the exploitation of hip-hop is quite often to take sides against the hip-hoppers themselves—even though in the end that exploitation is certain to prove a juggernaut that the hip-hoppers (and even the exploiters) can't control. To counsel purity isn't impermissible, but it's certainly complicated, with ramifications that stretch far beyond the scope of this review, or indeed of any piece of writing of any length on any similar subject that has ever come to my attention. Reviewing gamely on, I must conclude that the attractively straightforward is-it-honest-or-not approach cultivated by *Hip Hop* and *Fresh* does scanter justice to cooptation's complications than does *The Rap Attack*'s sly postmodernist delight in cultural dislocation. If only Toop were less evasive about the details and mechanics and extent of these dislocations. If only he shared Bambaataa's affection for the commercial culture he transmogrifies, or understood in his heart why Grandmaster Flash looks up to Rick James.

These if-onlys aren't rhetorical. As books, the cultural objects at hand are limited in both outreach and immediate impact, and so their complicity in hip-hop's exploitation is no big deal. They merely take an honest profit on an established phenomenon. But as books, they are relatively permanent, and thus will help define a tradition, a way of thinking about this particular subculture. Just because they're honest, loving, and knowledgeable, their failures will bear fruit along with their successes. I don't blame them, or claim to have done any better myself. But I am sure of this: however labyrinthine the resultants, the tensions between dissemination and exploitation, reaching out and selling out, must sooner or later be graphed accurately and sympathetically. If they aren't, we're never going to get a handle on how we talk to each other and change the world.

Village Voice, 1986

Making Out Like Gangsters

Preston Lauterbach's *The Chitlin' Circuit and the Road to Rock 'n' Roll* | Dan Charnas's *The Big Payback: The History of the Business of Hip-Hop* | Ice-T's *Ice: A Memoir of Gangster Life and Redemption—From South Central to Hollywood* | Tommy James's *Me, the Mob, and Music*

Although it's long made room for a few idealists and many fans who are in it for love, the music industry is not for the faint of heart. On the contrary, it's always been long on tough guys and worse, for reasons that are not hard to figure out. Cash businesses conducted at night in places where alcohol is served would have their shady side even in nations where the liquor trade wasn't illegal for fourteen crucial years, and although jukeboxes didn't catch on until well after Prohibition, the Mob was positioned to take them over, and get its mitts on record distribution in the bargain. Nor is it all about the Benjamins. If by popular music you mean domestic palliatives from "Home Sweet Home" to Céline Dion, OK, that's another realm. But most of what's now played in concert halls and honored at the Kennedy Center has its roots in antisocial impulses—in a carpe diem hedonism that is a way of life for violent men with money to burn who know damn well they're destined for prison or the morgue.

Most music books assume or briefly acknowledge these inconvenient facts when they don't ignore them altogether. But they're central to two recent histories and two recent memoirs, all highly recommended. Memphis-based Preston Lauterbach's *The Chitlin' Circuit and the Roots of Rock 'n' Roll* relishes the criminal origins of a mostly southern black club scene from the early '30s to the late '60s. Journalist-bizzer Dan Charnas's history of the hip-hop industry, *The Big Payback*, steers clear of much small-time thuggery and leaves brutal LA label boss Suge Knight to Ronin Ro's *Have Gun, Will Travel*, but plenty of crime stories rise up as profits snowball. Ice-T's *Ice* devotes twenty-five steely pages to the lucrative heisting operation the rapper-actor ran before he made music his job. And '60s hitmaker Tommy James's *Me, the Mob, and the Music* is an artist memoir distinguished by its substantial portrait of American pop's most legendary gangster, Morris Levy.

Owner of Roulette and countless other labels as well as the jazz club Birdland and the Strawberries record retailing chain, Levy is said to be the model for Hesh Rabkin of *The Sopranos* and deserves fuller treatment than James's fast-moving 225-pager. After he died of cancer while appealing an extortion conviction in 1990, a few of Levy's machinations were detailed in the likes of Dorothy Wade and Justine Picardie's Ahmet Ertegun biography, *Music Man*, and John A. Jackson's Alan Freed biography, *Big Beat Heat*. But James's stories are the most closely observed to date. IRS men examine Levy's books for so long that he gives them their own office at Roulette, where low-level enforcers and future Genovese boss Tommy Eboli stroll in and out. Levy roughs up James's first manager and threatens James himself. When James gets his draft notice, Levy phones a friend who's on the board of both Chemical Bank and the Selective Service, and James is classified 4-F. Finally, in 1972, with the hits dried up anyway, James confronts Levy in a pill-fueled rage and walks out with his knees intact.

James hated Morris Levy. Yet he also loved him, and he's not the only one. With James, maybe this is understandable. Although he and his Shondells were no Paul Revere and the Raiders quality-wise, he was a smart, ambitious, hardworking kid compelled to learn the music business at nineteen, and so Levy inevitably became a father figure—a father figure who robbed him of millions in royalties while overseeing a five-year run where James made his own pile touring, served as a youth advisor to Hubert Humphrey, and married a Mob-linked Roulette secretary whose dad forwarded the kids pharmaceutical samples from his post office job. But Levy had more sophisticated fans, especially in jazz, which he greatly preferred to rock and roll.

Count Basie, Dizzy Gillespie, and Nesuhi Ertegun are among the many to testify to his kindness and generosity. James simply says, "He was more fun to be with than anybody."

Levy—who also shows up in *The Big Payback* when he acquires the groundbreaking hip-hop label Sugarhill in a usury scheme—is the only white crook with a prominent role in these books. This is demographically unrepresentative. The Mob had its hooks into MCA, long America's dominant booking agency, and Levy's notorious predecessor Joe Glaser, who managed and fleeced both Louis Armstrong and Billie Holiday, was only the best-known of the many Mob-linked operators who controlled the nightclubs that became such a big deal as of the '20s. For the most part, however, these were northern clubs, because the North was where jazz fans had money and where white gangsters were organized. Preston Lauterbach tells the story of their black counterparts in the South, where ruder music was germinating.

Lauterbach's kingpin is Denver Ferguson, second in Indianapolis's Bronzetown only to that seminal black capitalist, hair-straightening queen Madame C. J. Walker. Ferguson was a numbers tycoon from a frugal land-owning family in a predominantly white Kentucky town whose printing business generated a specialty in gambling devices called "baseball tickets." By the early '30s that operation, plus the real estate it bought, led to his brother Sea Ferguson's Cotton Club and his own Trianon Ballroom, and these ventures to the Ferguson Brothers Agency a decade later. Lauterbach cares plenty about music, offering insightful descriptions of, among others, Little Richard, Louis Jordan, Johnny Ace, Gatemouth Brown, and journalist-bandleader Walter Barnes, whose well-embellished *Chicago Defender* columns on the South's many bronzetown "strolls" did much to raise African-American cultural consciousness in the '30s. But what he emphasizes about Ferguson is his workaholic organizational capacities. Although Ferguson accrued capital breaking the law, he was basically a businessman, and a responsible one: "He collected black dollars in underworld trade and gave back to the community at large, carving economic independence out for himself and employing black locals."

At times Lauterbach finds his material so colorful he can't resist providing prose to match, and he obsesses predictably on the ineffable southernness of rock and roll. But these are forgivable tics given what he's achieved—a coherent, musically savvy history of a performance culture that until now was known only piecemeal. In addition to Denver Ferguson we get the low-down on Houston's Don Robey, remembered because he owned a record label, and Memphis's Sunbeam Mitchell and Bob Henry, uncelebrated because they didn't. We also get revealing glimpses of unsafe havens where black men who knew damn well the white man was keeping them down could have more fun than anywhere—where music imparted spiritual concord to wine, women, and craps.

A redolent factoid is the name of the fraternal organization that staged the Baby Doll Dance at Natchez, Mississippi's Rhythm Club on April 23, 1940: the Moneywasters Social Club. How better declare your dissent from the Puritan ethic than by calling yourselves the Moneywasters? Unfortunately, the reason these spendthrifts are remembered is the 209 people who died that night in a one-exit venue where Spanish moss had been doused with kerosene to disperse mosquitos—including Walter Barnes, who had seen lots of fires and kept playing in a doomed attempt at crowd management. Also unfortunately, what has been dubbed the Natchez Dance Hall Holocaust would have been less deadly had not the Moneywasters boarded the windows and padlocked the back door to thwart freeloaders. But that's the kind of tradeoff you live and sometimes die with when you aim to have more fun than anybody.

Although most of the chitlin'-circuit impresarios went to their rest in more comfort than they'd been born to—and more comfort than their artists, especially the earlier ones—none of them got rich; Don Robey ended up selling Duke-Peacock for a hundred grand and a leased Cadillac. Two generations later, their successors have profited rather more spectacularly, marketing a rock and roll offshoot that began as un-southern as any African-American music this side of Anthony Braxton. The even tone of Dan Charnas's account of this big payback differs markedly from Lauterbach's. A Boston University summa whose thesis was titled "Musical Apartheid in America" and who always capitalizes "Black" and "White," Charnas was an early contributor to *The Source* and worked in the record business for much of the '90s. *The Big Payback* fuses these complementary orientations in a swift, detailed, thoughtful narrative that stands tall alongside Jeff Chang's canonical hip-hop overview *Can't Stop Won't Stop*. At well over six hundred pages, it weaves substantial portraits of at least fifty artists, businessmen, and radio pros into a story that isn't quite encyclopedic—it fast-forwards from 2000 and pretty much skips the Dirty South—but justifies its grand conclusion: "*Hip-hop succeeded not by being correct. It succeeded by being.* In its materialistic ubiquity, hip-hop won. . . . It is takeover. America has officially been remixed."

Half a century after Denver Ferguson opened the Trianon Ballroom, Afro-America had been changed drastically by an entrenched civil rights movement, an expanding economy that stalled just as the black middle class was taking off, and the partial breaching of racial barriers by rock and roll itself. Maybe the runners and enforcers who manned the chitlin' circuit weren't all that different from the many casual drug dealers who find a better way in Charnas's book: among them, in roughly ascending order of seriousness, Russell Simmons, Jay-Z, Damon Dash, Biggie Smalls, and Chris Lighty (plus the very casual young Ice-T of *Ice*, well before he figured out that robbing jewelry stores with a sledgehammer was a better deal). But the general mood was certainly angrier and more polarized—fatherless children were everywhere, and so were guns. Although hip-hop refutes the Lauterbach-approved Jane Jacobs truism that public housing projects destroy "*innovative economies*" (her italics), none of the thuggery described by Lauterbach, James, or any other pop historian approaches the murders of Tupac and Biggie. And those are merely the most spectacular examples of what Charnas calls "hip-hop's cycle of violent one-upmanship," which made the beatdown a social currency.

In *Ice*, Ice-T observes that this cycle began with escalating hostilities among LA's gangbangers. But these were obviously cranked up by the profits at stake in the inner city's innovative response to Reaganism's entrepreneurial imperative: the drug trade—especially, as Ice-T also observes, "once crack hit." Of the small-time dealers named above, several of whom sold only weed, Simmons and Dash were born businessmen on their way to safer hustles. Ice-T was an army veteran and a non-deadbeat dad who preferred to keep his ambitions reasonable—once he went into the crime business, he refused to use a gun on the job or traffic drugs. Biggie and Jay-Z, on the other hand, had much bigger dreams than street dealing could satisfy, and turned to music to fulfill them, as did two less casual dealers, 50 Cent and Wu-Tang headman RZA. Who knows whether any of these men had what it takes to become a crime boss—probably not, we hope. But they kept their eyes on the prize, which was untold wealth. And except for the slain Biggie, all made bigger bucks rapping than any but a few of the African-American musicians who preceded them. That is, all made out like gangsters, including the moderately talented 50, who cashed out of his VitaminWater deal with as much as $100 million and has a net worth Charnas estimates at nearly half a billion.

One of Charnas's most fascinating portraits is of supermanager Chris Lighty. His absentee dad an FBI agent, Lighty may be the one guy here with the makings of a crime boss—like Morris Levy, he's proven "calm, but completely capable of carnage." After one particularly fraught beatdown early in a career that began with his Violators crew providing muscle for DJ Red

Alert, Russell Simmons's Israeli-born partner, Lyor Cohen, told Lighty: "You have to make up your mind. Do you want to be *that* guy, or *this* guy?" Lighty chose *this* guy, but when necessary—convincing Suge Knight to OK a Def Jam video, say—he became *that* guy. Charnas says Lighty got into hip-hop because he "was interested in girls and thrills." He took 15 percent of 50 Cent's Vitamin Water money and may well be worth as much as his client.

The Big Payback documents the phenomenal talent, faith, and enterprise that went into hip-hop's takeover. Little Richard and Louis Jordan were musical titans, but Jay-Z and Wu-Tang belong in their company, and even adjusting for history, Chris Lighty and Puffy Combs as well as Jay-Z the label exec dwarf Denver Ferguson and Don Robey. And though there were quite a few whites and middle-class blacks in the hip-hop mix, many crucial innovators came up from circumstances as daunting as those of Ferguson's time. Charnas celebrates their admirable achievements without sensationalism or sentimentality.

Yet though he's not a political idealist on the order of fellow historian Jeff Chang, the onetime student of musical apartheid sees hip-hop's limitations. Economically, "there is still no great Black-owned major record company, no film studio. The winning paradigm . . . seems to be the joint venture." And culturally, the man who again and again depicts gangsters finding a better way—the scariest of Lighty's Violators now has his master's and a guidance counselor job—is less sanguine about gangsta rap, starring those hyperreal villains who became hip-hop's commercial mainstay by pretending to be ordinary thugs and sometimes acting like same. Charnas believes that what got Tupac killed was his pursuit of a "street credibility . . . measured by money, violence, brutality, and blind loyalty."

Such gangsta images as the gun and the beatdown have gradually lost ground to a carpe diem hedonism long on a sexist sexual candor that offends its female fans far less than feminists of either gender would prefer—no more "correct" than gangsta, but less deadly in its generalized escapism. Hip-hop accommodates many other kinds of expression, and I'm gratified when it makes them work. But at hip-hop's core is a dissent from the Puritan ethic that achieves its own kind of spiritual concord. And behind it, as behind many popular musics before it, are more or less shady businessmen with a special appreciation for girls and thrills.

Barnes & Noble Review, 2011

Money Isn't Everything

Fred Goodman's *The Mansion on the Hill: Dylan, Young, Geffen, Springsteen, and the Head-On Collision of Rock and Commerce*

Like Fredric Dannen's 1990 *Hit Men: Power Brokers and Fast Money Inside the Music Business*, *The Mansion on the Hill* tells a great story that's weakened by a humdrum thesis—or, to be more precise, tells a bunch of great stories that cry out for a thesis strong enough to hold them together. Lacking Dannen's convenient suspicion that rock and roll is a Mafia plot, the best Fred Goodman can do for a narrative and analytic thread is to cry somewhat incoherently in his beer about the long-lost '60s. His advantage is that by eschewing the page-turning True Crime Tales that help make *Hit Men* so much fun, Goodman's research ends up seeming somewhat more substantial. But where Dannen strives to pinpoint murky relationships between minor record executives and the Mob, Goodman—a business reporter who, unlike Dannen, has always made music his beat—sticks to far more significant bizzers who don't need crooks to help them win at information capitalism.

Foremost among these is David Geffen, as of 1990 the industry's first billionaire. Bruce Springsteen and his producer-manager, lapsed rock critic Jon Landau, place a clear second. Note, however, that the other star attractions proffered by Goodman's subtitle, Bob Dylan and Neil Young, play exemplary roles no larger than those of, for instance, Dee Anthony, a hilariously (if chillingly) unclassy manager few potential readers have ever heard of, or Dylan's legendary handler Albert Grossman. Stars move product, and Times Books is in the entertainment business too—as is Goodman, this publication, and your humble reviewer. The differences among us, decisive though they may be, are matters of style and degree—a truth that Goodman glimpses intermittently if at all.

Geffen is a fascinating figure, and if no one has yet satisfactorily explained his synthesis of solicitous empathy and ruthless greed, much less what it portends about the way we live now, that's excellent reason for Goodman to try. He organizes the facts expertly, with special attention to both the fiscal machinations underlying Geffen's empire and the unflappable charisma that has discouraged any but the most foolhardy from getting in his way. Starting off at Hustler U., a/k/a/the William Morris mailroom, Geffen discovered—as had Grossman, several of whose acts Geffen briefly booked—that a passion for music was a shrewd businessman's most bankable asset in hippie-era rock. Having established his bona fides with his immensely remunerative representation of Laura Nyro and Crosby, Stills, Nash & Young, Geffen created a record label he dubbed Asylum for such Los Angeles soft-rock icons as Joni Mitchell, Jackson Browne, and the Eagles. Delighted to have a killer dealmaker shielding them from the stink of lucre, these unsullied souls were shocked when he sold their safe haven to Warner Bros. for seven million in 1972. But this was hardly the first time—or the last—that big-money transactions for Geffen's clients ended up profiting him even more.

Goodman leaves little doubt that it's been twenty years or so since Geffen cared for one of his "significant artists," to use his pet phrase, the way he loved Laura Nyro in 1967. His enduring passion and genius is financial. Worth thirty million by 1980, he took twenty-five million Warner dollars and parlayed Geffen Records, where younger hirelings nurtured the multiplatinum, into his billion. Now he is a Broadway angel, Hollywood producer, philanthropist, and liberal macher who brutalizes perceived rivals while skillfully manipulating his own legend. What makes him tick is probably a gift for power itself. No wonder nobody understands him—the very few who share this ability don't waste time writing about it. Still, Goodman might have noted that other billionaires exert their largess less humanely, and wondered why Geffen doesn't.

The author's small interest in such distinctions very nearly wrecks the Springsteen sections, where it is difficult not to suspect some unstated personal animus against the artist and especially Jon Landau. Since Goodman is a stickler about conflicts of interest, I should note that I knew Landau slightly way back when and was once close to his sometime associate Dave Marsh, an intimacy that suffered a permanent crimp in 1975 when I publicly accused Springsteen of not being God. He isn't, and no matter when you think he peaked, it's reasonable to believe his best years are past. Nevertheless, Springsteen has proven both more vital and more moral than skeptics would have deemed possible. While a return to the wordy sprawl Landau excised from his music in the late '70s might be refreshing long about now, Goodman's attempt to paint this uncommonly honest and idealistic rock star as an irrelevant hypocrite simply isn't convincing. A failure to vote is hardly proof that you don't care about the working class.

The author's grudging admission that Springsteen "provided entertainment value in an extremely ethical manner" merely muddles his story further. Relying on such sources as a rejected early fan who confides that Bruce "isn't very bright" (an opinion that—even in the unlikely event it's true—might help explain why he was rejected) and a faithful lighting designer who develops "a bad cocaine habit" after Springsteen fires him (leading one to wonder whether it was merely mild before), Goodman can't get over the inevitable fact that Springsteen isn't the wartless paragon hagiographers like Marsh claim.

Thematically, this obsession connects to Goodman's belief that what made rock a form of unparalleled promise was its roots in the hippie counterculture, where, according to Goodman, it "assumed the mantle of meaning and intent from folk music." He can see that hippiedom's wuzzy vision of peace and love had even less chance of coming true than the Movement's inflamed fantasies of overthrowing capitalism. But that doesn't stop him from blaming Jon Landau for refusing to act on these illusions. Landau has always believed that the best thing about rock and roll was the musical spark that originally made it such a hot commercial item, not its noble links to Joan Baez and Pete Seeger. Hence he's concluded that only within the music business can rock and roll make its impact as rock and roll. This vision has severe limitations, especially in its resistance to formal innovation and cultural weirdness. But Landau and Springsteen have made lots of remarkable music out of it, not all of which has been calculatedly market-ready.

Don't misunderstand me. For any longtime fan, it has been confusing and often disheartening to watch a popular form get rationalized into a twelve-billion-dollar business—to watch the meaning of "commercial," a term Goodman tosses about with unseemly abandon for a business reporter, change from something like, "If we do this, kids will like it," to "If we do this, we can maximize our audience share and/or optimize our profitability." My nomination for the bleakest moment here comes when Dee Anthony drills his charges in Al Jolson's stagecraft—for twenty-five years I'd wondered why fools from Peter Wolf to Peter Frampton suddenly started milking the same shtick at the same time. But I'd understand if more casual observers cited Goodman's succinct, damning account of rock's international corporatization. Similarly, I understand why many prefer Neil Young's eccentric career to Springsteen's. I do myself. But eccentricity is the opposite of a political or social solution, which can only begin with a cogent analysis of the cultural contradictions well-meaning artists like both Springsteen and Young are living through. Regrettably, this ain't it.

Los Angeles Times Book Review, 1996

Mapping the Earworm's Genome

John Seabrook's *The Song Machine: Inside the Hit Factory*

Think of John Seabrook's *The Song Machine* as a sequel to his annoying but entertaining work of middlebrow cultural theory, 2001's *Nobrow: The Culture of Marketing/The Marketing of Culture*. Unsurprisingly, the keyword "Nobrow" is seriously fuzzy around the edges, so I'll just indicate what it symptomizes: Seabrook's fascination with the ongoing shifts in concepts of value that have been disrupting aesthetic pleasure and meaning ever since modernism began crumbling in the '60s. What is art and what isn't—and even worse, what is good art and what isn't? If you're as hung up on the au courant/hip/cutting-edge/whatevs as Seabrook, such conundrums can drive you to dream up your own cultural theory. But if you hang that theory off sharp pieces on George Lucas, David Geffen, and your father's clothes closet and fold it all into a memoir of Tina Brown's *New Yorker*, you've repaid your debt to society.

A clearer, subtler, and more skillful reassessment of Seabrook's ongoing anxiety about aesthetic worth, *The Song Machine* traces circa-2010 radio pop back to the '90s and forward to its Spotify tipping point. Framed by a memoiristic device that has him conversing with his son fore and aft, the first half is new, the second built from *New Yorker* reports on Spotify, Seoul K-pop, and superproducer Dr. Luke. As a music historian, Seabrook is the dilettante you'd figure—especially as regards hip-hop, the book is riddled with errors—but he knows how to write a profile. So on the surface this is an informed, witty, effetely unpretentious celebration of what Seabrook sees as an altogether new way of creating pop music. Yet if you care enough about popular music to ride the swells of his narrative, you'll feel undercurrents he knows are there.

In this context, "pop" and "popular" aren't nearly synonyms. By "popular" I mean the full panoply of non-classical music, including death metal, gospel, Celtic revival, hiplife, kroncong, New Age, and countless other variants. "Pop," on the other hand, indicates music aimed squarely at radio airplay and the singles chart. *The Song Machine* gives short shrift to the popular, which can be annoying too. But it's less annoying than the way fans of other popular genres dismiss the spectrum of today's radio music as unlistenable unless it catches them unawares on the dance floor—a testing ground half these prunes seldom get near. There's never been a time when this attitude hasn't been ipso facto philistine, and it's hit a nadir. Denying the attractions of Kelly Clarkson's "Since U Been Gone" is for ostriches only.

Nobrow's opening scene describes the cognitive dissonance that beset Seabrook on January 20, 1997, as he listened to the Notorious B.I.G. unfurl penis metaphors on his Discman while watching Bill Clinton taking the oath on the Times Square Panasonic Astrovision LED. That kind of putative ambivalence haunts the book—in an especially annoying scene, he declines to buy a well-made coffee table at Pottery Barn ("cheap" at 299 bucks in 2000, sez he) on the general theory that "mass-produced furniture" is "tacky." *The Song Machine*, however, begins with Seabrook overcoming just such ambivalence; although put off at first by the repetitiveness of a radio format that features closer to ten songs than forty, he finds that "the initially annoying bits . . . become the very parts you look forward to most in the song."

Less concept-driven than *Nobrow*, *The Song Machine* profiles song technician after song technician, although "technician" is too modest and concrete a word to suggest how conceptual their work is—and also, to be clear, how creative. These are gifted, obsessive, music-mad eccentrics whose well-told tales are worth the attention of anyone who cares about postmodern aesthetics or short, catchy songs with a good beat. Ditto for the artists, almost none male, who Seabrook believes are more "vocal personalities than singers," and the businessmen, not one female, whose mania for music has nothing on their affinity for money.

The technicians include Swedish DJ turned remixer turned hitmaker turned fountainhead Denniz PoP; classically trained Swedish metalhead and math whiz Max Martin, now one of the bestselling songwriters of all time; Stargate's Tor Hermansen and Mikkel Eriksen, once "the only two guys who listen to urban music in Norway," who become Manhattan fixtures after a single audience with Jay-Z; and guitarist turned superproducer turned scary monster Dr. Luke. Featured artists include icebreaking Swedes Ace of Base, *American Idol* rockist Kelly Clarkson, backsliding Christian Katy Perry, "teenage nightmare" Kesha, and Rihanna, whose charisma only caught up with her ambition when Chris Brown slammed her into a scene from her parents' abusive marriage. The bizzers include forever magniloquent Clive Davis, Backstreet Boys Svengali and imprisoned felon Lou Pearlman, digital false saviors Daniel Ek of Spotify and Steve Jobs of you-know-where, and happily retired Clive Calder, who sold Jive Records for two-point-three billion just as the biz was going bust.

The Song Machine bears its title because Seabrook believes all these people except the digital-music guys are deeply invested in a twenty-first-century songwriting method that recalls Motown's Holland-Dozier-Holland not much more than it does Tin Pan Alley's Irving Berlin and is utterly alien to the rock-era free-for-all normalized by Bob Dylan and Lennon-McCartney. Anyone paying attention senses this, but Seabrook is onto something major and explains it well. There are glimmers of what he calls track-and-hook songwriting in the circa-1985 rise of the "song doctor" and hip-hop sampling's evolution into hip-hop beatmaking. But he's right to trace its formalization to Denniz PoP's Stockholm studio.

Traditional pop songwriting usually came tune first, with words molded to melodic contours that might then be retrofitted to accommodate the words—although sometimes the lyric got things started, and Dylan and his lessers often devised music for pre-existing songpoems. Either way, melodist and lyricist split the royalties. Since rock was beat-driven by definition, this Eurocentric formula has long seemed worse than old-fashioned—just ask yourself how many songs draw their life from the clave mojo Bo Diddley worked on the old shave-and-a-haircut beat. And now that kind of Eurocentrism is biting the dust.

One good thing that's come of track-and-hook is that finally rhythm creators are getting their financial due. Less good is that they hog the proceeds almost as much as the ASCAP elite once did. In track-and-hook, songs begin with beats that producers construct digitally with zero input from live musicians unless the producers' own instrumental skills come into play. Once a beat is created—generally many at a time, most ultimately discarded—"topliners" are asked to lay on not one but several hooks. Since Berlin himself, hooks have been what Seabrook calls pop's "bliss point," a marketing term sampled from the snack food industry, and radio hits have sported multiples for decades. Track-and-hook hits, however, bristle with them, spiffing up an underlying beat that vamps seductively yet repetitively, at least a hook apiece for "intro, verse, pre-chorus, chorus, and outro." If the beat is promising enough, as many as fifty topliners may be emailed the MP3, and several of them may wind up with a composer credit for one bit or another. "Producers," Seabrook notes, "generally speak of a song's 'melodies.'"

As for the words, well, occasionally a lyrical idea or even a verse will get the party started, but usually lyrics are afterthoughts at which some topliners are better than others, just as some specialize in verses or bridges. Often they're just scraps of language pieced together—Seabrook's favorite topliner, the irrepressible Ester Dean, travels with a scribbled notebook of them. I know you're appalled, so let me agree that absolutely it's depressing and then add that sometimes it isn't. If you don't believe revitalizing the colloquial is one of popular music's signal accomplishments, read Christopher Ricks on Bob Dylan, and if Ricks doesn't think that means what Max Martin did for "I want it that way" or, hell, what The-Dream did for "umbrella," he's an arriviste anyway. Seabrook himself, however, doesn't worry much about what some might regard as the end of true song, much less about the music he as an old Nirvana fanatic grew up with. Sure he feels Clarkson's commercially doomed struggle to express herself. But she didn't have what it takes to write "Since U Been Gone," and if the end of the rock model she loves is what it takes to keep such bliss points coming, that's the historical reality and he's down.

Only then comes the K-pop chapter. Korean pop is so prefab it makes One Direction look like a vanguard hidden in plain sight, and Seabrook begins by hinting excitedly that this "cultural technology" might just explode the "distinction between real and manufactured music—which is fraught with so many logical inconsistencies and built-in biases." But as his praisesong runs up against the regimented vapidity of a teen-idol-in-training pipeline that holds thousands of young hopefuls in glamorously robotic servitude, he starts asking himself why American kids would prefer this "overproduced, derivative" stuff to the "more original" homegrown variant. Capper: "In the end, as Denniz PoP used to say, sometimes you have to let art win."

And for the rest of the book, art shows signs of doing just that. Jay-Z signs Rihanna because "her eyes—her determination" convince him she's "a star." Having chortled impolitely when Clarkson failed to turn her earnest outcries into hits, Seabrook likes the ribald up-from-nowhere sparkplug Ester Dean so much that you can feel his dismay when, like almost every topliner with an eye on the prize, she can't make her star-time dreams come true. Agog at first at the compulsively ambitious Dr. Luke, Seabrook ends up making him look like the abusive tyrant his radically untrustworthy protegee Kesha tells the judge he is. And when the now fourteen-year-old son whose enthusiasm for Flo Rida's "Right Round" kicked off this saga tells his dad he's getting into the Smiths, one senses that the fickle Seabrook may be headed for a retro bliss point.

For all its willful gloss and offputting mannerisms, *The Song Machine* performs an important news function and does useful cultural work. Streamed from the Spotify playlist they deserved, the songs he homes in on did indeed engender the earworms the hypersensitive despise and I think of as pets—but significantly, not all of them. Seabrook acknowledges one reason for this—track-and-hook still isn't an exact science, and not every release the song machine slots as a sure shot gets over. The other he acknowledges but sidesteps—not only did Jay-Z sign Rihanna because he thought she was more than a "vocal personality," she had to suffer in public before her full allure shone through. Star power remains difficult to calibrate, and for me, Kelly Clarkson is too cloddish to ever be much more than "Since U Been Gone." Not so with serial sinner Katy Perry or track-and-hook skeptic Pink, whose self-conceptions and -presentations remain unpredictable works in progress. And what about dance-oriented rock chick Lady Gaga, who breached the charts without track-and-hooking at all? Machine-processed or not, these women blur the distinction between popular artist and pop star, as the best pop stars always have, yet Perry fan Seabrook barely mentions the other two. Let me add, too, that in the midst of a ruinous economic downturn for popular music, it continues to generate more quality albums than anyone can fully absorb—almost all of them there for the streaming on, you know, Spotify.

Seabrook must get all this. But beyond the once-in-a-lifetime chance to turn a fourteen-year-old Smiths fan on to the music of his youth, beyond even the dilettante's compulsion to move on, the root of his disquiet comes clear in the Spotify chapter. It starts by praising how Daniel Ek broke down "traditional genres" so that "the song is once again king." But then it discusses economic matters, not with Spotify-boycotting Taylor Swift but with two artist-activists known for the kind of quality albums referenced above: art-country icon Rosanne Cash and avant-pop guitar god Marc Ribot, who for almost 700,000 Spotify streams between them have been paid just under three hundred dollars. Well, Seabrook rationalizes, at least they can still tour. But believe it or not, due to the way Spotify negotiated its label permissions, its songwriter payouts are even skimpier. So Seabrook does the math and concludes that if this trend continues, "the whole hit-making apparatus of the song machine is doomed."

Uh-oh. No wonder he's on the lookout for a new bliss point.

Barnes & Noble Review, 2015

In Search of Jim Crow first published in *The Believer*.

Bwana-Acolyte in the Favor Bank originally published in *Salon*.

Review of David Wondrich's *Stomp and Swerve*, October 9 issue © 2006, *Seattle Weekly*.

PART III
CRITICAL PRACTICE

Beyond the Symphonic Quest

Susan McClary's *Feminine Endings: Music, Gender, and Sexuality*

Feminine Endings is a musical version of the feminist deconstructions that have rocked aesthetic ideology since Laura Mulvey took on the gaze in 1975. Susan McClary counts as allies Tania Modleski and Mary Ann Doane in film, Teresa de Lauretis, Sandra M. Gilbert, and Susan Gubar in literature, Judith Lynne Hanna in dance—every one (along with many others) gratefully cited in an eloquent, contentious notes section a third as long as the 166-page text. But her book should come as a relief even to readers with no special use for multi-culti counteranalysis—criticism fans, pop egalitarians, committed anti-idealists, accountants and English teachers who think Schubert's *Trout* has something to do with water, or fish. Digging out from under music theory's genteel evasions, nutball positivism, and general delusions of grandeur, she articulates a point of view that often resembles common sense. In music theory, abstruse-to-arcane by linguistic nature, and feminist deconstruction, rooted in Lacanian gobbledygook and sworn to strip away surfaces at any cost, this achievement borders on the miraculous.

We're not accustomed to regarding what McClary calls "so-called serious composition" as a particularly sexist preserve. If anything, classical music ("longhair" music, in pre-Beatle Americanese) has always carried with it a whiff of the feminine, and in this century female musicians and singers proliferated. Female composers, however, have been even rarer than female painters or sculptors, and if anything women have fared even worse in the study of music. Among the seventy-eight key books and essays by fifty-six authors in the bibliography of Joseph Kerman's 1985 *Contemplating Music: Challenges to Musicology*—a sanely progressive overview by a scholar-critic praised in McClary's notes and thanked in her acknowledgments—precisely two are by women: one a musicologist who shares authorship with her pianist husband, the other an up-and-coming iconoclast who McClary reports was "severely chastised" for exposing American music departments to the Adorno virus.

McClary suggests that classical music's effeminate reputation is one reason men monopolize its ideology as well as its composition. Male longhairs feel pressured to defend their masculinity, and despite their insistence that the music they love operates on a formal-cum-spiritual plane that towers above mere signification, their metaphorical habits—epitomized by the common practice of designating such unresolved elements as nontonic keys and "weak" beats "female" and its often "climactic" harmonic and rhythmic closures "male"—leave no doubt that that's what they're doing.

It's typical that this defense is often reflexive and unselfconscious. Even for adepts, McClary makes clear, classical music functions as a sublime escape, providing spiritual and philosophical comfort all the more effective because it's nonverbal and therefore immune to news from the other side. And just because music's formal principles are beyond the ken of most listeners, it's anything but transcendent, abstract, or value-free. In fact, McClary believes, it's the opposite—a powerful and rather insidious socializing agent. Most of us assume that tonality's tension-and-release structures conform to a fundamental pattern of life. McClary says one reason we believe such patterns are natural is that we've been absorbing them musically since before we could talk.

This is common sense? Of course not—this is deconstruction. The common sense part is, first, McClary's insistence that music means anything at all, and second, her belief that there's important music outside as well as inside "so-called serious composition." Like Kerman's *Contemplating Music*, *Feminine Endings* is an argument for music criticism, a discipline long out of fashion in academia, where it's been superceded by the supposed objectivity of music history, science, analysis, and theory. Before she can establish that music is male chauvinist (or undertake any "socially grounded criticism"), McClary is compelled to attack the obfuscations that permit musicology to "fastidiously [declare] issues of musical signification to be off-limits to those engaged in legitimate scholarship."

This she does with more evident relish than Kerman (although compared to lit crits she respects her adversaries). And however unorthodox it may be for her to attribute "content" to musical "form," her basic contention—that sonata-allegro procedure, the crowning rationalization of tonality and the basic principle of symphonic construction, is obviously a species of mythic narrative—rings true. In view of the requirement that modulations return to a "home" key, an even more inescapable metaphor than "feminine" cadence, why should anyone think tonality is too good for the quest story that holds the rest of European culture in its thrall? But many believe just that, and feeling isolated in her unorthodoxy, McClary joins forces with other Others. First she observes that *Carmen* isn't exclusively devoted to the taming of Woman: Bizet seems equally fascinated and terrified by nonwhites, and by popular culture. Shortly thereafter she shifts her attention from Monteverdi, Tchaikovsky, and Donizetti to Diamanda Galas, Laurie Anderson, and Madonna.

Feminine Endings is both convincing and entertaining throughout, and hardly exhausts McClary's arsenal—her dissection of rock musicology with her husband Robert Walser is very nearly the best thing in Simon Frith and Andrew Goodwin's enormous *On Record* anthology, and I trust her "On the Blasphemy of Talking Politics During Bach Year" will keynote an essay collection soon. But that's not to say this book effects as many closures as one might hope. McClary writes acutely about sex—her comments on the "erotic friction" of Monteverdi's trios are but one example of her point that the dalliance of melodic foreplay often beats the imposed ecstasy of harmonic completion—but never comes out and says just exactly how overrated she thinks orgasms are. Her final positions on both order and tension-and-release also remain cloudy—she does sometimes threaten to fall into the deconstructionist trap of tearing down the house before she's put up the tent. And while I'm impressed by her harmonic analyses of Anderson and Madonna, whose music is almost always ignored in favor of their performances, I'm left wondering how common such patterns might be among less august artists.

McClary remains a creature of her training. She has nothing to say about jazz or any other black music, little to say about rhythm beyond asserting how crucial it is. And she's spent so much of her life with classical music that when she turns to pop icons she's sometimes overimpressed with tricks the media-saturated have learned to take for granted, even deconstruct—the fade, say, or the bare ass. Nevertheless, this is a major book by a writer I would eagerly read on any cultural subject. Not only do I admire her audacity in introducing the independent thought virus to American music departments—I get off on it.

Village Voice, 1991

All in the Tune Family

Peter van der Merwe's *Origins of the Popular Style: The Antecedents of Twentieth-Century Popular Music*

Since its three hundred pages make room for over half that many "musical examples," as writers designate those inaudible staves-covered-with-squiggles, maybe you shouldn't read *Origins of the Popular Style* unless you also read music. But anyone with an interest in the history of popular music, especially its blues-based variants, should take the plunge anyway. I don't read music myself, and can't claim to follow everything van der Merwe says, especially the details of "parlour harmony" toward the end. But it's no trick to intuit this South African scholar's points: many of his ideas make sense, which aids comprehension, and a number of them are unorthodox, which adds entertainment value. Especially if you have a weakness for musicology jokes.

Although van der Merwe hides his delight behind an academic irony that's almost tweedy, he recognizes that his ideas are funny ha-ha as well as funny peculiar. "The triumph of the blues is one of musical history's best jokes," he declares, and while other classically trained heretics have spoken kindly of this unanticipated turn of events, few of his precursors have found so much humor in the way "American gutter music" became "the most potent musical force of the twentieth century." Circumspectly, van der Merwe refuses to equate triumph with "progress": "I have a great deal of sympathy with whoever it was who described the history of music from the eighteenth century to the present as 'downhill all the way.'" But anyone who can devote decades to such a vast and idiosyncratic project is obviously motivated by unstated personal interests. Since he manages to cite "Long Tall Sally" five times in a book that supposedly ends in 1900, I'm betting he's a closet r&b fan.

In the tradition of such like-minded musicologists as New Zealand–born Christopher Small in *Music Society Education* and South African exile John Blacking in *How Musical Is Man?*, van der Merwe decries the European bias of musical canons that make harmony the measure of all things. But by getting down to cases, he goes a step further. And since musicological myopia isn't confined to the Bach-Boulez crowd—Alec Wilder rambling on about quiddities of key and structure in musical comedy songs or Wilfred

Mellers separating the Dorian from the Aeolian in Beatles tunes are almost as culture-bound—the sharpest pleasure of *Origins of the Popular Style* is its undeclared war on harmonic pieties.

Van der Merwe takes the structural lessons of all repetition-prone music so seriously that he discovers in notes that change their pitch a "melodic dissonance" that is "rather analogous to harmonic dissonance," and finds "resolution" in coinciding cross-rhythms. He considers supposedly "flatted" blue notes more ambiguous than most commentators would have you believe. He debunks the commonplace of assigning Greek mode names to folk tunes when modes so often "shade into one another," or "resist classification because they lack certain notes," or simply have no tonic (which renders harmonic analysis ridiculous rather than merely dubious). He prefers to speak of "levels" rather than "chords," "shifts" rather than "changes." And he concludes a dazzling cross-cultural tour of such "tune families" as "Frankie and Johnny" and "John Henry" with a generalization that, whether he knows it or not, stands Adorno's critique of standardization on its head: "Why were [these] patterns so fruitful and important? Part of the answer lies in their great strength and flexibility. They not only *permit* extensive variation, they positively *demand* it. With most classical tunes, if you get a note wrong you spoil the whole. This is not true of these great folk tune patterns. With them it is always possible to substitute something new with perfectly good effect."

Van der Merwe respectfully abjures "the socio-economic-political approach to the arts" as impossibly unscientific and overapplied to popular culture, but this liberal white South African does have his little subtext: he wants to prove that miscegenation is the way of musical growth. I agree, but I'd accept his case more confidently if he was out front about his motives, and am sorry to note that he tends to romanticize American racial relations. Given the thinness of his few strictly historical observations, however, his stubborn formalism is just as well, yielding goodies way beyond its uncanonical improprieties. He adapts Alan Lomax's concept of the "Old High Culture" to posit a "Near Eastern style" that survived in European and African folk music and helps explain the peculiar Afro-British congruences that came together in America. He summarizes African music (especially African rhythm) with surpassing clarity and is superb on the evolution of blues. He's tart about the harmonic banality of Wilder's "American popular song" and the "deadly predictability" of its thirty-two-bar format.

And for his final number, van der Merwe demonstrates that the vulgarians who went wild over blues wanted much the same thing as the genteel escapists who swooned for the Victorian ballad—not more rhythm, not at the outset, but more melody. Van der Merwe isn't the first to say something like this, as he isn't the first to make many of his points. But like the inventors of blues, he's assembled them with an instinct for the hook.

Village Voice, 1990

Bel Cantos

Henry Pleasants's *The Great American Popular Singers*

So John Rockwell and I were trying to figure out just when we ferried Henry Pleasants to Shea Stadium in my Toyota. A hot sunny day in 1974 or 1975, only London-based classical music critic Pleasants was wearing a trench coat as he took the traffic jam in stride and spoke warmly of Gladys Knight. He was in his early sixties, with the reason I'm here today just behind him: *The Great American Popular Singers*, published by Simon & Schuster 1974, reissued by same 1985, now out of print although findable used. I'd gotten one in the mail through John; we both reviewed it, him in the Sunday *Times* and me in one of my last *Newsday* columns. Although I only reread it in toto to write this paper, I have read *in* it hundreds of times since then, especially after I started teaching music history at NYU. So I was surprised when John mused: "Does anybody know who he is except you and me?"

Then I began checking indexes and realized he could be right. No Pleasants in biographies of Louis Armstrong, Billie Holiday, Nat King Cole, Jimmie Rodgers, Hank Williams, Johnny Cash, B. B. King, Ray Charles, Aretha Franklin, Frank Sinatra, or Bing Crosby, most of whom Pleasants's masterwork describes incisively, a few adequately, and one atrociously. There's one citation total—a definition of "mordent"—in Will Friedwald's *Jazz Singing*, and zero in Friedwald's big Sinatra book, although there is one in the Sinatra chapter of Roy Hemming and David Hajdu's 1991 *Discovering the Great Singers of Classic Pop*. I am obliged to acknowledge that Gary Giddins, who I edited for thirty years, never ever mentions Henry Pleasants, not even in connection with Ethel Waters, subject of the 1977 column that marked Giddins's transition from inspired jazz highbrow to discerning jazz democrat. Nor is Pleasants cited in David Brackett's pioneering musicological survey *Interpreting Popular Music*. So let's give it up to Barney Hoskyns, whose 1991

From a Whisper to a Scream: The Great Voices of Popular Music quotes Pleasants twice. And respect to the always thorough Peter Guralnick, who at least includes the otherwise unmentioned Pleasants in the bibliography of *Last Train to Memphis*. But note that Guralnick felt no need to buttress his celebration of Elvis Presley's many gifts by citing this renowned opera expert's assertion that, for instance, "Elvis has been described variously as a baritone and a tenor. An extraordinary compass and very wide range of vocal color have something to do with this divergence of opinion. . . . Elvis's is . . . an extraordinary voice—or many voices."

I don't have a definitive explanation for this negligence, except to observe that Pleasants's lifelong identification with classical music leaves him out of the loop for most of the rock and pop chroniclers who've surfaced in the half century that rock criticism hasn't been a contradiction in terms. But Pleasants's obscurity does lend some urgency to my practical goal here, which is to make sure *The Great American Popular Singers* doesn't disappear altogether over the next half century. Because while it's far from perfect, and has in some respects been superceded by the acres of prose its twenty-two subjects have inspired since 1974, I've found it invaluable as a writer and a teacher. Pleasants's calculation that the high end of the voice is attained far less often than we carelessly or ignorantly assume is why I don't call many singers tenors or sopranos. His unshrinking observation that Holiday had "a meager voice—small, hoarse at the bottom and thinly shrill on top" prompted my observation that the same voice was also "round, firm, even plump, and gorgeous"—not that my impressionistic praise had anything on Pleasants nailing her "way of wrapping a sound around a word or syllable, enveloping it, so to speak, in an *appoggiatura*, a slur, a mordent or a turn" and "her habit of widening the vibrato during the life of a sustained tone." And he's been invaluable to my teaching. His Bessie Smith chapter supplanted Amiri Baraka's. His Sinatra proved a clearer and pithier complement to Gay Talese's "Frank Sinatra Has a Cold" than anything I could extract from Friedwald. And when I taught a '50s course his takes on Presley and Cash stood proud alongside Marcus's and Hilburn's.

Pleasants was a doctor's son born in 1911 who grew up in Philadelphia's Main Line suburbs. He never attended college, instead studying voice, piano, and composition at the Philadelphia Musical Academy and the Curtis Institute, but his singing career was derailed by a five-year case of laryngitis. So by age nineteen he was working at the *Philadelphia Evening Bulletin*, first as a stringer who combined police reporting and music reviewing, although by twenty-five he was the paper's music editor. In the journalism of those days, "music" meant "classical music," but late in life he told an interviewer that he sometimes reviewed pop music there too, adding the dismaying footnote: "I didn't always get paid for it, but that didn't matter. I loved it." Presumably his income comprised an editing stipend plus piece-rate reviews, with a pop-side focus on swing bands white and black. *The Great American Popular Singers* quotes George Simon, the ranking pioneer of that beat, on Ella Fitzgerald, Nat King Cole, and Peggy Lee.

Pleasants also did radio work for the *Bulletin*, where he, and I quote, "learned to pronounce all the German and Russian names" (what Russian and German names?), and then took a Berlitz course in Russian (why?) to augment the German he knew from his time in Austria (wait a second, what time in Austria?). And in 1942, with the U.S. fighting in World War II, he joined the army as well as marrying the harpsichordist Virginia Duffy, who his *Guardian* obit says he'd met in Hungary. He served first in Alaska as a liaison with the Russians and later in Italy, where he was trained as an interpreter and interrogator. Plus, to quote again: "I was also a specialist in the German order of battle, that I knew from memorization, which I'm good at." Oh.

So after the war Pleasants pursued two distinct careers. The first of his many journalistic positions was central European music correspondent for the *New York Times*. But that was avocational—his money gig was with the U.S. government. Exactly what he did when is hard to determine from the scant record. But this much is clear, because it's in the renowned 1964 CIA exposé *The Invisible Government* and Pleasants owned up when pressed a little. Officially, he was a top-level S-1 foreign service officer. But for some time, conceivably as long as 1950 to 1964, he was in fact station chief of the CIA's crucial Bonn office, where he handled SS-identified ex-Nazi Reinhard Gehlen, Hitler's Eastern Front point man and the biggest asset in the U.S.'s anti-Soviet intelligence operation, who Pleasants lived with and presumably vetted for months. Gehlen is plausibly regarded by many observers, among them SDS's Carl Oglesby, as a crucial promulgator of the Cold War. In 1963, three of his ex-Nazis were exposed as Soviet moles, and soon Pleasants's government career had ended. By 1970, he was at work on *The Great American Popular Singers*.

Not that music journalism didn't remain part of the station chief's cover and dear to the thwarted singer's heart. In 1955, in fact, he ran some serious distraction with the controversial *The Agony of Modern Music*, a treatise that looked askance at all so-called "serious music" since Wagner and was venomous about Schoenberg, Webern, *und so weiter*. It argued that by privileging the composer over the musician and harmonic complexity over melodic appeal, "serious music" had abandoned the audience to what Pleasants usually identified as jazz but wasn't shy about calling popular music, which delved into many underexploited seams of melody, some of which inhered in various harmonic developments. I liked this book more in 1974, when challenges to classical hegemony were rare, than now, when I realize that the Webern piece that Pleasants cites as a horrible example evokes the B sides of Bowie's Eno albums. But I'm still in fundamental agreement. More such polemics followed: 1961's *Death of a Music?: The Decline of the European Tradition and the Rise of Jazz* and 1969's *Serious Music and All That Jazz*, which Gary Giddins tells me got his colleagues' dander up by classifying Andy Williams as jazz. And in between, after Pleasants and his wife had settled down in London, came his signature work, a groundbreaking survey of operatic vocal technique called *The Great Singers*.

I hate opera and doubt I'll ever read *The Great Singers*. But I like the way its introductory pages extract from contemporary descriptions a theory of bel canto, the seventeenth-century school of opera singing that the *Harvard Concise Dictionary of Music* says valued "beauty of sound and brilliance of performance rather than dramatic expression or romantic emotion"—that is, rather than the stuff I hate about opera. Pleasants takes this official definition further by insisting that bel canto *was* in fact dramatically expressive in an era when performers not composers were relegated the responsibility of enriching characterization with "ornaments, embellishments, roulades, trills, portamenti, arpeggios, octave skips, melodic deviations and alterations, variations, cadences, and so on." He also holds that the elitist intimacy of early opera venues encouraged and even required singers to affect a conversational modesty that was rendered old hat by the scale of nineteenth-century grand opera, which compelled singers to project loudly and magniloquently. *The Great Singers* often cites the seventeenth-century soprano and vocal theorist Pier Francesco Tosi. But the best Tosi quote I've found in Pleasants is the advice to singers he quotes in re Sinatra in *The Great American Popular Singers*:

> *Let him take care that the higher the notes, the more necessary it is to touch them with softness, to avoid screaming.*
> *Let him learn the manner to glide with the vowels, and to drag the voice gently from the higher to the lower notes.*
> *Let him take care that the words are uttered in such a manner that they be distinctly understood, and not one syllable lost.*
> *In repeating the air, he that does not vary it for the better is no great master.*

Whoever does not know how to steal time in singing is destitute of the best taste and knowledge.
Oh! How great a master is the heart!

Pleasants accounts Sinatra, an autodidact who himself cited bel canto as an influence, the very greatest of his twenty-two designees. Crucially, however, both Sinatra and Pleasants would say that Sinatra's greatest influence wasn't some castrato, it was Billie Holiday for melodic shading followed by Tommy Dorsey for legato endurance. This is typical of *The Great American Popular Singers*, which is driven by three theses: that classical music's evolution into a composer-dominated harmonic laboratory has left melodic exploration to the pop realm, that the invention of the microphone made the elitist intimacy of early opera available to anyone, and, most important, that almost all the great white American popular singers, even Cash and Streisand, owe a debt to African-American melodic and rhythmic innovations. For most of us who love black music, rhythm comes first. But while Pleasants certainly highlights singers' time, he's less interested in propulsion than in what Tosi calls *stealing* time, exemplified by the nonpareil Holiday, with her uncanny ability to linger perilously behind the beat only to end up right *there* at the end of the measure. And he's even more taken with the way black singers vary the air for the better, whether with audacious Armstrong-style improvisations or the infinitesimal microtones of a Bessie Smith, a Billie Holiday, a Frank Sinatra.

But Pleasants doesn't merely celebrate the African-Americanization of bel canto. He's at once more technical and more entertaining, sometimes both at once. Invariably, and uniquely in my reading, he sets himself the task of mapping each singer's range. So we learn that Smith, Holiday, Hank Williams, Judy Garland, and Ethel Merman had barely an octave, while Sinatra, Fitzgerald, Presley, and Streisand had more than two and Ray Charles had three if you count his falsetto, which Pleasants usually sets aside for special comment but can't with Charles or B. B. King either, because they live up there. Like most pop singers, with Sinatra an unsurprising exception, they leap into head voice where classical singers train their laryngeal muscles to negotiate what is dubbed the passage into tenor or soprano with no sense of athleticism or strain. But unlike most pop singers, Charles and King remain in their high range for whole verses or longer. And now let me execute a reverse and mention that while Pleasants once wrote of Johnny Cash, "He often misses, i.e. doesn't reach a pitch, because *it doesn't matter to him. He doesn't try to reach it!*," he also says of Cash that he often inhabits "a subterranean area hostile to even the deepest of opera basses."

Nor is the technical analysis confined to pitch and time—again and again Pleasants calculates the weight of the singer's breath on the vocal cords and the precision of her or his enunciation. These concerns do sometimes expose his weaknesses—generationally, he has severe limits, which he acknowledges with typical politesse. But Pleasants's democratic worldview extended to his tactics as a writer, where both his training and his proclivities were journalistic. So every chapter includes a mini-biography, which even when dated or overfamiliar is invaluable for students and contextualizing for experts. Moreover, his formal calibrations never determine his final judgment. He hears each singer as a living, breathing artist he hopes to describe in colloquial human terms. Like f'rinstance:

Jolson: "By moving into the audience he was, in a sense, crashing the party, usurping the privileged status of those he was being paid to entertain." Jimmie Rodgers: "Jimmie wanted the listener to get not only the words and the story they told, but also the *feel* of the story." Crosby: "Bing's biggest contribution was his lowering of the voice, not in pitch but in intensity, to a conversational level." Nat King Cole: "At his best and most characteristic, Cole was not so much a singer as a whisperer, or, as one might put it, a confider." Ethel Waters: "Her genius was for characterization, and characterization, in song, begins with language. Her diction was immaculate and flexible." Ray Charles: "It is the singing either of a man whose vocabulary is inadequate to express what is in his heart and mind or of one whose feelings are too intense for satisfactory or conventionally melodic articulation. He can't *tell* it to you. He can't even sing it to you. He has to cry out to you, or shout to you, in tones eloquent of despair—or exaltation." Armstrong: "It would be unjust, probably inaccurate, to suggest that he was ever anything but serious in his approach to a song. But it may be permissible to suggest that he rarely, if ever, took a song seriously." Fitzgerald: "Like Louis, she has always seemed to be having a ball. For the listener, when she has finished, the ball is over. It has been joyous, exhilarating, memorable, but hardly an emotional experience." Mildred Bailey: "What one heard was admirable and delightful. The sheer virtuosity, however, sometimes overshadowed the articulation of a lyric and the probing of textual substance." Garland: "One keeps coming back to that word *innocent*, again and again. It was not just an innocent sound. More importantly, it was a sound innocent of anything that smacked of artful management." Holiday: "What you had when she finished with a song was not just invention tempered by superb craftmanship, although there was plenty of each, but untempered autobiography." Sinatra: "The absence of any appearance of art was imperative to his style. His accomplishment in avoiding it was the most compelling evidence of his stature as an artist. He was not presenting himself as an artist. He was presenting himself as a person."

I topped off my catalogue with Holiday and Sinatra because in twentieth-century singing those two are the ultimate, because both comments link the concealment of artifice to the intensification of self-expression, and because I love the fact that, in these moments, Pleasants cannot resist the temptation to equate the singer with, as he says of a Sinatra he also claims "lived the life he sang about," the "person." Almost always with Sinatra and Holiday except in the general way singers conjure memories to call up relevant feelings in themselves, I would usually prefer to say singers aim for the *illusion* of self-expression, and usually Pleasants knows this—with singing actors like Waters and Lee as well as pure musicians like Fitzgerald and Armstrong, he never forgets it. But other times he's sucked into the illusion, as we all are and all want to be. And even though this weakens his thinking a little, it strengthens his book.

What does weaken his book, sometimes a lot, is his generational prejudices—and also his cultural limits as a trained envoy of "serious music." Despite the enthusiastic nod to Presley, who I say is best understood as transitional between '40s pop and the rock and roll he came to symbolize via genius and historical happenstance, *The Great American Popular Singers* is a pre-rock book. Pleasants singles out the "lowering" of Crosby's voice because Crosby was the first great microphone singer, and what Pleasants most treasures, even more than African-American musicality, is pop's return to the lost intimacy and subtlety of bel canto as he conceives it. In the Ray Charles chapter you can feel his fear of the Genius's proudly and loudly elaborated excesses. And although Aretha Franklin is, nominally, one of Pleasants's twenty-two "great American popular singers," he has trouble saying anything nice about her. This is a terrible loss, because some tech stuff from Pleasants would be such a great start in explicating the most indescribable of great voices. Instead we get one useful graf about a non-falsetto range of two-and-a-half not four octaves, general praise that leans too heavily on the word "lovely," and considerable complaining about how, and I quote, "everybody nowadays is hollering and shrieking and screaming." The adjectives "appalling" and "abominable" both come into play.

As with soul, so with rock proper. The introduction dismisses all folk singers except opera-trained Odetta and classical pianist Nina Simone as "amateurs ingenuously celebrating their amateurism." And a brief coda manfully acknowledges: "I have to remind myself that our younger singers are singing to younger listeners bred to a higher decibel count than I find agreeable, or even tolerable." Lennon versus McCartney? The lean subtleties of Lou Reed? The howls of Chester Burnett? The yowls of Janis Joplin? The dozen voices of belated Bing fan Bob Dylan? The self-taught laryngeal discipline of Michael Jackson? Great singers all, I'd say. But Pleasants will leave them to me and especially you, since chances are excellent that you read music better than I do. It's a task eminently worth undertaking. I can only hope that you read Henry Pleasants's *The Great American Popular Singers* before you go about it.

EMP Pop Conference, 2016

The Country and the City

Charlie Gillett's *The Sound of the City: The Rise of Rock and Roll*

Although you'd never know it to read him, Charlie Gillett grew up on a farm. When his parents divorced in 1947, five-year-old Charlie stayed with his mother, who raised prize-winning Jersey cows on a smallholding in northeast England, 250 miles from London and seventy from Leeds although fairly near the steel town of Middlesbrough. But he and his younger brother did occasionally get to London, where they'd visit their father, and even from the farm you could hear Radio Luxembourg and read *Melody Maker* and buy records, especially if your mom was a music fan who took you to see Buddy Holly and Lonnie Donegan when they came north. Charlie attended a local grammar school, got an economics degree from Cambridge in 1963, and then studied education in Bristol, where his future wife Buffy Chessum was in art school. In 1964, they moved to New York so Charlie could get a master's from Columbia Teachers' College. Most Columbia students settle uptown in Morningside Heights, but having checked in with radical documentarian Norman Fruchter, who was married to Charlie's cousin, the couple instead rented an apartment on Rivington Street on the Lower East Side, where they lived, as Fruchter puts it, "close to the bone": a bed, a desk Fruchter gave them, a small kitchen setup, a small TV, a radio, and a phonograph.

Buffy was quickly hired as an assistant at a nearby Jewish daycare center, and soon legendary Columbia sociologist Herbert Gans offered Charlie a research job at his Center for Urban Studies. Charlie earned thirty-two credits at Columbia, worked as a fill-in soundman on Fruchter's prize-winning

SDS Newark Project film *Troublemakers*, and listened to the radio, including free-form WBAI, where the slightly older Charles Hobson devoted a show to what he calls "music white folks wouldn't have heard," with gospel quartets prominent. As the son of Jamaican Episcopalians, Hobson wasn't reared in this music, but he had a passion for it. So after Charlie reached out to him, the two spent hours at Hobson's place talking and listening.

By then it was early 1966 and Charlie had gotten Gans's go-ahead to research a thesis on, as he later wrote, "a subject that seemed odd at the time": a history of rock and roll. Laboring through *Billboard* microfiche, he'd come across artists he hadn't heard—Orioles, Flamingos, Five Royales—and contacted Hobson primarily to learn about these names. For Charlie the meeting ended up having major ramifications. It both focused his understanding of how culturally definitive music was for African-Americans and broadened his understanding of everything that music could be. Remarkably, Charlie had trouble conceiving "the bird groups," to use Hobson's term, as black music at all. He still identified black music with the bluesier strains of r&b and soul. The bird groups had to be pop of some sort, he thought. So Hobson schooled him.

Having finished writing his thesis in New York after Buffy returned to England to give birth to their first child, Charlie then pecked out the final draft on a Center for Urban Studies typewriter. In a story he told many times, a nearby secretary was so moved by his ineptitude that she volunteered to finish the job, which took her two days and cost Charlie a box of chocolates. Back in England Charlie landed a teaching job, but was unable to resist further revisions, which often surfaced as historical essays in *Record Mirror* and the soul magazine *Shout!*, and were then corrected by collectors and amateur experts previously unknown to him. After several years came an unexpected letter from the boss of Charlie's volunteer typist, Harris Dienstfrey, who had left the Center for Urban Studies to co-found a publishing house called Outerbridge & Dienstfrey. As Charlie told it, Dienstfrey had read what his secretary was working on over her shoulder and thought it might make a book. First published in 1970 under a title Charlie devised, that book gave this year's EMP its name: *The Sound of the City*.

Way too young at sixty-eight, Charlie Gillett suffered a fatal heart attack two years ago. Harris Dienstfrey, who as it happens brought my first collection to Penguin in 1972, doesn't remember the secretary and also recalls his editorial suggestions as minor where Charlie has gratefully described them as extensive. But what strikes me about the history of this seminal work is how many bystanders contributed to its fruition. Although unsung experts like Hobson and the collectors who good-humoredly fact-checked Charlie are the kind of angels who grace every successful research job, all were clearly nursing a pent-up need to see this art they loved get some respect. Neither Gans nor Dienstfrey, meanwhile, was much interested in music—the conceptual focus they shared was pop culture. Dienstfrey brought a history of comics and an Arlene Croce book on Astaire and Rogers as well as Peter Guralnick's first collection to his short-lived house, and in 1974 Gans published a study called *Popular Culture and High Culture: An Analysis and Evaluation of Taste*. As for that secretary, Buffy thinks her first name was Margaret. Maybe she was a rock and roller, maybe not. Either way she felt the call, and either way we owe her.

This book so many people wanted to happen exceeded all reasonable expectations. It's had a remarkable five iterations: the 1966 master's thesis, the 1970 Outerbridge & Dienstfrey version, a slightly revised mass-market paperback with Dell in 1972, a greatly revised and expanded version with London's Souvenir Press in 1983, and a 1996 Da Capo reprint with new intro and end matter that remains in print. Charlie's *New York Times* obit reported sales of a quarter million copies. Dienstfrey thinks that sounds high. But it's certain that until Ed Ward's *The Fifties and Before* volume of *Rolling Stone*'s *Rock of Ages* appeared in 1986, *The Sound of the City* had no serious competition. There were books too useless to name, there was fifty pages of Nik Cohn's stylish and even classic but radically underresearched 1969 *Rock from the Beginning* a/k/a *Awopbopaloobop Alopbamboom*, and there was Arnold Shaw's biz-savvy 1974 *The Rockin' 50s*, a useful and amusing inside story in which the historical context is boilerplate and the critical insights are far sparser than in Shaw's essential history of post–World War II r&b, *Honkers and Shouters*. There were also a few biographies, and in 1976 *The Rolling Stone Illustrated History of Rock & Roll* collected quality essays on specific artists. But *The Sound of the City* was the standard history for rock criticism's first two decades.

My account has exploited the elasticity of the term "rock and roll"—which initially designated the commercially insurgent, teen-targeted, r&b-derived pop of the late '50s, fell into abeyance as Bob Dylan and *Rubber Soul* inspired collegiate post-teens to call their beat music "rock," rose again in reaction against the bloated thing that "rock" became, and has now receded along with "rock" in an era whose terminological chaos defies all parsing. Gillett's subtitle would seem clear enough: *The Rise of Rock and Roll*. But in fact he was cagey about what was and wasn't rock and roll, not least by apostrophizing the "and" in the early edition's title and spelling it out for the revision. Gillett argued explicitly that rock and roll was gone by 1958 or 1959 as "the industry, with typical sleight of hand, killed off the music but kept the name." But he also argued that around 1962 it was revitalized, with Britain "a major source of the new music." And in the revision he explained that if the original seemed a little awkward around the music of the late '60s, that was because he'd lacked the advantage of hindsight.

Maybe, maybe not. Gillett was clearly enthusiastic about the Dylan-Beatles-Stones triumvirate, but even with them his enthusiasm peaks early. Few observers of Gillett's orientation are big *Sgt. Pepper* fans, but to dismiss its songwriting in two words—"obscurely surreal"—and dispense with the thing in a paragraph isn't just bad criticism, it's myopic history, just as it's strange not to mention *Beggars Banquet* and *Let It Bleed* till you get to producer Jimmy Miller. So beyond a few not-so-secret sharers—the Band, Creedence of course, Van Morrison—and some surprising praise for Joni Mitchell, he turns into a stick-in-the-mud fast. The Hollies are "traditional show business entertainers" and the Who are going downhill by 1967; Randy Newman is "too subtle and sophisticated," Neil Young a "morose and morbid" "acquired taste." Et cetera. In soul he's pro-Sly and sharp and thorough on Atlantic Records, about which he would publish *Making Tracks* in 1974, as well as Curtis Mayfield and, briefly, Al Green. Motown not so much except for Smokey Robinson—the Temptations, Marvin Gaye, and Stevie Wonder get short shrift, and the Supremes are dismissed altogether.

So for Charlie Gillett, maybe the term rock and roll isn't so elastic after all. The opening sentence of the 1996 introduction where he claims hindsight makes that clear enough: "When the first edition of *The Sound of the City* was published in 1970, it felt as if the rock 'n' roll music of the mid-fifties was about to become just another dim memory from a bygone era." Note that in this sentence, no matter how Da Capo and Souvenir spelled it on the cover, Charlie once again uses the *'n'* in the course of acknowledging his defining passion. My own preference is always to spell out the "and," which in my opinion announces that the music has become something to write about, as it manifestly has. But if you think I'm overemphasizing this nicety, then why is the apostrophized spelling the subject of the very first sentence of Part I of the book proper? Later, Gillett illustrates the "industry"'s "sleight-of-hand" by reporting that the 1959–62 period was when the spelling changed, to wit: "The abolition of the apostrophe was significant—the term looked more respectable, but sounded the same. Perfect." Or as I would apostrophize: The term sounded the same, but the music didn't. Perfidy.

None of this is to dismiss the post-1958 portion of *The Sound of the City*, which occupies more than half of the expanded edition. A lot of it concerns music that escapes industrial takeover, and not just r&b—he likes the Beach

Boys, for instance. And even when it doesn't, his basic structural device, which is to organize his history in terms of labels and producers, often provides a refreshing vantage, as when he describes the Byrds as Terry Melcher's successor to Paul Revere & the Raiders and names all the studio musicians on their debut. Nevertheless, it's as a historian of "the rock 'n' roll music of the mid-fifties" that Gillett excels.

One advantage of organization by label was that it was, as Gillett put it, "readily available to the armchair and library researcher who wrote the first edition." But the device ended up determining his thesis and eventually his title. Simply put, Gillett argues that where the pop music rock and roll displaced was generated by "major recording companies" whose "distributing systems . . . ensure[d] that each of their records would get to every retail market," rock and roll was local, overseen by visionary small businessmen with an ear for talent who ran the independent labels that incubated rock and roll. Insofar as is practical he isolates regional sensibilities. But the local doesn't matter as much to him as the urban itself—the city's cultural connectivity and electrified modernity. As Buffy wrote me: "Being brought up on a farm, isolated, no late buses, no shops, no electricity (at first), the lure of town or city was huge, and always remained so, and what that did to the music."

That Gillett was the only early rock critic with a rural background seems to have armed him against the countervailing anti-pop of our generation: the folk music that attracted so many supposedly forward-looking teenagers with a secret penchant for pastoral romanticism and cultural purism. He recognizes that the Chicago bluesmen were indebted to Robert Johnson and the rest of the Clarksdale posse. But it isn't the likes of Muddy Waters and Howlin' Wolf who inspire his best writing. Gillett emphasizes that the primary source of rock and roll was rhythm and blues, and that in r&b, as he put it, "the prevailing emotion was excitement." But as teenagers everywhere get excited, he's just as good on white artists as on black ones. And although *The Sound of the City* was written in a critical and scholarly vacuum by a twenty-four-year-old with no musical or musicological training, nuggets that emerge throughout its first half continue to top or materially augment all the words expended on the same artists since. This young amateur avoids any Romance of the Negro as well as the broader primitivist assumptions that inflected so much early rock criticism. He assumes the dignity and intelligence of craft and self-knowledge that inform even art where the prevailing emotion is excitement.

Spinning Big Joe Turner, Gillett hears a "good-natured" Southwestern optimism he's read about in Ralph Ellison where Nick Tosches hears "the sound of the Devil chaining his third wife down." And if literary shock jock Tosches is too obvious a target, Gillett also hears in Jerry Lee Lewis "a sophisticated technique of varying the emotional pitch of his fast songs" where Jim Miller emphasizes Lewis's "unquenchable spontaneity" and "pointless but exhilarating glissando runs," even wonders—in a turn of phrase you just know he'd like back—whether he's "a white man with a black soul." Bill Haley's "rhythm dominated the arrangements much more than it did in the Negro records." Eddie Cochran's "thick, aggressively rhythmic guitar sound became an important ingredient in the 'heavy rock' sound [of] the Kinks and the Who." Fats Domino "sang with a plaintive tone that did not seem so adult and alien as did the tone of his contemporary rhythm and blues singers." The Five Royales' Johnny Tanner cultivated "a vocal tone similar to [Clyde] McPhatter's, slightly more hesitant and less melodic, more mature with a harder drive at fast tempos." And get what Gillett discerns in Percy Mayfield's "Please Send Me Someone to Love": "With a rare sense of balance that entirely avoided self-conscious irony, Mayfield brilliantly evoked the common dilemma of understanding the significance of others' problems yet being unavoidably bound up in objectively lesser but privately more important personal issues."

That level of psychological detail epitomizes the seriousness Gillett prized in teen music. Like almost every early writer about rock and roll, he cared too much about authenticity—not as the abstract noun, which only arises toward the end of the book, but as the various virtues secured by the then-unexamined adjective "authentic." "Authentic" specifies the superiority of Danny & the Juniors to Paul Anka and of Freddie Bell and His Bellboys to Georgia Gibbs. It honors the studio band Harold Battiste assembled at Liberty and the idiomatic bar blues of the Vee-Jay roster. Inside ironic scare quotes, it also mocks the purism of the early Stones, the prissiness of the folkies who would have liked Chuck Berry and Buddy Holly fine if only they'd stood there with an acoustic guitar. But one time it very nearly epitomizes his value system, which guards against "the substitution of sentimental pleasantries or sensational effects for a more authentic consideration of relationships and experience." For better or worse, Gillett wasn't really a pop fan—he's so suspicious of hooks that his favorite term of derision is "singalong." Instead he has a special passion for blues-based artists who deliver subtlety and a mature outlook.

Yet Gillett's readiness to integrate bird-group quasi-pop into his r&b schema once Charles Hobson explained it to him is just one example of his openness and breadth—when his hero Jerry Wexler complains tediously about doowop's crudity, Gillett steps aside to praise this "urban folk music"'s "natural presence" and "illusion of intimacy and sincerity." After he actually met some bizzers, Gillett began to notice how many indie proprietors were crooks while such organization men as John Hammond and Milt Gabler stood out as heroes of a sort. Still, the pro-indie line was a crucial insight that's now more relevant then ever. And just as important, Gillett played a key role in separating the reflexive praiseword "authentic" from the pastorale with which other proponents of vernacular music regularly linked it. That the city is as real as the country is taken for granted today. But like so many truisms it initially had to be fought for. That's why Herbert Gans started the Center for Urban Studies.

Does the music of the country feed into that of the city? Absolutely. It happened all the time in '50s rock and roll, particularly in Memphis and on Chicago's South Side but also as Carolinans and such imagined doowop. It happens now in Nashville, although less consistently than Music Row pretends. For decades it's happened internationally in the world music strains to which Charlie devoted the last three decades of his life. And hey, sometimes the music of the city needs a breath of fresh air—think Merrill Garbus, the Waco Brothers, Oneohtrix Point Never. Nevertheless, simply by entitling his seminal book *The Sound of the City*, this transplanted farmboy drew a line in the dirt—and on the concrete.

EMP Pop Conference, 2012

Reflections of an Aging Rock Critic

Jon Landau's *It's Too Late to Stop Now: A Rock and Roll Journal*

In "Confessions of an Aging Rock Critic," the final essay in this collection, Jon Landau says: "Critics are often failed artists of some sort. Most of the rock writers I know play an instrument; several have been in bands." Now, this is true of Landau himself, and no doubt of his acquaintances, but it is not true in general. It is not true, for instance, of me and my acquaintances. In fact, there isn't one failed musician among the rock critics I admire most.

Frustrated novelists, perhaps, although most of us write about rock because fiction hasn't compelled us for a long time. Rock seems so much more—please pardon the expression—relevant, its intrinsic excitement trailing unnumbered cultural connections. Ignorant of music theory, we write about popular music simply as members of the populace.

Landau was one of the first rock critics, working at the beginning for *Crawdaddy!* and then moving on to *Rolling Stone*. He writes as a record producer and ex-musician. As an analyst of the guts (or machinery) of rock and roll he has no peer. This can be very useful. It's nice to go back to a record you've enjoyed casually and understand how a drum break or stereo separation that Landau noticed makes it work, and even though technical expertise isn't necessary to such insights—musical illiterates like Greil Marcus and Lester Bangs make them all the time—it certainly helps. And only a critic like Landau can observe authoritatively that, for instance, the Motown sound depends on sophisticated chord changes and a "relentless four-beat drum pattern." He is especially acute when he applies both kinds of analysis to music he really knows and loves, as in his definitive piece on Wilson Pickett.

Let me emphasize that example. Landau's essay on Wilson Pickett is definitive. Yet when I gave it to a Pickett fan not long ago, I came back five minutes later and found the fan asleep. This did not really surprise me. For one thing, Landau is not a very interesting writer. Over the years, his style has evolved from the clubfooted to the pedestrian, but even now it is always colorless and frequently graceless. (A late random sample: "Through his demeanor, speech and attitude, Sly conveys the impression of a man teetering on the brink.") More important, he seems disinclined to link music to culture with any vigor. His long analysis of Motown never explores the relationship between black music and white market that the observation I cited so clearly indicates. He doesn't suggest how the chief musical virtue of Carole King's *Tapestry* (clean, forceful production) might mesh with its verbal emphasis on the value of simple friendship. And so forth.

Landau does have a good head for the thematic core of an artist's work as well as for technique. My complaint is that he doesn't connect them intricately enough. Larger connections are even harder to find in his work, especially the connection between the critic himself and the music he loves. The admixture of black music and white audience is the most basic mystery of rock and roll, and few critics would be better qualified to discuss it than Landau, whose involvement in black music is so intense. Yet he never does.

I suppose this amounts to a presumptuous suggestion that Landau write a different kind of criticism than he has chosen to write. Very well then. The crucial presumption of this "different kind of criticism" is that such suggestions are a critic's real work. In the '30s, leftish partisans like Lionel Trilling and Philip Rahv used the tools of the rival New Critics to construct a more broad-based sort of cultural analysis around literature. In rock, where the artistic content is somewhat less abstruse and the cultural impact so massive, a similar project is required, and it's clearly one that Landau could undertake.

It is significant that by these different standards the best piece in this book—in which Landau deals with questions of a size he rarely attempts, such as how a star's self-image and public image affect each other and the star's art, how art affects audience, and even Landau's personal stake in the work—concerns boxing, about which Landau is knowledgeable but not expert. I wish he would write about music that way—with his technical perception, he would be the complete rock critic. But it may just be that in popular culture, expertise inhibits ambitious thought rather than encouraging it.

Book World, 1973

Pioneer Days

Kevin Avery's *Everything Is an Afterthought: The Life and Writings of Paul Nelson* | Nona Willis Aronowitz's (ed.) *Out of the Vinyl Deeps: Ellen Willis on Rock Music*

It's a little silly for me to do the full-disclosure tap dance around the books at hand. I'm quoted ten times in Kevin Avery's Paul Nelson biography-collection-tribute, *Everything Is an Afterthought*, and thanked prominently in the acknowledgments. Paul and I were friends in the '70s, although he had many closer ones, and I edited a few of the pieces Avery chose; Paul helped me move into the apartment where I'm writing this and was directly responsible for the recording career of my beloved New York Dolls. And with Ellen Willis I have no "objectivity" whatsoever—we were a couple from 1966 to 1969, and except for my wife no one has influenced me more. Six years younger than Nelson, Willis died four months after him in 2006, when she was only sixty-four. At a memorial colloquium the next year, I called for a collection of the rock criticism she'd written decades before, and I meant all of it. Overseen by her daughter, Nona Willis Aronowitz, *Out of the Vinyl Deeps* is pretty much the omnibus I imagined. I blurbed it. I'm in the video.

I believed Willis was a better critic than Nelson before I read these books, and for whatever my objectivity is worth, I still do. But I believed even more that both collections deserved to exist before their authors attracted attention by dying. From where I sit inside the whale, '70s rockmags and alternaweeklies generated a lost trove of American criticism. With Willis and Nelson added to the smattering of other names now compiled one way or another—Lester Bangs, Greil Marcus, Robert Palmer, Dave Marsh, Jon Landau, Richard Meltzer, and myself—the early record is in a sense complete. *The Village Voice*, *Creem*, and *Rolling Stone* archives could yield multi-author miscellanies that document the democratic babble of that brief era with the diversity it deserves. But Willis and Nelson cultivated distinct voices that merit consideration on their own terms—very similar in their passion for lucidity, very dissimilar in their ideological impetus.

Re-encountering these voices in book form years later differs radically from meeting them in their journalistic moment, and although I originally edited parts of both books, I'd never read most of either. Willis and I split up in late 1969, and she was the one with the *New Yorker* subscription, so I picked up on her column haphazardly after that. (If this seems weird, I'm sorry—I did really prefer both *Creem*, which came free, and *The Nation*, which was cheaper.) Nelson's reviews I checked out regularly in *Rolling Stone*, but not his profiles nor, obviously, the previously unpublished work Avery has unearthed. Moreover, half of *Everything Is an Afterthought* is a biography Avery heroically assembled from years of interviews with Nelson's friends and boxes of interview tapes Nelson left behind.

Both books are better than you might figure. With Willis, the red flag is that it comprises all of her published rock criticism, and completist omnibuses are not generally how to do collections—some pieces always work better than others and some get old quick. Yet despite a few sequencing glitches and a handful of outright failures, *Out of the Vinyl Deeps* reads strong start to finish, its more casual concert reviews humanizing the focused intellect Willis soon trained exclusively on her sex-positive vision of left feminism and feminist leftism. With Nelson, the wild card was Avery, an unknown from Utah whose national track record starts here. But he's done inspired, diligent work. Constructed from a greater proportion of direct quotes than is normally deemed proper, the biography is doubly gripping as a result: as Avery sadly and scrupulously establishes, Nelson spent the last two decades of his life as a blocked, depressive loner, so the warm affection and unblinking realism of admirers from Jackson Browne to his boss at the video store says worlds for his inner worth. And though the critical analyses that triggered this admiration shone less brightly than I'd hoped, the narrative writing I'd put less stock in compensated.

Willis's book, out since May, has been widely and enthusiastically reviewed, which is gratifying even if the collective amazement that *this woman once wrote among us* speaks poorly of how well kids today do their homework. Pub date on the Nelson is November 18, eight weeks after its astonishingly thorough Avery-edited companion *Conversations with Clint: Paul Nelson's Lost Interviews with Clint Eastwood*, so reviews are sparse as I write. But my guess is that Nelson will finish second in this race, and would have even if Willis's feminist cred didn't give her such a head start.

Nothing illustrates Nelson's cult status more impressively than the fact that Jonathan Lethem, whose foreword to *Conversations with Clint* describes his tour as the master's cinematic apprentice, based *Chronic City*'s central character on Nelson. But in the end, Nelson's critical vision, especially as regards music, does have a cultish quality. An escapee from the laced-tight confines of a small Minnesota town, Nelson maintained a longer career in journalism and the music business than you'd predict for such a screwed-up guy. A neurotically painstaking writer who wasted years on unfinished articles, books, and screenplays, he was also a hopeless romantic silently tormented by both guilt (over his split with his high school sweetheart and their son) and rejection (by the other woman, a beguiling folksinger who told Avery: "He wasn't a complete person. You know, Paul's interests really were in three areas: music, books, and movies"). But none of this negates how readily artists took to his laconically encyclopedic cool, or how awestruck colleagues were by his high-principled, dryly humorous, reference-dropping style.

"There was a gentleness and compassion in everything that he did," says Nelson's great bulwark, critic-turned-screenwriter Jay Cocks. "I think it was unique in rock writing, that kind of compassion." Compassion is there if you look for it, and you can see its wellsprings in a biography that helps explain Nelson's weakness for sensitive cad Jackson Browne. But up on the surface is his never-ending quest for the kind of rugged yet thoughtful American hero who came to the fore as Ford and Hawks, Chandler and Macdonald were adjudged classic. Nelson wasn't insensible to music per se—as his life ran down, there were long, long spells when he obsessed on Chet Baker and Ralph Stanley. But from Minneapolis scavenger Bob Dylan to Dolls mastermind David Johansen and beyond, all his rock heroes were rock poets, and all were white men. The only female Avery highlights is Patti Smith, via Nelson's pan of her "pointlessly pregnant" *Horses*. Even worse was Muhammad Ali fanatic Nelson's utter indifference to African-American music—I once assigned him a Millie Jackson album on the optimistic theory that she was a hell of a lyricist, but to no avail. A generous man, r&b adept Lethem diagnoses this vast lacuna as an "autism."

Like most rugged individualists, Nelson was staunchly apolitical, a tendency accentuated by his early immersion in the folk movement and his tour as managing editor of *Sing Out!* under Irwin Silber, whose commitment to socialist realism survived his 1955 departure from the Communist Party proper. This didn't distance Nelson as much as you might think from Willis, who like most radical feminists was staunchly political, but also an individualist, plenty tough if not literally rugged. Willis couldn't stand Silber's aesthetic either. His sober moralism seemed to her a repressive, objectively counterrevolutionary burden just waiting to be swept away by some hedonistic-libertarian analysis. That she should find herself getting paid to develop that analysis for a ruling-class outlet of notorious gentility exemplified the pop contradictions it was her mission to resolve. Whether the gig made her, as her *New Yorker* heir Sasha Frere-Jones calculates, the most widely read of America's few working rock critics depends on how many subscribers actually perused "Rock, Etc." The really big deal was that out of nowhere, this obscure twenty-six-year-old had a beat.

The dealmaker was one long, painstakingly turned essay published first in (I kid you not) *Commentary*, and then in the short-lived weekend-hippie slick *Cheetah*. Its subject was Bob Dylan, its focus his image(s), and it remains one of the richest things ever written about the artist or the '60s even though it was formulated without benefit of historical perspective. "Dylan" leads *Out of the Vinyl Deeps*, as it did Willis's 1981 collection, *Beginning to See the Light*, and then come every "Rock, Etc." column she ever published—forty-seven of them, dated 1968 to 1975, with a falloff during her 1969–70 stint running an antiwar coffeehouse for GIs in Colorado.

There's been a lot of kerfuffle over how personal, casual, and fannish these columns seem. But in fact the first-person anecdotal was a standard ploy in early rock criticism—Willis just knew how to make it signify. The laid-back Colorado reflection "Stranger in a Strange Land," for instance, is every bit as thought through as it is peaced out, a rigorous examination of the limits of rigor. Even at her most contemplative, Willis is in command of something she valued more than tone: ideas.

Because Willis was writing so early, her concepts are sometimes crude and her facts under-researched. Because she devoted so much attention to icons who have since been analyzed down to the molecules, not all her critical insights come as revelations. Still, read her on Randy Newman or Black Sabbath or *Blood on the Tracks*, to name just three, and find stuff that never occurred to you. Ponder her notes on Bette Midler's camp and rethink your views on interpretation. And tucked away in the back is her fourth *New Yorker* column, the audaciously theoretical "The Star, the Sound, and the Scene," a post-communist manifesto that celebrates celebrity, praises mass culture, and puts virtuosity in its place. I was right to want it all. Having never read most of this book before, I've now read most of it twice, and I'm not done yet.

Willis was a pioneer, feeling her way through the underbrush like all of us who treasured '60s notions of freedom. She was perceptive enough to call out utopian nostalgia as it arose. But she writes a whole hell of a lot about the usual suspects: Dylan, Stones, Beatles, Who, and Creedence (who she considered dance music). Inconveniently for a radical feminist, all are men. Nevertheless, she didn't miss many major women artists, either—Grace Slick I guess, Raitt and/or Ronstadt, and Gladys Knight, who she name-checked but never tackled. Knight's absence is especially unfortunate, because beyond an imaginative Stevie Wonder report and a halting Aretha Franklin review, too much crucial black music does get missed. More perplexing omissions than the generally neglected James Brown are failed hippie Sly Stone and politico-sexual obsessive Marvin Gaye, and I could go on (AlGreenAlGreenAlGreen). Still, compared to Nelson she was a polymath.

Nelson was a pioneer, too—I wish Avery had made room for some work from *Little Sandy Review*, the folk journal Nelson co-founded in 1960, which I don't know (his best-remembered folk piece is his gantlet-throwing Dylan-at-Newport defense for *Sing Out!*). But between 1974 and 1982, when he and *Rolling Stone* underwent a bitter divorce, Nelson had the run of the ranch. It's to his immense credit that he recognized the literary cowboy under David Johansen's glam, and certainly his tastes ranged wider than his big pieces suggest. But those tastes were very narrow for a major critic. That's why I came away less taken with his reviews than with his magnificent Warren Zevon profile and Clint Eastwood interviews, which would mean far less without their critical underpinnings. As I told Avery, Nelson "liked what he liked." Too bad his Neil Young book was never written and his Rod Stewart book was passed off to Lester Bangs.

Different as they were, Willis and Nelson shared two things. One was that they prized clarity. Willis strove for an elevated plainstyle that at its most finished—best exemplified not by her columns but by ambitiously worked essays like "Dylan," her Velvet Underground exegesis for Greil Marcus's 1979 *Stranded*, and the title piece of *Beginning to See the Light*—made abstractions seem part of the natural world. Nelson was more poetic, endlessly pursuing rhythm and overtone. But neither was much for describing physical facts, and as a result neither much conveyed how music sounded—a common enough challenge that rock criticism's pioneers defeated in their own ways as they stuck at it. This brings us to the second thing Willis and Nelson shared. They didn't stick at it.

About sticking at it I am even less objective than I am about my old companions Ellen and Paul. I am rock criticism's champion lifer, churning out two hundred record briefs a year as if I still thought it was fun, which I do. But I can say this much. Although both turned out some of their best rock criticism after they retired—in Nelson's case an account of his five-year tour at Mercury Records written in the mid '90s—I suspect that their failure to get to the nub of music per se helps us understand why they quit.

Willis's partisans aver that she got out while the getting was good, while Nelson's mourn the loss of his genius. I believe the opposite. Nelson was right to get out. Rock's hero quest has been a dead end since circa 1980—there's Springsteen, that's one, and then there's, well, Bono, who it's impossible to imagine Nelson taking seriously for a host of reasons good and bad. But I think Willis would have been better off staying. She was a powerful thinker, and though she never wrote enough she almost always wrote well when she did. But as someone who spent fifteen years extricating himself from her politics and is so glad he did, I say continued attention to her beat would have changed those politics for the better, sensitizing her to mass pleasures, countercultural anxieties, class antagonisms, and racial contradictions she lost touch with. Mere attention wouldn't have done it, though—she would have had to enjoy it. And it's my guess that for writers as gifted as Willis and Nelson never to have found language to describe music means that in the end they didn't enjoy music for all it's worth. When Ellen and I were feeling our way through the music of the '60s, we scoffed at such notions. But we were wrong.

Barnes & Noble Review, 2011

Impolite Discourse

Jim DeRogatis's *Let It Blurt: The Life and Times of Lester Bangs, America's Greatest Rock Critic* | Richard Meltzer's *A Whore Just Like the Rest: The Music Writings of Richard Meltzer* | Nick Tosches's *The Nick Tosches Reader*

To can the first-person taboo and proceed to the main event: fuck yes I have a personal interest in the books that follow. Not just because all involve rock criticism and I am Der Dean, but because in two of the three I am explicitly and persistently attacked. So, having been offered extra space by this journal's editor-in-chief—he wanted a cover piece, me scowling in my Special Ed T-shirt: IF MELTZER DISSES THE DOLLS AGAIN I WILL FUCK UP HIS HARD DRIVE—I would be disingenuous not to address a couple of grating factual issues.

Listen up, Jim DeRogatis. When I threw that piece of pie (not my "dinner," the food line was *long*) at Ellen Willis, it wasn't because, as Willis with her Handy Dandy Theory Generator lets you suggest, I wanted to maintain the sexist status quo of "gender relations in rock-critic land." The motives I experienced were no more noble but a lot more personal, and to find out what they were (and then assay their credibility) you need merely have asked. I know you're big on journalistic ethics, so write this one on your wrist: Check The Source. (It's real useful when you have an unidentified third party provide uncorroborated off-the-record poolside repartee by someone—not me, Neil Strauss, remember?—who makes you so jealous you could shit.) (Reached by telephone, DeRogatis denied that he was jealous of Strauss.)

As for Richard Meltzer, right now let me say this. Meltzer complains, bitterly, that "30–40 times" over "seven years," he asked me and the true inventor of rock criticism, Richard Goldstein, whether he could "FUCKING WRITE FOR THEM" (i.e., US, presumably HERE). I don't recall this, and neither does Goldstein, not least because neither of us was a *Voice* editor until 1974. We could put in a word for someone we loved, as I did for my dear friend Tom Smucker, an equally eccentric and valuable voice back then, and when Goldstein had his own mag briefly, Meltzer was in it. But we couldn't assign until we became editors. Whereupon we acted. Meltzer led the second music section I edited, 8/8/74 (Vince Aletti on the Jackson 5 got 8/1), one of his three appearances before 10/1.

I dunno—maybe Meltzer's from Triton and I'm from Uranus. 'Umble Queens boys though we both were, at some one-on-one level we never did relate. Which is why Meltzer has it 180 degrees wrong when he begrudgingly allows as how I liked him "personally . . . and to some degree professionally." Truth is, I considered Meltzer an antisocial jerk, and please read "Handsome Dick Throws the Party of the Century" before calling me a goody-goody. As a writer, however, I thought he was terrific. And it turns out he was only warming up.

In a famous phrase—it rhymes—James Wolcott once dubbed Lester Bangs, the subject of DeRogatis's *Let It Blurt*, and Meltzer, whose "rockwriting" has now been collected as *A Whore Just Like the Rest*, "the Noise Boys." And while Bangs's drinking buddy and Meltzer's drinking best friend Nick Tosches serves a sterner muse, his bedrock faith in "the saxophone whose message transcends knowing" places *The Nick Tosches Reader* in the territory even though it's less than half music writing. The three never blew the same horn; as DeRogatis quips, they were "individually dissimilar." But they were all partisans of rock at its noisiest—culture as ecstatic disruption. "Fuck the tradition, I want the Party," Bangs declared in 1971. "A touchstone of genuwine *liberation*," Meltzer recalled in 1986. Maybe even, as Tosches recollected in the forced tranquility of 1991, "a cold hard blue-veined cock right up under the tie-dyed skirts of benighted sensitivity." And the minute rock stopped delivering the requisite Skullbustium, the Noise Boys shouted their pain. As usual, Bangs was softer on this than the other two, enmeshed in a life-drama of musical betrayal and reconciliation until he goddamn died. But like Meltzer and Tosches he dreamed of escaping rockcrit and becoming a "real writer."

Tosches has succeeded royally. A master crime reporter whose manner yokes Homer, Hemingway, and some '60s tit magazine I'm not literate enough to ID, author of a comical, biblical Jerry Lee Lewis bio that trumps Albert Goldman coming and Peter Guralnick going, he is just shy of famous—his Dean Martin book on its way to the movies, an investigative assignment inflated into the current *The Devil and Sonny Liston*. Meltzer has failed brilliantly. A writer of barbwire hilarity and recondite formal daring whose Kantian yawp doubles back on itself three times a sentence as it blows all decent expository standards up the hemorrhoids of history, he's pure cult figure, so strapped for cash he's still compelled to concoct a dadaist preview squib for seventy-five of the *San Diego Reader*'s cheapskate Georges a week. As for Bangs, he should be so unlucky. When he died in 1982, he was still churning out record reviews as he dreamed of (and worked on) novels, memoirs, stream-of-consciousness screeds, and treatises exposing man's inhumanity to man. Although his legend as a substance-ingesting fabulous character exceeds Tosches's and Meltzer's combined, nothing in his work or story, including the craving for transcendence all three have known too well, suggests that he wouldn't rather be alive.

Instead he got his best-of early: *Psychotic Reactions and Carburetor Dung*, edited (solely) by Greil Marcus, published in what would have been Lester's thirty-ninth year, 1987, and not yet pecked to death by the many geese who've stuck their yellow noses in. And now he gets a biography as well. The legend is a lousy substitute for the words—my best hope for *Let It Blurt* is that it will spark a second anthology. Still, DeRogatis has gathered his facts with gusto. As someone who knew Lester, I found the account of his early years poignant and then some, and, whatever my quibbles, the rest of the narrative is readable, scrupulously researched, and fair enough—affectionate without romanticizing Lester's tragic, destructive . . . not "excesses," to hell with that, *vices*. Wonderful photos, too. But—well, here comes the first person again. Early on, DeRogatis quotes me as saying, "His critical ideas were not the strength; it was the language that was the strength," then stoutly ripostes, "I disagree." I braced myself, but the follow-through never came. The few ideas DeRogatis cites at all—boo irony, boo academia, the beauty of ugliness, rock's democratic imperative—are elementary. Even Bangs's style is barely explored; I wonder how many who weren't there will suss that he was one of the funniest writers on the planet. The book's few striking critical insights come from interviewees, particularly Meltzer. And be this journalistic principle or intellectual aptitude, the result is a less than critical biography that assumes Lester's writing and raves on about his legend.

It was to refocus on his words that this piece was initially conceived. Just how good was Lester Bangs, and why? Marcus, that sobersides, famously claimed of *Psychotic Reactions*: "Perhaps what this book demands from a reader is a willingness to believe that the best writer in America could write almost nothing but record reviews." Note that this is not the same as claiming Bangs was the best writer in America—and that Marcus wouldn't mind if you got that idea. On the other hand, after Meltzer belittlingly compares Bangs to such "*dregs* of beat" as Ray Bremser and Ted Joans, he doubles back, grandly and slyly adding: "(He also of course found USE for Céline and Bukowski.)" No admirer of Bukowski or fan of Céline, I don't find that especially far-fetched. Then again, I do have a weakness for record reviews, and would be hard-pressed to gainsay some lit crit who found Bukowski and Céline more "relevant." But Bremser and Joans? In my dream world, even a lit crit could make that call. And although Tosches pumps Meltzer's big Bangs piece as the class of the field, I prefer his own little one, which fondly sums up the "hayseed"'s three obsessions—writing, music, and communication—and concludes: "He was a nice guy."

This basic observation doesn't partake of DeRogatis's "St. Lester," a straw myth no one believes in. It simply respects the openheartedness people fell for, in person and on the page. Meltzer is so set on reestablishing the self-abuse, hostility, egomania, and b.o. the nice guy and his legend made too much of that he short-changes the sweet stuff, and so there's something conflicted about his g'bye. Lester's writing—his self-mocking confessionals, left-field generalizations, free-form metaphors, effortless epithets, and boffo laugh lines, all flowing like a river of Romilar or a Coltrane solo—touched readers in a place his legend never reached. Between the two he became more notorious and beloved than Meltzer ever could while ringing changes on a method of outrage Meltzer isn't crazy to think he got to first. But Meltzer has never come near Bangs's well-nigh Dickensian flow—few have. And for a long time he didn't approach Bangs's heart either. It was his heart, heart that never compromised his tremendous intelligence and always fed off his humor and his endless love of music (here signifying merely "his subject," or "the world"), that made Bangs the wonder he was.

One rock and roll thing about Bangs was his gift for juicing commonplaces—hype! alienation! spontaneous bop prosody! (youth! sex! the big beat!)—with the freshness of his idiom and the intensity of his convictions. That's why I believe his language subsumes his ideas. But he was also a gusher of musical connection and description who in the right mood could hear just about anything anew. In the right mood, Meltzer can be an even better, very different critic-qua-critic. *The Nick Tosches Reader*, however, gives us something else—a great music reporter with narrow tastes and an overview captured in its entirety by the title of his Bangla-Desh putdown: "The Heartbeats Never Did Benefits."

As a devotee of the journalism collection, yes I said yes I will Yes to the Michele Sindona prolegomenon, the Carly Simon interview, the Burroughs-Hoover tour de force, the meta-ironic send-up of *Love Story*, the monumental George Jones profile *The New Yorker* rejected in its infinite gentility. In toto, however, this six-hundred-pager is a bold-faced mishmash, full of dull stuff (much of it from men's magazines, although the stump-fucking fantasies 'tis rumored he penned for *Penthouse Forum* are absent) calculated to prove how much realer a writer he's become. In controlled doses I love the high-low particularities, heroic rhythms, and sardonic bite of his prose. But after 593 pages—plus the skillful 1988 literary thriller *Cut Numbers* and *The Devil and Sonny Liston* heaping contumely on Muhammad Ali and the pinkos who love him—I was plumb worn out. If you believe Philip Roth, Peter Matthiessen, and Hubert Selby, Jr. are our only great living writers, Der Dean isn't gonna stop you from making "There is no new thing under the sun" your fucking mantra. But what kind of careful craftsman repeats such a wheeze over and over? A writer who prides himself on going against the grain should recognize that anyone who devises a fresh way to say the world cannot change will eventually be rewarded by rich people who hope he's right. Tosches's novel-in-progress looks strong. I sincerely hope it goes against the grain. And if instead he gets mired in his "vision," he was still right to forsake rockwrite. The passion is not in him.

With Meltzer this is a far more complicated question. Although I helped select him the Association of Alternative Newsweeklies' 1995 music critic of the year, that three-article submission was all I'd seen of his non-*Voice* journalism since he moved to L.A. in 1975; I didn't even know he'd published 1988's accurately titled *L.A. Is the Capital of Kansas*. So I downed that 244-page collection after polishing off the 575-page *A Whore Just Like the Rest* and enjoyed it fine—the hamburger reviews, the boxing piece, the sexcapades, and especially the tender "Silent Nite(s)" and the nothing-happened ". . . and Crazy for Loving You" toward the end. But *A Whore Just Like the Rest* is so superior to this alien-in-paradise miscellany as to render Meltzer's vituperative contempt for current music and its criticism something like a tragedy.

Now, since almost all the many things Meltzer says about me and mine are, not to call him a bad word, misunderstood or misremembered—*Stranded*, Greil's *Aesthetics of Rock* intro, my Little Richard T-shirt, my intimacy with his oeuvre, and his place at the *Voice* (where I'll give him half of Eric Dolphy)—maybe he's equally untrustworthy across the board. But although he does go on about Truth, he's not in the trust business. He's selling ideas by the bucketful, mockery of that there, jokes for jokes' sake, a word born every minute, a childish refusal to curb his orality, his own pud-pulling, panty-snagging genius. He wasn't a token of my tolerance, much less (so defensive!) "a vulgar exhibit" in my "proto-multiculture briefcase." He was an essential argument, the most extreme available, for what I'll retrospectively dub impolite discourse, a concept that encompasses all rock criticism then and (Anthony DeCurtis excepted, of course) much of it now—only marginally more unacceptable to literary bowwows than Tom Smucker or Ed Naha, but manifestly more brilliant and offensive, hence much harder to take. If you weren't threatened by noise, Meltzer wouldn't bother you. If you were, you would have to confront the likelihood that this Yale-dropout barbarian could beat you at Scrabble with one hand and finish off your Jack Daniel's with the other.

Egomaniac that he is, Meltzer doesn't want to be anyone else's argument, certainly not mine. Yet the disgracefully cheap *Voice* was the nearest thing to a money gig available to a guy whose behavior and oeuvre were epitomized by his great line in a Redd Foxx review: "(Tastes rather like beef Redd and the texture sure beats sushi!)." Subject of sentence: assholes. His writing wasn't and isn't unpublishable, but at its straightest it's extremely eccentric—not even dollar-a-word stuff, especially given the author's kneejerk contempt for all editors. Impressed by the literary bad boy Tosches nails as a "con man," Meltzer has never understood why he shouldn't achieve fame and fortune commensurate with William S. Burroughs's, and his inevitable failure to do so, while improving his politics the way poverty does, has further curdled his always sour media analysis. This analysis never made him any easier to assign, not because media-bashing is verboten (these days it's the tedious coin of the rockcrit realm), but because music critics are supposed to be interested in music and Meltzer started with the rock-is-dead shit in *1968*. Young people scoff when I tell them this, but although he flirted with country and fell for punk and remains an avant-jazzbo, Meltzer repeats the date many times in *A Whore Just Like the Rest*—all but eighteen pages of which were published 1969 or later.

Professional ressentiment fed this conceit—*his* topic, stolen by hustlers! But basically, the egomania involved was spiritual. Rock had been Meltzer's whole world—no one has ever heard the Beatles better—and when the illusion faded he blamed rock rather than contingency, mortality, life. As a result, *A Whore Like All the Rest* is rife with pans of meaningless music he may not even have heard, especially in the early '70s and again in those squibs, my favorite of which boldfaces the Cigar Store Indians (?) in an addendum to a list of fifty-five extinct soups: Olive and Watercress, Spaghetti and Mole, Fat-Free Pantyhose, Chicken with Starch, Dawg . . . Yet for all his utterly fucked, generationally banal inability to hear Sonic Youth, Youssou N'Dour, Ol' Dirty Bastard, Mouse on Mars, or Juliana Hatfield, the music criticism here has so much vitality—an offhand take on his friends the Blasters, an insulting dead-on description of Lester's voice, a rave about the Germs (who I hate), the Bud Powell fantasia *mit* dump memoir he gave the Association of Alternative Newsweeklies, the aleatory "Ten Cage Reviews" (his last true music column at the *Reader*, which fired him before he got his award).

There's more, too—*Voice* stuff he hates/resents, the two other AAN submissions, jazz writing I've only heard about.

Meltzer used to spew everything first-draft. But in the late '70s he started "composing" laboriously, and while his prose still has the old jismy dazzle, it's also clearer, denser, less shticky. It's not all equally good, though. Journalism is that way, and although Meltzer insists indignantly that he's not a journalist, all the '90s stuff here, including a left-of-rad rant on the '92 riots, first appeared in the *Reader*. Maybe he can generate novels, memoirs, stream-of-consciousness screeds, and treatises exposing man's inhumanity to man. But the great virtue of journalism is that it gets writers out of themselves. Nothing will stop Meltzer from writing about himself; nothing ever has. He's always performed great tricks with his egotism, and from somebody who's become a much nicer guy, personawise—vulnerable, compassionate, evincing considerable, how about that, heart—we wouldn't want it any other way. But since I'm convinced he and music still have something special going after all these years, I would like respectfully to suggest that somebody assign him, I don't know . . . some jazz reviews? He needs the money. A second collection is probably too much to expect in this media economy; this one's miracle enough. But you never know.

One more thing. Possessed of his own Handy Dandy Theory Generator, Meltzer suggests in the long, climactic "Vinyl Reckoning" that me and Marcus give everything we praise "COOTIES." We devalue it, scare the uncontaminated away. That wasn't my intention; I loved his book long before I got there. But if I've made his head itch, well, as we used to say at Junior High School 16: "SUF-FUR!"

Village Voice, 2000

Journalism and/or Criticism and/or Musicology and/or Sociology (and/or Writing): In Honour of Simon Frith

Although few rock critics have dallied so long in the higher reaches of academic abstraction than Simon Frith, it's equally true that few have insisted so actively or theorized so proactively that music is a physical experience, something you *hear*. This impulse dates to his early days as a reviewer, when he was also one of the few to enjoy post-soul and schlock-rock for what they were. The Chi-Lites' "Have You Seen Her," 1973: "The joy of the record lies in the way [Eugene] Record *milks* this sob story—talk-in intro, clanging guitar and, above all, the magical use of the Chi-Lites group voice, ooing and bupping behind the action." The Moody Blues, 1973: "The Moodies (or at least their producer) have a feeling for sound qualities which can't be sneered away. Every track has its stirring moments (especially in the use of the guitar as a genuinely electronic instrument)." The Miracles' "Love Machine," 1976: "At home, in the armchair, you hear the beat and its insistence is numbing and mindless. But on the dance floor it's taken for granted by your feet, and your head, freed by the haze of movement, can notice everything *else*—the snatches of instrument, the cross-vocals, the mutters and murmurs of machines. That's when you can hear a good disco sound and it's suddenly gripping, complex, surprising."

Yet at precisely the same time the academic Frith was conceiving and realizing a grander context for his powers of observation: 1978's *The Sociology of Rock*, soon revised into its commercially published 1981 American iteration, *Sound Effects*, which put into general circulation truisms that many have forgotten—and that more reiterate without knowing they're Frith's. Foremost among these were two observations about lyrics. First was that lyrics are physical as well as verbal signifiers, always inextricable from the sound of a human voice (and also, as he might have fleshed out some, the contour of a melody), and contextualized by such "nonverbal devices" as "accents, sighs, emphases, hesitations, changes of tone." Second was that in not just rock and roll but the Tin Pan Alley that preceded it—to demonstrate which Frith cheats a little by deploying Ira Gershwin's atypically colloquial "Nice Work If You Can Get It"—the basic poetic strategy of the pop lyric is to freshen familiar language, not to heighten it crimson-flames-tied-through-my-ears style.

Sound Effects was like that. As a cool-headed academic who made the most of his library privileges and a warmhearted fan who enjoyed listening, Frith's command of pop music fact and theory were unequalled. Thus he was equipped to explain how Tin Pan Alley's conception of romance as means to a connubial end evolved into rock's conception of sexual relationships as an ongoing engagement with serial identity. To argue strenuously that the inevitable failure of rock pleasure to be as innocent as it pretended didn't render its consumption merely passive. To observe balefully way back in 1980 that rock had become "old people's youth music." And he saved his masterstroke for last. Rock's history, he concluded, "like the history of America itself, is a history of class struggle—the struggle for fun." As not just concept but phrase, "struggle for fun" proved so redolent and useful that these days it gets a million-and-a-half Google hits. As the Beastie Boys rewrote it a few years later, and don't bet they hadn't read *Sound Effects*, "You've got to fight for your right to party." After which Chuck D said, "Party for your right to fight." And Atmosphere ten years after that: "Party for the fight to write."

Only problem was, *Sound Effects* might have struggled for more fun itself. The lucidity and serviceable grace of Frith's version of academic prose is more welcome than ever after thirty-five years of jargon-besotted and -beclotted theory. He understands full well that such non-Latinates as "sighs," "jokes," and "mouth" convey both the sound of lyrics and lyrics as sound in a way academese and social science boilerplate could not. But with no editor committed to the common tongue looking over his shoulder, too often he resorts to language worn dull by overuse: "One result of this diversification" followed next graf by "Another result of this diversification" followed next sentence by "The final results on a company's balance sheet," to choose a result that popped up when I opened the book at random. In addition, he declines to beef up the prose with concrete descriptions of individual artists and their audiences. So following *Sound Effects* with 1988's *Music for Pleasure* was a propitious move.

Published by Routledge, the go-to trade house for left-leaning professors seeking a civilian audience, this collection got less ink than *Sound Effects* and soon fell far out of print. Formally, it's unusual, mixing seven properly footnoted scholarly essays, four of which exceed twenty closely printed pages, with twenty-seven much shorter journalistic pieces including seven Britbeat columns he wrote for *The Village Voice*. Aimed at pop intellectuals broadly conceived, *Sound Effects* blended its tone accordingly. In *Music for Pleasure* the scholarly essays are designed for scholars, for whom essays are jobs to be buckled down to rather than language for pleasure. But this is hardly to suggest that its journalism is middlebrow entertainment or limits itself to succinct, sharp-witted, thought-provoking reviews.

That's partly because this thing called journalism can rope in so many different audiences. Not only wasn't *Marxism Today* the *Sunday Times*, but the punk-intellectual *New York Rocker* wasn't the world-music-plus fanzine-qua-little-magazine *Collusion*, where the five-pagers on Gracie Fields and Ennio Morricone first appeared. Nor was the aesthetically alert but soberly center-left *New Society The Village Voice*, where the politics-covering front of the book was far less radical than a culture-covering back of the book devoted to art for pleasure and the struggle for fun. Read consecutively, the seven Britbeat two-pagers Frith premiered there exemplify what the great American book reviewer John Leonard once called "the 800-word mind" while ranging further than Leonard's dense, well-informed mini-essays. It helps that Frith feels obliged to explicate his organically Anglocentric context to readers with scant knowledge of British culture, occasioning lead generalizations like "In Britain 1984 turned out to be the year of the miners' strike and Frankie Goes to Hollywood" and "The central myth of British pop is style."

What's happening in *Music for Pleasure*'s journalism is that Frith is seldom just a reviewer—he writes criticism as an academically trained sociologist. Although far more musically sophisticated and engaged than most sociologists, he evokes musical details primarily to illustrate larger points and shows no interest in establishing canons—his introduction reports that he never again played some of the pieces of musical fun the collection preserves in bound pages. In a way, this is cool—but not entirely. Reviewing Jon Landau's pioneering rockcrit collection *It's Too Late to Stop Now* back in 1973, he schematized his impatience with Landau's pedestrian prose, stolid taste, and apolitical auteurism-once-removed into the dubious theorem that "Music grows new meanings in new times, criticism doesn't." Unless he was the only young rock critic who didn't get het up about Pauline Kael's *I Lost It at the Movies* and Susan Sontag's *Against Interpretation*, this is patently absurd. Maybe he just needed a hook with his deadline bearing down—that happens in journalism.

One way to justify collections is to ease their flow from patch of prose to patch of prose with organizing conceptualizations, as Frith does by declaring *Music for Pleasure* "determinedly post-punk." His musical taste has changed so much as of 1988 that he finds "something *essentially* tedious these days about that 4:4 beat and the hoarse (mostly male) cries for freedom." Perhaps that's why he failed to include his dissection of the Rolling Stones' *Beggars Banquet* in *Stranded*, where Greil Marcus asked twenty critics to celebrate their desert-island discs. Although by 1979 Frith's kind of musical description had caught on, his *Beggars Banquet* breakdown excels as usual at that part of the job. The contrasting grooves of "Parachute Woman" and "Salt of the Earth," the distinct vocal affects of "No Expectations" and "Prodigal Son" aren't just vividly rendered. They're verbalized to buttress Frith's larger purpose: explaining how the Stones' intellectual (from Frith a compliment) bohemianism (from Frith not so much) "celebrates the reality of capitalist pleasure and denies its illusions." The Stones' commitment to this kind of double consciousness, he argues, is what makes them politically germane—devoid of "commitment to party or class, but powerful and critical all the same." By then many of us had thought in print about this apparent paradox. Few if any solved it more elegantly. Yet ten years later it was clear that this sort of elucidation wasn't to be Frith's path as a writer.

Read today, *Music for Pleasure* has a leave-taking air. While he found himself "more intrigued by the old journalism than by the 'lasting' scholarship," he also made clear that he'd had it with rock criticism's political presumptions, then wheezing on as if Margaret Thatcher didn't hold the winning hand. While he's never taken in by the intellectually vacuous anti-"rockist" rhetoric that transfixed British music journalism in the '80s, his own sympathies too are with music that slots pop, which is why he's happy to include records no one remembers if they noticed them in the first place. So the very year of its publication he elected to devote himself fulltime to enterprises that transform a field of battle where he's confident he can remain relevant: the academy. Thus he took his sociology PhD to the English department of Glasgow's Strathclyde University and its John Logie Baird Centre for Research in Film and Television.

Eight years later ensued *Performing Rites*, clearly his masterwork by the standards of the career he chose—and also the only book of his I've had trouble warming to. Much more than *Sound Effects*, *Performing Rites* is an academic tome. Having made his decision for the university, Frith writes to the university—if not exclusively, then primarily. Hence his obligation to address the postmodernism that was such a byword in the humanities departments of the mid '90s, and also to address theory—although except for one stealth parenthetical that gets Derrida in the neck, he cannily and discreetly sticks to Barthes and Bourdieu, both clearly essential to any academic book subtitled "On the Value of Popular Music." Hence also his extended attention to what I know I'm not supposed to call classical music so let's make it highbrow music. Hence the chapter on music and time, which I understand no better than any of the many other disquisitions on this topic I've labored through as I pursued my muse. And hence an analysis in which sociological ways of thinking subsume those of cultural studies, literary theory, and highbrow musicology—or maybe even defeats them.

Performing Rites is not on the surface a polemical work. Even more than his journalism, Frith's academic writing strives for a quiet, unshowy plainness of style that attracts attention only with the subtle crackle of ideas that come faster than its tone and syntax prepare you for. Without warning you're stopped short by a sentence like: "The point is that as speakers we create meaning through stress; therefore, music creates meaning." Or: "Amplification has enabled us to hear the detail of loud sound in quite new ways, and if the distinction between music and noise depends on our ears being able to find order in chaos, then technology, in allowing us to attend to previously indistinguishable sonic detail, has greatly expanded our sense of what music is and can be." Or: "Student music (as record companies realize) must fit student life, fit the student rhythm of collective indulgence and lonely regret, boorishness and angst, and also draw on shared teen memories and the sense of exclusiveness that being a student (at least in Britain) still entails." Or: "It has always seemed to me ironic that the academic effect of Jacques Derrida's musings on what it means to treat a text as an event has been the systematic study of events as texts."

By similar stratagems, *Performing Rites* comes to praise various academic shibboleths and then demolishes them. After many shows of politesse he follows that Derrida knock by observing: "I'm sure, similarly, that postmodern theorists (also much concerned with performance issues) have more to learn from a study of popular music than popular music theorists have to learn from postmodernism." He goes on to point out that the "instability and questioning" for which one postmodernist extols avant-garde dance and theater have already been established in this very book as hallmarks of "popular performance—something as much to do with the social basis of the event as with the intentions or principles of the performers." And the respects Frith pays highbrow music, which you come to realize are extended more freely to its audience than to its creators much less its guardians, function as feints. They establish his right to dismiss the philistine elitism of those guardians and to eviscerate the nineteenth-century ideology of Eduard Hanslick more recently taken up by Roman Ingarden—an ideology in which Hanslick combats "the tyranny of the ear" by declaring that true music is the score you read not the performance you hear, and in which Ingarden posits that "so-called dance music" designed "for keeping dancers in step" probably isn't music at all.

Nonetheless, I believe *Performing Rites* both overstates and fudges the firmness and clarity of so-called genre identities and especially taste communities. And while I agree that "the rhythm-focused experience of *music-in-the-process-of-production* . . . explains the appeal of African-American music and not its supposed 'direct' sensuality," I'm not therefore convinced that African-based rhythms lack any sexual homology or component—the fact that playing a harpsichord is no less physical an act than dancing to soukous doesn't mean both are physical in equally sexual ways. Similarly, when Frith asserts with uncharacteristic finality that "No listener could have thought that either [Jerry Lee] Lewis or [Mick] Jagger was black; every listener realized that they wanted to be," I can only jump up and down and say not me buster. Later for self-identified "stylist" Jerry Lee, but Jagger's vocal strategy, especially at first, was to contextualize his slurs and drawls by aping blackness with an exaggeration whose distance from its model was a joke his true soulmates were in on. And while it's righteous enough for Frith to bear down on the key concepts of voice and performance, I say he gets the emphasis wrong.

Offering a fourfold analysis of the voice as instrument, body, person, and character, Frith short-changes body and proves surprisingly uncritical about person and character. Addressing Barthes's "grain of the voice" under body, he suggests briefly that perhaps a grained voice might simply be one "with which, for whatever reasons, we have physical sympathy" and then proceeds. To me, capturing the details of such sympathies in language, and trying to explain their reach and spread, is one of the central tasks of popular music criticism, which nonetheless has altogether failed to elucidate, to choose the most glaring exception I'm aware of, exactly why so many find Aretha Franklin's voice irresistible or even gorgeous. And although Frith may be feinting with his talk of voices as persons and then characters, it takes him too long to admit that "in pop it is therefore all but impossible to disentangle vocal realism, on the one hand, from vocal irony, on the other"—that is, to pinpoint the difference between an expression and an enactment when the chances are excellent that you're hearing some incalculable combination of both.

And then, in a linchpin chapter called "Performance," Frith avers that for him—personally! in his mind! and I quote!—"to hear music is to see it performed, on stage, with all the trappings." Although he does immediately make clear that this vision coexists with a "full knowledge that what I hear is something that never existed," I honestly don't know whether this variation on double consciousness bespeaks brilliance, personal taste, or sheer oddity. But I can say that I almost *never* do this, not even with a live album. The assumption that performance means something done onstage rather than a more general kind of self-making strikes me as a very sociological kind of perception. In fact, much of *Performing Rites* seems fundamentally that way, making me suspect the whole book is Frith's quiet and unshowy way of imposing on the "humanities" his life-defining social scientist's conviction that nothing is more important than what happens between human beings. That as he once told rockcritics.com, "people are as instinctively social as individual, sociable as competitive." That "curiosity is a more important human motivator than fear."

Performing Rites, however, was not Simon Frith's final book. Published in 2007, the unaffordable *Taking Popular Music Seriously: Selected Essays* I hustled a review copy of is part of the Ashgate Contemporary Thinkers on Musicology Series, and as a connoisseur of collections I found it a poetic object—the offset reproductions of the nineteen selections, each in the typeface of the journal where it first appeared with the periodical page as well as the book page indicated, say so much that's sad about the increasingly esoteric marginality of the critical essay and print itself. But it's also a redolent introduction to the sly, putatively modest way Frith's mind works. At its best the prose, not all of it musically focused, is irresistible. There's suburbia as "a place where people live but don't work; rest but don't play," disorienting the offspring who so rarely get to leave it; there's "leisure as an experience of freedom so intense that it becomes, simultaneously, an experience of loneliness"; there's "youth experienced . . . as an intense presence, through an impatience for time to pass and a regret that it is doing so, in a series of speeding, physically insistent moments that have nostalgia coded into them." The poetry and empathy of such passages feel more like literature than historical sociology.

My favorite, however, isn't very sociological at all: "Towards an Aesthetic of Popular Music," published in *Music and Society* nine years before *Performing Rites* and, in my view, compatible rather than congruent with it, a kind of alternate mix. It begins with a switch designed to undo the rhetoric prevalent in both traditional mass culture theory and academic musicology, to wit: "In analyzing serious music"—which I've labeled highbrow music because I think most music is serious one way or another—"we have to uncover the social forces concealed in the talk of 'transcendent' values; in analyzing pop, we have to take seriously the values scoffed at in the talk of social functions." Don't think Frith doesn't know two contrasting uses of "serious" are cheek by jowl there—the program he's proposing is to interpret pop music aesthetically and highbrow music sociologically. And then he develops an idea articulated but left undeveloped in *Performing Rites*: "Everyone in the pop world is aware of the social forces that determine 'normal' pop music—a good record, song, or sound is precisely one that transcends those forces!" Exclamation point in original.

A guy can dream. At the very start of *Performing Rites*, Frith takes out of the closet what he calls his "rock critic's hat" and devotes two pages to a detailed, specific, quite witty critique of what I'd guess is his favorite band ever, the Pet Shop Boys—a band masterminded by a rock critic, as it happens. It's an uncharacteristically spectacular demonstration of the critic's craft, and one of the few times after he made his decision for academia that he's done what I was missing as of *Sound Effects*: describe individual artists and their audiences. So my modest proposal would be that Frith devote a portion of his golden years to writing about favored bands and musicians.

Unfortunately, I happen to know that Frith has his own program: a collaborative history of live music in the British Isles. In other words, the social scientist in him has prevailed. But somehow I doubt the results will be quite as one-dimensional as that.

Keynote, Studying Music–An International Conference in Honour of Simon Frith, 2014 · Condensed and revised

---

Serious Music

Robert Walser's *Running with the Devil: Power, Gender, and Madness in Heavy Metal Music*

Expertly straddling a fence few were aware existed, *Running with the Devil* is a rich, intelligent, audacious little book. In fewer than two hundred pages of text, Robert Walser, a musicologist who's been known to wow his students by illustrating fine points on electric guitar, does three things worth doing. First, he devises a compelling formalist account of a rock genre—not an easy trick, as Wilfred Mellers's deeply eccentric treatises on the Beatles and Bob Dylan and Tim Riley's dully middlebrow workouts on the same artists prove. Second, he defies academic convention by honoring noncanonical music outside the safely esoteric boundaries of the ethno, and by defining his musicological mission as polemical criticism rather than positivist "science." Third, he offers a tour of contemporary cultural studies. Woven into his argument are the iconoclastic ideas of music scholars Christopher Small, Susan McClary, Philip Tagg, and John Sloboda; youth sociologists Simon Frith and Donna Gaines; and cultural theorists John Fiske, Stuart Hall, George Lipsitz, Terry Eagleton, and Marshall Berman. And that's only to name the big guns.

Admittedly, this last feature may put off not just the average Van Halen fan but also a goodly portion of the audience *Running with the Devil* deserves. Ordinary readers willing to put aside their comfortable notions of what culture should be rarely have much patience with the carefully mapped, jargon-laden position papers favored by cultural studies specialists. But Walser has an exceptionally sharp mind and writes more gracefully than most; when he recapitulates other people's theories, he picks good ones and goes about his task with clarity and dispatch. Note, too, that he prefers Fiske's extreme populism and Berman's unrepentant humanism, neither especially modish these days, to, oh, Pierre Bourdieu's austere speculations. He's his own man. After all, this is someone who's been known to listen to Judas Priest for fun.

Walser's primary aim is legitimation. His evidence that heavy metal musicians are serious, highly skilled, given to minute aesthetic discriminations, and knowledgeable about "that assemblage of disparate musical styles known in the twentieth century as 'classical music'" will not only come as a shock to his colleagues in musicology, an academic calling of devout insularity, but will also be news to many pop fans who pick up this book. Metal is a world of its own, and even listeners who grew up hearing Led Zeppelin or Quiet Riot on AOR radio rarely combine an appetite for difficult ideas with a continuing passion for such music. Rock intellectuals prefer "alternative," even rap, and their disdain rankles the metal faithful—for instance, Deena Weinstein, whose valuable if less than scintillating "cultural sociology" *Heavy Metal* is Walser's only academic competition. Walser shares this resentment, and indulges in the defensive overstatement it invariably sparks—you'd never guess that many of the young critics who grew up hearing metal remain selectively sympathetic. But the intellectuals who really get his goat are his own professors—anybody in authority who ever gave him a hard time about his plebeian passions.

You don't have to love metal to enjoy watching Walser puncture the pretensions of cultural gatekeepers. His case for the frequently disparaged notion that musical usages have emotional meaning—based mostly on the observations of musicians themselves but shaped by the concept of permanently provisional "discourse" that is one of poststructuralism's most essential insights—is thorough and sophisticated without betraying the idea's commonsense roots. And his notated bar-and-measure breakdowns of a few key songs, most of which exploit groundbreaking technique to achieve effects that might qualify as deathless art played by the right people on the right instruments at the right time, will be legible even to the musically illiterate.

As one of those rock intellectuals, however, I remain unconverted. Walser scores some points about glam androgyny, but cops out when he argues that metal sexism is "shaped by patriarchy" like everything else in this society—in fact, the intensity of its phallic narcissism has few parallels outside X-rated movies, toilet art, and (oh yes) rap. Though his discussion of horror and madness is recommended to anyone who gives the slightest credence to the canard that metal bands drive their fans to murder or suicide, most anti-metal crusaders are so silly that too often he's reduced to shooting down gnats with ack-ack guns. And most important, he writes from so deep inside the aforementioned "assemblage of disparate styles" that he pays too much attention to metal's now obsolescent neoclassical strain and too little to the punk-influenced schools that succeeded it. It never seems to occur to him that, for many of us, metal's classical affinities are the very thing that renders it unlistenable—that we feel the instrumentally dexterous, rhetoric-drenched, and often melodramatic approach to meaning the two musics share is what rock and roll was put on earth to save us from. But even when it seems unlikely that metal is as smart as Walser is claiming, his own brains shine through. Only a bigot could deny that his openness to coexisting musical languages is more humane than the exclusionary standards of the so-called humanists he takes on.

City Pages, 1994

Fifteen Minutes of . . .

William York's *Who's Who in Rock Music*

"*Who's Who in Rock Music* is an attempt to compile in one volume the essential facts about the recording career of every individual and group in the history of rock music," begins William York's brief preface. After averring that his "over 13,000" entries will include "virtually . . . every individual who has performed on a rock album," York goes on to explain that his book is strongest "from the 1960s onward," and that his coverage of "soul" is limited to "artists whose work affected rock musicians." One more thing: "Notice of errors, oversights, and additions will be welcomed."

Well, we shall see. Having spent fifteen minutes browsing, I've learned that neither Funkadelic nor Earth Wind & Fire affected (or are) "rock musicians"—no surprise, the usual racist arrogance. I've also learned that Al Green and an obscure funk band called Crackin (Crackin', actually) did. Hmm. To my surprise, York got the first three obscure '60s bands I could think of—the Wind in the Willows, Chrysalis, and Autosalvage. But then he missed the Hobbits, Morning Glory, Nova Local, and the Equals ("soul," I guess—no Desmond Dekker either). On Mercury, Mercury, Decca, and RCA, if memory serves.

I'm not showing off my knowledge of trivia here—I don't think a knowledge of trivia is worth boasting about, and mine is limited. But I expect it from those who undertake insane projects—why bother if you're not a genuine obsessive? (I just checked, and all four of these groups are in the February 1970 Schwann, a pretty basic source. I got two of the labels wrong.) An interest in spelling is also recommended. Even Andy Fairweather Low isn't always sure his last name begins with L, but he's positive—just has to check the album jackets on which York supposedly based his research—that it isn't Fairweather-Lowe. It's not John Entwhistle, it's Entwistle; it's not Mickey Newberry, it's Newbury. Jesus.

Since York did teach me that Chicago was once called Big Thing, I'll inform him that Freebo is better known for his work with Bonnie Raitt than with Peter C. Johnson or Catfish Hodge, that Gram Parsons first recorded with the International Submarine Band, that Tory Crimes is listed as the drummer on the first Clash album, and that Chunky, Novi & Ernie, God help us, made two albums. I fervently hope these errors will not appear in his next edition, because I fervently hope his next edition is not forthcoming. Librarians, please note: this took me *fifteen minutes*. Jesus.

Village Voice, 1982

The Fanzine Worldview, Alphabetized

Ira A. Robbins's (ed.) *The Trouser Press Guide to New Wave Records*

I opened this book with the irritable trepidation known only to writers whose labors have been superceded in time by those of an unsimpatico rival, and was disarmed by its diligence, intelligence, and sound judgment. What a useful piece of work—and it's almost as thorough as it claims to be. Not only are the spellings and dates of excellent quality, but the reviewers seem actually to have heard the records they write about, and more than once at that. If this seems like faint praise, I refer you to Dave DiMartino's classic *Creem* pan of *The Rolling Stone Record Guide*, now just revised. To the dozens of errors he located in half an hour's perusal, I'll add my own little horror story, in which Dave Marsh not only dates tiny-voiced folkie Alice Stuart's 1971 and 1972 folk-rock albums in "the mid-Seventies," which is simply inaccurate, but calls them "West Coast funk," which is either irresponsibly imprecise writing or inexcusably lax listening. For resisting both kinds of carelessness, the *Trouser Press* crew deserve the respect of everyone who cares about popular culture scholarship, which is what they're involved in whether they like it or not.

"'New Wave' is, admittedly, a pretty meaningless term," begins Ira Robbins's introduction, which goes on to posit a unifying "sense that rock music should be explored, enjoyed, attacked, converted"—not a bad way of putting it if you bear in mind that such approaches can be faked and marketed like anything else. Having staked out its turf with suitable vagueness, *The Trouser Press Guide* then strives to cover it all. To avoid the sisyphean fate of B George and Martha Foe—whose *Volume 1982/83: International Discography of the New Wave* runs 736 tight pages even though it's nothing more than a listing—Robbins limits his survey to twelve-inch discs comprising at least four tracks and doesn't try to review all "international" (non-British and -American) or independent releases. I've spotted a few major omissions (e.g., Lester Bangs, Charlie Burton, Legal Weapon, and the Angry Samoans, who sure do make a lot of enemies) as well as some gloriously silly ones (e.g., the Fabulous Poodles, Sue Saad & the Next, and TP's own beloved Pezband). And I must complain as usual that by deferring to a racist definition of "rock music" he's never shown any inclination to combat, Robbins ignores hundreds of black artists who explore, enjoy, attack, and convert, including more than a few who've actively pursued the "new wave" audience. (If Was (Not Was), why not Sweet Pea Atkinson? If Steel Pulse, why not Black Slate? If Grace Jones, why not Linx? If Prince, why not Michael Jackson?) But the book is remarkably comprehensive on its own terms.

Most impressive, its reliability extends to its assessments. De gustibus and so forth, but there really are catchy songs and dull ones, and over the course of an LP, critics' idiosyncrasies usually even out to permit a rough consensus. Of the four principal reviewers here—Robbins, Scott Isler, Jon Young, and Jim Green—only Green seems deficient in this area. (Not surprisingly, Green has the most adventurous tastes of the four—an appetite for novelty can deafen you to received achievements, which is why Green believes his indifference to Blondie's *Parallel Lines*, the Police's *Ghost in the Machine*, and ABC's *Lexicon of Love* is more than a quirk.) Despite the chasms that separate *TP*'s sensibility from my own, the book alerted me to a hundred mostly import albums that look interesting and another fifty domestics I'd already dismissed after a fairly careful listen. A check reveals unsuspected virtues in Stiv Bators's *Disconnected* and the Equators' *Hot.*

Of course, an outsider might well wonder how much that means—a few extra B plus albums in the world obviously aren't going to change it much. Indeed, I bet one reason this guide declines the consumer courtesy of a grading system is to avoid specifying how small the pleasures it honors are. Which begins to suggest the major critical failing of a useful enterprise. Writers who value thrills, laughs, and surface originality above all ought to brim with such goodies themselves, but the prose here is usually serviceable and very rarely more, almost devoid of verve or laughs. (Jokes are often indicated by parentheses at the end of paragraphs, *which I suppose is better than italics.*)

Moreover, although the analyses are fairly accurate as far as they go, after reading 389 pages about 962 acts, I doubt I've come away with a dozen new ideas about the lot of them. The reason is elementary—not one contributor seems to care about what any of this work might *mean.* Lyrics are assessed strictly on their avoidance of cliche; I was struck by how the cant term "decadence" is used non-normatively, as if it were just another rock subject, like romantic love only not so played out. When catchy songs aren't the issue, which given the general pop bias isn't often, musical singularity is praised for its own weird sake as long as it isn't "pretentious"/"self-indulgent." In short, the assumption underlying all this putatively unideological description is that the function of rock and roll is delivery from boredom—and nothing else.

The roots of this attitude probably lie in *TP*'s origins as a fanzine. The typical fanzine is the brainchild of a white, middle-class teenage male who spends an inordinate amount of time holed up with his stereo. For such kids, the delights of marginal differentiation become obsessive—with pop music a crucial index of identity, there is an irresistible temptation to establish your uniqueness by latching onto records that no one else in your school has even heard. Like many (although not all) rock critics, the *TP* boys have pretty much outgrown this syndrome—that's why their judgments about well-known artists are trustworthy. But they're slaves of the formalism fandom leaves in its wake. It's one thing to make rock and roll your passion, another to leave the impression that it's an end in itself.

These are the people the mass culture theorists warned us about. They're far brighter and more dedicated than those doomsaying fools ever anticipated, and they do serve an invaluable function—in a true democracy, it's important to know what supposed small fry like Stiv Bators and the Equators (and Alice Stuart) have been up to. But *The Trouser Press Guide* is also living proof of what I take to be "new wave"'s secret message—that no matter how great rock and roll may be, it ain't enough.

Village Voice, 1983

Awesome

Simon Reynolds's *Blissed Out: The Raptures of Rock*

It was 1986, and twenty-three-year-old Simon Reynolds was sore afraid—afraid he'd missed "the last big rave-up." For him that meant punk, for other young Britcrits the exhilarating false spring of Culture Club et al., but overriding such details of taste was a longing for one of those magic moments when "an old musical order is dis-established but nothing stable has yet taken its place." All over the UK music press, earnest rock had been shown the door by the smart "subversions" of self-conscious pop; every week, image-wise hopefuls—soul boys black and white, trashy fops glad to be glam, showbiz bohemians, neat guitar bands with their smattering of poststructuralism and revolution-from-within—gave interviewers what for. But Reynolds wasn't buying any. Too perverse or discerning for the latest variation on songful eclecticism, scornful of retro, cut off from the exotic roots and alien authenticities of the world-music option, he'd had it with antirockism. He saw what too many young alternative types did not: most of the smart-pop folks were full of shit from the git, not just after their cover story became a dustbin liner. Even those who talked a good game couldn't put it in the grooves.

Then the miracle occurred, for the umpteenth time. Whaddaya know—rock hadn't died after all. It had merely "suffered a neglect that allowed it to breathe again." And how did its breath smell? Like wine, like ambrosia, like wacky tobaccy. "All the glorious incoherence and Dionysiac gratuitousness that Nik Cohn had first divined in pop, had somehow resurfaced in rock, with a spate of brilliant groups, *of which The Young Gods, Throwing Muses and A.R. Kane were the most glaring examples.*" Italics mine, in case you had any doubt. Who are—or were—the saviors of rock and roll? The Young Gods, Throwing Muses, and A.R. Kane, of course. Who else? I mean, how can you not love this guy?

Reynolds recognizes the eccentricity and impermanence of his judgments. "A supernova," he calls that brief season when his faction at *Melody Maker* took up the cudgels for an inchoate constellation of musicians who were at a bare minimum both pretentious and irresponsible—a supernova that soon ionized, its incandescence visible months or eons too late here in the colonies, where Reynolds has just published a collection that's almost as crazy as Lester Bangs's, almost as solid as Simon Frith's, and considerably more contradictory than either. *Blissed Out* is described by its author as "an argument about noise" and "an argument about bliss." It doesn't argue the way books argue, however. The effect is more like newlyweds flinging the dinner set at the wall—the dinner set being the all too practical legacy of the punk that a born cultural radical like Reynolds was born too late for. He missed its fucked-up anarchy, because fucked-up anarchy doesn't endure. Commitment endures; profit endures; the productive and progressive endure. And so, ten years after, the liberal sincerity of U2, punk's very own arena-rockers, was proving indistinguishable as social program from the cannily mock-ironic worldviews of dozens of song bands aiming to infiltrate pop from the avowed left like Paul Weller—except that unlike Paul Weller, they weren't rich and famous. Yet.

Most of these bands remain unknown here for excellent reasons—I defy anyone outside college radio to name two songs by the Christians, or Danny Wilson, or Wet Wet Wet, or Hue and Cry. But Reynolds hates the talented ones most—when schemers like the Housemartins or the Pet Shop Boys actually top the charts, his sarcasm is scathing. He can't stand mature pop, pop as theory—pop should be crazes, fantasies, slavish devotion, antisocial noise, the grain of the voice, pretty boys frittering away their stipends while crooked managers conceal ill-gotten gains in Bahamian bank accounts. He opposes naturalism, logocentrism, journalism, "the merry street dance of egalitarianism," "off-the-peg self-improvement." He defends Morrissey's self-pity and doesn't bat an eye when Kristin Hersh allows as how she never liked having a body or My Bloody Valentine boast that only two of their songs mention suicide. He'll take id over ego, ego over superego, mad romance over "love as contract." He valorizes Roland Barthes's "'voluptuous infantilism' of languor," Nick Cave's neomedieval passivity in the face of horrible fate. He wants "vastness," "re-mystification," "the vertigo of rapture." He wants adolescent solipsism, psychedelic schizophrenia, an underground that never gets on the telly. He wants vision. He wants excess.

If you find these values limited or illusory, bully for you. Occasionally so does Reynolds, who at one point admits he votes Labour. He's a bit of a poser, our Simon, a poser without apology, as befits the uncampy flamboyance of his style and thought. Anyway, as an American I doubt he could name once put it, a foolish consistency is the hobgoblin of little minds. Reynolds keeps tripping over Britcrit's rock/pop distinction only because it's his unconscious plan to destroy it (in the nick of time, too). And if he's of several minds about regression, artistic growth, and the ineluctable modality of the electric guitar, that just means he's no simpleton—in rock and roll, these are complex concepts that merit complex responses. True enough, Reynolds never exactly formulates the responses—although he's worked to make the pieces flow and cohere, he's comfortable with the pomo cut-and-paste of the anthology format, and he doesn't worry too much about repetitions, contradictions, or loose ends. "We preferred the singular moment of awe to rock discourse's long-term scheme of amelioration," he says of himself and his sometime collaborators at *Melody Maker*. How better compliment his criticism than to say it provides precisely what it praises?

In fine, Reynolds is the upstart this old fart has been waiting for—at last someone to explain all the formally recalcitrant weirdness I knew couldn't be as stupid or arbitrary as it sounded, someone to renew my faith in human progress by proving that not everyone who swears by the Cocteau Twins and My Bloody Valentine is a faddist or a fool. As Reynolds acknowledges, the stunned, dreamlike intoxication he celebrates makes more sense for whiteboys "trained to be aspirational and competitive" than for "those excluded from status and opportunity (blacks, women, gays etc)." And it's pretty much youth-specific—hard on going to work in the morning, hell on parenting. But where so many young critics, especially the ubiquitous fanzine and tipsheet reviewers, just stamp their feet and state their druthers, Reynolds writes in a context. Even though he defines the music he likes as "a local culture rather than any doomed attempt at a global overhauling," he's possessed by its philosophical and political relevance and well-read enough to explicate it. A postyippie propagandist surrounded by antiyuppie defeatists, he manages to combine the inspired willfulness of a Gerard Cosloy or Frank Owen with the reasoned overview of an Ann Powers or Rob Tannenbaum, partly by keeping his distance from the rock discourse that underpins most rock overviews. Going along with the critical wisdom more than he lets on (although his historical command is spotty), he nevertheless suspends belief in its truth value.

Unfortunately for him, or at least his pride, rock discourse is dripping with truth value, and infinitely absorbent too. Needless to say, Reynolds and his posse were determined to escape cooptation, and they had their pathetic rhetorical strategies—the refusal to dictate taste, "writing that fervently seeks out its own limits," and so forth. And insofar as they failed to convert the world, I suppose they succeeded. But four years after, as he watches callow Britcrit imitators regurgitate the litany without partaking of the sacrament (an ancient complaint, of course), *Blissed Out* assures that Reynolds's truths will join the discourse. There *are* words for Throwing Muses' "places there are no words for," as the act of criticism so often demonstrates in spite of itself, and Kristin Hersh's teenaged angst reveled too luxuriously in its arty misery to touch simple Smiths fans or complicated rockwriters. But here's betting that the Young Gods, a Swiss sampling band I'd filed as anonymous industrial Eurodisco, will grow in stature as Ministry-style metal machine music achieves its place in the panoply. And A.R. Kane, tipped by Greg Tate in these pages, very nearly live up to Reynolds's impossible description of "The Sun Falls into the Sea": "a mermaid lullabye not so much 'accompanied' as almost drowned out by a sound like an immense quartz harp the size of a whale's ribcage, from which harmonies disperse and scatter as haywire as sunlight refracting under the ocean's surface."

Is it really that good? Well, not quite—a little too textural, as you might imagine. I prefer the beatier "Spermwhale Trip Over," which precedes it on 1988's *Sixty Nine*. But something's happening there for sure. Anybody who's listened to an "alternative rock" DJ segue songful guitar bands and felt stuck in some folk club with stale draft in the sawdust—not so much aurally, praise Thomas Edison and Leo Fender, as in the smug reverence accorded a subgenre on life support—will perhaps notice that in both the Young Gods and A.R. Kane the guitars sound like synthesizers and the songs sound like . . . call them tracks. Slightly more rock and roll are, of all people, My Bloody Valentine, whose suicide song on 1988's *Isn't Anything* is unlikely to be construed as an incitement to same and wouldn't necessarily be bad if it was. If you think the Jesus and Mary Chain have nothing more to tell us, you're probably right. If you think they're a dead end, as I always have, My Bloody Valentine would like to get in your earhole. A terrific album, and I missed it—but now, contextualized by Reynolds, it goes on my current shelf, right near *Interiors*.

Rosanne Cash is on my mind because I saw her at the Bottom Line while writing this and wondered what Reynolds, who's currently balancing love-as-contract and mad romance by shuttling between a job in London and a girlfriend in New York, would make of her. Not much, probably, but chances are he'll get someplace similar eventually—all mockery of Good Songs notwithstanding, Cash can tell a body more about relationships than Updike or Angela Carter, not to mention Bataille or Kristeva or the rest of the pomo highbrows who inform Reynolds's cool. My own taste in cultural theory still runs to Raymond Williams, who if pressed would call Cash "residual" and My Bloody Valentine "emergent" and share Reynolds's skepticism about any possible "co-incidence between desire and responsibility, ecstasy and concern"—from the opposite direction. And it's that coincidence that rock discourse keeps searching for nevertheless. Transcendence equals oblivion, we know that. But if you don't risk oblivion you soon end up nowhere. Pass the arkana.

Village Voice, 1990

Ingenuousness Lost

James Miller's *Flowers in the Dustbin: The Rise of Rock and Roll, 1947–1977*

There's a rare unguarded moment in the impressive discography-bibliography to James Miller's *Flowers in the Dustbin: The Rise of Rock and Roll, 1947–1977*, when he comes upon "a really esoteric item featuring Jimi Hendrix playing with a UK group called Eire Apparent, 'The Clown.' Wow." By ordinary standards of rockcrit wild-ass, that "Wow" may not seem like much. But for all Christopher Hitchens's dustjacket praise of Miller's "vivid and ironic prose," *Flowers in the Dustbin* doesn't exactly sparkle with bright informalities. From *The Real Paper* to *Newsweek*, Miller was never the most demonstrative of rock critics, and nothing in his current perch as a New School dean is liable to bring out the lover in him. For reasons of personal proclivity and professional decorum, he means to keep his cool about an art form that was once his passion. And it is this, more than the deliberate selectiveness of its historiography, that renders Miller's rockbook dangerous and dislikable.

Miller says he wanted to assess the disenchantment with rock that made him quit *Newsweek* in 1991, but it's hard to imagine he wasn't also attracted by a commercial and intellectual vacuum. For while academia has spawned a spate of would-be textbooks, the only writer of Miller's skill and stature to attempt such a thing since before his cutoff date is the late Robert Palmer, in *Rock & Roll: An Unruly History*. Like Palmer, Miller concluded that the sane way to organize a subject so vast was not to tackle all of it. So from secondary sources and his own experience he assembled forty-five quintessential vignettes, fourteen of them Elvis-Beatles-Stones-Dylan. This method assumes major omissions. Anyone tempted to infer musical biases from narrative judgments should bear in mind that in *The Rolling Stone Illustrated History of Rock & Roll*, which Miller originally edited and which remains the finest rock overview extant, he himself grabbed the entries on the Beach Boys and Led Zeppelin, and that his desert island disc in Greil Marcus's *Stranded* is a Phil Spector album. Nevertheless, one omission seems inextricable from the other formal peculiarity of *Flowers in the Dustbin*, which is that it ends with the Sex Pistols and Dead Elvis.

Miller lists James Brown among the artists he was sorry to pass by, and I'm sure he's some kind of fan. Who isn't? But his failure even to reference JB's infinitely fruitful rhythms does facilitate that 1977 cutoff. If you want to argue that the Sex Pistols inaugurated a system in which bizzers exploited a never-ending procession of "bands so new they could hardly play," well, you're twisting facts, but Christopher Hitchens will never know. Were you to hint that "Papa's Got a Brand New Bag" and its countless progeny have been renewing rap and r&b for two decades, however, people might start asking questions. Did your chewing gum lose its flavor on the bedpost overnight? Whither disco? And how come you don't get to 1960 till halfway through? Why so fascinated with beginnings, Jim?

It's about time I noted that "Jim" isn't just Miller's abandoned rockcrit byline. It's what I've called him during an intermittent professional relationship in which he's often been my benefactor. But as I've gotten older I've come to see how feuds among old allies develop, and I do sense danger in this book—not the cheerful irresponsibility of Palmer's overstated *Unruly History*, which is a good kind of danger, but the pall of hegemony. Except perhaps for Simon Frith, Miller wields a cultural authority exceeding that of any other rock critic. He's held down prestigious jobs in both journalism and academia, and has published three well-regarded works of history and political theory. The two I've read—the award-nominated SDS chronicle *Democracy Is in the Streets* and *The Passion of Michel Foucault*, a quietly obsessive biocritical tour de force that gets double points for outraging Foucauldians and cultural reactionaries alike—are lucid, balanced, and credible, deeply respectful of their subjects even when faulting them. *Flowers in the Dustbin* is also lucid, balanced, and credible. But too often its dry tone comes across cynical and belittling. While Miller asserts his affection for the music, he rarely explains it and seems unwilling or unable to express it—perhaps because that's not the way of authority, perhaps because he's sick of the stuff.

From the episodic structure a thesis emerges, a piecemeal theory of innocence ever more irretrievably lost. Miller keys his origin myth to Wynonie Harris's 1947 "Good Rockin' Tonight," but in a nation where show business began as minstrelsy he's suspicious of the comforting notion that rock and roll opened up a new era of racial crossover. As culture, he judges the music fundamentally white, its defining magic more a matter of youth than of race: "the surprise of untrained amateurs, working within their limits, finding a voice of their own." But Miller completes this thought in a typical turnaround: "Without an air of ingenuous freshness and earnest effort, rock as a musical form is generally coarse, even puerile—full of sound and fury, perhaps, but characteristically spurning the subtle creativity and seasoned craftsmanship that is the glory of such other mature vernacular pop music genres as jazz and the blues, country and gospel." Relieve the language of its overtones, pretend that "coarse" leads to "puerile," and the generalization has truth value. A lot of exciting rock is "coarse" in the sense of "unrefined," of consciously rejecting refinement; properly inspired and/or realized, its "puerility," taken to mean merely the "childishness" or (better) "childlikeness" of "untrained amateurs," is something to treasure. Problem is, the sentence's weight is all in its connotations. It's a measured insult, a calm criminal charge that should have been a lament.

This kind of rhetorical device pervades the book. Over and over Miller deploys pejoratives like "crude," "ugly," "brutal," never with any backspin; "nihilism" is adduced more loosely than is suitable in a poli sci professor; straddling the Velvets' reach, or reggae's morality, or even the Beatles' impact, the tired "for better or worse" always seems to land on the downside. The tone remains detached, authoritative, as if crudity were as objective and value-free a quality as color or chart position. This is how the controlling discourses Foucauldians bitch about operate. Despite some lovely countervailing passages—describing the first Beatles records ("the sullenness and sweetness, the aggression and nostalgia, the country plaintiveness and the bluesy bravado . . ."), summarizing what teens got from '50s rock ("their own brand of Dionysian revelry, watered down and trite, but genuinely uplifting at the same time")—the irony of a mandarin who has put away childish things prevails.

As with style, so with content. Manifestly less original than the SDS book, with its many interviews, or the Foucault, with its sustained immersion in the philosopher's texts and lives, *Flowers in the Dustbin* has its acute moments nevertheless—discussions of Fender guitars and "The Tennessee Waltz," surprisingly fresh insights into Elvis and the Beatles, sharp references to Talcott Parsons and "The White Negro," the almost tossed-off and *un*pejorative final account of rock and roll as "a novel kind of consumer religion." And usually it recycles the old stories deftly enough. But sometimes it's wrongheaded or just wrong. No way did W. C. Handy invent the fox trot (*Handy* said it was James Reese Europe) or Pat Boone "croon" "Ain't That a Shame" (he has the hernia to prove it). No way is the nostalgia quotient of individual pop songs determined by airplay saturation—"Home Sweet Home" was the original golden oldie, and if musical quality weren't a prime factor, Boone's "April Love" would be more famous than "Hey, Bo Diddley." The most telling botch of all is the Velvet Underground chapter, rotely unperceptive on music and influence and a flagrant example of Miller's tendency to be overimpressed by behind-the-scenes conceptualizers (Andy Warhol, here counted a "rock and roll Svengali") and classical training or pretensions (John Cale, in the club with Wagner buff Alan Freed, Sex Pistols producer Chris Thomas, and fifth-through-eighth Beatle George Martin, among others).

This is significant because it prefigures Miller's disregard for the alt-indie subculture that has engendered most of the good white rock since his cutoff date. It's also significant because it typifies the elitism that powers his book. At one level Miller is another tragic victim of Sixties Syndrome. He thought his generation was going to revolutionize the world, and instead of moving on has devoted his life to figuring out how he could have been so wrong—how the Port Huron Statement led to the Weathermen, how "The Green Door" and "Night Train" led to Marilyn Manson and the Wu-Tang Clan (whom he equates in the epilogue). Beneath the surface of his books he's tormented by this question. This renders *The Passion of Michel Foucault* a mind-blower, because while Miller's politics have evolved/degenerated from principled anarchism to a cautious liberalism whose outlines he leaves obscure, he continues to half-share Foucault's Nietzschean conviction that all morality is constructed on a terrifying, thrilling, unknowable void. But Foucault was both well educated and a genius. SDS adventurist Jeff Shero, the bete noire of *Democracy Is in the Streets*, was merely clever, and so exemplifies how Tom Hayden's fellowship of humane intellectual seekers was wrecked not just by the intractability of the capitalist order but by the self-indulgent incomprehension of their recruits. And when we get to Jim Morrison, well, he was "a monumental jerk," simple and plain.

Right, Morrison was a jerk—it wasn't me who thought "The End" "seemed bold and brave" in 1967, it was Miller. But *The Doors*, where the jerk is finding "a voice of his own," remains a redolent piece of music, and so do the multihued contributions of thousands of arty guys and gals who came after. The strange thing isn't that overexposure undermines "wonder and surprise," that chewing gum loses its flavor on the bedpost overnight. It's that reinventions and rediscoveries continue in an aesthetic realm whose "subversive social significance," which Miller claims is all that makes the rock critic's job "interesting," inheres largely in their living insistence that mandarin refinement and the wisdom of controlling discourses are never enough—that uncomprehending jerks must be heard. Especially since this ongoing miracle isn't at its most magical right now, the line that its "general patterns" are "perfectly predictable" is precisely the sort of thing that can discourage arty guys and gals from giving it a whirl. God, does this mean I have to write my own textbook? Somebody help, please.

Village Voice, 1999

Rock Criticism Lives!

Jessica Hopper's *The First Collection of Criticism by a Living Female Rock Critic*

With a righteous boost from an indie-rock buddy who's also in the indie-book business, Jessica Hopper's *The First Collection of Criticism by a Living Female Rock Critic* was what its title claimed when it came out in 2015 and always will be. None of the four possible exceptions she acknowledges in an eight-sentence preface qualifies: the 1981 part-rockcrit Ellen Willis one, the posthumous all-rockcrit Ellen Willis one, Caroline Coon's Britpunk overview *1977*, or Lillian Roxon's herculean *Rock Encyclopedia*. But though Hopper has every right to bewail the paucity of women in the rockcrit business, one upshot of this paucity is that few other women have amassed enough ace essays, profiles, and reviews to merit a collection—only Ann Powers for sure, although if Vivien Goldman, Carol Cooper, Evelyn McDonnell, Danyel Smith, or some brave woman not in my recall memory tried to prove me wrong I'd certainly check out the result. In the meantime, however, let me mention an equally accurate and striking title that comes to mind: *The First Collection of Rock Criticism by Anybody Born after 1970*.

Here I see two challengers, both of which I rate higher than Hopper's book. John Jeremiah Sullivan's mind-boggling 2011 *Pulphead: Essays* includes five "essays" on music, but making an exception for the best Michael Jackson piece you'll ever read, he doesn't write rock criticism even if some rock critics like to claim him. He writes masterful, eccentric, outrageous, incorrigibly personal, incorrigibly literary reportage that also addresses such topics as the Tea Party, the revolt of the animals, and life after death. A more plausible candidate is Touré's 2006 *Never Drank the Kool-Aid: Essays*, even though it only comprises sixty percent music pieces and sixty somewhat different percent celebrity profiles, because Touré identifies as a rock critic who recognizes hip-hop as a proper locus of the calling—one who by labeling his reported pieces essays insists on their intellectual ambition. Greg Tate having launched *Flyboy in the Buttermilk* in 1992, Touré couldn't have bum-rushed the title *The First Collection of Rock Criticism by an African-American*. But his race, like Hopper's gender, is one good thing you can say about rock criticism in the twenty-first century. I wish there were more.

God it's a mess out there—I sure don't have a grip on it, and I doubt anyone does. There are too many online "publications" stiffing too many rushed reviewers, and although insightful work certainly gets done, sift it out, I dare you. It's gratifying that the hip-hop press has defined itself as a self-sustaining world dominated although far from monopolized by black writers, but it generates less quality criticism than one would hope. And in every area, plenty of words and too few well-chosen ones has been the rule, with none other than *Pitchfork* Exhibit A. Although cred-wise it surpassed *Rolling Stone*'s circa 2005, it was years before someone (imported professional editor Scott Plagenhoef, I've always assumed) started requiring reviewers to sum up each artist's history and single out key tracks, simple adjustments that drastically enhanced its use value. Yet as long as it remained the snarky boys club Ryan Schreiber devised in 1995, the only major critics to land at *Pitchfork* were Philip Sherburne, well after he'd established his techno expertise elsewhere, and arguably Nitsuh Abebe, now a cultural generalist on staff at the *New York Times Magazine*.

Only then, in the early '10s, *Pitchfork* stopped being such a boys club and took a quantum leap. The standouts were Lindsay Zoladz, Carrie Battan, and Amanda Petrusich, all writers you wanted to read as writers, in part because they outclassed the pedestrian *Pitchfork* norm, but also because as women they offered long overdue perspectives just as female artists were dominating the quality pop *Pitchfork* was finally paying some heed and coming to the fore in the punker and progger precincts of alt-rock. Was Zoladz wrong to compare Lana Del Rey's *Born to Die* to "a faked orgasm"? Hopper would say so, and Zoladz herself ultimately recanted. But were the boys of *Pitchfork* wrong to make the assignment? Hell no—they were lucky to have her available. And they were luckier still when Zoladz turned in a pained 2014 investigation of Justin Timberlake's intellectual theft of the slogan "Take Back the Night," an appropriation he declined to acknowledge even by donating a few grand to the rape prevention foundation of the same name that made those words ring in his target market's ears.

But good writers are hard to find, and before long all three of these women had graduated to the slicks where they belonged—Zoladz to *New York* and then the online *Ringer*, Battan and Petrusich to the *New Yorker*. Of *Pitchfork*'s remaining female regulars, only Meaghan Garvey stands as tall. Respect to all of them, obviously; respect too to Craig Jenkins, an African-American critic who came up through *Pitchfork* with a stop at *Vice* on his way to replacing Zoladz at *New York* as other black journalists rode the hip-hop wave into other species of mainstream cred. But the woman this review is about followed a rockier path, She blogged, she freelanced wherever, she established a foothold at the *Chicago Reader*, she edited at *Rookie*, she kept freelancing and blogging, and finally she landed game-changing gigs at first the bound-paper *Pitchfork Review* and then MTV News—gigs that were snatched away in turn by money-changing suits at Condé Nast and Viacom. So let's excavate that title one more time.

What else are we to notice about *The First Collection of Criticism by a Living Female Rock Critic*? The last two words: "rock critic." That's because "rock critic" is dying terminology; I stick with it myself at least in part out of do-not-go-gentle bloody-mindedness. Fact is, although the idea of "rock" survives in what is still designated alt-rock as well as in metal-etc. and to an extent bro-country, it signifies guitar-bass-drums too much to suit most "music critics," not to mention "music writers" or the already fading "pop critics." Zoladz, Battan, and Petrusich are music critics. Hopper, on the other hand, claims rock critic. She claims a rhetorical tradition where music with a common touch, an excited edge, and a chip on its shoulder unites you with people who may not agree with you about Lady Gaga but still want the world to change in pretty much the same way you do.

Hopper grew up in Minneapolis and lives in Chicago, where she and her husband are raising two sons. Both of her biological parents are journalists. Although she's so petite she could still pass for a teenager in dim lighting, she's older than the *Pitchfork* troika—born in late 1975 if you extrapolate from the drolly unembarrassed sexual-cum-musical-awakening reminisce "Louder Than Love: My Teenage Grunge Poserdom," which culminates when the teenager stops pretending she's into Soundgarden and discovers Bikini Kill. But though a punk identification runs through her work—see especially the 2003 "Emo: Where the Girls Aren't" and the 2004 Vans Warped Tour report—she's militantly unnostalgic about it. "Riot-grrrl wasn't the end result, it was the catalyst," she lectured bleeding hearts in a 2010 post on her Tiny Lucky Genius blog. "How current feminist work honors older feminist work is with progress and new paths. That is all we should ask of it as feminists: BLAZE THE FUCK PAST US."

So leaf through her book and find Lana Del Rey and Rickie Lee Jones, St. Vincent and Lady Gaga, Coughs who are long gone and Frida Hyvönen who you never heard of. No surprise that the final section praises six women including two of the above. But perhaps a surprise is that those six bring Hopper's artist selections not quite up to gender parity. Repeat: she's a rock critic. Her thing for Van Morrison is why she begins by dancing in the dark to *T.B. Sheets* and finds a home for a late-night *Astral Weeks* swoon someone cooler would have saved for her diary. She praises Bruce Springsteen, Michael Jackson, Nirvana, Pearl Jam, and Superchunk. She praises M.I.A., No Age, Chance the Rapper, Kendrick Lamar, and apostate Christian rocker David Bazan, who she once did PR for. She disses Miley Cyrus, Dinosaur Jr., Animal Collective, Tyler the Creator with his "faggot"-dropping "Imma-rape-you steez" (twice, yay), and a useless twentieth-anniversary *Nevermind* box: "Cobain is not our Jimi—he's our Jim. Nirvana, punk bona fides be damned, has become an analogue for today's stoned, misunderstood teenagers: a died-young druggie poet-totem." (Let the record show that Hopper was staying at Kurt's place the morning he shot himself in an outbuilding.)

As you probably didn't notice because she comes to it so naturally, the Hopper quotes that cap my two previous grafs are in the first-person plural, her rhetorical home. In a sense that's the most rock critic thing about her—not the editorial we, the cultural we, which for Hopper is the political we as well. For her, music isn't just a private pleasure or a journalistic leg up. It's a calling, which is something one feels in Touré even as he hustles TV gigs but not so much in Zoladz's honed professionalism. And that's what makes Hopper a gem. She does like to go off, as in the dust-up she once staged with Stephin Merritt, who she accused of racism for admiring Disney's *Song of the South* at the very moment Merritt was explaining that he didn't in the auditorium she'd just exited so she could live-blog this outrage *right now*. And she could certainly use some of Zoladz's editorial savoir-faire. That eight-sentence preface slips into the solecism "should of come first," and my copy-editing pencil kept X-ing syntactical gaffes somebody should have smoothed over before they were transferred to these 201 tallish, gilt-edged pages that for some bad reason are paragraphed with line spaces, internet-style. No editor anywhere should publish the phrases "It was made in the time where" or "Her drifting orientation from the Mouse mothership" once, much less twice. But in twenty-first-century rock criticism, editing is vestigial, if you're lucky.

See for instance "Old Year's End," a Tiny Lucky Genius post dated December 2007 that begins: "No year-end lists to contribute to for any publication this year. Budget constraints, art constraints, being freelance are most of the reasons." As Three 6 Mafia has never rapped and never will, "It's hard out there for a rock critic." But Hopper has persevered. I don't rely on her opinions any more than I did on Lester Bangs's. But I value her spunk, her spirit, her belief that she's in the justice business as well as the music business. So as much as I admire the Nirvana and Pearl Jam and Frida Hyvönen reviews, my two favorites pieces of rock criticism in this collection are rock criticism in a rather broad sense. As is fitting for the first female rock critic to publish her own collection, they're not about Van Morrison or Chance the Rapper, neither a paragon of post-sexist consciousness anyway. They're about the kind of guys who give dicks a bad name.

One is a long *Village Voice* interview with bad rock critic Jim DeRogatis, who years ago made up for that asinine Kill Your Idols thing by leading the legally fruitless charge against "accused" sexual abuser R. Kelly. It consists of DeRogatis emoting cogently about all the victims he's interviewed and Hopper interjecting the occasional felt, relevant comment, such as: "It's often uncool to be the person who gives a shit." The second is a blog post that describes a punk ladies-mud-wrestling night at a Chicago warehouse in cool, patient, disgusted detail—the vomiting, the screaming, the gyro meat and beer raining from the singer's mouth, the boner the raffle winner sports when he gets to wrestle two of the ladies, and then the three rather different men who assume Hopper is tricking as she waits for the bus and the drunk girl on said bus begging a kiss from her drunk boyfriend. Every time

I read it I'm ashamed to share a gender with these asswipes, these ginks, these baboons.

Yet even after those two pieces Jessica Hopper still wanted to be a rock critic. Somebody pay her a living wage to keep it up.

Previously unpublished, 2018

Emo Meets Trayvon Martin

Hanif Abdurraqib's *They Can't Kill Us Until They Kill Us: Essays*

I don't want to go overboard here. Hanif Abdurraqib isn't as masterful a stylist as Dave Hickey or Jonathan Lethem, whose finest collections bear down on music, or straight-up rockcrits Greil Marcus or Ellen Willis. Nor is he as deft as Touré or as dazzling as Greg Tate or as original as his acknowledged inspiration Lester Bangs. And yes, there are other notable youngbloods out there, most of them women. But as someone who'd as soon read a good essay collection as a good novel, I don't want to understate either. *They Can't Kill Us Until They Kill Us* establishes Abdurraqib as a major rock critic—polished and deft and original in a searchingly unpolished way and, if you'll grant that the word need be no more race-specific than "rock critic" itself, more soulful than any of the above except Bangs. Yes, he's less funny than Bangs—we all are. But in Abdurraqib's case that comes with the concept.

Abdurraqib is a thirty-two-year-old African-American from a struggling lower-middle-class family in Columbus, Ohio, who owes his Arabic name to parents who converted to Islam in the '70s. Although never devout and no longer observant, he was the only Muslim at the local college he attended on a soccer scholarship. A third of the sixty poems his website links to reference music, which is also the subject of half the twenty essays there. He's got a gig at MTV News, where a dozen of these selections first appeared; others surfaced in *Pitchfork* and the *New York Times*. But whatever their provenance, Abdurraqib has worked hard to make this book their natural home.

An opening section sequenced Chance the Rapper-Springsteen-Carly Rae Jepsen-Prince-ScHoolboy Q-Weeknd establishes his cross-racial orientation and his black identity simultaneously, only not quite as you might expect. Yes, the ScHoolboy Q piece unpacks the rapper's insistence that white fans who buy his ever pricier tickets get over it and utter the word "nigger." But Abdurraqib's thoughts on Springsteen, whose delvings into mortality, work, and the American Dream he admires avidly, are just as race-conscious—only a day before the show, he'd put mortality in perspective by visiting Ferguson, and he can't help but notice that, speaking of work, he's the only black person at the Meadowlands who's there for the concert rather than a j-o-b. Yet arrayed around Springsteen are the explicitly happy beginning of a candy-colored, gospel-soaked Chance the Rapper event and, happier still, a Carly Rae concert—which does, he mentions, attract some black couples—where fans are kissing, truly kissing, in Manhattan's brutally industrial Terminal 5.

If you're expecting more of the eclectic same, though, Abdurraqib then pulls a switch, because it turns out he was an emo kid, a follower of the punky, hooky, hyperemotional pop-rock subgenre typified by Dashboard Confessional and Fall Out Boy that dominates section II. Its built-in male narcissism rendered even ranker by its trademark self-pity, I was always too old for emo, but Abdurraqib's report from the front is something to treasure. Emo is such a white scene that he was often the only black kid at shows where moshers thrashed in full-fledged clubs and sweaty basements alike, and so he begins by outlining his eventual progress to the Afropunk movement. But that clarified, he turns his sympathies to the lost white suburban Midwesterners who were his brothers in pain, in particular his friend Tyler, who surfaces by name in the jumbled eight-part tour de force "Fall Out Boy Forever." In the beginning, tall Tyler strides into the pit to rescue short Hanif, sprawled below the leaping throng. In the end, troubled Tyler commits suicide. The lesson being that the unlistenable emotions emo indulges are literally too much for many who hear their own anguish there.

Although almost every black American lives closer to death than almost every white American, Abdurraqib is probably more blessed than Tyler was. But not by much. Several other emo deaths haunt him; he lost his mother overnight when her bipolarism meds killed her in her sleep; his 2015 "My Demons and My Dog and This Anxiety and That Noise"—not included here, perhaps because he didn't dare expose himself so nakedly—is an excruciating account of his own anxiety disorders. And so the bulk of the book culminates with a long final section, most of it previously unpublished, that hews close to music as it lays out a piecemeal autobiography. Most of it takes place post–Trayvon Martin, who was slain the night Abdurraqib drove to Minnesota with a companion I take to be his future wife to witness a typically stirring show by white alt-rap lifers Atmosphere.

I don't agree with all his analyses or feel all his tastes, but every one gains not just poignancy but heft from personal particulars that are also, inevitably, political. Abdurraqib always remains a critic who deals in textual interpretation and aesthetic judgment. But the urgency that infuses music for him, often captured in a few articulated details, is what criticism ought to be for and too often isn't.

Thus the "shiny suit" rap of the Notorious B.I.G.'s "Mo' Money Mo' Problems" moves him because he knows his just-deceased mom would fall for its Diana Ross sample. Thus the Bataclan massacre evokes first Muslim teens seeking in live music "an escape from whatever particular evil was suffocating them" and then Muslim rapper Lupe Fiasco. Thus man in black Johnny Cash, who never shot a man in Reno, parallels suburban trap-rappers Migos, who never dealt crack. Thus the interlude when Atmosphere's Slug pauses his nonstop set for a brief "I need y'all to know that we're gonna be all right" foreshadows both "The White Rapper Joke," which surveys seven of the ungainly beasts and reserves special praise for Macklemore's "weaponization" of his excess fame, and "They Will Speak Loudest About You When You're Gone," which juxtaposes white outrage about racist police killings against white failure to see living African-Americans, like the New Havenite who peremptorily dumped her bags in his lap and then got on her cell to gab about Freddie Gray—an image Abdurraqib says he recalls often, as will I.

They Can't Kill Us Until They Kill Us, which takes its title from a sign Abdurraqib spotted in Ferguson, is on balance a rather dark book. His anxieties can't be much fun, his marriage falls apart as his story ends, and he's seen too much death without becoming inured to it like a gangsta sporting a teardrop tattoo. But let's not kid around. The era of African-American good feeling that began with the election of Barack Obama—which generated what "The Obama White House, a Brief Home for Rappers" calls an "optics of equality"—was radically disrupted by white supremacist George Zimmerman and demolished by white supremacist Donald Trump. Abdurraqib assigns himself a mission of celebrating music's "love and joy"—his Columbus elders with their Sunday soul parties, his emo pals discharging pent-up torment, the Baton Rouge rapper Foxx igniting his only hit with a profligate "I pull up at the club VIP/Gas tank on E/But all drinks on me," those provisionally carefree Chance and Carly fans. He ends with a meditation on the wheelies gleeful kids are practicing in the parking lot behind his apartment. But it isn't just his anxiety disorders that compel him to dwell as well on all the injustices that surround and subtend the same music. It's a sense of the moment all too few can figure out how to put into words.

Abdurraqib doesn't write zingers—his power is cumulative, preacherly even. I've told you how he ends, with those innocents and their wheelies. So let me end with how he begins. Goes like this: "This, more than anything, is about everything and everyone that didn't get swallowed by the vicious and yawning maw of 2016, and all that it consumed upon its violent rattling which echoed into the year after it and will surely echo into the year after that one. This, more than anything, is about how there is sometimes only one single clear and clean surface on which to dance, and sometimes it only fits you and no one else. This is about hope, sure, but not in that way that it is often packaged as an antithesis to that which is burning."

Barnes and Noble Review, 2017

PART IV

LIVES IN MUSIC INSIDE AND OUT

Great Book of Fire

Nick Tosches's *Hellfire: The Jerry Lee Lewis Story* and Robert Palmer's *Jerry Lee Lewis Rocks!*

As the world's biggest rock criticism fan, I have no doubt that rock and roll inspires lots of good writing, but as an English major who married a novelist I'm compelled to acknowledge that in the fifteen years since I took up the trade it hasn't produced much good literature, by which I simply mean good books. Admittedly, this is only fitting: I love rock and roll because, unlike literature, it's not caught in the cerebral, self-referential, and ultimately defeatist cul-de-sac of highbrow modernism. Physical and popular, it points the way out of (or at least waves at) a cultural dilemma in which only prodigious feats of deep feeling can achieve the political and economic equality the world depends on. And although it's much narrower than film, which is also physical and popular, its special connections to Africa and to evangelical (hence democratic) religion provide angles of attack that movies just don't command. Yet the good books about movies far outnumber those about rock and roll, or even American music in general.

Admittedly, this, too, may only be fitting: movies are more like literature than rock and roll is. But that I don't regard the book as the definitive cultural form doesn't mean I buy any hokum about electronic villages. We need prodigious feats of literacy, too—of extended analysis and narrative commitment—and I see no reason why rock and roll shouldn't be where some of them start. Yet if you'll pardon the litany, the only candidates are Greil Marcus's *Mystery Train* (dissenting criticism far more authoritative and formally original than, say, Parker Tyler's), Geoffrey Stokes's *Star-Making Machinery* (a less cynical counterpart of Lillian Ross's *Picture*), and maybe Simon Frith's *Sound Effects* (more ambitious ideas than Andrew Sarris's more dauntingly expressed). No highbrow modernist myself, I'm not above seeking out gems among drugstore cheapies and trade paperback pictorials. But I'm chagrined to admit that pickings are even slimmer and more predictable in trashy contexts. And since no rockbooks disappoint more consistently than rockstar bios, I'm especially pleased to add one to the genre's tiny pantheon: Nick Tosches's *Hellfire*.

I can't claim to be much of an expert on rockstar bios, and I pity anyone who can. Not that there are no handy homilies, especially regarding the mixed rewards of fame itself, to be garnered from the experiences of celebrities. But rock stars rarely inspire good literature, good self-help, or even good trash, because rock biographers are rarely good hacks, much less good writers or (heaven forfend) good critics. Given a dearth of as-told-tos and ghosted or genuine memoirs, all juicier forms, semi-pros whose main interest is the rest of their advance glut the racks with official and unofficial life stories. A certain quantum of candid revelation is de rigueur, but the emphasis is always on sex and drugs rather than love and money—that is, on epiphenomena. Deep thinkers need not apply.

Nevertheless, in this individualistic culture we're in the forgivable habit of criticizing art via artists, and so rockstar bios constitute the largest subclass of rock books. As such, they've engendered critical hierarchies of their own. In my view, it's mainly the abysmal competition that accounts for the inside reputations of John Goldrosen's authoritative but staid *The Buddy Holly Story*, David Henderson's inspired but wildly uneven *Jimi Hendrix*, Dave Marsh's comradely but adulatory and rather sloppy *Born to Run: The Bruce Springsteen Story*, and Lester Bangs's eloquent but wrongheaded *Blondie*. At least these authors cared enough for their subjects to try and write good books about them, and except for Goldrosen all had something to say about the art as well as the artist. The results in each case are admirable and useful. But while the music involved is most certainly up to the standard of *The Wizard of Oz* or *The Thief of Bagdad* or *Some Like It Hot*, not one of the books is within two leagues of John Lahr's portrait of his father Bert or Richard Schickel's analysis of Douglas Fairbanks or even Norman Mailer's ruminations on Marilyn. And neither are such profitable tomes as Jerry Hopkins and Daniel Sugerman's *No One Here Gets Out Alive* (which claims Jim Morrison as a god and then describes him as a jerk) or Albert Goldman's *Elvis* (the hepster calling the bopcat square), although both are more solid than Dave Marsh or Greil Marcus would have you believe. In fact, it's not impossible to understand why Myra Friedman's priggish, condescending *Janis Joplin: Buried Alive* is regarded by the ignorant as the best biography in the field—in terms of sheer craft, it is. Or rather, it was.

Blame money first: most rock biographies, and indeed most rock books, are written fast because they're written cheap—big-advance subjects like Janis and Jimi are rare. But they're also written fast because they're sold fast—editors who assume all rock stars are headed for instant oblivion press for instant copy. So Marsh and Bangs executed variations on the quickie, turning out their forty thousand or so words (cut from eighty-five in Bangs's case) with the alacrity of craftsmen confident of their right to a decent hourly wage. And thus they managed to get cherished ideas about rock and roll into *Books in Print* if not between hard covers, while most of the best rock writing remains buried in yesterday's papers. Their quickies were also labors of love—Marsh's love of Springsteen, Bangs's love of spouting off. They were rockstar bios as exemplary/expedient rockbooks.

Both Tosches and Robert Palmer, author of another current Jerry Lee Lewis bio, have taken a different route to the rockbook in the past: the pop text. Not surprisingly, neither elected to cover rock and roll per se—unless you count *Sound Effects*, Nik Cohn's *Rock From the Beginning*, a history published more than half the music's lifetime ago, remains the only honorable attempt at that sisyphean undertaking ever essayed by an individual acting alone. Tosches's 1977 *Country: The Biggest Music in America* is pure gonzo scholarship, so outrageous that I felt let down when jacket copy that began "If you're looking for a cogent, comprehensive history of America's moat popular music . . ." didn't continue ". . . then steal Bill C. Malone from the library, sucker." Alternating garish anecdotes, many apocryphal and several completely made up, with the kind of catalogue-number fanaticism only record collectors can read without artificial stimulants, *Country* attempts to prove that America's most conservative popular music is in fact its most radical. Where Marxist George Lipsitz makes a similar case by doggedly documenting the music's class origins and consciousness, Tosches's book is all fucking and fighting and getting high. As history, it's partial and absurdly distorted. But as vision, it's hilarious and instructive, a perfect rockbook combo; it's not the key to country music, but it breaks down some doors.

Palmer's *Deep Blues*, published in 1981 and just out in paper from Penguin, is something else entirely—the best book available on a subject that's always inspired passionate erudition. Although I'm not enough of a blues scholar to attest unequivocally to its originality or accuracy, I guarantee its scope, coherence, and grace. Tracing the blues back to Will Dockery's plantation in northwestern Mississippi, where in the 1890s guitarist Henry Sloane (teacher of Charley Patton, student of ???) was heard to play something quite similar, Palmer follows the tradition to its international present with an admirable sense of proportion except when he overplays his good source Robert Junior Lockwood. Because Delta blues is his subject, he barely touches on the East Texas strain, but that's regrettable only because he would have made such a good job of it. He completes his self-appointed task superbly, especially the stopover in Chicago with Muddy Waters and his numerous nephews. This is a pop text, yes, but it's also where to start exploring the source of all rock and roll. A rockbook and then some.

Palmer's critical virtues have always been on the ethnomusicological side—he appreciates madness, style, and sleaze, but he's never shown any inclination to incorporate them into his writing. So for the same reason that the star lecturer isn't always the life of the faculty party, it's no surprise that Palmer brings off a history with more pizzazz than he does a quickie. His *Jerry Lee Lewis Rocks!* began its life in 1980 as a memorable *Rolling Stone* profile, but stretched out for the rockstar bio people at Delilah, it's little more than the usual excuse for photographs, many of them wonderful. Sure the facts are here, as well as a lot of historical background and a few of the authorial reminiscences that Bangs always made a specialty—Palmer grew up in Little Rock and had his life changed, he says, by "Whole Lot of Shakin' Going On." But he doesn't put a whole lot of thought, or heart, into his thesis that "maybe rock and roll can save souls as well as destroy them." And while in *Deep Blues* he applies his musical expertise to one of the key enterprises of rock criticism—establishing the technical brilliance of inspired primitives—he never does the same for Jerry Lee's pumping piano, surely one of the great instrumental signatures. Too bad—I would have liked him to parse those boogie rolls.

Hellfire feels like it was written fast, too—but not ground out like a quickie, really *written*, in what I envision as a month or two of icy lyric fury. Even at the end, when what begins as heroic narrative breaks down into a string of clipped little items that might just as well have been lifted whole from the trades, the police blotter, and the secret diary of Oral Roberts Jr., the book has the kind of trancelike coherence that has overtaken every writer at the dawn of a specially blessed all-nighter. Basically the tale of the archetypal Southern backslider, it's been described as Biblical and Faulknerian, and it should be. But Tosches, who has lots of just-the-facts hack in him, sustains a page-turning pace that intensifies its of-a-pieceness. And his tone partakes of the grand, inexorable distance of a genuine epic as well.

Such things cannot be, of course—the epic is of the past. All the oral tradition south of the Mason-Dixon line can't bring it back unspoiled, and anybody who thinks different is ignorant, pretentious, or both. So *Hellfire* can only succeed as some kind of mock epic, the chronicle of a would-be hero in an antiheroic age. And indeed, Tosches does cut King James English with journalese; he does mix straight reporting and bent faction with the stuff of legend; he does disfigure his story with the mean details of Lewis's vanity, cruelty, and crazed sense of humor. But *Hellfire* isn't mock anything. Without hewing foolishly to the usages of a dead form or trying to write like someone he isn't, and without presenting Lewis's excesses as merely cool, colorful, or demidivine, Tosches limns the life of a doomed hero as if that hero deserved our respect, and his. As a dedicated classicist who is also a former snake hunter and a contributing editor to *Penthouse*, he rejects the notion that there's something debased or devalued about the mongrel rhetoric he exploits. It's just there, with all its peculiar virtues and drawbacks, and it's Jerry Lee Lewis's mother tongue.

Not that this avowed Pindar fan doesn't respect the past—not even that he doesn't believe there-were-giants-in-those-days. Like most rock critics with a specialty in roots music, he disdains today's pop, and his Jerry Lee is driven by his heritage as "the final wild son" (Tosches's phrase) of a family with "a big history" (Lewis's). Nor is *Hellfire* at all solemn—in fact, it's very funny indeed. Lewis's excesses aren't merely cool or colorful, but they're at least that—this wild son has done a lot of exorbitant things in his life, and he's some interview: "I mean Elvis this. Elvis that. What the shit did Elvis do except take dope that I couldn't git ahold of? That's very discouraging, anybody that had that much power to git ahold of that much dope." Furthermore, Tosches does play his story for laughs, often finding punch lines in the grand rhythms of his rhetoric itself: "She caressed Jerry Lee and soon told him that she was pregnant. He told her that it was no seed of his that had rendered her so. They lifted their hands in anger anew." Nevertheless, Tosches never makes fun. This is a humor not of derision but of delight.

I'm making big claims for Tosches's complexity of tone, and I'm sure not everyone will read him that way. His elevated periods can be dismissed as rodomontade, his jokes as sarcasm, his compact narrative and penchant for interior monologue as proof he didn't do his homework. Then again, you can also dismiss Jerry Lee Lewis as one more unholy roller, or pigeonhole his achievement as a couple of classic rock and roll songs, a piano insignia, and a fling as a country star. But I would argue—having listened long and hard, I would swear—that there's a lot more there. Lewis's offhand arrogance, candid insincerity, and unshakable sense of destiny are not qualities commonly found in any artist. He's very much a modern, set apart not so much by the elementary truth and transcendent power of his singing and playing as by his self-consciousness itself. His distance from his own show of fervor can seem positively eerie upon reflection, yet it in no way diminishes that fervor—if anything, the distance helps the fervor penetrate and endure.

Tosches has absorbed this sensibility if he didn't share it all along. In *Country*, he avers (pace Bird and JB) that Jerry Lee Lewis's mastery of twentieth-century rhythm is rivaled only by Faulkner's, but what author has learned from subject hardly stops there, and where it ends is with that same synthesis of distance and fervor. This is why Albert Goldman's half-truths about rock's attitudinal roots in "the put-on and the take-off" are so irrelevant—it's radically unlike "*Mad* or the routines of Sid Caesar" because its formal roots are in the ecstatic vernacular music of the American South, just as Tosches, who is touched with the spirit, is radically unlike Goldman, who has all the largesse of an unemployed gag writer.

Lewis believes that the source of his fervor is beyond question. "I got the Devil in me," he told Sam Phillips just before cutting "Great Balls of Fire." "If I didn't have, I'd be a Christian." And while he's hardly the first Southerner possessed by such a notion, no one else has ever had the genius to dramatize Christ's defeat so graphically. Not only is Jerry Lee a sinner, he's a proud sinner, and not only is he a proud sinner, he's a bored sinner; he's always interpreted the breakup songs, for instance, as if no period of suffering would ever bring him around. You win again, he seemed to say—and you'll win again after that. And what does it matter? I'm still the Killer. Grrrrrr.

What Tosches believes is harder to know. I suspect, however, that the source of his own fervor isn't secondhand—isn't just his passion for Jerry Lee Lewis. Tosches's account of Pentecostal fundamentalism maintains an objective if not skeptical tone. But like everything else in this terse, intense book, it never gets theoretical, never sociologizes, and although that's formally appropriate, I'm left wondering. Not only does it seem that Tosches envies Lewis the simplicity of his Manichaeanism, which is bad enough, but it also seems that in a less literal way he counts himself in thrall to the same dichotomies. Tosches makes no bones about the wages of this belief, always linked so intimately to romantic agony in extremis—he leaves Lewis unloved and without male issue, his career and his IRS account in tatters. His judgment, however, is muted. If Lewis has traded an eternity in Hellfire for some great music, it's possible Tosches feels he's gotten a fairly great book at comparable cost.

As a skeptic in the matter of eternity, I don't really believe that myself, of course, even though *Hellfire* is fairly great indeed—the finest rockstar bio ever and up with *Mystery Train* among all rockbooks. But as such it raises philosophical questions, for it reminds us that even the much more reflective *Mystery Train* is rooted in—and perhaps limited by—the Puritan tradition and/or the Great Awakening, which between them sometimes seem to ground all American culture. Because Nick Tosches, Greil Marcus, and Jerry Lee Lewis each takes this heritage seriously, each creates work that isn't mock anything, that connects us with an epic, heroic, deeply felt past. But in escaping modernism's cul-de-sac they don't escape modernity, which is why it's worth remembering that in the end neither *Hellfire* nor *Mystery Train* is epic all. They're tragedies of damnation—a damnation I always thought rock and roll was put on earth to help us get the better of.

Village Voice, 1982

That Bad Man, Tough Old Huddie Ledbetter

Charles Wolfe and Kip Lornell's *The Life and Legend of Leadbelly*

Until 1934, when he was forty-six, the seminal folksinger Huddie Ledbetter made his mark in an almost totally African-American world. The only son of hard-working sharecroppers-turned-smallholders in a parish near Louisiana's Texas-Arkansas border, Huddie was a serious, somewhat spoiled child who grew up fast. By sixteen, he was a prodigious cotton picker, an absent father, and a notorious rounder—a songster in demand at local dances for his powerful voice, extensive repertoire, fancy stepping, and virtuosity on guitar, mandolin, piano, accordion, and harmonica. He contracted gonorrhea working the Shreveport red-light district, recovered, married and moved to Dallas, went partners with the not-yet-famous bluesman Blind Lemon Jefferson, and retreated to a Texas farm near his birthplace. And that's when his troubles really began—troubles that eventually led to worldwide fame after collector-impresarios John and Alan Lomax discovered him in prison.

Although the details remained fuzzy, much was made of Ledbetter's criminal record and supposed propensity for violence when he was first celebrated as an entertainer, and Nashville-based music historian Charles Wolfe and Smithsonian archivist Kip Lornell don't soft-pedal the facts, adding a previously unreported teenage shooting incident (cleared up by his father, who'd given him the pistol) to three better-known imprisonments for murder and assault. But they do minimize their subject's image as the "murderous minstrel" of a 1935 *Time* profile. They point out that Leadbelly lived in a frontier environment where violence was an accepted part of life. They argue that his sole homicide conviction was clearly self-defense. And they establish that the crime for which he did hard time in Louisiana's brutal Angola Penitentiary was refusing to take guff from a white man—for ultimately, of course, his African-American world was controlled by European-American racists. Still, examine the vitae of other bluesmen and songsters with dangerous reputations and you'll find one prison term each for Son House, Bukka White, and Lightnin' Hopkins, and none for Robert Johnson, Charley Patton, Tommy Johnson, or the much older Henry Thomas. Unless Leadbelly had exceptionally bad luck, he must have been one tough customer.

The authors' willingness to skirt this embarrassing likelihood typifies the failures of an honest, authoritative biography that provokes as many questions as it answers. Wolfe and Lornell are excellent on the varied sources of Leadbelly's music. Their detailed history of his renowned "Goodnight Irene," which appears to have originated with a racially integrated pop songwriting duo of the 1880s and undergone uncounted oral transformations before it reached the man who gave it back to the world, quietly demolishes music-of-the-folk romanticism, in which songs are created spontaneously by vague collectivities, or by anonymous geniuses unsullied by education, industrialization, or modernity itself. They've found out as much about his virtually undocumented early life as seems possible almost a century later. And their account of how he suddenly became a sometime darling of white academics and progressives—of his dealings with the Lomaxes, the nascent New York folk scene of the '30s and '40s, and the Communist Party—is balanced and thoroughly researched. But they never take it up a notch.

More than any bluesman, the artist whose career most closely parallels Leadbelly's is the folk-music movement's other star exhibit, Woody Guthrie, who grew up less than three hundred miles from Leadbelly and even sponged a bed off him for a while in New York. It's not entirely fair to compare *The Life and Legend of Leadbelly* to Joe Klein's *Woody Guthrie: A Life*. Whereas Leadbelly died in 1949, Klein did his digging barely a decade after the 1967 death of his subject, a compulsive scribbler who left millions of unpublished words behind him. Klein knew he had the makings of a great book, and he wrote one. Nevertheless, his work points up what's absent here: not just the psychological depth that can be attributed to privileged access, but any concerted attempt to assess the evolution of folk music as a theoretical concept and urban phenomenon, the cultural ferment surrounding the Communist Party, or, indeed, Leadbelly's place in musical history. By declining to venture critical analyses of his music—of his vocal and instrumental style, his writing, the changes he worked on found material—the authors make that music seem like a natural phenomenon rather than willed, conscious art and/or entertainment, which is precisely the kind of mystification their research usually corrects for.

Finally we're left with what must have been a surreal inner journey: a mature black man plucked from the self-contained world of the black South—a world that he (unlike Muddy Waters, say) never showed any desire to escape or transcend except when enmeshed in its penal system—and transformed, in about a year, into a near-famous New Yorker whose professional and social relationships were primarily with well-meaning white people, many of whom regarded blacks as noble savages even so. Wolfe and Lornell do a good job of limning this complex story, but they're understandably chary of filling in the outline. A fuller account would clearly require empathy as well as sympathy—a leap of imagination into Leadbelly's racial conflicts that would almost certainly have been facilitated by more candid interviews with surviving African-American witnesses as well as the personal experience of bias. It would be simplistic to suggest that any black writer could have provided such insight. But I'd love to see the right one try.

New York Times Book Review, 1993

The Impenetrable Heroism of Sam Cooke

Peter Guralnick's *Dream Boogie: The Triumph of Sam Cooke*

Peter Guralnick's *Dream Boogie* follows *You Send Me*, Daniel Wolff's serious and authoritative Sam Cooke biography, by ten years. It's nearly twice as long—too long, like so many doorstops before it, including *Careless Love*, the second volume of Guralnick's life of Elvis. But it draws on research that would have justified an even more monumental book. Guralnick doesn't add much to Wolff's thesis. Both argue that though the soul singer who predated soul music made many records that fell short of his artistic potential, he was nevertheless a heroic figure, topping a voice that for the many who loved it was liquid magic—cool, relaxed, infinitely inviting—with a questing intelligence and cultural ambition startling in a teen idol whose most important compositions included "You Send Me" and "Twistin' the Night Away." As Cooke strove for pop success, he funded one of the most resolutely black labels the record business has known. He supported the civil rights movement in word and deed. He studied black history. At the time of his death in December 1964, he really was a hero, cut down in his prime at thirty-three, and Guralnick's sense of this man, and of the lesser men and women who surrounded him, is vastly more complex than his predecessor's.

That Wolff is no hack hardly puts him in a league with Guralnick, who alongside the more eccentric and intellectually ambitious Greil Marcus is the prestige brand in rock authordom. By 1986 Guralnick had published two major profile collections and *Sweet Soul Music*, which remains the go-to history of the style. Yet only with the 1994 publication of Elvis I, *Last Train to Memphis*, did many outside the specialist audience recognize his gift. Even in the intermittently clumsy 1971 *Feel Like Going Home*, where five of the eight subjects are bluesmen, Guralnick's self-effacing eye lent a cinema verite authority lacking in, for instance, Michael Lydon's hipper and slicker collection *Rock Folk*. By 1979's *Lost Highway*, which focuses on country and rockabilly, he was a master of the journalistic portrait. Yet for Guralnick, who until the 1990s made his living running a summer camp he'd inherited, journalism was only a means to literature. Despite a few shortcomings, *Last Train to Memphis* justified his ambitions—it's a book that grows in the mind. I can't see how any reader could come away unmoved by Elvis Presley's intelligence, musicality, and sense of spiritual adventure, or still crediting the character assassinations of Albert Goldman's *Elvis*, which Marcus once predicted would be conventional wisdom in perpetuity.

Formally, *Last Train to Memphis* represented a major change. In the profiles, Guralnick aimed for the intensive reporting of New Journalism, but he also exploited the freewheeling first person of sixties rock criticism. While he was most often the nerd in the corner, jotting down details as his subjects lived their lives and, occasionally, answered his questions, at moments—in introductions, conclusions, afterwords, interjections, and sometimes whole essays—he became the A student dazzled by meeting one of his highly unsuburban heroes, or explaining what makes that hero tick, or figuring out how rock and roll changed his life. From the first he had confidence in opinions he adjusted as he learned more. Over the years, however, he grew more discreet about revealing them as such—where in *Sweet Soul Music* the narrative he was compelled to impose on a welter of secondhand evidence also proved a story of personal discovery, in *Last Train to Memphis* Guralnick disappeared entirely, avoiding the "I" and limiting psychological interpretation and critical judgment.

The book tells Presley's story you-are-there fashion, with he-said-she-said at a minimum, and dazzles anyway because Guralnick's interviewing persona—where he presumably maintains his admirer-not-expert pose—induces people to tell him things they maybe shouldn't. Arcing up toward infinity before crashing to the death of Gladys Presley and Elvis's induction into the Army, *Last Train to Memphis* is an unflinchingly affectionate argument for democratic genius. But Guralnick found it harder to extract tragedy from Presley's decline into drugged isolation, and although *Careless Love* was praised profusely, even gratefully—rock and roll's challenge to the reading classes exposed as a sham—its accreted detail becomes as boring as the second half of the King's life. Because Cooke's life didn't divide down the middle, *Dream Boogie* fuses the moods of the two Presley volumes. But in the end it's diminished—not drastically but markedly—by Guralnick's reluctance to say what he thinks, an MO in which formal principle and professional convenience are difficult to distinguish.

Sam Cooke already envisioned a musical career as the six-year-old lead tenor in the Singing Children, the family gospel group organized by his hard-hustling preacher and factory worker father, and as a young teenager he was both bookish and charismatic, one of those people who convinces anyone he talks to that he's there only for him—or her. Clean-cut and ingratiating, he was consciously set on stardom even then, and not just black stardom. The gospel equivalent of a matinee idol by age twenty-two, he spent four years figuring out how to breach the pop market, which he conquered when the simple vocal showcase "You Send Me"—the B side of his first secular forty-five, a version of "Summertime" released under a pseudonym that fooled no one in the gospel world—turned him into an instant idol, adored by girls black and white. With young male fans he was never quite such a hit, but despite an ill-timed flop at the Copa in 1958, white adults took to him, and for all his ups and downs he was a consistent commercial presence: not the first gospel-trained singer to go pop, but until Aretha Franklin the biggest.

But Cooke's opaque and compulsive sides also surfaced early. Exhibit A is the womanizing that would end with the race hero shot dead in his underwear by an ex-madam in a cheap southwest LA motel. Even when he was the seventeen-year-old leader of the fledgling Highway QCs, his sexual appetites stood out on a gospel circuit that never equated holiness with chastity. By the time he'd joined the much bigger Soul Stirrers, Cooke was a well-known dog. Multiple witnesses recall his taste for orgies and much greater danger—once, in Texas, he had sex in the shower with the wife of a white radio man, who was passed out on Cooke's motel bed. He drank, too. He saw a continuing street connection—playing craps with the boys, greeting winos in the alley—as integral to his black pride. And like many driven charismatics, he held even intimate friends at a distance, in his case with "an inscrutably cheerful and impenetrable calm which, for all they knew, might merely have masked the simple fact that it was all as much a mystery to him as it was to them." That unknowability took other forms, including sudden rages all the more troubling for their infrequency. And then there was the way this affable, generous, idealistic guy screwed one manager, agent, and label head after another.

Most of the peripheral characterizations that bring *Dream Boogie* alive are of African-Americans. There's Cooke's wife, Barbara, who avoided Guralnick for years before opening up. There's his singing brother L.C., his player brother Charles, and his relentlessly striving father. There are satellites and running buddies like replacement Soul Stirrer Leroy Crume and Cooke's protege Bobby Womack, who married Barbara two-and-a half-months after Cooke died. The colleagues include civil rights pioneers like staunch NAACP supporter Clyde McPhatter and bandleader Harold Battiste, whose visionary musicians' collective became the house band at Cooke's SAR label. But most are on the wild side: gangster-friendly singer Lloyd Price and pugnacious Cooke imitator Johnnie Taylor; lost proto-soul balladeer Little Willie John, who would die in prison, and night-crawling Johnnie Morisette, who preferred pimping to singing. There are disc jockeys, promoters, and pros—fast-talking Bumps Blackwell, Cooke's longtime advisers S. R. Crain and J. W. Alexander. But beyond Barbara Cooke and Bobby Womack, Guralnick's chief supporting players are white businessmen.

From the start this Jewish kid from New England knew how to draw out unlettered Southerners. But researching *Sweet Soul Music*, he came to realize that another class of middle-class white people shared this knack: the marginal entrepreneurs and music lovers who ran the companies that recorded such artists. That book celebrated not just Stax's Jim Stewart and Estelle Axton and Otis Redding manager turned Capricorn Records founder Phil Walden, all of them white, but, through them, the de facto integration of the soul industry as Guralnick defined it—which excluded the poppier Motown and Philadelphia substyles, both masterminded by black bizzers. And some of *Dream Boogie*'s most memorable descriptions are of white businessmen: in addition to many lesser figures, Specialty Records' Art Rupe, the liberal gospel enthusiast who chiseled his artists a bit less than was customary and was so affronted when they chiseled back that he quit the business; Hugo Peretti and Luigi Creatore of RCA, whose unbridled crassness in no way interfered with their candor, intelligence, or sense of fun; and Allen Klein, the accountant turned manager who wrested Cooke's catalogue away from RCA and ended up controlling it himself—as he does, for instance, the Rolling Stones' sixties music.

This is a mark of quality, and an impressive leap for Guralnick, initially a folkie romantic for whom Elvis "never recaptured the spirit or the verve of those first Sun sessions." To reread Wolff's received takes on the above-named is to understand why not being a hack is never enough—there's no sense of these human beings' humanity. Still, Guralnick's taste in bizzers has to make you wonder. At stake isn't just the conundrum of why white executives dig gritty putative authenticity more than black ones, and whether this predilection doesn't arouse untoward sympathy in folkie romantics (not to mention observers who've mocked folkie romanticism for decades, like me). In this book, there's also the Allen Klein problem.

Klein is one of the most widely mistrusted figures in the history of the music business. In late 1963, with Cooke an established star who craved total autonomy, Klein formed a dummy corporation to receive Cooke's payments from RCA, named it after Cooke's daughter Tracey, installed Cooke as president, and reserved the entirety of its ownership for himself—an arrangement that, after Cooke's death, had a dire effect on the extended family Cooke had always propped up. By 1968, according to Rolling Stones chronicler Philip Norman, there were fifty lawsuits against Klein, who by then had his mitts on half the British Invasion, and much later he did two months for income-tax evasion. But although Guralnick details the Tracey setup, he pays less mind to its consequences than to Klein's financial genius in devising it. He stresses that when Cooke died intestate he was emotionally estranged from his wife. He pooh-poohs rumors that Cooke hoped to dump Klein as he had first manager Louis Tate and crossover-guru manager Bumps Blackwell, Specialty's Art Rupe and Keen's John Siamas, sixties manager Jess Rand and sixties booking agent Jerry Brandt. And by establishing Cooke's taste for reckless sex and, occasionally, prostitutes, he forestalls speculation about the singer's death, which some fantasists have even tried to pin on Klein.

As Guralnick says, it's "impossible to know exactly what happened" at that motel, although I wish he'd gone somewhere with the possibility he leaves open that prostitute Elisa Boyer and manager Bertha Franklin were in cahoots. Like him, however, I buy the semi-official version, in which Cooke had his money and clothes stolen by Boyer and was then shot by Franklin when he went looking for the thief (perhaps in one of those rare rages, Guralnick implies). But although *Dream Boogie* offers more interpretation than the Presley books, Guralnick continues to disdain speculation and unanswerable questions. Thus he never points out what is obvious—that whatever his feelings about Barbara, Cooke would certainly have preferred to leave his assets to some version of his family than to Klein. Nor does *Dream Boogie* engage the animadversions Wolff and others—especially Arthur Kempton, whose 2003 *Boogaloo* isn't even in the bibliography—level at Klein, who in Guralnick's portrait is a prince of a fellow, if a bit of a rogue, who was deeply touched by Sam Cooke. Since Guralnick makes clear that the book couldn't have been written without Klein and his archive, this smells bad. It's one thing to ignore Albert Goldman while you demolish him. Goldman was a liar and a cad. Wolff and Kempton are neither. You-are-there aesthetic or no you-are-there aesthetic, they deserve more respect—and Klein deserves less. By declining to defend Klein—and I don't assume he's indefensible—Guralnick effectively whitewashes him.

Guralnick's reluctance to polemicize doesn't merely reflect his humble subservience to the material. It also keeps him above the fray—especially the critical fray. He seems to regard himself as beyond disputation. So where his early work implied an informed version of the old blues-and-country-had-a-baby theory of rock and roll, writing about former Soul Stirrer Cooke—as in *Sweet Soul Music*, but not the Presley books—he has little choice but to emphasize rock and roll's more recently recognized gospel roots. Ex-gospel performers go pop by the dozen in *Dream Boogie*, while Guralnick's beloved blues is barely mentioned even though Cooke grew up in Muddy Waters's Chicago and sang the bejesus out of Howlin' Wolf's "Little Red Rooster." Because blues implies an outlaw ethos while gospel carries with it images of sustained social responsibility, blues-versus-gospel has become a contentious issue in rock history. Guralnick has the range and, here, opportunity to concoct a unified field theory. He doesn't.

In the end, what's most frustrating about this redolent story of a black hero killed by his irresistible attraction to—or principled refusal to abandon—"black" (or is it?) street life isn't a mere music writer's inability to convey tragic psychological imponderables. The imponderables render the book compelling in any case. Nor is it the Klein matter, which shouldn't be ignored but (as Guralnick might argue) is peripheral to Cooke's larger meaning. The frustration has to do with music. For sure, Cooke was a black hero cut down in his prime. But one must ask whether he was also a great artist cut down in his prime. And if he wasn't, how does that inflect his heroism?

Too proud to forswear the white audience, Cooke presaged the soul style without bringing it to fruition, and his prolific songwriting, as Kempton is one of the few fans to say flat-out, mixed much corn with the likes of "Bring It on Home to Me," "Good Times," and the unquestionable masterpiece "A Change Is Gonna Come." So more than any other major rock artist—more even than Al Green or Aretha Franklin, and certainly more than any other charter member of the Rock and Roll Hall of Fame—his artistic power is bound up in how the individual listener responds to the physical reality of his voice. Guralnick works hard to pin down the specifics of this voice, isolating the genesis and impact of his yodel and analyzing his fusion of white-identified crooning techniques with the contained passion of his epochal Soul Stirrers predecessor Rebert Harris. As often happens with great voices, however, he's reduced to metaphors when it comes down to cases, and they don't always suffice: "flexible and *playful*," OK, that's important, but "aching sense of loss, of lostness" won't ring as many bells. By now Guralnick knows Cooke's music better than almost anyone, so there's assuredly some truth value there. But it's not the kind of universal truth value Cooke aspired to. What is it about Sam Cooke? We still don't know.

In fact, it seems possible, despite how late Guralnick came to church music, that he's one of those who deep down prefers Cooke's Soul Stirrers recordings to his pop output. Although he has the wisdom to fight it, Guralnick is a folkie at heart, moved to his bones by pastoral versions of the simple, the true, and the real. Intellectually, he gets this—he's not jiving when he praises the late Elvis milestones "In the Ghetto" and "Suspicious Minds." But emotional connection comes harder—he can explain what made "Everybody Loves to Cha Cha Cha" a hit, but designating it "irresistible" doesn't help everybody love it. This is probably why *Dream Boogie*'s assessments of Cooke's music fall short.

What kind of story would it have been if, despite some masterstrokes and a few performances like the 1963 Miami show Guralnick annotated back in 1985, the most durable art the hero left behind predated his brave crossover quest? What kind of story would it have been if the price of the cultural triumph Cooke never fully achieved was musical compromises and trial balloons his truest believers can't get their hearts around? As someone who prefers Aretha Franklin's "You Send Me" to the original, no contest, and whose own response to Cooke's voice suggests that it's no more magical than that of the young Dionne Warwick, dissed in passing by Guralnick here, I believe those are stories worth being told. And like Greil Marcus after Goldman's *Elvis*, I fear they never will be. As monumental as *Dream Boogie* is, it could have been more monumental still.

The Nation, 2005

Bobby and Dave

Bob Dylan's *Chronicles: Volume One* and Dave Van Ronk's *The Mayor of MacDougal Street*

Averse to nostalgia in general, folkies in particular, the Americana tendency in middlebrow rock criticism, and the Bob Dylan industry, I skipped Martin Scorsese's *No Direction Home* to write, escaping periodically to go watch TV. Every time, though, some grizzled adept of acoustic authenticity sent me back to my labors. Arresting though it was to see Dylan speak in an apparently straightforward manner, and fond though I am of some individual informants, old farts patting themselves on the hem of Dylan's garment made a lousy circus act. Admittedly, the average rock-doc is much worse—old farts exuding vanity, yeucch. At least Scorsese's guys are honorable bohemians. But like most bohemians, they put too much stock in their long-gone moment.

Only then I belatedly inhaled Dylan's *Chronicles: Volume One*, which made me wonder. The book has inspired endless hosannas, many dumb and some far from it (as well as a few dismissals, all dumb), so quality-wise I'll just say great-not-good, oughta stand as a literary landmark and, due to its drop-dead mastery of the semiliterate tone, probably won't. Contentwise, however, it boasts two virtues overlooked in the kvelling over Dylan's eloquence and the head-scratching over his elusiveness e'en now. One is his recollection of the early '60s folk scene as a wonderland on the order of 52nd Street, Swinging London, the Loft, or CBGB—"a paradise that I had to leave." The other is music criticism that nails Ricky Nelson, Roy Orbison, Harry Belafonte, Mike Seeger, Bobby Vee, Hank Williams, Joan Baez, Woody Guthrie, Ramblin' Jack Elliott, Dave Van Ronk, and Brecht-Weill's "Pirate Jenny," among others. Maybe not "Pirate Jenny," actually—Dylan, elusive devil, is more confused by Jenny's murderous misanthropy than the man who wrote "The Lonesome Death of Hattie Carroll" should be. But he compensates by explaining how his misprision spurred him to become the songwriter he became—along with a test pressing of Robert Johnson's *King of the Delta Blues Singers*, which inspires the very best writing I know about Johnson. Dave Van Ronk, Dylan reports, found Johnson derivative on first hearing.

I mention this because Van Ronk has his own memoir—Da Capo's posthumous *The Mayor of MacDougal Street*, begun in Van Ronk's well-worked prose and expertly completed from fragments, interviews, and such by Elijah Wald. Five years older than Dylan, Van Ronk was one of the few native New Yorkers among Village folkiedom's big names. After departing "Our Lady of Perpetual Bingo" in the staidest corner of Queens, Van Ronk turned anarcho-Marxist out of orneriness and common sense. Initially a Dixieland banjoist who doubled on foghorn vocals, he was an interpreter who mastered blues and kept going. His repertoire encompassed not just his mentor Gary Davis and the Harry Smith canon but old pop, jazz, and vaudeville material, a few self-penned gems, and, soon enough, the cream of the singer-songwriters he insists were folk only by loose-thinking association. He was an ace guitarist who made up in practice what he lacked in dexterity and a brainy arranger whose book was raided on his protege Dylan's Columbia debut.

Chronicles means to repay debts to old allies used up and cast aside. So not counting the apropos Johnson story, Dylan is very kind to Van Ronk, who "came from the land of giants" and "towered over the street like a mountain but would never break into the big time. It just wasn't where he pictured himself." Van Ronk is, shall we say, more measured. He has no use for the "purists" who attacked Dylan for going electric ("forty years later Bobby is still out there making music, and they're all dentists"), and despite the "contrived primitivism" of Dylan's songs anoints them "far and away the best on our scene," let there be no mistake about that. But he wants us to know that Tom Paxton invented "the new song movement" and that Phil Ochs knew more about chords. He complains that "All Along the Watchtower" doesn't parse because you can't travel "along" a watchtower. In the end, he prefers Joni Mitchell.

Well to the rear of Dylan and Peter Stampfel, Van Ronk is my third favorite MacDougal Streeter. I appreciate his politics. I share his preference for literal songwriting even if "you should never say anything in poetry that you would not say in prose" takes it way too far. I always enjoyed him live and found his albums, as he liked to say, consistently inconsistent. Even the Wald-compiled "rarities 1957–1969" CD—*The Mayor of MacDougal Street* on Lyrichord/Rootstock—is far less frustrating than most such hodgepodges, because eclecticism was his way. The cross-label comp Rhino surely has in the works should include one of the 1957 living-room recordings, the Trotskyite "Way Down in Lubyanka Prison," and the W. C. Fields routine about serpents and maraschino cherries. It should also include the disco-era rewrite of his

Davis-derived signature song, "Cocaine." But I note with interest Wald's report that one of the tracks he passed up for this collection was a live 1961 version of Robert Johnson's "If I Had Possession Over Judgment Day."

Is Dylan, elusive devil, fibbing? Or did Van Ronk change his mind? I'd guess the latter, and anyway, as a convinced fingerpicker he never did get into Delta or Chicago blues. He had his standards, did Van Ronk. But they were idiosyncratic, equal-opportunity standards—loved Bing Crosby, yet opposed the well-groomed cabaret folkies of the Josh White and Theodore Bikel generation, many of whom he liked personally. Where Van Ronk was catholic, however, Dylan was totally absorptive—Dave Guard of the Kingston Trio gets a few sentences, nightclub-folk king Belafonte several paragraphs. And then Dylan obsessed on a Brecht-Weill song and completed the puzzle with Robert Johnson: "It's not that you could sort out every moment carefully, because you can't. There are too many missing terms and too much dual existence." So much for poetry and prose. Soon he would obliterate cabaret folkiedom on the back of its Peter, Paul & Mary apotheosis. Unbelievably in retrospect, folk svengali Albert Grossman offered Van Ronk the chance to be Paul, which he wisely turned down. Then Grossman signed Dylan, solo. He was just getting set to leave a paradise where he'd found a key to the past that would explode pop music's future. Talk about the big time—time doesn't get much bigger than that.

Village Voice, 2005

Tell All

Ed Sanders's *Fug You: An Informal History of the Peace Eye Bookstore, the Fuck You Press, the Fugs, and Counterculture in the Lower East Side* and Samuel R. Delany's *The Motion of Light in Water*

I've been reading a lot of memoirs lately, for two reasons. The first is the glut of rockbooks written by boomer musicians with time on their hands for boomer fans with memories deteriorating. The second is that I'm writing a memoir of my own, and always immerse in work that might clarify the project at hand. Ed Sanders's *Fug You* fits both bills: the Missouri-born poet, publisher, classics major, and peace creep who led the band that provides his title lived within blocks of me in the East Village for the entirety of the high '60s, and I knew him slightly. Originally published in 1988 and reissued twice since, Samuel R. Delany's *The Motion of Light in Water* is a less obvious case. But science fiction meistersinger Delany, author of *Stars in My Pocket Like Grains of Sand*, *Triton*, the beloved *Dhalgren*, and many others, is like me a product of the New York public school system born in April 1942, and was also a Lower East Sider for much of the '60s. In his 1979 memoir/"essay" *Heavenly Breakfast*, he recounts his six 1967–68 months in a 2nd Street commune with the never-recorded band that provides his title. *The Motion of Light in Water* reaches back earlier. Although never more acute than when revisiting the Bronx High School of Science, its main event is Delany's four-plus years, summer 1961 to autumn 1965, in "squalid" apartments on 5th and then 6th between B and C with his wife, the poet and Bronx Science graduate Marilyn Hacker.

Two things about memoirs often annoy me: they go on too much about the nature of memory and there's not enough sex in them. Memory is indeed unreliable; memory does oft support alternate, nay, contradictory narratives; memory speaks loud and ineffable to our mortal selves' longing for an immortality that would drive us nuts if it proved our fate. Got it. As for sex, it's not because I like pornography, which I do. Nor is it because I'm nosy, which I am, and aren't you? It's because in my experience sex and the love that generally comes with it—a big qualification, I know, but even memoirists who've had a lot more loveless sex than I have either include sex in their primary love relationships or should explain why they don't—plays a determinative role in most lives. Trying to avoid this evasion in my own book, I soon came up against the logic of discretion—however ready I may be to give up my own privacy, I don't have the right to demand that of anyone else. Nevertheless, it's a formal problem that cries out for a solution.

Rereading two classics I've long admired—Malcolm Cowley's *Exile's Return* and Thor Heyerdahl's *Kon-Tiki*—I was struck by how thoroughly both authors avoided describing their wives, but those were troubled relationships in more circumspect times. Less acceptable is how few of the contemporary memoirs I've downed recently do justice to the power of sexual fulfillment and domestic partnership. Christopher Hitchens's *Hitch-22*, for instance, profiles so many bigshots I think I'll just can my Mick Jagger story altogether, but never reveals when or why he married either of his wives, the second of whom helped him through quite a lot as I understand it. Major exceptions are Richard Hell's tell-all, David Carr's scabrous *The Night of the*

Gun, and Joyce Johnson's *Minor Characters*, which counterposes her affair with Jack Kerouac against auxiliary relationships I found just as interesting. And of these, only the supposedly titillating Hell provides much sexual detail.

Since the '60s Fugs may have been the raunchiest rock group ever—Sanders's "Slum Goddess" intro began, "She's lying down in viscid, skooshy strands of cherry Jell-O, buttocks popping in arpeggios of lust . . ."—one might expect Sanders to be like Hell, but no. He cheerfully describes the lost 16-mm footage he shot of couples copulating on the floor of the "secret location" where he mimeographed *Fuck You/A Magazine of the Arts*—a chip-on-shoulder poetry outlet that once designated itself "the magazine of street-fucking"—and in the Allen Street apartment where he handed out speed to speed the filming of the never-seen *Amphetamine Head: A Study of Power in America*. He recalls many occasions musical and political when he implored his public to "grope for peace." But does he himself grope once in here? He does not.

With no access to the real dirt, I'm certain that sometimes he was just kidding, as when a police sergeant who hates him on principle fails to find "the Ankh symbol tattooed on his penis" and "the first 53 hieroglyphs of Akh-en-Aten's Hymn to the Sun Disk on his nuts" even though both delights were attested to in his pornrag. I'm also certain that in later years, after the successfully revived Fugs had recorded an extraordinary twelve-minute suite on polymorphism, mortality, and mating for life called "Dreams of Sexual Perfection," he had second thoughts about the band's sexy bits, just as *Fug You* regrets the needle imagery he fooled with. And I note that a special hero of the memoir is his wife of fifty-two years, Miriam. Three times she talks him down from bad trips, and though she appears seldom elsewhere, Sanders's last paragraph begins: "The 1960s had ended, and Miriam and I were still together. We had survived the Revolution. I was very grateful for that."

A pack rat taught by Allen Ginsberg "to clip articles. I mean oodles of articles," Sanders holds his meditations on memory down to a prefatory pledge to settle no scores; after all, "I was sometimes imperfect in my behavior toward others, tending at times toward arrogance and egotistical smugness." His approach is flatly factual, based on his archive and broken down into hunks of a page or a paragraph rather than flowing narratively or developing thematically (and illustrated with the "glyphs" he used to draw freehand on mimeo stencils). Expedient though this method might seem, I loved the bite-sized pieces myself—as with pistachios, there's a just-one-more effect.

I was pleasantly surprised to learn of Sanders's longtime bond with Andy Warhol. A radical pacifist turned rabble-rousing anarcho-utopian who's now a "European-style social democrat," he also admired JFK and RFK. Having helped found the Yippies, he was appalled to hear Jerry Rubin call RFK's assassination "good news" because it meant the absurdist politicos could proceed with their Chicago plans. That was a turning point. But it didn't stop him from immersing in Chicago or testifying in Rubin's defense.

As regards memory, Delany is Sanders's opposite—from its title on, *The Motion of Light in Water* is bound up in instability, stepping aside to undermine its own reliability with disquisitions on "parallel narrative" that come naturally to a creator of imaginary worlds who's immersed in structuralism and its brainspawn since the '60s. He's Sanders's thrice-dislocated opposite in other things too—homosexual (although polymorphous enough to sleep with women and marry one), African-American (although middle-class and light enough to pass), and acutely dyslexic (although he too has studied Greek). And as regards sex, well, he leaves Sanders behind. As a lifelong erotic adventurer who believes sex is always "personally difficult" and usually "socially difficult," of course Delany writes about it. *The Motion of Light in Water* is full of explicit encounters, most of them gay and what some would call impersonal, a characterization Delany vehemently denies, but warmest and also hottest in a menage he and his wife share with a rough-hewn male friend. Around when Sanders was introducing "Slum Goddess" in 1968, Delaney followed the nine science fiction novels and novellas he'd then published with Ace Books by concocting the semiotic, arousing child-and-death-porn minisaga *Equinox*.

Although I myself value the Fugs' legacy not much less than, say, the Byrds', history will probably rank Delany's art higher than Sanders's. But he's never made much of a living writing—long an academic without BA, he teaches because he needs the money—and although each man proved himself a titan before the high '60s even began, they were very different statuswise back then. Where the Peace Eye Bookstore was a community center, the Fugs the first indie-rock band to breach the *Billboard* album chart, and Sanders's unflinching 1971 Charles Manson report *The Family* a bestseller, Delany's feat of publishing his first novel at nineteen left him neither rich nor famous, and for most of the '60s he got by busking in folk clubs and buckling down to straight jobs. From their different vantages, both writers recount everyday kindnesses and heroic shows of mutual support that seem more historically significant in retrospect than the counterculture's inevitable destruction by war creeps zeroing in on its weaknesses, and both praise rent control, a left-populist leftover that succored hungry artists as watered-down rent stabilization would not. Still, it's Delany who has the kinder and lower-rent tale to tell.

At its core *The Motion of Light in Water* is the story of two young artists who marry long before they're ready—Hacker gets pregnant, then miscarries—and try to love each other in an open relationship that even a doctrinaire monogamist like me finds emotionally credible. It's a book about no lock on the street door, about reading *Middlemarch* in a day to forget how scared you are, about the man doing the housework, about sexism in jeans design and the book trade, about the endlessly courteous W. H. Auden and Chester Kallman coming to dinner, about how many truckers you can suck off in a night, about visiting your wife's lover's much nicer place, about shutting down an argument by talking literature, about stolen goods and health crises and the rat on the sink and friends dropping by to mess up your night or your life, about not being able to stand her another day and hanging in for four years because you love this blocked poet so much you quote her published and unpublished work twenty-five times (and it's all good too). It's exceptionally novelistic and more evocative than *Fug You*. I only got to East 9th Street six months before Delany left Marilyn—with whom he later had a daughter—and flew to Europe. But the marginal life he celebrates feels like the East Village I moved to.

By 1967, many things had changed, for me and the neighborhood, and I expect I would have been unconvinced by a visit to the musical commune Delany reconstructs from his notebooks in *Heavenly Breakfast*. But though some may find this benevolent microcosm harder to believe than *Triton*, I feel enriched to have encountered it. Delany has said that one incontrovertible social benefit of literature is that it teaches compassion, and compassion, often for human beings most readers would do their best to ignore, rises to the surface of almost everything he writes.

In yet another memoir—the charming, sexually explicit *Bread & Wine: An Erotic Tale of New York*, illustrated by Delany's friend Mia Wolff when it was first published in 1997 and now reissued by Fantagraphics with illuminating addenda—Delany tells how he got together with the love of his life, a homeless bookseller with whom he's now lived for twenty-two years. Three of its forty-four pages are devoted to how filthy Dennis was when Delany brought him to the Skyline Hotel the first time they had sex—the innermost of his three pairs of socks had decayed to oozy shreds on his feet. Yet Dennis—like Sonny and Bob, nice guys some would dismiss as rough trade who play major roles in *The Motion of Light in Water*—comes alive as both sex object and autonomous subject. He's a good man and an appealing love partner. I hope I can write as well about the women I've loved. It's part of the job.

Barnes & Noble Review, 2013

King of the Thrillseekers

Richard Hell's *I Dreamed I Was a Very Clean Tramp*

The best proof of how brazenly punk yoked New York's post-hippie avant-garde to rock and roll is two albums by Richard Hell: 1977's *Blank Generation* and 1982's *Destiny Street*. Not Talking Heads, who in the interest of comity Hell barely mentions in his new book. Not his enabler Patti Smith, whom he compliments unstintingly given that he also calls her "a hypocritical, pandering diva." Not Television, the band Hell co-founded with bosom buddy Tom Verlaine, who forced him out in a much-debated dynamic Hell recounts evenly and convincingly. Not Blondie or the Ramones, who as Hell observes outsold the other CBGB bands (although not, let me note, Talking Heads) because their individually distinct aesthetics respected the pop verities as those of the other CBGB titans did not.

One way to conceive Hell's *I Dreamed I Was a Very Clean Tramp*, which ends just post–*Destiny Street* in 1984 with a brief addendum covering a relapse that lasted 1988 to 1990, is as the full story of how two historic albums grew from the artistic chip on his shoulder. A true memoir for as long as it lasts, it spends a hundred pages detailing Richard Meyers's childhood, adolescence, and extended tour of duty—beginning Christmas 1966, when he was barely seventeen—as a Lower Manhattan bohemian of intense if intermittent ambition and tiny renown. It's half over before the slacker self-starter can dub himself "the king of the Lower East Side." It's two-thirds over before his longtime drinking, smoking, dropping, and chipping has evolved into the full-on junkiedom that pervades without dominating the rest of his story. And basically it ends when he kicks, the second phase of which it summarizes in a paragraph, with a two-sentence paragraph right after explaining that he abandoned music along with heroin, repurposing himself as "a professional writer" to make sure he stuck with the program.

Hell dates his "junkie mentality" to before he was actually using—to Theresa Stern, the hooker poet he and Verlaine invented and impersonated in their collaborative 1973 collection *Wanna Go Out?*, and even to his early anthem "Blank Generation." So another way to conceive the new book is as a substantial substance abuse memoir. But my theory is that Hell had something to prove and needed to get on the stick with it—needed to finish this project because in a publishing business now officially scared of its own shadow, the rock memoir could be as over as the substance abuse memoir in a year or two. And though I doubt Hell was vain enough to think he could top Dylan's *Chronicles: Volume One*, the pandering diva he gives her due won a National Book Award for *Just Kids* in 2010. That must have rankled, and must also have seemed within reach.

Which it was. I love *Just Kids*, but it does self-mythologize; for all its shows of humility, Smith's book-length love letter to Robert Mapplethorpe is grandiose. Hell's ego is as big as Smith's, but because his artistic strategy has always been to throw himself off balance, this book feels and to some small extent probably is casual and tossed off, which only makes its roughly chronological wealth of private reminiscences, subcultural anecdotes, character sketches, critical sallies, and metaphysical generalizations harder to resist. Equally disarming is his decision to rebuild burnt bridges—like Dylan, making an effort to thank rivals he may have disrespected in the past. Hell recognizes that, even though it was Television who established CBGB as a rock venue, it was Smith whose rushing river of ambition and charisma opened the punk floodgates. He understands that just like guitar votary Verlaine with Television, he rejected the collectively conceived Heartbreakers because he needed to run a band of his own. He agrees with all the CBGB chauvinists who bitch that Malcolm McLaren and John Lydon stole his "short, hacked-up hair and torn clothes," his "safety pins and shredded suit jackets and wacked-out T-shirts," yet still knows that Johnny Rotten "was about the whole world; I was about myself."

This counterpoint of modesty and self-regard is the essence of Hell's charm. He's an embodiment of hipster cool who explains why he isn't cool at all: "I'm cranky under pressure, I'm a mediocre athlete, I get obsessed with women, I usually want to be liked, and I'm not especially street-smart." Immediately after declaring himself king, he qualifies the claim: "The crown was mine largely by virtue of my appreciation of the realm and because I hated royalty." In this second instance, I should add, Hell's modesty is false flat-out even if you extend the "appreciation of the realm" part to his immersion in the neighborhood and its artist denizens—he was especially devoted to the New York School poets, in particular such second-generation obscurities as Bill Knott, Tom Veitch, and future uber-agent Andrew Wylie. Basically, Hell was king because he'd generated a sensibility so many could emulate and run changes on. Only the Ramones were as seminal, and they were half cartoon.

Although he's self-deprecating about it of course—mocking his early incompetence, shrugging that he "knew how to pick 'em"—Hell was New York punk's great ladies' man, and here again he scrupulously acknowledges his debts. Although his portraits of male musical buddies—Tom Verlaine, Robert Quine, Johnny Thunders, Dee Dee Ramone, Lester Bangs, Peter Laughner—are equalled only by Dylan's in the rock memoirs I've read, he's even more impressive honoring major girlfriends for a few paragraphs or pages: Patty (Mrs. Claes) Oldenburg schooling the artist as a young man; Marisol assistant Anni cushioning their amicable breakup; Aphrodite-with-money Jennifer Wylie and her nice apartment; gracious scenester-photographer Roberta Bayley ("the prettiest breasts I've ever seen"); Stiletto and "slut (like me)" Elda Gentile; supergroupie Sabel Starr ("She truly lived for fun and joy, and the thing that was the most joyous of all to her was to make a meaningful rock musician happy"); lifelong beloved Lizzy Mercier ("hair so wild and abundant it looked like it would have leaves and twigs in it"); "psycho fiend" Nancy Spungen before she bagged Sid Vicious; dominatrix turned sub Anya Phillips before she bagged James Chance; rent-a-punk Paula Yates before she bagged Bob Geldof, shagged Michael Hutchence, and OD'd; photographer and future Mrs. David Johansen Kate Simon ("I didn't treat her right"); big-hearted John Waters/Nan Goldin fetish object Cookie Mueller; childlike Dutch prostitute Liva; and the "stupendously generous" Susan Springfield of the Erasers, who my wife and I would watch from our corner window walking sweetly hand-in-hand with Hell toward his apartment a few blocks east.

Although Hell's title is a childhood memory and it takes him fifty pages to quit high school, exactly or even approximately what turned the kid into such an original remains unclear. Academic father drops dead when he's eight, mom earns Ph.D. while he runs wild, end of unrevealing story. But wild he was—in one jaw-dropping sentence-and-a-half, he signs up for a driveaway car to Texas and totals it drunk in Illinois—and also something special. At goddamn seventeen he hated *Sgt. Pepper* and thought be-ins were corny, but soon he loved the surreal demotic of the New York poets, not least because they were "funny," a favored honorific. On the one hand he believes: "All there is are the entertainments, pastimes, of love and work, the hope of keeping interested." That is, unrequited life's a bore. Yet he's also seen the top of the mountain: "All through this book I've had to search for different ways to say 'thrill,' 'exhilaration,' 'ecstatic.'" Somewhere in between lie both his junkie mentality and his rock and roll genius.

About those two albums, let me quote a passage at length after reining myself for thirteen hundred words, because it's something I've tried to say myself without getting it so right:

> I love a racket. I love it when it seems like a group is slipping in and out of phase, when something lags and then slides into a pocket, like hitting the number on a roulette wheel, a clatter, like the sound of the Johnny Burnette trio, like galloping horses' hooves. It's like a baby learning how to walk, or a little bird just barely avoiding a crash to the dirt, or two kids losing their virginity. It's awkward but it's riveting, and uplifting and funny.

Hell achieved that racket by writing New York School lyrics in rock and roll dialect, by tormenting and tricking and twisting his chronically off-pitch voice into a skewed emotionality with no aspirations to "soul," by egging guitarist Quine into stretching the songs' strictures and wringing their necks so that on the basis of these two albums alone Quine is remembered as an all-time astonishment. I liked those albums when they came out without imagining that they'd be acknowledged classics three decades later, different yet of a piece. Crankily, Hell decided a few years ago to re-record *Destiny Street* with fifty-nine-year-old vocals and avant-garde virtuoso Marc Ribot sitting in for the dead Quine. It still sounded great.

Hell did indeed become "a professional writer." He's published two spiky little novels, a now out-of-print miscellany, some smaller reclamation projects, and a bunch of reportorial and essayistic journalism including an eccentric but knowledgeable movie column stupidly axed in a staff bloodbath, as well as annotating a variety of curatorial projects. Especially in the context of *Destiny Street Repaired*, however, it's significant that two of the latter were retrospectives of his own music assembled for Matador in 2002 and Rhino in 2005. (My wife and I helped out on the latter, although in the end our most important service—which I should emphasize I'm proud of—was commentary so prosaic by his standards that he felt compelled to improve on it, which he did.) And it's even more significant that this book is certain to outsell his autobiographical novels—and that it's better-realized than those novels. There's a sense in which he's stuck with a genius that came in spurts—a genius that coincided inconveniently with his addiction, dismissive though he may be of the pin-eyed lie that heroin is good for your art.

Likely the main reasons Hell chose to end his memoir in 1984 were discretion and respect: "the closer I get in the story to the present day the more problematic it gets to describe situations frankly." He never mentions his twenty-six-year-old daughter by rocker-not-to-be-confused-with Patty Smyth (of Scandal, now wed to John McEnroe) and praises the "incalculable impact" of his wife of ten years without volunteering her full name. But the kicking-heroin-plus-*Destiny-Street* coincidence remains striking. Early on Hell tosses off the commonplace that rock and roll is "the art of teenagers," and although he doesn't riff on this idea much, it does pop up—in Quine's record collection, crammed with one-of-a-kind rockabilly solos, and in a CBGB mythology that's never killed off the know-nothing fallacy that punk was just a faster version of '50s rock and roll. One might ask Hell what kind of a teenager he was when he released *Blank Generation* at twenty-seven and *Destiny Street* at thirty-two. Maybe he'd respond "a self-created one"—he's big on self-creation, as he's earned the right to be. But would that mean the professional writer has lost part of his access to this essential aesthetic capacity?

"A writer's life is fairly uneventful," Hell insists. And compared to the life of a DUI teenager who totals a driveaway, there's a sense in which it is. But there's also a sense in which it's anything but. I'd like to see Hell write about that sometime.

Barnes & Noble Review, 2013

Lives Saved, Lives Lost

Carrie Brownstein's *Hunger Makes Me a Modern Girl: A Memoir* and Patti Smith's *M Train*

To get right down to it, Carrie Brownstein's new memoir *Hunger Makes Me a Modern Girl* is about a life saved by rock and roll and Patti Smith's new memoir *M Train* isn't. Granted, you could say there's an excellent reason for this, and you'd be right. Punk materfamilias Smith, who at sixty-nine is twenty-eight years older than Brownstein and helped invent the music that made Brownstein's titanic Sleater-Kinney possible, took care of the theme in her National Book Award–winning 2010 memoir *Just Kids*, where the last third traces the Patti Smith Group's rise to stardom before culminating with the AIDS death of Smith's fellow kid, first love, and lifelong inspiration Robert Mapplethorpe. But that's too easy, because *M Train* never mentions rock and roll at all. It presents itself as the diary of the year-and-a-half when Patti Smith bought a house—a decrepit bungalow near the Rockaway boardwalk. The year in question was mostly 2012, as we know because (and only because) her real estate adventure is half wrecked by Hurricane Sandy. Yet although *M Train* reports that she toured Europe hard that summer so she could pay for her house, the few performances it details are lectures. We never learn that in September Smith released *Banga*, her first album in five years, or that she was performing with her band and sometimes her son Jackson from June to October. For punk's materfamilias, these are striking omissions, especially in a book that makes so much of her solitude and, by extension, loneliness.

Maybe in twenty-eight years Brownstein will publish something equally sidelong—she's already established herself as a master of ironic indirection in *Portlandia*, the IFC post-sitcom that won her more fame than Sleater-Kinney. Nonetheless, *Hunger Makes Me a Modern Girl* is a straight memoir that begins with Brownstein's childhood and proceeds in engaging, well-paced chapters to Sleater-Kinney's 2006 "hiatus," with a three-page epilogue devoted to their 2015 revival. And although she declines to tell us much about her love life, Brownstein compensates by briefly but incisively describing the uneasy sexual experiments of her youth. But the most formally unconventional thing about her memoir is the rock criticism—reflections on Sleater-Kinney's music woven into a tale dominated by the band's rise to a historical stature every bit as solid as the Patti Smith Group's. Post-hiatus and pre-*Portlandia*, Brownstein contributed a record blog at NPR, and this is a first-rate breakdown, the most insightful writing I know about the band Greil Marcus told *Time* magazine was the best in America in 2001. Marcus is hardly the only critic worth reading to try to explain why his famous rave might be true. Most of us have. But compared to my own labored attempts, certainly, Brownstein's analysis is so sharp and inside it's thrilling.

She explains how Corin Tucker's "completely arbitrary" C-sharp tuning established "a sourness, a darkness that you have to overcome if you're going to create something at all harmonious." How Corin's and Carrie's shared responsibilities for the trio's bass register made their guitars clash as well as intertwine. How dueling guitars joined with vocal countermelodies—which they chose over harmonies without ever discussing it—to set listeners the puzzle of deciding "what to follow" in a song that "sounded like a tightly bound entity, fragments clinging to each other for dear life." How their lyrics addressed issues rather than suggesting stories, often from a meta perspective that examined the band's aesthetic practice. How in 1996 power drummer Janet Weiss—"the most musically gifted member of the band, the one with the largest musical lexicon"—led them into greatness by "translating the secret handshake into a more universal greeting."

But as compelling as Brownstein's rock criticism is, it barely suggests how her life was saved by rock and roll. That's why the third of the book devoted to her upbringing isn't just well told and engaging—swift yet detailed, often funny yet in the end no joke—but formally essential. Although most of Smith's personal history is laid out in *Just Kids*, it's a major presence as well in *M Train*, where her father appears often, and the contrast is striking. Smith reports she grew up so poor her family could afford to take her to the Philadelphia Art Museum only once, thus transforming her life. Yet her factory-worker father was a book-lover who read Plato aloud, her mother gave her a Diego Rivera biography for her birthday, and everyone pitched in when a teenaged Patti conceived out of wedlock and gave the baby up for adoption.

Brownstein, on the other hand, grew up comfortably but also wretchedly upper-middle-class just outside of Seattle—her dad was a corporate lawyer. Although I tend to snort when alt-rockers bemoan adolescence in the lifeless suburbs, Brownstein's is undeniably a horror story—her mother severely anorexic, her father a long-closeted homosexual, the emotional temperature dipping from chilly to frigid by the time her parents split in her mid teens. Add her chronic anxiety, her history of obsessive fandom, and her lifelong compulsion to perform and it's easy to understand why rock and roll was such a good fit for her: "I could play at bravery in the songs, I could play at sexiness or humor, long before I could actually be or embody any of those things."

Thus she became braver, sexier, and funnier. But rock and roll wasn't there to stay. *Hunger Makes Me a Modern Girl* begins with a prologue in which Brownstein's anxiety has manifested in a severe case of shingles that compels her to "destroy" Sleater-Kinney, "the first unconditional love I'd ever known." Her portrayal of the physical and emotional pain of Sleater-Kinney's farewell tour is as harrowing as her tale of the family dog dying of emotional neglect. Having come through the breakup ordeal, Brownstein slowly healed into a successful young arts professional. Yet it's no surprise that this up-and-comer wasn't content with NPR and *Portlandia*—that she felt the need to assemble, record, and tour with the excellent all-female Wild Flag in 2011 and 2012. And it's more than fitting that the book ends by recounting Sleater-Kinney's reunion: "Tears stung my eyes. Corin started the first notes of 'Price Tag,' the opening track on the new album. Two bars later, Janet and I came in. I was in my body, joyous and unafraid. I was home."

Sleater-Kinney's mythic period lasted eleven years, ending when Brownstein was thirty-one. The Patti Smith Group's was much shorter. Since few have mythologized rock and roll with such intensity, aesthetic abandon, or, to quote the author, "abundance of romantic enthusiasm," it's strange to remember that Smith closed her band down after only five years—in 1979, when she was thirty-two. It also signifies that Smith's mythologizing had a distinctly sexual dimension, albeit shamanistic rather than self-objectifying—she invoked sex rather than acting "sexy"—and that in addition she was the less than secret lover of Mapplethorpe, of Sam Shepard, of Tom Verlaine, of the Blue Oyster Cult's Allen Lanier. It was quite a switch when she threw away the star power she'd sought and the Manhattan of *Just Kids* to marry a working-class rock and roller with a much smaller place in punk's genealogy: onetime MC-5 guitarist Fred "Sonic" Smith, with whom she was raising two children in the modest Detroit suburb of St. Clair Shores when her husband died of a heart attack in 1994. *M Train* is indeed about Smith's new old house. It's about her love of coffee and TV detective shows. It's about the art heroes—Genet, Plath, Kahlo, Osamu Dazai—whose graves she visits. It's about the many Polaroids that illustrate it. But haunting it all is the absence of Fred "Sonic" Smith.

This is not an easy book to describe, and naysayers who feel Patti Smith is too full of herself by half will find corroboration within. Those lectures "scrawled," as she puts it, on the napkins of the cafes where she takes her spartan nourishment? A major Patti fan I know witnessed her distracted Pratt commencement address and came away feeling that this was someone who'd learned she could get away with anything. But the reflections and experiences she scrawled for *M Train*, in notebooks she wasn't fated to lose like her faithful camera and her treasured raincoat and the MetroCard she so resents, transported me. There are dreams here, and flashbacks, and digressions, and pointedly quotidian occurrences. There are critical observations about Plath and Bolaño, about Horatio Caine and Kurt Wallander and *Midsomer Murders* and *The Killing*'s Sarah Linden, about Japanese writers too obscure for little old me. There's a laconic imaginary cowpoke uttering apothegms. There are lacunae that announce themselves. But there are also lacunae that don't, prime among them rock and roll. Lenny Kaye, identified as her old friend rather than her old bandmate, gets a fond cameo. But while these are the reflections of a born artist, an artist by inescapable psychological necessity, that artist's life wasn't saved by rock and roll except in the sense that music remains the foundation of an income that's nothing to write home about and a miracle anyway.

Like most of the bunch of albums Smith has recorded since her return to New York in 1996, with Fred two years gone and her fiftieth birthday rushing up, *Banga* rides just enough striking songs to keep a fan's hopes up, with neither the conquistador meditation "Amerigo" nor the blithe trifle "April Fool" sparking nearly the magic of the Neil Young cover "After the Gold Rush." Many rock and rollers make terrific music after fifty, but with important exceptions (Lou Reed, say) it tends to be rock and roll mostly by historical association. Unsurprisingly, the belief that you can get up, over, and out by emoting about it over the right beat proves difficult to sustain. And so it's been with Patti Smith, whose post-mythic material tends reflective, elegiac, at best exhortatory—seldom fast or funny and almost never kick-out-the-jams, as the MC-5 once put it. But she knows kick-out-the-jams made her a myth, and anyone who figures this mode is lost to her altogether should hear the live 2004 remake of her seminal, quasi-orgiastic "Land: Horses/Land of a Thousand Dances/La Mer(de)," which rocks harder for twice the length of the nine-minute original without an extraneous moment. Clearly she still gets it. But it's no longer how she defines her life.

It's easy to forget that in the wake of "Land" *Horses* closes with a brief, fluting envoi called "Elegie" that ends: "I think it's sad/It's much too bad/That our friends can't be with us today." In 1975, this was somewhat anticlimactic. The 2004 version, also twice as long, isn't. It's deeper because both Smith's voice and her hyperactive emotions have deepened, and it names names: Jim Morrison, Jimi Hendrix, Robert Mapplethorpe, her brother Todd Smith, Fred "Sonic" Smith to serious applause, bandmate Richard Sohl to equal applause. In the wake of *M Train*, however, this hardly seems Patti Smith's last word on such matters. Her life was made by rock and roll. But she was a writer first, and it's as a writer that she prefers to express her older, more mortal self.

Presented as a memoir, *M Train* reads more like some kind of poetry. Images, feelings, and characters recur, and the big ones intensify as the book rises brokenly to a close. We read of Fred's funeral and then a month later the sudden death of her bulwark in that moment, Todd. A chapter considers the execution by network fiat of Sarah Linden. Fred looms larger, finally exiting in a dream where he rescues Smith from a precipice and then disappears chasing a clock with no hands. As she remembers her father to begin the final chapter, the sense of loss is pervasive. Smith has laid the groundwork for this sequence some forty pages from the end: "We want things we cannot have. We seek to reclaim a certain moment, sound, sensation. I want to hear my mother's voice. I want to see my children as children." But by the very last paragraph she's managed to understand her life, for that moment at least, as a cosmic gift: "I was my own lucky hand of solitaire."

So how will she deal the next hand? "I'm going to remember everything and then I'm going to write it all down."

Barnes & Noble Review, 2015

The Cynic and the Bloke

Rod Stewart's *Rod: The Autobiography* and Donald Fagen's *Eminent Hipsters*

Quiet as it's kept, the early '70s were not the dark ages of rock'n'roll. They were its economic heyday. Pop music is too big to shrivel up artistically overnight, and with the record business booming more confidently than it ever would again, the magic of venture capital was juicing durable artists of enormous potential and profitability. Think Joni Mitchell, Randy Newman, Bonnie Raitt, John Prine, Linda Ronstadt, all creating music of substance as they embarked on long career paths about whose quiddities we are free to quibble, and all flowering between 1970 and 1975, before punk and disco rendered them passe without tempting them to find another line of work.

In *Rod: The Autobiography* and *Eminent Hipsters*, early '70s arrivals Rod Stewart and Donald Fagen bear witness to their own artistic choices and the career opportunities that ensued in what no one will be surprised to learn are very different books. Credited to Stewart alone, *Rod* is a straight-down-the-middle celebrity memoir presumably put on paper by the only person name-checked in its ninety-seven-word acknowledgments section, "wonderful editor and confidant" Giles Smith of the *London Times*. Written entirely by the auteur himself, Fagen's slim *Eminent Hipsters* is memoiristic only in passing. Its first eighty-five pages sequence ten critical essays, eight previously published, to trace a rough chronology of a "rotten little bookworm's" early life: Boswell Sisters, Henry Mancini, science fiction, Jean Shepherd, '60s jazz clubs, jazz DJ Mort Fega, Ennio Morricone, Ray Charles, Ike Turner, four years at Bard. Although only the Charles and the Morricone flop totally, these pieces tend slighter than I'd hoped from a very bright guy who can write, and I didn't look forward to the 2012 tour diary with which Viking has larded them into a book. But that diary proved an exceptionally sharp and entertaining inside overview of life on the road.

Stewart predated Fagen by a few years. A Scottish plumber's son born in London in 1945, he was singing for his keep before he was twenty, hit the States fronting the Jeff Beck Group in 1968 (at an enthusiastically received Fillmore show where I booed his every overstated white-blues affectation), released his first solo album in 1969, and was propelled into stardom in 1971 by a long, chorusless reflection on May–October romance called "Maggie May." A Jewish accountant's son born in 1948, Fagen is an escapee from the Jersey suburbs who hooked up at Bard with his equally jazz-obsessed partner, Walter Becker. After college the two worked as contract songwriters and then as backup musicians for the biracial Jay and the Americans. Shortly thereafter, they named a band for William Burroughs's favorite dildo and began Steely Dan's unlikely chart run with "Do It Again," a devilishly catchy 1973 hit about self-destructive obsession.

I know it's hard for those who weren't there to understand, but both Stewart and Fagen were counted art heroes in an era when prog, boogie, country-rock, and singer-songwriter mawk were vying for next big thing status. Stewart's *Every Picture Tells a Story* and Steely Dan's *Can't Buy a Thrill* and *Pretzel Logic* are great albums straight up. Moreover, both were accounted "hard" before that word was taken over by the metal that was also rearing its head—"hard" meaning merely not soft like all that other crap. Steely Dan were hard by virtue of their concision, their cynicism, and Fagen's unshowy vocals, Stewart by virtue of his simple eagerness to rock—in the dynamically Band-like band who backed his solo sessions and especially on his job fronting raucous road dogs the Faces, who broke up only when the Stones poached Ronnie Wood and whose running-around-and-falling-over box set should be heard by anyone who thinks *Five Guys Walk into a Bar . . .* is as evocative a title as I do.

Everybody but the millions of fans who attend Rod's shows thinks he was never again as good as solo on Mercury and clowning around with the Faces pre-1975, and I agree. True, I'd say something similar of every other artist named up top while granting that, Mitchell excepted, the drop-off was somewhat more drastic with Rod. Whether the same applies to Steely Dan, however, is a trickier question. Steely Dan were and remain perfectionists, chord-obsessed jazz nuts who in 1974 made what seemed a rational economic decision—they quit the road to turn out better and better records, because records were where the money was (and also because they're neater). Commercially, their coup was 1977's *Aja*, which apotheosized the sonically opulent AOR aesthetic at a level of difficulty glossy rivals like Supertramp and Journey couldn't approach—and which won them a jazz-lite following that makes their original fans very nervous, because we're not suburban cornballs and want everyone to know it.

Stewart, meanwhile, recorded a lot and toured a lot, sporting his rooster haircut and peacock finery all the while. Soon he came to symbolize corporate-rock sellout via two number-one singles: 1976's seductive "Tonight's the Night," where rather than Maggie May showing her age Rod's sex object is a "virgin child," and the deal-killer, 1978's flat-out disco "Do Ya Think I'm Sexy?" Because I had nothing against megahits and considered punk's disco problem small-minded, I liked these records. But I never thought either matched up to "Maggie May" or "Every Picture Tells a Story" or "You Wear It Well" or Jimi Hendrix's "Angel" or especially Mike d'Abo's "Handbags and Gladrags," which won me over to Stewart in 1970 by protesting the generation gap from a granddad's p.o.v. And by the '80s, Stewart's few keepers were covers.

Rod doesn't admit it got this bad, but you don't have to squint to see it happening. I only wish Stewart had told us why he got into music to begin with. Fagen had a swing-singing mom and club-hopping cousins and explains how an adolescent jazz snob might turn to rock in college if enrolled there from 1965 to 1969. Rod the Mod is a football-mad youngest child transformed utterly by Bob Dylan's debut album for reasons he may not even grasp himself, just as he doesn't seem to understand his vocal knack except as a "quirk of fortune," on the one hand claiming kinship with the ductile Sam Cooke and on the other responding to a request to clear the frog from his throat by exclaiming, "Oi, that isn't a frog. That's my voice." Nevertheless, the reckless abandon of the long and terrific Faces chapter makes his long subsequent career seem like a natural fact. For once we meet a rock star who not only loves performing, preferably with a drink or two to loosen him up, but loves touring.

Admittedly, he also loves making more money than most mortals would know what to do with (hint: collect enough "pre-Raphs" to decorate all four of your houses). And he loves many, many fabulously beautiful, unfathomably long-legged blondes (and one redhead)—thee of whom he marries, three more of whom he might well have married, four of whom bear him seven children (plus the one he gave up for adoption when he was eighteen), and every one of whom is a warm and genuine human being, you bet. He also did coke for thirty years without buying a line, and steroids for his voice until he was saved from that perdition by the invention of the earpiece monitor. And somewhere amid all the showbiz drama, the songwriting that never came easy got lost altogether. The best he could manage was the occasional generalized bestseller like his fatuous rewrite of Dylan's "Forever Young," a major comedown from, say, the anti-gaybashing tale "The Killing of Georgie," a gratifyingly unlikely hit in 1977.

But if you're thinking the punks were right about his sellout after all, not so fast. I hate the rich more than you do, but I didn't emerge from *Rod* hating Rod Stewart. Instead I admired his persistence, enthusiasm, and chutzpah, its latest manifestation a much-mocked series of mega-selling twenty-first-century *Great American Songbook* albums that I praised back in 2005 for marking pantheon standards as rock with that Cooke-smitten croak rather than "interpreting" them. I also admire his blokedom—quite a lot of this book is about football, the sport he's not just followed but played into his sixties, and the subculture where he finds his best pals. The least appealing of his blondes is social climber Alana Hamilton, who, Stewart notes with cocked eyebrow, regularly inquired as to the rest of the guest list whenever they were invited out. Warm and genuine human being though she may be, he doesn't seem to have come out of that one craving more of the same.

One reason I ended up so impressed by Stewart's cheerful cheek was the contrast it provided with Fagen's sour puss. Don't misunderstand—the man's mordant dolor has always been tonic at its best, and one virtue of *Eminent Hipsters* is its glimpses into the elective affinities of a sixty-five-year-old cynic who has a life even so. His terse recounting of his stepson's suicide, for instance, leaves no doubt that he bleeds like you or me. Still, for me the most striking essay wasn't the most informative, which would be the one connecting science fiction, L. Ron Hubbard, and something called general semantics. It was the sketch of radio raconteur Jean Shepherd, who, with his voice "cozy yet abounding with jest," inspired me as he did so many teenage "nonconformists" in the metropolitan area of the late '50s and early '60s, and who Fagen followed all the way to a petulant late '65 lecture by a Shepherd turned "aging diva," whose "'hipness' was revealed as something closer to contempt."

Contempt is the great peril of mordant dolor, and the foremost virtue of Fagen's tour diary is how he sometimes indulges, sometimes sidesteps, and sometimes transcends it. This was not one of the Steely Dan tours Fagen and Becker reinstituted in 1993, major profit-takers that induced them to record two more albums decades after falling back exhausted from 1980's stillborn *Gaucho*. But Fagen—accustomed to a level of affluence well below Stewart's and well above most people's, less savvy economically than he once thought, and a musician to his bones in the end—has also toured intermittently in a de facto r&b band co-led by fellow old-timers Michael McDonald and Boz Scaggs. The latest edition, dubbed the Dukes of September Rhythm Revue, spent the summer of 2012 zigzagging in six buses and two trucks between what Fagen emailed his nasty little manager were "dumps"—amphitheaters, arts centers, hotels, resorts, music sheds, music tents, pavilions, bandshells, and ordinary theaters in greatly varying states of refurbishment. Having reported that Scaggs and McDonald often sack out on their respective buses to economize, he also devotes much literary attention to sleeping accommodations that too often become insomnia accommodations as he sinks into ATD—Acute Tour Disorder.

In his affection for touring, Stewart is the exception. Hating touring is state-of-the-art. But few have diagnosed its symptoms—including, among others, panic attacks, stage rage, flashbacks, memory loss, paranoia, diarrhea, and the inevitable insomnia—with Fagen's penetrating eye. Nor does Fagen's cynicism help him cope—as a grouchy old man in autumn plumage, he seethes with contempt for "TV Babies," subliterate young casuals oblivious to "In the Midnight Hour" who use their infernal internet skills to purloin the laboriously perfected tracks to which he sacrificed his youth. I'm grouchy enough myself that I often sympathized. But that was possible because the contempt proved anything but unmitigated. Fagen isn't in it for the money—not exclusively. A part of him loves performing. He's not a blithe spirit like Stewart; he's neurotic as hell. But as a musician he always loves it when the band grooves, a miracle impossible to predict, and as an artist who against all odds believes art requires "a certain level of empathy," he usually loves it when the audience has a good time, a less technical matter. Touring is hard. ATD would seem an inevitability. But it's more complicated than that, and richer. "Every night in front of an audience, no matter how exhilarating, is a bit of a ritual slaying. . . . On some level, you're trying to extinguish yourself. Because, corny and Red Shoes-y as it may seem, that's what you are, and they need it."

Career paths do differ. Cynicism more pathological than Fagen's looms for some. But it says worlds for pop music's vitality that two men as different as Rod Stewart and Donald Fagen could find it so sustaining for so long.

Barnes & Noble Review, 2013

His Own Shaman

RJ Smith's *The One: The Life and Music of James Brown*

My favorite of the many excellent stories in RJ Smith's *The One* describes a gun hustle devised by James Brown's father Joe Brown, to whom Smith devotes more detailed and unfavorable attention than any other Brown biographer to date. Joe Brown and a confederate would approach any man visibly packing and challenge him to shoot them. When he didn't, they would take his gun. Simple once you think of it, right?

This tale told me something I hadn't fully grasped about the roots of Brown's arrogance, which was as unmatched as his sense of rhythm in a calling that has made self-regard its currency since long before Little Richard or Al Jolson—since Charles Dibdin, say, or one of the Himalayan shamans Smith links plausibly to Brown. *The One* tells us more than we may want to know about Brown's people skills. It establishes that Joe Brown brutalized his son, who loved him all his life, as well as James's mother, who Smith believes was less absent than the singer always claimed. It documents James Brown's lifelong gun use, sometimes on the women he brutalized in turn—the Tammi Terrell sequence, which involves a hammer, is especially hard to take. It makes clear that he always supplemented his income from the multiple jobs he was working as of age eight by stealing whatever he could, and argues convincingly that his three years in youth detention taught him what he needed to know about the discipline he imposed on his bands for fifty years. It reports that his faithful guitarist Jimmy Nolen ordered his wife to convey to Brown his dying wish: that Brown treat his replacement better than he treated Jimmy Nolen.

Yet *The One* is no debunk, as even those who worship this incomparably crucial musician should understand. That's because—unlike Michael

Jackson, say—Brown isn't loved as a saint but admired as a titan. All Smith does is put flesh on the control freak we already knew was there. And that isn't by any means the best, freshest, or most diligently researched thing about *The One*, because Smith excels in both his portrayal of Brown's specifically "Georgialina" and then also "Affrilachia" southernness and, even more important, his comprehension of Brown's art. He uncovers two crucial early Brown drummers: French Quarter-born Charles Connor and Clayton Fillyau, a Tampa-based Creole who got a life-changing lesson in the rhythmic concept of "the one" from Huey "Piano" Smith drummer Charles "Hungry" Williams. This prepares the way for a superb breakdown of the decisive tandem of the late '60s, when Brown was inventing funk and modern music: Mobile's Jabo Starks, steeped in both New Orleans second line and the stuttering float of Holiness soul-clapping, and Memphis's Clyde Stubblefield, whose straight eight provided a "strong, broad back for New Orleans drummers to climb on." But he's equally good on cheerful, acid-tripping troublemaker Bootsy Collins, who transferred the funk first from the drums to the bass and then from James Brown to George Clinton.

Although Brown got religion as his public power diminished, Smith makes the crucial point that when it came to gospel Brown "was of the music, but not quite of the faith." This is another way of saying he was his own God, his cape ritual an enacted rebirth that does indeed track back to shamanism even though Brown thought it up himself. He makes the link between Brown's nonstop touring and his prowess as a dancer who incorporated local moves from all over America into a single ever-evolving routine. He demonstrates that for all Brown's talk of black capitalism he was a terrible businessman—"analytic" to his bones, he couldn't delegate because he couldn't trust. But though he treated most of his musicians even worse than he treated Jimmy Nolen, his bandleading was beyond genius. "If you were with Brown for any length of time," Smith writes, "you understood what you would get out of it, and what would never be yours. If you wanted to be a star, this was not the place to be. If you wanted to get rich, or record your own music, or see your name on an album, that was not likely to happen. But if you wanted to see the world and play some amazing music for crowds huge and small, you could not do much better."

In fact, you could not do any better. Amen, Jimmy. Amen, Jabo. Amen, Clyde. Amen, Bootsy. Amen, Mr. Brown.

MSN Music, 2012

Spotlight on the Queen

David Ritz's *Respect: The Life of Aretha Franklin*

The "Also by David Ritz" page of *Respect: The Life of Aretha Franklin* is set in two columns, making room for precisely fifty titles. Only three are biographies per se, and the Marvin Gaye, *Divided Soul*, would also have been a co-authored autobio if Gaye had lived. Although his oeuvre also includes a dozen novels, three co-written with Raelette-turned-reverend Dr. Mable John and two with rapper T. I., Ritz's specialty is the as-told-to, to use a term he likes. His collaborators include the celebrity concert pianist Lang Lang, Don Rickles twice, and matched schlock-rockers Scott Weiland of Stone Temple Pilots, his brother in addiction, and Scott Stapp of Creed, his brother in Christ. But he is especially renowned as a chronicler of black music. Although Ritz has gotten good ink out of Atlantic Records' Jerry Wexler and songwriters Jerry Leiber and Mike Stoller, most of his best-known books are as-told-tos with African-American performers—some as world-historical as junkie geniuses Ray Charles and Etta James, some as dubious or obscure as rap-beating sex creep R. Kelly or gay disco anthemeer turned gay Christian clergyman-activist Carl Bean.

Famously and indeed outspokenly, Ritz is a mouthpiece, not a reporter. He regards it as not only his job but his mission to put his collaborators' version of the past in their own words—words he not only admits but asserts are seldom verbatim, because "literalism" isn't the road to truth. But by no means does the mouthpiece whitewash. On the contrary, because he's earned the trust of so many artists and bizzers, because he's both a sinner and a believer himself, and also, I suspect, because his lifelong stammer opens holes in any conversation while making him seem more vulnerable than he actually is, his collaborators have a long history of telling him all. Thus his work is at least as valuable a historical resource as, for instance, that of the famously scrupulous Peter Guralnick. But there's long been a blot on Ritz's record: the 1999 Aretha Franklin as-told-to *From These Roots*, whose most startling revelation is its use of "gown" as a verb. At Wexler's 2009 memorial service, Ritz—whose stammer renders him a pin-drop public speaker—apologized for having midwifed it into the world. And now he has redeemed himself. *Respect* is a major biography, and unauthorized in the extreme.

Beyond recluses like Axl Rose and Kate Bush, there is no greater enigma in popular music than Aretha Franklin. And however misleading her lack of candor might be for a musical titan millions believe is singing her joy and pain straight from her soul to theirs—and whose artistic and commercial success is based on that effect—you could say that's her right. One reason I interview so little myself is that I don't believe the public's right to know extends to anyone's private life. But that's more unequivocally true of artists who, like Bush and Rose, shun the spotlight. This has never been Aretha Franklin's m.o. As *Respect* demonstrates, she covets the spotlight; since the '60s, she's given *Jet* in particular regular exclusives that amount to press releases. This is less egomania than career management. Until she dies, she intends to be queen. Abdication is not in her.

So however disrespectful it may seem, *Respect* is what she had coming. And ethics or no ethics, anyone who cares about her music will be glad a thoroughly researched account of her life is finally available, not just because facts are gold but because gossip is fun. But although both facts and gossip abound in this fast-reading tome of nearly five hundred pages, there's more. For one thing, fewer than half the words that fill those pages are Ritz's. Having started interviewing his vast black-music network about Franklin long before he embarked on *From These Roots* in 1994, he lets his sources do the talking, and many emerge as full-fledged characters. Foremost is Ruth Bowen, Aretha's on-and-off friend and booking agent until her 2009 death, who Ritz got to know when initiating his as-told-to career with Ray Charles in the mid '70s. And right behind are three Franklin siblings.

Every Aretha fan knows the queen is the daughter of Detroit-based preacher and civil rights activist C. L. Franklin, whose recorded sermons made him a celebrity throughout black America. Most are aware that her backup-singing sisters Erma and Carolyn had notable recording careers of their own, and that Carolyn wrote Aretha's "Ain't No Way." A few have heard tell of her brother and manager Cecil, too. But I at least had never pondered what a hell of a family this must have been. In *Respect*, Erma, Carolyn, and Cecil emerge as supersmart individuals better-educated than the equally intelligent Aretha. And all began spilling the beans on their sister long before Ritz signed up to write *From These Roots*. Cecil, who had a doctorate, and Carolyn, who was a lesbian, both died in their forties of cancer, in 1989 and 1988; Erma became a youth social worker and died of cancer at sixty-four in 2002. All were original and accomplished, and all had tempestuous but loving relationships with their genius sister, just like everybody else she's ever known. Aretha is soulful by definition—fifty years on she epitomizes the concept. But she's also, let's say, emotional. File her under diva if you like. Ritz chooses to go deeper.

In Ritz's analysis, six-year-old Aretha was the sibling most traumatized by her mother's 1948 split from her gallivanting father—nightclub gospel singer Clara Ward proved C. L.'s chief consort, but there were many others. Ritz sees Aretha's choice of a first husband, the abusive gentleman pimp Ted White, as a man strong enough to free her from C. L., who she nevertheless looked up to all her life—and who in Ritz's view deserved her admiration whatever his faults. Ritz establishes that despite her rampant insecurities, Franklin was always strong-willed, ambitious, and acutely competitive, and concludes empathetically that her insecurities were amplified unbearably first by the five-year coma that preceded her father's 1984 death and then by the triple deaths of Carolyn, Cecil, and her matriarchal paternal grandmother Bertha. He praises her conquest of alcohol and chronicles her unending struggle with her weight. He reckons that she's hamstrung her career with a fear of flying that has been absolute for three decades, impeding the cash flow of a gown-obsessed spendthrift who never lets her handbag full of Benjamins out of her sight, even onstage. He reports that she wanted to sue Steely Dan over a couplet from their classic May–September love song "Hey Nineteen": "Hey nineteen, that's 'Retha Franklin/She don't remember the Queen of Soul."

But although the Queen of Soul has to feel violated by these details, and although Ritz was so dismayed by *From These Roots* that he'd have to be Jesus himself to know no schadenfreude now that he's published what he calls his "version" of her story, *Respect* tenders plenty of respect. As both an intellectual and a recovering addict, Ritz has his own ideas about how psychology works. But having spent his life turning half-truths into testaments, he doesn't blame Franklin for her rose-colored evasions: "Idealizing her past was her way of hiding pain." He minimizes mention of the four sons whose privacy she has every right to guard, and reproaches his pal Wexler for spreading the widespread and in Ritz's well-researched opinion demonstrably untrue rumor that the two born while she was a teenager were sired by C. L. (Ritz, who names the likely biological fathers, isn't jiving about Wexler—I was among the many Jerry told that story, way back in 1967.) And most important of all, he writes better than either Guralnick in *Sweet Soul Music* or Franklin herself in *From These Roots* about the precious thing our nosiness springs from: her music.

We know about the power and range and ease of her voice; its grain and timbre, two slightly different things, are more resistant to cognition, so we love them even more. But the irresistibility of her voice only magnifies the temptation to think of her as, to use the phrase Wexler came up with, a natural woman. So Ritz enlists his informants to document her musical acuity. Wexler credits her with inventing the "stop-and-stutter syncopation" that made her "Respect" more epochal than Otis Redding's: "Her taste in vocal riffs and licks was absolutely flawless." Atlantic producer-arranger Arif Mardin praises her "fabulous taste" in songs. Luther Vandross glows about a songwriting ability that set her apart from his adored Diana Ross and Dionne Warwick. Ritz himself celebrates her primacy as a pianist—her own most sensitive and compelling accompanist, renowned for working out arrangements of almost every song she recorded. More gingerly, he also acknowledges that, unlike so many aging stars, she never stopped taking an active interest in the hit parade, perhaps because she realized that her failure to meet disco halfway very nearly stalled her career.

Ritz has done well to recount the life as a whole. Sure he devotes more space to Franklin's ascension and early reign, and it couldn't have helped that so many sources passed prematurely, but he takes the story well into this decade even so. Moreover, his contention that "methods of denial . . . perfected over a lifetime" have shrunk her world is reasonable enough—worlds do shrink, she does have her depressive tendencies, and all the loved ones she's lost are her fate, not her fault. But I'm not convinced things are quite as dire as Ritz believes, in part because we hear her precious music somewhat differently.

Now seventy, Ritz is imbued with all the African-American musics he bonded with coming up, multiple strains of gospel and jazz as well as the r&b that evolved into soul and its offshoots. This is one reason he prefers early Aretha. I'm not talking Atlantic's '60s soul classics, which everyone pretty much prefers. I mean more of the pre-Wexler Columbia kitsch than I can abide, although I've come around to the sweet and pure soprano that swings her bluesy jazz with the Ray Bryant Trio, and have been convinced by Ritz to enjoy pieces of Atlantic's overcrowded big-band *Soul '69*. I also know that if he wants to count the grave two-LP 1972 gospel extravaganza *Amazing Grace* as Aretha Franklin's recorded peak, the market agrees—it's her all-time bestseller. His adoration of 1977's Curtis Mayfield-produced *Sparkle*, on the other hand, is an outlier—the mildly political, audibly gospel Mayfield was Ritz's kind of genius, but far from a sure-shot songwriter. Instead I believe he should have paid more mind to the albums I play most, 1970's casually funky *Spirit in the Dark* and 1972's upwardly mobile *Young, Gifted and Black*, whose daydreaming Aretha original "First Snow in Kokomo" is as serene a domestic fantasy as American pop has produced.

The keyword is "pop," which Franklin considers her rightful realm and Ritz thinks unworthy of her gifts and heritage. Without a doubt Franklin's music has slackened since she joined pop sachem Clive Davis in 1980. Her comeback albums with Luther Vandross and Narada Michael Walden were narrow if effective, and she committed some total crap on Arista as well. But Ritz believes the title track is pretty much where 1998's subtle nuevo-r&b masterstroke *A Rose Is Still a Rose* ends, and slags the very same 2002 Radio City concert I strong-armed my *Village Voice* editor into letting me rave about. I believe these judgments reflect his biases, and it's conceivable that he's made similar mistakes about the life.

When I attended Ritz's book party to congratulate him, he was kind enough to congratulate me in turn—for enjoying, as he could not, RCA's (and Davis's) new *Aretha Franklin Sings the Great Diva Classics*, a return to form I fantasize mightn't have happened if the artiste hadn't known a terrifying tell-all was on its way. It includes Aretha's version of Gloria Gaynor's "I Will Survive," disco four-on-the-floor and all. Gaynor's version survives. But Aretha has dibs on it now. And for sure she's done more than survive herself.

Barnes & Noble Review, 2014

The Realest Thing You've Ever Seen

Bruce Springsteen's *Born to Run*

So what else was he going to call it, asked one reviewer of the big new Bruce Springsteen autobiography *Born to Run*. "Born to Run," as you may know, was the title song of the 1975 album that put Springsteen on the-covers-of-*Time*-and-*Newsweek*, whence he became the freewheeling, hard-touring American hero we know today. But as often happens with this man of the people, the song is trickier than it appears—the lyric more about feeling trapped than breaking free, the music an exhilarating up that's all about escape. You could say it's too grand—Springsteen cites rebel-rousing guitar-twanger Duane Eddy, operatic rockabilly Roy Orbison, and convicted megalomaniac Phil

Spector as inspirations. But its grandeur is subsumed by the layered momentum of eighty-five-mph drums, blood-rousing piano, and tinkling glockenspiel. Is it true, as Springsteen feverishly declares, that he and Wendy plan to die together in their "suicide machines"? Only metaphorically, the music insists. They were born to run again—and then again.

Of course, Springsteen could have chosen a parallel title more in keeping with his grandiose side: *Born in the U.S.A.*, after the title song of the 1984 album he went decaplatinum on, which framed a dark antiwar lyric inside a solemn, deceptively martial groove. Although soon misprised by Ronald Reagan and lesser liars, it's the ur-source of all the Springsteen books whose titles sport phrases like "American poet," "American song," "American soul," and the inevitable "American dream." Yet Springsteen still called his autobio *Born to Run*, and properly so—he's not really a pretentious guy, and anyway, the title serves to emphasize a running metaphor. More times than I had the wit to count, he feels compelled to get on his motorcycle or in his car and race around this U.S.A. he was born in, often for days or even weeks at a time. Then he comes home, generally in a better mood. After thirty-plus years of psychotherapy, he's still running.

That's right, psychotherapy. By now even his most ardent fans have figured out that their hero isn't just a fun-loving bundle of energy fronting three-hour concerts that exhilarate you for your money, and in 2012, David Remnick honored his complexity with a massive *New Yorker* profile in which therapy played a crucial role. But *Born to Run* doubles down on the gambit. It reads like it was written by an analysand—he thanks his shrink by name, in the text rather than the acknowledgments—and that's good. This is someone who's thought a lot about his upbringing, and not just the brooding father sitting in the dark kitchen with his six-pack and smokes who was a fixture of his stage patter from the beginning.

Far more incisive than any biographer's version, Springsteen's account of his early years—say pre-Beatlemania, which hit when he was fourteen—lasts over fifty pages. Although his parents both worked, his mother steadily as a legal secretary and his father usually as whatever he could get, to call the Springsteens lower-middle-class would be pushing it: when he was young, a single kerosene stove provided all the heat in the house. Yet his mother came from money even if it was damaged money—her thrice-married father was a lawyer who did three years in Sing Sing for embezzlement and held court thereafter in a proverbial house on the hill. But it's even more striking that his paternal grandmother was young Bruce's primary caregiver, indulging him so unstintingly that he refused to live with his parents even when he reached school age, sleeping down the block in his grandmother's bed with his grandfather exiled to a cot across the room. "It was a place where I felt an ultimate security, full license and a horrible unforgettable boundary-less love. It ruined me and it made me."

There are no typical childhoods, but this part of the book, which I wish was even longer, cracks through the working-class/South Jersey typology that has long encrusted Springsteen's myth. It's *weird*. And it's also *written*. Put aside your literary preconceptions and taste the two sentences I just quoted. They're a mite awkward, the three commaless adjectives barely in control. But they make a big point loud and clear. Autobiographer Springsteen doesn't command the brash fuck-you eloquence of rock memoirists Bob Dylan, Patti Smith, and Richard Hell, each quite distinct yet all of a piece in their aesthetic verve and acuity. He's cornier. But there's a life to his prose that such high-IQ rock autobiographers as Pete Townshend and Bob Mould don't come near, a life redolent of the colloquial concentration and thematic sweep of his songwriting. Sure he bloviates sometimes. But the book moves, and carries you along.

In Remnick's profile, Springsteen's manager-for-life, intellectual mentor, and dear friend Jon Landau (who as the world's wealthiest former rock critic could have supported more pages, though he gets his share) calls Springsteen "the smartest person I've ever known." Intimates could probably say the same of Dylan, Smith, Hell, for that matter Townshend and Mould. But never think Springsteen has less brain power than these art heroes. Insofar as his book is corny, that's a conscious aesthetic choice he's made for the entirety of his career. It's just that as he's matured he's gotten more conscious about it—and even smarter. Sure he's all about Jersey, as he should be. But his first Jersey was the late '60s one where a hospital in Neptune refused to treat the head injury of a long-haired teen named Bruce who came in after a serious motorcycle accident—there are outsiders everywhere, and the longhair gravitated to them and knows he owes them. Moreover, he also tenders many thanks to Greenwich Village—as a human being, because it bristled with life-changing alternatives to Jersey's manifold limitations, and as an artist, because its poesy-spouting singer-songwriters and bohemian esprit lured him far enough away from his home turf to reflect on it with perspective.

Born to Run is a true autobiography, a thorough factual account of the author's life until now. But since it's an artist's autobiography, it can't do that job of work without telling us stuff about his art. For some this might mean the twelve out of seventy-nine chapters whose italicized titles match those of albums he deems worthy of individual attention, which I found merely useful except as regards his overrated post-9/11 *The Rising*, which indicates that much of it was written pre-attack and then retrofitted to the catastrophe New Jersey's poet laureate felt compelled to address, where the much sharper 2012 *Wrecking Ball* was protest music from its conception. Others will savor the celebrity gossip that's always a selling point of these books—Sinatra knowing a paisan when he sees one, or "the GREATEST GARAGE BAND IN THE WORLD" prepping his "Tumbling Dice" cameo at their 2012 Newark show with a single five-minute rehearsal-space run-through that blows his fanboy mind. But for me both were dwarfed by his reflections on persona and performance.

Never in *Born to Run* does Springsteen claim the mantle of "authenticity" he's forever saddled with. "In the second half of the twentieth century, 'authenticity' would be what you made of it, a hall of mirrors," he says, but also, mirror fans: "Of course I thought I was a phony—that is the way of the artist—but I also thought I was the realest thing you'd ever seen." And if you'd prefer your analysis straighter, there's: "I, who'd never done a week's worth of manual labor in my life (hail, hail rock 'n' roll!), put on a factory worker's clothes, my father's clothes, and went to work." No matter how you slice it, it's an act, or to use a word he loves, a show: "You don't TELL people anything, you SHOW them, and let them decide." To convince them, he works *hard*, Jack, exerting himself as unrelentingly as any manual laborer, because only the audience's boundary-less love can satisfy that deep, ruinous emotional hunger. Yet what you think you see is not necessarily what you're getting. The book's most dazzling single passage is a phantasmagoric two-page recollection of the frighteningly self-conscious "multiple personalities" who battled within him during his very first European performance, at London's Hammersmith Odeon in 1975. Ordeal over, he returns to his hotel room "underneath a cloud of black crows" and feeling like a failure. Only he was wrong—the performance became legendary, and when he worked up the guts to watch film of it thirty years later all he saw was "a tough but excellent set."

Impinging even on these aesthetic reflections, however, you'll notice the familial history that provides not only this full autobiography's substratum but its true subject. You may want more about, say, Pete Townshend, who is quoted fruitfully on how the rock band makes de facto family members out of people you happen to meet as a kid, and his old pal Steve Van Zandt gets plenty of ink, as do departed saxophone colossus Clarence Clemons and departed organ grinder Danny Federici. But Springsteen leaves no doubt that although the show is his lifeline and he may die running, his love life in the broadest sense is what got five hundred pages out of him. Offstage he's been loved and loving from an early age, but between his unconditional grandmother and his silent father, learning to stick at it has been quite the sentimental education. Clearly Dr. Myers was his best teacher until he finally settled on homegirl turned backup singer Patty Scialfa in 1988 and married her in 1991. But although he's not bragging, much of the credit redounds to him.

Full autobiographies generally portray elders more acutely than youngers for the obvious reason that the elders are dead—they can't stop you and their feelings won't get hurt. But in *Born to Run*, Bruce's father Doug ends up packing more mojo than Van Zandt or Landau or Clemons or even Scialfa, and that's unusual. The story returns to Doug when it doesn't have to—no one would have missed that fishing trip. The account of his senescence, when he was finally diagnosed with not one but two major psychological disorders, is topped off with a bravura description of his body—"elephant stumps for calves and clubs for feet"—in the final hours of his life. Which in turn is topped by a briefer tribute to Bruce's miraculous mother, still radiating "a warmth and exuberance the world as it is may not merit" as she navigates Alzheimer's at ninety-one.

Scialfa doesn't resonate as vividly as his parents—discretion no doubt intervened, and is presumably why the redolently homely divorce case naming Bruce as a respondent goes unmentioned. Nonetheless, she's the silent hero of this book. Springsteen was never a dog, but from his teens he was a serial monogamist with lapses who acknowledges with less vanity than chagrin that he went through a lot of women, including his first wife, the model Julianne Phillips. Scialfa benefited from Dr. Myers's spadework as well as the failed Phillips experiment. She's no beacon of calm because that wouldn't work at all—she'd better the hell stand up to him. But she gives her husband the superstar version of a normal life he's clearly craved since a childhood that taught him he couldn't have one—a life both his maturing art and his everyman politics impelled him toward. Even the three kids are richly described, with discretion well served by focusing on their very different early years—in a passage few autobiographers would adjudge worth their literary while, Scialfa jawbones him first into getting up with the kids and learning to make pancakes and then into giving young Sam his late-night bottle-and-story. As he puts it: "She inspired me to be a better man, turning the dial way down on my running while still leaving me room to move."

Born to run, yet happy with room to move. The artist's story is worth telling. But so is the man's.

Barnes & Noble Review, 2016

All selections identified as having originated in *The Village Voice* are reprinted by permission, copyright the year indicated by *Village Voice*, LLC.

Some of the articles in this book originally appeared in *The New York Times* and are reprinted here by permission.

"The Impenetrable Heroism of Sam Cooke: Peter Guralnick's Dream Boogie," previously published as "In Search of Sam Cooke" © 2005, *The Nation.*

"His Own Shaman" originally appeared on MSN Music, Microsoft's online music website located at http://music.msn.com/.

PART V
FICTIONS

Writing for the People

George Orwell's *1984*

I've now read *1984* three times—once as a Queens teen in the '50s, once as a budding leftist in the '60s, and once as a pop pundit a year before the final gun approaches—and if anything I've been more affected by it each time. Yet because the pundit in me hasn't given up the lessons of his lower-middle-class origins or his radical coming of age, he feels a little defensive about this. In the silly tug-of-war over the current political affiliation of a man who died three years before Stalin, *1984* and *Animal Farm* are the chief exhibits for the opposition—Norman Podhoretz in *Harper's*, for instance. Those leftists who don't believe he and Podhoretz deserve each other reply that Orwell never stopped calling himself a socialist, or thinking like one. But they're clearly more comfortable with the Orwell who wrote *Homage to Catalonia* in the late '30s—the freedom fighter whose commitment to working-class revolution snapped into place at the same time as his opposition to the Soviet Union, during the Spanish Civil War.

It's silly to speculate about where Orwell would stand in today's politics because we don't prize him for his positions—we prize him for his independence. His understanding of economics was sketchy, he seemed unaware that women (much less homosexuals) might constitute an oppressed group, and although he was a passionate and prophetic anti-imperialist, it's hard to imagine him feeling any less disdain for the mess of third-world politics than, let us say, V. S. Naipaul. But he hated repression of any sort so viscerally that it's equally hard to imagine him mouthing neoreactionary rationalizations in which torturers are transformed into the bad best hope of Latin American democracy. So as he approached eighty, Orwell would no doubt still be a maverick, valued most of all, as always, not for his political content but for his attitude, his persona, and his writing itself.

Since Orwell believed very emphatically in letting "the meaning choose the words, and not the other way about," this may seem needlessly paradoxical. But in fact Orwell's obsessive ideas about prose constituted a metaphysic that was the ground of his authority. Springing as it did from his deepest political convictions, this metaphysic was the source of his political credibility.

The clarity, candor, and common sense of Orwell's style made a kind of transcendent ideal out of ordinary English decency. Amid the rhetoric and romanticism of literary Marxism he strove to speak for plain people whose lives were dedicated mostly to getting on. A colonial and Etonian with a taste for slumming, he probably never knew those people as well as he wanted or claimed—V. S. Pritchett once commented that he had "'gone native' in his own country." But if only because it was in him to try, he got a lot closer to them than most of his peers, and you could feel that in his words. Thus his forebodings about authoritarianism always seemed more down-to-earth than those of Arthur Koestler (or later, Hannah Arendt). And thus would-be populists of the left and right still think he's worth squabbling over.

Because Orwell died in 1950, just a year after *1984* was published, it's come to seem his last word on man's fate, which it wouldn't have been, if only because most of its prophecies were incorrect. Certainly Orwell's vision of an earth ruled by three superpowers was prescient (although he did underestimate the third world's potential for autonomy). But he had the big picture wrong in three crucial respects. First, he was convinced that the '50s would bring worldwide atomic war (one reason he grew so attached to his farm in the Hebrides was as a haven). Second, he partook of the traditional left awe of technology, which he considered illimitable (never wondered about energy) and capable in principle of meeting all human needs (never wondered about food). Third, he believed Stalin's U.S.S.R. and Hitler's Germany represented only the primitive beginnings of totalitarianism, whereas they have thus far proved its nadir. Not that electronic surveillance doesn't now facilitate thought control, or that Pol Pot's Cambodia and Khomeini's Iran and Pinochet's Chile aren't unspeakably horrifying, or that the Gulag and for that matter the Chinese educational system don't qualify as totalitarian. In thirty years, however, nobody has matched both the scale and the sadism of Hitler's or Stalin's lust for control. Small comfort, and I'm not holding my breath. But I'm also not predicting that the Hitler/Stalin spirit must inevitably dominate the planet the way it does in *1984*.

Yet as it happens the truth value of this proposition is beside the point, because regardless of its realism or lack of same, regardless of how it distorts Orwell's best message, a fixation on the will to power is the secret of the novel's artistic triumph. And it's this triumph, of course, that well-meaning leftists wish they could pick holes in. In *1984*, even more than in the relatively digestible (and dismissible) *Animal Farm*, Orwell achieves the popular contact his political instincts always drove him toward; to attribute the novel's enormous, unflagging appeal to the machinations of anti-Soviet propaganda barons is to indulge in the left's customary cultural elitism and myopia. Where *Darkness at Noon* now seems a terrifying period piece, *1984* reveals less as a satire than as a feat of pop sensationalism not all that different in effect from such sci-fi dystopias as Richard Fleischer's *Soylent Green* or John Brunner's *The Sheep Look Up*. Insofar as the novel escapes the usual critical insults—"manipulative," "melodramatic," etc.—it's protected by Orwell's serious and humane persona. He's so obviously a high middlebrow on the same level as those who favor such antipopulist rhetoric that he's immune to charges of commercialism, although not to ad hominem speculations about his dark fascination with the sadistic and the authoritarian—speculations that I figure might just as well be true, because I make it an article of faith that books that carry a real emotional charge tap something deeper in a writer than mere craft. And the hold of this book is so widely acknowledged that I suspect those who resist it of having something to hide, like those who claim to be bored by pornography.

Perhaps what they're hiding (or hiding from) is the old paradox of power on the left—seeking it in order to dismantle it. There would seem to be a logic, after all, in which those who succeed in dismantling their own power will ultimately fall under the control of those who don't, or who never intended to in the first place. This premise is what makes *1984* even scarier than the typical futuristic horror-show, although Orwell, like any good thriller writer, doesn't reveal it until he's thirty pages from the end. "The Party seeks power entirely for its own sake. We are not interested in the good of others; we are interested solely in power. Not wealth or luxury or long life or happiness: only power, pure power." The idea that a version of this premise might be true, or even possible, is the Room 101 of left intellectuals, and some of them will never forgive Orwell for making it come alive.

But nobody suffers more under Ingsoc (Newspeak for English socialism) than Orwell himself. *1984* is a nightmare of his own devising, a suffocating, self-enclosed system that embodies all his worst fears, every one of which proceeds or at least gains plausibility from the notion that "the object of power is power." Orwell's attachment to the abiding details of daily life, his conviction that change must begin with the needs and desires of ordinary people, and above all his faith in clarity, candor, and common sense—all are turned on their heads. Because the Party won't utilize technology for "the good of others," there are no simple comforts under Ingsoc—everything is cheap, broken, stunted, ersatz, unavailable, as if the deprivations Orwell experienced on the down-and-out side of the Depression have imposed their texture on all of history. The people have become the proles, as incapable of improving their lot without leadership, which is methodically and gleefully weeded out from above, as were the lumpen with whom a younger Orwell roughed it. And for someone who lives through language, the world of *1984* is worse than a nightmare: it's a madhouse without doors or windows at zero gravity, with nothing, nothing at all to hold on to.

Clearly, then, the physical and social dimensions of Orwell's nightmare can be dismissed as one man's bad dream, although certain specifics make more sense than they usually get credit for—notably, the joyously expedient carnality of Winston Smith's love affair with Julia and the condescending depiction of the proles (who are always viewed through the eyes of Smith, a slummer like Orwell with more excuse). But while it makes some sense to accuse Orwell of metaphysical crudity—a priori and a posteriori get confused in the book's argument at times—his linguistic analysis grounds the novel as decisively as his will-to-power premise, and it's just as substantial. Given the author's fervent belief that meaning precedes language, the process whereby Smith is persuaded that a photograph he just saw never existed or that two plus two equals five obviously terrified Orwell beyond all reason, but it's an evasion to pass off his terror as irrational. Bernard Crick wonders whether social encounters with logical positivist A. J. Ayer mightn't have set off some of his fears, but there can be no doubt that their root inspiration was the means-justify-ends flim-flams (doublethink, you can call it) that so many left intellectuals engaged in during the Stalin era—and which all principled supporters of revolutionary terrorism, myself included, have flirted with for close to two decades. If A. J. Ayer gave Orwell the willies, ponder for a moment what he would have thought of structuralism.

I hope my allies don't misunderstand my position here. I still support revolutionary terrorism in extreme instances (such as South Africa, where it almost always targets infrastructure not people), and have no doubt the structuralists are onto something real; unlike Winston Smith, I treasure emotionally integrated sex, and I respect the proletarians I grew up with, too. But my reservations about the first pairing—terrorism should be a last resort, linguistics should supplement common sense rather than superseding it—are linked to my awareness of how contingent both my sex life and my class consciousness are: neither would have developed naturally, if at all, in a repressive society. For left intellectuals to pretend that plain Americans are brainwashed into fearing repression above all else is a distortion—if anybody's brainwashed it's the Americans plain and fancy who don't. In short, both the power and the paradoxes of *1984* are worth taking very seriously.

It's a cautionary image of a world we don't want to make. And if we think we're safe just because it hasn't literally come true, we don't deserve to call ourselves leftists *or* intellectuals.

Village Voice, 1983

A Classic Illustrated

R. Crumb's *The Book of Genesis*

Not to belabor the obvious, but *The Book of Genesis* is the first book R. Crumb has published that isn't funny. Awright, I'm ignoring the cityscapes and posters and flyers and record covers and blues cards, not to mention the straight portraiture that dots the seventeen volumes of Fantagraphics' *The Complete Crumb Comics* and Fantagraphics' ten Crumb *sketchbooks* and also dominates the three collections of placemat drawings published as *Waiting for Food*—portraiture that although derived from cartooning's funny-animals tradition also justifies the Daumier and Hogarth comparisons with which the smut-mongering master draftsman is now routinely explained to the gallery market. So make that *narrative* book, and remember that funny needn't imply hilarious or knee-slapping—it can also be wry or sly or mischievous or, to get back to Daumier and Hogarth, satiric.

Good satire is rarely knee-slapping because it already hurts too much. That's sure how it is with *The Complete Crumb Comics Vol. 17*'s "People . . . Ya Gotta Love 'Em," in which an atypically bare-chested Crumb grapples and excuse-mes his way through fifteen largish panels crammed to their freehand borders with other similarly unclothed human beings before finally reaching his goal, the "43 percent toxic" sea. And ready or not it also describes the notorious "A Bitchin' Bod," which gets thirteen full-color pages in *The R. Crumb Coffee Table Art Book*. Premise: Mr. Natural stuffs the head of belle ideal Devil Girl into her body so Flakey Foont can adore and abuse her nether regions without impediment.

The Book of Genesis Illustrated has way more than draftsmanship going for it and it's not satiric—it's objective, almost sober. Relying respectfully but critically on onetime *Commentary* editor Robert Alter's scholarly, literary translation, Crumb hand-letters every word of Genesis onto the page and depicts them all. Although Christian conservatives will deplore its wealth of goodly breasts, scattering of modest penises, and occasional R-rated sex panels, these no-nos are all described or implied by a text the artist refuses to bowdlerize. It's *Classics Illustrated* done right, and as such will be hailed as Crumb's crowning achievement, especially by the Daumier-Hogarth crowd.

What won't be much noted is that it's also a retreat. Try to count how many adepts of a low, entertaining, supposedly cheap or simplistic genre have set out to prove they were capable of greater things: Charlie Chaplin's *Limelight*, Woody Allen's *Interiors*, Duke Ellington's sacred music, Green Day on Broadway, comics icon Will Eisner devoting his golden years to a graphic novel exposing *The Protocols of the Elders of Zion*. Some of these works are better than others, but all betray a longing for status and "substance" also apparent in Crumb's Genesis. What's more, Genesis also represents a retreat from Crumb's other artistic gift, for in addition to being handy with a Rapidograph he can write—that's part of the craft. True, Crumb often collaborates with his wife, cartoonist Aline Kaminsky—the visual disparities were stark at first, though she's narrowed the gap—and illustrated some of his Cleveland buddy Harvey Pekar's early work. But he's always scripted his own stories. And that hasn't been getting any easier.

In fond retrospect, the Crumb of the '60s stands as a beacon of toughmindedness distinctly delineated against the enticing haze of Haight-Ashbury hippiedom, an artist who partook more of East Coast pop than West Coast psychedelica and regularly punctured San Francisco's flower-power naivete and mystical hoodoo. But when you reread his comix colleagues, you realize that from gag writer Gilbert Shelton to zapped surrealist Bill Griffiths they were all satirists who targeted counterculturists as well as straights. What distinguished Crumb (and made him seem so pop) was his technique—his firm line and honed detail, the cuteness ingrained in him by his apprenticeship in the greeting-card business. And turning his satire up a notch was his own weakness for hoodoo. With his shortish hair, suit jackets, and purist distaste for loud modern music, the Philadelphia-raised Crumb never identified as a hippie. But he took acid early and arrived in San Francisco hungry for dope and free love. Acid, whose effects he conveyed with matchless sardonic zest, directly engendered his signature characters—the males aspects of himself from trickster guru Mr. Natural to square-looking seekers like Eggs Ackley, the females built to his sasquatchian sexual specifications—and the big-footed "Keep On Truckin'" shtick that made *Zap Comix* such a sensation.

Crumb's '60s comics are stoned fables about the goofy perils of getting stoned and stoneder fables about the goony perils of staying straight. They generally end in a what-me-triumph? shrug that tweaks the limits of hip comedy, the dark master themes Crumb has in him kept in check by the prevailing cultural optimism and the upsurge in his personal fortunes. Soon enough, however, sexual obsession and existential despair came to the fore as his content turned overtly autobiographical. By his own account, Crumb was churning it out in the early '70s, and his uneven output since then suggests that this problem persisted. Yet though his level of inspiration fluctuated—the Bob-and-Aline stories especially seem tired sometimes—Crumb's productivity remained impressive, and jaw-droppers continued to arise from his febrile subconscious.

Consider the thirty-eight-page "Bad Karma" in 1999's *Mystic Funnies No. 2*, where a new character named The Moron trods in his work shoes over hurting fields of upturned human faces, falls into the abyss, finds himself reborn in the arms of the callipygous Fairy Godmother, enjoys eleven pages of explicit sex that climaxes on one of her boots, gets dumped for a handsome blond guy, and goes to seek his fate in a wilderness of impassable brambles. This marriage of hell and heaven could only happen in Crumbworld. But you can see why its creator might hanker for spiritual truth that has some finality to it. The Bible, for instance.

Like me, Crumb was a serious churchgoer into his teens. Because he was a Catholic and I was a born-again Presbyterian, he probably read the Bible less than I did, and in the Douay version, which is less poetic than the King James. Nevertheless, I presume from my own experience that scripture left its stamp on Crumb's sense of language, deepened by his active interest in the cosmic and the guilt that haunts him so. Yet I'm obliged to report that when I reread the King James Genesis as a warmup, I found it tough going—Ecclesiastes and even Joel proved markedly more pleasurable. The Genesis stories are very old and, especially as redacted by intermediaries with doctrinal agendas, remarkably obscure. It's one thing to dimly recall their unlikelihood and barbarism, another to re-encounter two conflicting accounts of the creation, to wonder where the sons of Adam found their wives, to do the arithmetic on the begats, to roll your eyes at the incest and polygyny, to look on as Levi and Simeon slaughter a cityful of just-circumcised Schechemites because Schechem lay with their sister Dinah, to see how Joseph gets rich by inducing Egyptian peasants to trade starvation for serfdom. Also, the language lacks flow, in part because documenting the children of Israel requires so many otherwise forgotten proper nouns. Next time you need to name two cats, male of course, how about Muppim and Huppim? Better than Serug and Arphaxad, right?

None of this fazed Crumb, who believes the world is a brutal place, keeps an open mind about all paranormal phenomena including God, and really likes Old Things. So he just drew the pictures. Except on the cover, these are strictly black-and-white, making the most of his phenomenal crosshatching. They're also, as noted, sober—evidence of Crumb's increasingly explicit commitment to realism, with the cuteness he's despaired of excising imperceptible except perhaps on Noah's ark. The women are hefty without looking like tryouts for "Baby Got Back," and the far more numerous men are painstakingly differentiated—arrayed like postage stamps across a two-page spread, the head shots of Jacob's fifty-eight grandsons could come straight out of the Damascus A&M yearbook. The sex panels radiate a playful affection absent from Crumb's porno, ya gotta love the crowd scenes, and what my King James calls "the battle of four kings against five" suggests a tapestry in which some medieval genius has miraculously solved the problem of motion.

To say Crumb's tone is objective is not to deny that he adds content. Because he's visualizing, he pretty much has to. Robes and tunics are ragged until hems come in with Abraham. Two drops of blood spatter into the bottom of the frame at Ishmael's circumcision. The Sodomite louts who storm Lot's house have the body language of chop-shop brokers at a sports bar. Schechem and Dinah gaze into each other's eyes. Sarah—this is a strange one—stands before Abimelech in a sheer top that shows off her nipples. Reaction shots abound—Adam and Eve abashed, Jacob fearful, Esau beaming, Joseph magisterial. And facially, Crumb provides plenty of broad characterization. Noah seems permanently dazed by the magnitude of his responsibility. Buffeted between Sarah and El Shaddai all his life, the submissive Abraham starts looking patriarchal as things go his way. Rebecca begins as a generous lass and ends up a scheming yenta. Joseph grows thoughtfully into his authority.

Funny, however, is not in him here, not even in the chapters where Jacob spends twenty years working for Rebecca's swindling brother Laban before he can return to Canaan married to his cousins Leah and Rachel. In his notes, Crumb calls this "bedroom-comedy relief," but unless you count the panel where Leah's youngest drives her bonkers or get a kick out of Jacob's mysterious tricks with the streaked and speckled goats, you'd never guess it from looking. Similarly, although Crumb's notes praise Savina J. Teubal's

Sarah the Priestess, which without having attracted the attention of supposedly encyclopedic annotator Alter argues convincingly that the Genesis stories are obscure because they've been doctored to hide their matriarchal content, that theory has to be inferred as well.

Supporting the inference are all those hefty women. Rather than mount a full defense of Crumb's supposed misogyny, an understandable but misguided charge, I'll just point out that Crumb's very public relationship with Aline Kaminsky as well as such unusual fetishes as thick ankles and wide feet indicate a man drawn to women who are strong. STRONG. If you think about it, Sarah, Rebecca, and Rachel, Teubal's "matriarchs," have a soulfulness and sense of purpose in Crumb's rendering that the patriarchs lack, not least because they're always cowering before the Big Patriarch—the Almighty, YHWH, El Shaddai.

Unlike Teubal in her agenda-driven moments, Crumb doesn't assume that these women are staunch in sisterhood or warmly communal. But neither does he figure out a way to hint at Teubal's best idea, which is that Genesis's true subject is a world-historical shift from matriarchal cooperation to patriarchal individualism. If that's what's going on with the sheer top, which by sexualizing Sarah's relationship with Abimelech shores up Teubal's highly speculative surmise that the Philistine king became Jacob's biological father in a hieros gamos ceremony with Sarah the priestess, no one will ever know. In some mix of formal discipline, intellectual modesty, and fear of failure, Crumb declines to turn Genesis into a either a comedy or a tract.

Thus Crumb's Genesis remains a sacred Old Thing, which is fine in one way and just slightly disappointing in another. Let others rail about misogyny; what bothers me most about Crumb is an extreme distaste for modernity that only starts with his limited musical capacities. This prejudice has been great for his drawing—in a cartooning whose mainstream is the design-heavy melodrama of superhero comics, Crumb's funny-animals tradition is retro in an exceptionally fruitful way. But for those of us taken with the patriarchal notion that it's good for humanity to marry outside the clan—a community of belief that includes Crumb and his proudly Jewish wife—the old ways are seldom the best. *The Book of Genesis Illustrated* has many virtues. But the best thing about it is that it exists at all, a reproach to anyone offended by the very notion that Christendom's murky origin myth is available to the mind and hand of the guy who invented "Keep On Truckin'."

Barnes & Noble Review, 2009

The Hippie Grows Older

Richard Brautigan's *Sombrero Fallout: A Japanese Novel*

Richard Brautigan inspired some foolish praise in his time, a time that ended almost as soon as it began, but he never angled for it and that is to his credit. He is a serious writer, certainly, but the mark of his seriousness is in his craft, especially as a stylist; he is not pretentious. Thus his 1971 novel, *The Abortion*, is dedicated to someone named Frank, apparently a slow reader: "come on in—/read novel—/it's on the table/in front room. I'll be back/in about/2 hours." And the protagonist of his new book is identified as a "very well-known American humorist." Not novelist or poet, not even writer—just humorist.

For at his best that is what Brautigan is. Compared to Doris Lessing or Frank O'Hara he's a midget, but he stands tall enough next to Woody Allen or even Robert Benchley or George Ade; on a small scale he has been an original and an innovator. As might have been predicted, however, *Sombrero Fallout* does not represent Brautigan at his best. Not only is it the least funny of his books, but its paucity of humor is intentional, capping a dilemma that would appear to be permanent: he no longer knows what to write about.

The three novels that brought Brautigan his fame around 1970—*A Confederate General from Big Sur*, *Trout Fishing in America*, and *In Watermelon Sugar*—were reprints. They were written in the early and mid '60s, when Brautigan was an impecunious, poetry-writing bohemian from northern California. It isn't likely that he foresaw the role bohemians from northern California were about to assume in the national imagination any more than anyone else did. But he will survive as the literary representative of that phenomenon in American culture known as The Hippies.

Brautigan's reputation is based on a surrealism notable for its grace, its matter-of-fact flow—his narrative technique is so conversational and pellucid that preternatural details and crazy coincidences don't even ripple its surface. (Certain rock lyrics, carried along on the beat, achieve a not dissimilar effect. In fact, Brautigan gets major competition in the realm of hippie art from the Grateful Dead, who make up for not being funny by being good to dance to.) But his best work—especially *A Confederate General from Big Sur*, but also *Trout Fishing in America* and the more memorable stories—is realistic much of the time, as remarkable for its content as for its form. Brautigan documented a way of life in which his style of surrealism was almost second nature, evoking '60s bohemianism far more intensely than Kerouac ever did the '50s kind. His world was passive and goofy; his voice displayed whimsical if not coy amazement at the most banal of events. As he teetered between the edge of comfort and the edge of survival, Brautigan was often sad but never pessimistic.

As the broad attraction of this gentle vision among the literate young became apparent, however, Brautigan found himself transformed from an impecunious bohemian into a successful popular author. It was a big change, and he knew it. Each of the three novels to appear after his success—*The Abortion: An Historical Romance 1966* (1971), *The Hawkline Monster: A Gothic Western* (1974), and *Willard and His Bowling Trophies: A Perverse Mystery* (1975)—is subtitled to indicate some sort of play with a popular literary form. What's more, after *The Abortion*, a bohemian novel much fatter and more perfunctory than the earlier ones, Brautigan tried to do what popular authors do—invent plots and characters. He has not proven to be especially good at this, and his failure seems to have cut into his optimism quite a bit.

The full title of the new book is *Sombrero Fallout: A Japanese Novel*. The subtitle is ambiguous; the book is dedicated to a Japanese novelist of the respectably perverse whose main similarity to the old optimistic Brautigan is his brevity. But if in two previous novels Brautigan has toyed with popular forms, this time he resorts to one of the most hackneyed of pretentious literary devices: the self-conscious, self-lacerating author/protagonist and his novel within a novel.

This self-laceration is not without interest. A feature of Brautigan's novels has been charming but finally unconvincing love affairs with pliant young women who are always very pretty and always good in bed. On occasion the affairs have been sad or failed, and last time there was even a tragic one (out of two); this time, however, the relationship is what you'd expect of a man who imagines women so pliant—candidly exploitative and neurotic, entirely defined by the "very well-known American humorist," whom Brautigan dissects with a fine, cruel hand.

Meanwhile, the novel within the novel—in which a surrealistic detail, a frigid sombrero, precipitates a disastrous mob action that takes thousands of lives—is so gratuitously nihilistic that Kurt Vonnegut takes on the weight of the prophet Jeremiah by comparison. Does this pessimistic turn merely reflect the derangement of his lovelorn protagonist? Or does the mob action also reflect the way Brautigan feels about the hordes of young people who read his books? One senses yet another artist who feels defeated by his audience and longs for simpler times. And one wishes to remind him that times were never that simple, and that the audience is out there affecting your life whether you know it or not.

New York Times Book Review, 1976

Comic Gurdjieffianism You Can Masturbate To

Marco Vassi's *Mind Blower*

Reading great pornography for aesthetic satisfaction is like getting laid when you want to dance—the desired consummation is available in the material, but unless you're very lucky it will distract you from the point. Which is why I hadn't ever read this book from cover to cover until now even though I almost know it by heart. For unlike all that airless French crap, *Story of the Eye* to *Story of O*, *Mind Blower* is designed to be used first and appreciated later. Published by French porn king Maurice Girodias during his American sojourn, Marco Vassi's first novel is about death, self-transcendence, and so forth, but most of all it relishes the facts of sucking and fucking. And in this supposedly sex-obsessed culture—in this world—there's nobody who always sucks and fucks with the relish those sacred, difficult, absurdly finite acts deserve.

Although Vassi's language and ideas tend purple, always a pitfall in ambitious porn, his structure and tone are at bottom comic. Set in Doctor Isador Tocco's Institute for Sexual Metatheatre, which like a Sade castle serves Vassi as a hermetic environment in which his ecstatic scenarios are protected from social and economic contingencies, *Mind Blower* is as '60s as its title. For Doctor Tocco, the immolation in pleasure that so fascinates pornographers suggests a Gurdjieffian mysticism; he prescribes discarding the concept of personality (hence romantic love, not to mention jealousy) so that it can be reclaimed at a more comprehensive level of consciousness. After the narrator, Michael, abandons his quest for a shared "image orgasm" (mere physical simultaneity is of course a snap), he joins three fellow metaphysicians in a climactic four-way that's one of the most intense and emotionally credible accounts of group sex in erotic literature. But then the joint is raided, and Michael is reduced once again to consorting with swingers in pickup bars. These are "not serious people," he muses disconsolately, and as he lies back to facilitate a blowjob vows that he will begin his "search for Tocco . . . tomorrow." Ellipsis in original. The End.

It's Vassi's willingness to take his orgiastic vision as seriously as its comedy permits that charges his descriptive writing. But it's his sense of detail that turns on a faithful earthling like myself. One of the few genuinely bisexual pornographers, which is hardly to imply that he's free of male bias, Vassi loves the little ridged cavern where scrotum becomes asshole as much as the pink pout of engorged labia, and explodes the philistine cliche that sexual organs (and acts) are all essentially alike. Not that there's anything but fear or prudery to prevent the reader from bringing the erotic energy he generates back home. But if necessary you can take it out to a pickup bar, or into your own hands.

Village Voice, 1981

Porn Yesterday

Walter Kendrick's *The Secret Museum: Pornography in Modern Culture*

Two interwoven arguments carry *The Secret Museum* to one overriding conclusion: that the censorship of sexually explicit materials is dangerous, foolish, fruitless, or at least ill-conceived. So Walter Kendrick seems to intend, anyway. The decisive evidence of what he thinks he's brought off comes in his next-to-last sentence, when he sums up the two arguments with a brevity that's both remarkable and typical of his exhaustively researched 239-page text: "'Pornography' is not eternal, nor are its dangers self-evident."

Before you ask what else is new, give the man room for the tone and context half a sentence can't convey. Since the planet itself isn't eternal, that word may look overblown, but when Andrea Dworkin et al. trumpet *Hustler* and *The 120 Days of Sodom* as the root of all suffering, they're the ones who endow pornography with power verging on the cosmic. Kendrick proves beyond a doubt that the term "pornography" dates only to the mid-nineteenth century, and makes a strong if not air-tight case that the cultural phenomenon it's come to signify isn't much older. If *The Secret Museum* accomplished nothing else, this would be an essential contribution to a controversy that definitely ain't over yet. Unfortunately, the same can't be said for "nor are its dangers self-evident," self-evident though it may appear. That's because it's a real argument, not just a sharp piece of research. Or rather, it ought to be an argument and isn't. Kendrick isn't good at arguing. Though he's a critic by profession, his narratives persuade more powerfully than his analyses. The surface of his abstract writing achieves a remarkable clarity, but exactly where it's going can be hard to figure out.

One problem is that *The Secret Museum* affords none of the customary discursive amenities: it begins at the lexicographical beginning, and after a chapter of backtracking proceeds to the present with never a preface, introduction, conclusion, or the-story-so-far. Compounding the confusion is its subtitle, *Pornography in Modern Culture*. Given Kendrick's long-standing fascination with Victoriana, it's no surprise that by "modern" he means twixt preindustrial and postmodern, but it is a disappointment; two-thirds of the way through he's still tarrying with Anthony Comstock, and he doesn't reach *Ulysses* until fifty pages from the end. Nor does he pay anywhere near as much attention to pornography per se as to its suppression. In substance, *The Secret Museum* is a history of scholars, crusaders, and jurists who are described and interpreted in more detail than any of the works that happened to excite their interest. The past twenty years, which most would describe as pornography's high-water mark if not golden age, are for Kendrick "the post-pornographic era"—except for *Hustler*, immortalized by its tireless PR rep Dworkin, not a single title is cited.

In fact, although he never says so, Kendrick's subject seems to be a cultural tendency, not a genre comprising individual, well, novels and other works of art, however formulaic and manipulative they may be. This tendency manifests itself as both sensibility and production. The sensibility evolves from pale seventeenth-century imitations of such masters of scurrilous obscenity as Martial, Juvenal, and the incomparable Catullus to a fascination with the lascivious that Kendrick traces to the cataloguing of certain frescoes and statues unearthed at Pompeii. Before the nineteenth century, he tells us, sexual imagery was almost always the servant of invective, intended to insult rather than arouse, to exploit as metaphor rather than render as fact. But as realism became a byword, more and more ruling-class men joined the tiny market that had long existed for prurient fictional or "autobiographical" sexual representations. Supply rose to meet demand. And as pornography's audience expanded and democratized along with every other reading public, censors emerged from closets everywhere.

For Kendrick, the keyword in this scenario seems to be "representation." I hear tell this term made its highbrow move during the film-theory debate that filled the pages of *Screen* in the '70s, a debate I've avoided like the collected works of Enver Hoxha, but if that's where Kendrick picked it up he never lets on. He just uses it like a normal English word, related to such formulations as "an apparently unstoppable drive toward the total availability of total detail" and "The real problem—though no one recognized this—was publicity itself, the permeation of culture by images." That is, the growth of pornography was simply one more instance of the proliferation of what Foucault (cited by Kendrick from a polite distance) calls discourse, and the content of pornography was of little if any moment; as McLuhan (ditto) put it, "The medium is the message," and hence: "*The Mysteries of Verbena House* and *The Little Flowers of St. Francis* are more alike than they are different. Both are printed books and hence influence their readers' perceptual organization in precisely the same way; that one praises flagellation, the other sanctity, is irrelevant."

Immediately Kendrick adds: "No one, perhaps, would be willing to adopt this proposition in its baldest form." But this sop to common sense is too little ("perhaps" my foot) and too late: once such a thesis has pranced across the page with its clothes off, its protestations of modesty aren't going to convince anybody. In a sense, Kendrick proposes to defend dirty books (and feelthy pictures, whose increasingly disproportionate prominence in the bluenose imagination he acknowledges but never engages) with the arsenal of contemporary academia's cross-disciplinary formalism. Oh, not really, I suppose. He must suspect that his descriptions of archcensor Comstock's insane shenanigans—cribbed from the kind of sources only scholars should read and spun into the kind of good yarn few scholars have the gift for—are every bit as instructive as his repeated denial that representation affects behavior. After all, if "history provides no proof" that life imitates art, history also offers no proof that the course of human events has been changed by right reason, this book included. For the stringent empiricist, in fact, history offers no proof of anything, because proof requires experimental controls that life messy life won't sit still for. Which I'm afraid throws us back on the common sense enlisted by such anti-porners as Richard Nixon and Edwin Meese et al. after science let them down. Common sense tells us that

Kendrick is right to disparage the "simple-minded" superstition that "representations direct our lives in ways we cannot govern or even understand." But common sense also tells us that representations feed into the tangle of factors that determine human action.

Astutely, Kendrick traces the censorship debate back to Plato, who saw art as "poison . . . accumulating in the system," and Aristotle, whose concept of catharsis suggested that art was more like "homeopathic medicine, to be taken as needed and put back on the shelf." But rather than suggesting that maybe these two possibilities cancel each other out, Kendrick relegates both to the scrap heap of history—he believes art neither misleads nor ennobles. What it does do, apparently, is provide diversion, amusement, pleasure, or perhaps something like Clive Bell's "aesthetic emotion." While Kendrick takes care to remove himself from the myth of "literature," and also from the myth of the alienated genius (which he believes arose "in tandem with" pornography), he often uses the word "art" as if he knows what it means, usually in connection with high craft. Such workmanship and formal sophistication he finds sadly lacking in most pornography, which he labels "tawdry," "of the lowest quality," "trash," even "vile drivel." And like so much else in Kendrick's impressive, useful, deeply frustrating book, this can only make the attentive reader wonder what the fuck he's driving at. I mean, if all representations are equal, then what induced Kendrick to write a book about sexual representations? Was it just solidarity with the young and the poor, whose desires he believes (astutely once again) are what really terrify the censors? Or does the stuff just give him a hard-on sometimes? And if so, is a hard-on behavior?

Kendrick's failure to say is typical of the maddening reticence of this book, and I hope it doesn't seem like name-calling to suggest that this failure has an academic look. Academics, after all, are responsible for most of the work that achieves the sweep and authority to which *The Secret Museum* aspires, not only because few other writers enjoy enough institutional support to undertake such projects, but also because academia remains this culture's chief repository of the grander intellectual virtues. Anyway, Kendrick isn't merely an academic—not to be coy about it, he was my colleague long before he took a leave from Fordham to help edit this newspaper's book section. His journalistic proclivities deliver him from the overkill that afflicts so many professors who can write—the habit of insuring accuracy by adding words and details until the whole sinks under the sum of its parts. Yet the dry distance of Kendrick's tone is distinctly professorial, and in tandem with his reluctance to underline his points clearly is sure to bewilder anyone naive enough to crave some sense of the author behind the text. You'd think that in the so-called postmodernist era academia would have banished irony, certainly the most cliched of modernist devices, but in writers like Kendrick irony has instead been elevated into a working assumption, a natural way of dealing with the world.

At its most innocent, Kendrick's irony takes the form of the implicit attribution responsible for the "eternal" in his summary sentence. Slipping into the voice of whomever he's targeting, he sounds almost but not quite as if he himself regards Sade as "dangerous," doesn't like "gross references to low characters and comic scenes," and believes that to thrust Rochester's poems "before a public composed of all classes and degrees of sophistication is in fact to make them more pernicious than their author ever designed." On the other hand, maybe he views one or more of these judgments with sympathy—I'm honestly not sure. And although his solidarity with the young and the poor would appear sincere enough, if only because he mocks those who fear them so stalwartly, that doesn't stop him from sounding superior again and again—to a fascination with "the mechanics and hydraulics of sex" or a nineteenth-century public that's "infantile and barbaric," to Margaret Sanger's ignorance of etymology or Judge Woolsey's pretensions to literary expertise. Writing about a wealthy abortionist hounded to her suicide by Comstock, he says: "a modern observer can hardly help pitying Madame Restell, however vulgar and venal she may have been." Us moderns are so big-hearted.

I'd like to hope that a bigger book could swallow up these tonal deficiencies, that in fact Kendrick's journalistic terseness is his undoing here. I'd like to hope that if he'd taken the space to outline and fill in his argument and paid unabashed critical tribute to the pornographic novels and stories I can only assume got him interested (as he says of early prostitution scholar William Acton, "the very fact that a writer had chosen obscenity as a subject . . . would impugn him"), the reader wouldn't have to scratch around for clues to his intentions. But it seems unlikely that I'll ever find out. Maybe that's because Kendrick doesn't think a book is obliged to perform such quotidian feats. Maybe it's because he'd really rather I didn't know what his intentions are. Or maybe it's because he doesn't know himself.

Village Voice, 1987

What Pretentious White Men Are Good For

Robert Coover's *Gerald's Party*

In certain influential circles, Robert Coover is put forth as something like a great novelist, a master of the "metafiction" also practiced by John Barth, William Gass, John Hawkes, Thomas Pynchon, and the list could go on. Now getting on into late middle age, these writers share another demographic, a striking one in view of their challenge to the cultural authority of slightly older Jewish novelists like Bellow and Mailer and the venerable southern grouping dominated by Faulkner: all are Wasps from the Northeast and Midwest. While this isn't enough in itself to put off many potential readers, it doesn't look good—unless you've bought pretty heavily into the academic avant-garde, it's hard to resist seeing these guys as mere mandarins. This is true even if, like me, you think most of them have done remarkable and sometimes engaging work—work that would be better served by less grandiose claims. In the end it's fairer to think of them not as standard-bearers of the fiction-making process, but as representatives of a significant subculture with a unique perspective on the world today. If we can speak of black fiction and women's fiction, surely we can speak of fiction by pretentious white American men.

"Pretentious" may seem unnecessarily snotty, especially with Bellow and Mailer huffing and puffing in the vicinity. All I can say is that I intend no pejorative; it's just that "ambitious" and "imposing" and "erudite," accurate though each is in its way, don't cut the mustard. Metafiction is narrative that means to destroy narrative's comforting delusions—its sequential logic, its omnipotent creator, its human beings made of words, its beginning and its middle and its end. It proposes to situate itself on the leading edge of avant-garde technique and yet "speak eloquently to our still-human hearts and conditions, as the great artists have always done" (Barth on Borges), to dissolve "that simple legendary world we'd like to live in, so that new values may be voiced" (Gass on Coover), to "unravel or discover or understand the basic underlying assumptions about the world" (Coover on Coover). A writer who sets himself such nearly impossible tasks is pretentious by definition unless he should happen to bring them off, and I don't mean in theory. But we can still value the way his pretensions help him speak to us, the pressure they put on our values and assumptions, or at least our aesthetic.

In theory, Coover stretches us every time out, nowhere more thoroughly than in *Gerald's Party*, the fourth novel of a prolific and varied two-decade career. Ostensibly an Americanized English murder mystery complete with shrewd sleuth and houseful of suspects, *Gerald's Party* reveals its recondite purposes almost as quickly as one of Coover's short "fictions," the controlled environments where he conducts his frankest experiments. Thus it's like all his novels, only more so. All of them tell a synopsizable story that parodies/subverts/exploits the folk/popular with explicit mythic/metaphorical intent; all descend from relatively calm and solid narrative into a whirlpool of violently orgiastic incident. But over the years each of these usages has shown the taste for its own tail that is to be expected from any artist with Coover's highly conscious interest in form as form. Plot—not to mention character—atrophies; folk/popular content transmutes into form; myth and metaphor parade around with their clothes off; calm seems less prelude than illusion, sex-and-violence not metaphor but the ground of all being.

In *The Origin of the Brunists* (1966), a superbly rendered realistic novel about a millenarian sect that draws heavily on Coover's knowledge of mining towns and newspaper work, the sex and violence are plausible outcomes of a plausible situation. *The Universal Baseball Association, Inc., J. Henry Waugh, Prop.* (1968) is almost as conventional in narrative technique, only most of the action takes place in Waugh's (Jahweh's, get it?) baseball league, which by the novel's sixth or seventh inning has generated a phantasmagoric social microcosm tied by no mathematical logic to the hits-runs-and-errors of Waugh's dice, a microcosm that eventually subsumes Waugh's life—and also the novel's. *The Public Burning* (1977) is half-crazed from the outset, interrupting chief narrator Richard Nixon's indistinguishable facts, factoids, and fictions in re the Rosenberg case with the hornswoggling palaver and braggadocio of Uncle Sam, a mythic figure everyone can see, who ends up cornholing Nixon in the aftermath of a three-ring execution where great Americans from Karl Mundt to Marilyn Monroe take down their pants. And in *Gerald's Party*, the whodunit quickly disappears beneath a bacchanal of snatched conversation, theatrical ritual, and of course sex-and-violence. When it's finally "solved"—almost by the by, mostly to prick our underlying assumptions—it's impossible and indeed inappropriate to care who murdered the first of the novel's numerous decedents, a nymph whose loss the male reader, at least, is inclined to mourn.

It isn't very metafictional of Coover to make Ros so lovable (for Ros is the name of this gorgeous blond actress who fucks so brilliantly, so all-embracingly). In fact, identifying with characters as if they were human beings is so frowned upon in this artistic microcosm that not just Ros but the novel's other sympathetic figures—host-cocksman-narrator Gerald, the nearest Coover's come to an autobiographical protagonist since Miller the newspaperman in *The Origin of the Brunists*; Gerald's flame, Alison, a paradigm of intelligent lust; painter Tania and author Vic, who philosophize with some cogency before the novel kills them—may well be missteps on Coover's aestheticist path. Of course, by choosing the metaphor of an arty party he's inviting identification from his arty readers, and as his partisans will no doubt huff, he's probably just testing us. Ros is a porn fantasy, Alison and Tania and Vic get theirs, and in due time the book undermines not only Gerald's credibility but the self-probing self-satisfaction that makes him sympathetic. We like Tania's or Vic's ideas, an affection enhanced by the skill of Coover's dramatization, and then make the mistake of extending this affection into some illusory characterological realm, where it's doomed to drown in the bathtub or get shot through the heart. Gerald's parties deliquesce inevitably into disaster, and his love for the ladies isn't so supreme that he can muster the wherewithal to protect Alison, who winds up getting gang-raped in the basement, or his loyal, hard-working, nameless wife, who a few hours after the cops have searched her rectum joins Gerald for a great lay and then pads off to sleep, leaving our protagonist in utter existential solitude as Ros yanks ferociously at his balls (don't worry—it's only a dream, or a rehearsal, or an image, or a mistake, or The End).

All the telegraphic description and dependent clauses of this synopsis don't begin to suggest the novel's hectic mood. It's impossible to keep the thing straight, which is what Coover wants. There are too many characters, some of whom go the way of all flesh by hearsay only, not even bothering to show their corpses. Ros's entire acting troupe commandeer house and guests in improvised obsequies. Though the novel is mostly dialogue, no conversation proceeds uninterrupted for even a page, and Coover enjoys sticking random remarks from passing onlookers into the middle of crucial and not so crucial utterances and ruminations. Yet at the same time, *Gerald's Party*, like all his novels, moves, something no one can claim for Hawkes's *Second Skin* or, God knows, Gass's *Omensetter's Luck*. And while Coover's transcriptions of speech aren't totally free of annoying condescension, his fascination with American idiom adds a richness of texture you won't find in Barth or

Barthelme or Hawkes, who for their various reasons are all more British in diction and/or rhythm than has been common in our literature. There really is something Rabelaisian in Coover's sense of humor, and his raunch is juicy enough to alarm reviewers. So we're hit with a potent combination—a formal scheme that makes a proper metafictional mockery of ordinary narratives yet doesn't disdain all the amenities we associate with them.

In theory, this is swell, but in fact, *Gerald's Party* is the least of Coover's novels. I suppose I prefer it personally to his most popular book, *The Universal Baseball Association.* ("Not to read it because you don't like baseball is like not reading Balzac because you don't like boarding houses," wrote Wilfrid Sheed. Unfortunately, to read it because you do like baseball is like reading Finnegans Wake because you like funerals—or *Gerald's Party* because you like parties.) But the formal intensifications of Coover's latest effort sell him short. The master of rhetoric who brings forth the dazzling fictions of *Pricksongs & Descants* and fleshes out *The Public Burning* hardly pokes through the tangle of dialogue here, and the crafter of flawless descriptive prose is choked altogether. Although Coover's political ideas are marred by an elitist's japes and an exile's exaggerations, I miss the humane impulses that inform much of what he's published in the last decade. And although it's unreasonable to expect stone genius of any writer, I admit that I was hoping for something on the order of *The Public Burning*'s Nixon, a mind-boggling creation not least because his namesake's status as a historical personage confounds the kind of empathy metafiction warns us to mistrust.

In the abstract, *Gerald's Party* is the poppest of all Coover novels; in fact—and probably as a direct consequence, given the distaste of pretentious white American men for full-fledged pop—it's the most rarefied. Though you have to hand it to Coover for continuing to produce novels in the face of the metafictional void, something only Hawkes has managed readily, *Gerald's Party* would seem to betray a certain groping around for material. Despite his fondness for the American idiom, Coover has spent large parts of his adult life in England and Spain, returning for the teaching jobs that now seem to have made him a permanent resident again, and his novels have manifested an accumulating distance—first a good philosophical yarn rooted in personal observation, then a more fantastic book reflecting his baseball-fan boyhood, then a researched historical novel, and finally an arty party, one thing fringe academics generally know plenty about. Considering what he's given himself to work with, it's small surprise that the non-ostensible subject of *Gerald's Party* turns out to be about as innovative as the wild party itself. If I'm not mistaken, it's Coover's hope to unravel or discover or understand our basic underlying assumptions about—oh dear—Time.

Maybe I'm too young to fully appreciate such things, but I've always felt that novels about Time succeed (Proust) or fail (*Ada*) irrespective of their metaphysical revelations. No matter what's contraindicated by subatomic physics or mystico-philosophical introspection, the events of which almost all these novels still (ostensibly) consist take place in something like a sequential, diachronic dimension, a dimension that's physically human (mammalian, say) in scale, and the novelist is hard-pressed to dislodge them without resorting to the kind of sci-fi devices that are beneath pretentious white American men. This isn't to dismiss such excellent Time-related themes as the intransigence of death, the persistence of regret, the inadequacy of memory, or the unfathomability of causation, all of which *Gerald's Party* does its erudite yet idiomatic bit with. I'll go along with Vic, for instance, when he argues that "rigidified memory, attachment to the past" is the only crime (only I wouldn't say only), and I kind of get why Tania insists that "art's great task is to reconcile us to the true human time of the eternal present, which the child in us knows to be the real one!" But I'm afraid Tania is getting a little too close to Inspector Pardew, who posits a world in which space is fluid and time fixed and eventually concludes that Ros was done in by a satyrical dwarf who makes his entrance well after the guests notice her body on the floor. Even worse, I'm afraid Coover is setting Pardew up to do the hard part for him—to jar events into a properly metafictional dimension, to deprive us of the teleological comfort that no reader dogged enough to get to the end of this book is likely to feel much need for. Maybe Pardew is just venting his anti-satyr prejudice, or maybe he knows something about the dwarf's movements that Gerald doesn't bother to mention. Maybe he's fitting facts to theory, or maybe he's creating truth with it. It's hard to know what Coover thinks. And impossible, or inappropriate, to care.

One reason it's inappropriate is the games Coover plays with authorial authority, but in general there's just too much self-congratulation built into metafictional practice. Consider Gerald's genius in bed. As in Hawkes's *The Blood Oranges*, a clearer and more disturbing book in which the narrator-protagonist is cooler about but no less possessed by his sexual prowess, it's a peachy metaphor for authorial omnipotence and—in Coover's case, not Hawkes's—its discontents. But either way it has the convenient side effect of making the author (as opposed to the narrator) look like an ass man. After all, mandarins generally think quite a lot of themselves. Just as in Beckett, the act of writing stands as a not-so-mute corrective to the nearly absolute pessimism of its (ostensible) message, so in Coover the act of showing off counteracts any pretensions to self-critical humility—which may be yet another conscious contradiction for us to chew over, and so what? It isn't Coover's doubts about his work that should impress us—we're capable of generating those all by ourselves, thank you. It's the broader humility that underlies his sizable gifts.

Coover is one of those select contemporary writers who is genuinely awe-struck by the pervasive power of the tools of his trade, an honorary citizen of structuralism's vast domain. As a pretentious white American man, he has no built-in beef with American society that Richard Hofstadter didn't win a Pulitzer for complaining about, and thus he's free to peer at it from outside and above, like an astronaut photographing the whole earth. He's a formalist at least partly because he was given the chance to be. Although like most formalists he's strongest when he struggles willy-nilly against formalism's confines, if you strip his ideas down you'll find a good many middlebrow commonplaces—his carefully ironized male chauvinism, his political despair, his black humor itself. So it's his focus on form, and on words themselves, that we read him for—less the way he breaks apart the comforting rigidities of conventional storytelling than the way he builds up the sharp, diverting pleasures of the other kind. Still, there's an attractive intellectual strand there, a skeptic's fascination with simple faith that's heartier and more democratic than anything comparable you can pick out in his colleagues, sort of a cosmic counterpart to his abiding passion for the words he instructs us not to believe in. If you happen not to be a convinced formalist yourself, you could even say his work has content. And maybe one way of explaining what went wrong with *Gerald's Party* is that his skepticism overcame his fascination and made the book brittle.

Or put it another way. I wouldn't say the best of Coover's work achieves any eternal present—that dream of synchrony is an old one among art-for-art's-sakers, obsessed as they are with focusing their frustrated religious yearnings, and as Coover makes clear, it's impossible. Perhaps, though, it offers a dirty glimpse of it. And perhaps in *Gerald's Party* Coover wants to make sure we concentrate on the window.

Village Voice, 1986

Impoverished How, Exactly?

Roddy Doyle's *The Woman Who Walked into Doors*

Long before Roddy Doyle's *The Commitments* became a movie about a better and duller band than the novel's Commitments ever were, I downed the whole thing on a flight to L.A. with my three-year-old squirming in the next seat. It was that quick and that compelling. Canon-keepers stodgy and hip may pigeonhole it as local color, but that's snobbish piffle—it's as major as a short novel can be. The closest precedent is Alan Sillitoe's jaunty report from the working-class '50s, *Saturday Night and Sunday Morning*, but Sillitoe isn't as funny or fast. And there's a bigger difference—except for "The Loneliness of the Long-Distance Runner," he never matched it. Doyle, on the other hand, has just published his fifth terrific book about the Dublin working class. And while *The Woman Who Walked into Doors* may seem more programmatic than *The Snapper* or *The Van* or *Paddy Clarke Ha Ha Ha*, it hits harder than any Doyle since *The Commitments*—and has at least as much juice and backbone as any competing report from the middle-class present.

The fiction of contemporary life is generally populated either by troubled professionals and their doubly troubled children or by bohemians, wanderers, wastrels, sociopaths, and other supposedly paradigmatic outsiders. Doyle's novels are about ordinary yobs who spend their lives in one place and watch too much television. Most of his adults have jobs or houses to take care of or wish they did. Incomewise, they're twentieth to fortieth percentile—very nearly middle-class at their peak, but more likely to slip than climb, although the young may rise via education and bohemia (or get wasted by misery and drugs). The welcome surprise is that Doyle doesn't believe his characters are what is called culturally impoverished. His genius is to construct a vernacular that does justice to the humor, empathy, resilience, savor, curiosity, and moral discrimination of their unexpectedly rich lives.

Not that Doyle has chosen to sustain the inspired optimism of *The Commitments* and *The Snapper*. The Booker Prize–winning *Paddy Clarke Ha Ha Ha* is at once a minutely rendered childhood memoir and the sad tale of how one bright lad withdraws as his parents rip apart. *The Woman Who Walked into Doors* attacks a still grimmer theme—even, perhaps, a Social Problem. Audaciously, Doyle assumes the voice of thirty-nine-year-old Paula

Spencer—charwoman, single mother, alcoholic, battered wife. Never long on plot or structure (both *Paddy Clarke* and *The Van*, three-hundred-pagers where the others are two hundred, slow down in the middle), he jumbles her story the way she might, beginning a year after a climax in which she routs her husband with the oversized frying pan her mother-in-law gave her, and continuing a year past that. Three brutal chapters toward the end, forty pages that stick with you like the taste of bad meat, contain nothing but abuse, seventeen years of it, sometimes in sentences and paragraphs that seem to repeat of their own accord, beyond the control of narrator or author. "He dragged me around the house by my clothes and my hair." "My back." "Ask me."

Typically for Doyle, however, half the book describes Paula's happier (and funnier) life before Charlo started hitting her. Unlike the earlier novels' Jimmy Rabbitte Sr., who knows exactly what he likes in a cup of tea or a scene from *Cocktail*, Paula's command of detail isn't always acute, but she homes in on the interpersonal, and the rules she devises to keep her alcohol addiction off the backs of her three remaining kids (the fourth's a heroin addict out in the world) are intricate and effective. Poverty grinds harder here than in Jimmy Rabbitte's tract-house Barrytown—Paula can't believe her luck when she finds a Danielle Steele in the trash she's emptying. Yet she's undefeated, and while it may take more than a frying pan to scare off most batterers, there's nothing pat about the resolve she achieves after she gets rid of Charlo—or about the love that still complicates her loathing. Roddy Doyle has the decency to understand that the most constrained human life is never simple, and the grace and guts to prove how unimpoverished the countless meanings of that truth can be.

Spin, 1996

Sustainable Romance

Norman Rush's *Mortals*

How can Norman Rush's 1991 *Mating* rank among the great twentieth-century novels? Let me count the ways. Rush is the rare male modern to imagine a female protagonist as vivid and complex as *Mating*'s unnamed lover-anthropologist-adventurer. Few if any white novelists have written so easily about the underrepresented turf of Africa. In an age of realpolitik rampant, *Mating* has the courage to posit a plausible utopia: Tsau, a fabricated matriarchy in Botswana's Kalahari Desert (yes, the action includes many political meetings). Add the bonus of the book's most spectacular accomplishment, an indelible account of the heroine's perilous one-woman trek to Tsau that lets us taste Rush's facility at bravura description. And then there's the touch that at bottom *Mating* is about what it says it's about—not animal sex, though that gets its due, but, oh dear, conjugal love.

Now twelve years later comes *Mortals*, at over seven hundred pages half again as long if slightly less magnificent. *Mortals* isn't about what it says it's about, except as a bonus. Instead it's about conjugal love again. Makes you wanna holler, Shape up, man—you're turning seventy, you started late and write slow, better move on to the serious stuff toot sweet: infinite epistemological regression, the buzz and tangle of information overload, the futile compromises of human connection. Granted, Rush does give alienation a fair shake. Where *Mating*'s Nelson Denoon was a visionary progressive, Ray Finch is out of le Carré: a pushing-fifty CIA operative cum literature professor in Botswana's capital, Gaborone. But although he's good (and moral) at both jobs, in neither does he find much human connection. That part of his life, as well as all the rest, he devotes to "the most beautiful white woman in southern Africa," his thirty-eight-year-old wife of seventeen years, Iris. And here's where Rush will run into trouble. Iris isn't just beautiful. She's also kind, funny, intelligent, and sexually uninhibited—as well as sexually inexperienced, childless, unemployed, and depressed. Yet sophisticated readers have been trained to doubt Ray's passion, or find it comic somehow, and doubt too that it's worth 712 pages. That's what sophistication is for.

Partly to counter such objections, but mostly to give Ray's love a chance at another seventeen years, or thirty-four, Rush mixes in two more major characters—both of whom, as it turns out, found their callings in the fallout of ruined marriages. Davis Morel is an African-American physician who emigrates to Gaborone with big plans to rid Africa of the scourge of Christianity; Samuel Kerekang returns to Botswana with smaller plans to teach his people cooperative agriculture and Victorian poetry, in particular Tennyson and William Morris. Iris falls for Morel, Ray's pig of a boss targets Kerekang, and the plot is in motion. Rush has said the subject of *Mortals* is Kerekang's accidental jacquerie—a word I didn't know meaning a doomed rural uprising that leaves the power structure stronger than ever. And maybe that's what he intended. But the love triangle weighs obsessively on Ray (and

Morel) even when Iris leaves the stage for three hundred pages while the three men take care of politics up north. Although the politics are substantial and intrinsic, what's most meaningful about them formally is how they inflect the marriage that gives *Mortals* its originality.

Exactly how original I lack the authority to say. If marriage hasn't been as central to the postwar American novel as one might expect, it's certainly been favored by chroniclers of suburbia one would rather not waste time on. Avoiding Updike, Beattie, and their well-spoken nieces and nephews like I avoid boite singers, I can only surmise that most of them share the belief that marriage is at best a glass half-full and at worst a hideous prison. A friend observes that the guy who invented this idea was Flaubert. I would add, surmising again, that Flaubert's template is badly worn, and note the coincidence (or is it?) that somewhere in the Kalahari Ray burns a copy of *Madame Bovary*.

That Rush treasures marriage doesn't mean he's palmy—he has no illusions about permanent bliss. We know from *Mortals* that the couple in *Mating*, eight thousand miles apart as the novel ends, marry after it's over; we also know their union is radically diminished by the failure of a subsequent project, yet heroic nevertheless. As for Ray and Iris, early on there's a two-page embrace so uxorious you just know Rush is still smitten with his wife of nearly fifty years. The forty pages that precede the final chapter are equally acute, however, and they're agony, capturing the horrible day-by-day crawl of a doomed relationship that for scheduling reasons hasn't yet physically broken apart. But in both books, the domestic details—the wordplay and long talks, the carnal knowledge and habits of support, the empirical verification that for living lovers there's usually something new around the bend—lift the couples out of the morass of failed imagination in which so much fictional marriage carps, glowers, and grinds.

Part of the secret is a lucid, luminous, proudly literary prose that aspires to neither pomo pyrotechnics nor the dogged clarity of Iowa-school convention. The marriages are alive because the writing is. But it's not palmy to conclude that Rush's political concerns nourish his commitment to sustainable romance. Well before the jacquerie, Morel and Kerekang enter a spectacularly well-informed argument about the uses of Christianity that makes the erudition of Rushdie or Franzen seem show-off frippery by comparison. Doubly spellbinding in a moment when fundamentalism is eating at the polity worldwide, it's as urgent as the Grand Inquisitor chapter of *The Brothers Karamazov*. Much later, Ray gazes at the faces of bivouacking Batswana and Bushmen and thinks: "Everyone around the fire was serious. They didn't know that was remarkable."

And though Ray has learned the limits of his parity with black Africans, such seriousness is key—because Ray and Iris have it, their marriage is remarkable. By this point Ray has decided that bringing down the Soviet empire and denying Taiwan the bomb don't counterbalance CIA evil in Guatemala; he's also helped destroy a squad of Boer mercenaries by literally weaponizing a manuscript. Iris has wanted him to quit for years, and soon he will—not so he can save a marriage he despairs of, but so he can be truly serious. Morel has said that he longs for "a place where the rude fact that we are all dying animals transfigures every part of life," and Ray has reached that place. He has no time to waste. He's accepted the basic wisdom that if you're going to put marriage first in your life, you'd better have more in your life than marriage. And maybe, just maybe, he can make that logic work.

Village Voice, 2003

Derring-Do Scraping By

Michael Chabon's *Telegraph Avenue*

Michael Chabon split his career in two with 2000's Pulitzer Prize–winning *The Amazing Adventures of Kavalier & Clay*. Before then he was a Respected Young Novelist whose widely praised, commercially robust *The Mysteries of Pittsburgh* and *Wonder Boys* mined the academic-bohemian nexus in the city where Chabon attended college. He also published two volumes of short stories, many of which initially appeared in *The New Yorker*. "Naturalistic," Chabon came to call this mode, especially in short-story form; stories of "disappointment, misfortune, loss, hard enlightenment, moments of bleak grace. Divorce; death; illness; violence, random and domestic; divorce; bad faith; deception and self-deception; love and hate between fathers and sons, men and women, friends and lovers; the transience of beauty and desire; divorce—I guess that about covers it." And although Chabon was never as dreary as this caricature, in *Kavalier & Clay* he became a different kind of storyteller—to use another term he means to reclaim, an entertainer. The title characters were two cousins who invent a comic-book superhero called—impudently, yet justifiably—the Escapist.

Audaciously brokering Chabon's mass-culture-meets-high-art IPO, *Kavalier & Clay* is some kind of masterpiece. Although its action is strictly realistic—nobody flies like the hero of Jonathan Lethem's *Fortress of Solitude*—it's also fanciful, panoramic, and full of laughs. The cousins' story maintains a comic book's what-next pace for over six hundred pages, packed with adventures almost as swashbuckling as those of the confabulations who make them moderately rich and famous—cartoonist Kavalier moonlights as a magician, defeats domestic Nazis, revives a dying Salvador Dalí, and jumps off the Empire State Building. And after it triumphed, Chabon went wild—a Sherlock Holmes novella, a YA fantasy about baseball, an illustrated action saga starring two tenth-century brigands provisionally dubbed *Jews with Swords*, and *The Yiddish Policemen's Union*, a four-hundred-page murder mystery set in a twenty-first-century Alaska that has been populated by pre-Holocaust European Jews just eight crucial years before the Palestinians' 1948 rout of the Zionists. Its alternate-reality premise won it a Hugo as the best science fiction novel of 2008.

In some respects Chabon's big new *Telegraph Avenue*, which he's dared to brand "naturalistic," calls a halt to such sensationalist frippery. It's set in 2004 near the Oakland-Berkeley border, where Chabon has long resided with his wife and kids, and features plenty of disappointment, misfortune, and loss, although in the end no divorce; insofar as it chronicles one of those liminal bohemias American cities throw up everywhere, it shares a milieu with the Pittsburgh novels too. But where those books were about students and literati, this one dispenses with such dreary conventions. It centers on a Jewish couple from Berkeley and an African-American couple from Oakland who share two business partnerships—the wives are midwives, the husbands proprietors of a used LP store. Its de facto protagonist is Archy Stallings, the estranged son of a fallen blaxploitation star named Luther Stallings whose verkakte attempt to revive his career stirs up much unnaturalistic incident amid the disappointment, misfortune, and loss.

The younger Chabon's novels had more than their share of color and intentional violence. The presiding spirit of *The Mysteries of Pittsburgh* plunges to his death after a Mafia-engineered police chase; the narrator of *Wonder Boys* drives around with a dead dog in his trunk before escaping his own death by heaving a dead boa constrictor at a thug with a nine. But the color didn't come near to obviating my big problem with those books, which was that I disliked all six of their major characters. Both are dominated by dashingly hedonistic homosexuals who I assume reminded Chabon of one or both of the men he's said he was in love with back then, and I'm so resistant to the charisma of these rather different guys—one a social-climbing student, the other a carousing editor—that I distrust the narrators who adore them. It's cool that Chabon has stuck with homosexual content through phase two—Clay is gay, the victim in *Yiddish Policemen's Union* is a homosexual Hasid, and the young teenaged sons of the record dealers discover sex together. But the irresistible wastrel is as tired a trope as quiet desperation, and *Telegraph Avenue* rejects them both. There's desperation, but it's loud; there are wastrels, but resisting them is a point of honor with Archy Stallings even when the wastrel is himself.

Among the many remarkable things about *Telegraph Avenue* is that this insistently Jewish novelist chose to focus on the black couple. There are key walk-ons for a villainous OB/GYN, a baby-bearing couple in the hills, and a wigger who litigates for whales to cover the three hundred bucks he spends on vinyl every month. Nevertheless, Nat Jaffe, Aviva Roth-Jaffe, and their son Julie are the only significant white characters in a book that devotes major attention to Luther Stallings, his Cleopatra Jones–channeling consort Valletta Moore, Hammond B-3 master Cochise Jones, a funeral director who runs black Oakland, and a retired quarterback whose Dogpile corporation has made him a mogul. Then there's Archy's son Titus Joyner, on his dad's hands at fourteen after his maternal grandmother in Texas passes, and his wife Gwen Shanks, a well-schooled daughter of the civil rights movement and the upper middle class. And there's Brokeland Records itself, which while it peddles anything it can move bears down on the pop funk and fusion jazz of the '70s, the most specifically African-American music of the rock era.

I'm white, so it's possible I've been hoodwinked. But with allowances for the narrative goodies we can praise Anansi that Chabon has no intention of abandoning, I found the tales and conversations he imagines convincing, engrossing, and relaxed. It helps that none of his characters presents the difficulty of being trapped in the underclass, because even Titus, who came all too close, and Luther and Valletta, who are homeless half the time, are well supplied with intellectual capital, as their conversations and interior monologues make amply clear. But bottom line, these folks are scraping by. The funeral director and the Dogpile magnate are good to go, and Aviva and Gwen have marketable if perilously countercultural skills—and in Gwen's case family money, which she needs when she decides it's time to beat the OB/GYN at his own game by going to med school. But the organist barely makes ends meet, the lawyer isn't raking in the hourlies, and the main plot involves the magnate's scheme to put Archy and Nat out of business. In short, this is among other things a novel of the endangered middle class—of people who've made something of themselves that may well be taken away. That story is different in the half-bohemian East Bay than in one of those Rust Belt ghost towns where doctors' offices turn into dollar stores, and it's not quite thematic. But as a substratum, it anchors the themes admirably.

Beyond cross-racial relations—a substratum mapped in terms of Gwen versus the OB/GYN and the fight for Brokedown, among other things—the theme is what to make of the dreams of youth as one reaches middle age. That Chabon finds this perplexity daunting is indicated by the title he devised for a 2009 collection of autobiographical reflections culled from a *Details* column: *Manhood for Amateurs*. He's daunted in part because as he nears fifty he remains a devotee of such kid culture as comic books, sci-fi, kung fu flicks, and Philip Pullman's *His Dark Materials*, which he celebrated in a *New York Review of Books* piece into which he snuck the hilariously un-*NYRB* sentence: "But it turns out that there are other ways to pass among the worlds than by Lord Asriel's costly method of child-sacrifice and transdimensional demolition." The main reason, however, is his personal variant of everybody else's—the experience of repurposing his career and fathering four kids over nine years with his second wife, whom he married at thirty in 1993.

Chabon was lucky—he got to steer his craft toward the Sea of Childhood, and without surrendering his *NYRB* passport either. Only that wasn't luck, it was skill, in fact genius, and none of his leads are geniuses—not even championship midwife Aviva, in need of a new partner after Gwen rejects a boutique profession of no material use to the poor African-American women she undertook to serve. Like Chabon, Gwen doubles down on her ideals, refusing to ante up even a perfunctory "I'm sorry" when she breaks the rules. Ultimately, however, her refusal to compromise means she goes straight—gives up the countercultural conceit of natural medicine for real people. And the men lose much more than the women, although Chabon reminds us subtly that as record retailers in 2004 their prospects were pretty sad anyway. At the end Nat is ready to take his trade mail-order, giving up the interracial day-to-day he so loved about his store. He'll probably rent his new space from Archy, who's getting his real estate license—a likely-looking trade that in 2004 is also headed for a major fall.

Chabon's inventiveness requires language dazzling and deft enough to put it across, and like most of his later work, *Telegraph Avenue* reads easy—I downed three hundred pages flying back from Denmark, stopping only to eat and nap. In addition to a twelve-page sentence from the point of view of a parrot, there are two areas where he always coruscates without letting the bravura blaze so bright you can't see the next sentence. The first is music, in the past such a casual and catholic matter for Chabon that I bet he had to research fusion as hard as midwifery. The loving savvy with which the Brokeland posse calibrate their enthusiasms could tempt a fella to reassess Creed Taylor, and Chabon's solo on Cochise Jones's Brokeland Creole reconstruction of *Jesus Christ Superstar*'s "I Don't Know How to Love Him"—music that exists solely in his words—is an illusionist's tour de force. Yet although *Telegraph Avenue* begins with male music palaver, as it should, it only goes into overdrive after a take-home exam in Chabon's other course of study, the topic a troubled birth that had me cheering and squirming and holding my breath for twenty pages of gynecological and sociological derring-do. And four hundred pages later Gwen's own birth scene puts this coup in its place. Late as usual, Archy arrives only an instant before his son drops, leaving Gwen's heart, as Chabon puts it, "starred like a mirror by a stone."

In the end, Archy kicks his doglike ways and Gwen forgives Archy and Titus forgives Archy and Luther kicks crack and Archy half-forgives Luther after finally whupping his ass and Nat gets off with community service when the Dogpile blimp he liberated lands harmlessly in Utah and Aviva keeps on being Aviva. Some might find all this pat. Chabon's first marriage was a rousing failure, and years after it ended his second story collection was filled with, like the man said, divorce. But as he pursued a happier union and turned himself into an entertainer—even a bit of a ham, albeit one it's easier to envy than resent—he also developed his version of the Hollywood ending: all three of his major twenty-first-century novels resolve by reconstituting a troubled marriage in a far more troubled world. Due to novelists' built-in egotism as well as storytelling's penchant for conflict, "serious fiction" is hard on marriage—considerably harder than the world is, which is saying something. Nevertheless, divorce happens, and in a world so troubled we'd better do more than just live in it, a part of me suspects that Chabon should change up his formula a little.

But another part recognizes that for all their shared mass culture heritage, his twenty-first-century novels change up pretty good no matter how they happen to end. My bet for what's next: a fantasy novel I'll find more readable and grounded than Philip Pullman. But what do I know? One reason I envy this guy is that I'm pretty sure he'll think of something I couldn't.

Barnes & Noble Review, 2012

Futures by the Dozen

Bruce Sterling's *Holy Fire*

Racing through the setup of the seventh novel by a scrivener who has earned his measure of renown from a subculture a step or two up the status ladder from the Trekkies, the English honors scholarship boy in me started hearing the old alarm bells. For the thousandth time, I wondered whether the thrill of a patently demotic work measured up. Was this what Clive Bell—dated now and a painting guy, I know, but such a hell of a stylist that his way of wording the truisms sticks with me—meant by "aesthetic emotion," "Significant Form"? As it happened, I'd just reread what I remembered as my favorite Faulkner novel—*As I Lay Dying*, not most people's number one but still Faulkner. I'd enjoyed it, too, sometimes very much. But for sure I didn't devour it in two days, and for sure its satisfactions, while perhaps subtler, were nowhere near as intense. Recollecting *As I Lay Dying* and *Holy Fire* in tranquility, I couldn't even say one book was "deeper" than the other—unless you still think depth is a function of what is called character.

Character is not Bruce Sterling's strength. Indeed, it's vestigial in most of the science fiction I've admired, although Sterling's close associate William Gibson shows a sub-Dickensian gift for caricature—see the toecutter Blackwell or the computer-mediated Zona Rosa in his just-published trifle *Idoru*. Sterling's previous novel, *Heavy Weather*, bravely attempts to address this absence by pinning its twister-tracker plot to two pairs of siblings, about whose interrelated psychologies it says nothing of any interest I could descry—although the main reason the book falls slightly flat is that, with a tip of the hat to their imagined virtuality gear and well-researched meteorological nitty-grit, the tornado-chasing chapters are all work and no play. On the other hand, *Heavy Weather*'s fictional environment—a functioning ecocatastrophe awash in private electronic currencies and "evacuation freaks" who live to share the "feeling of intense, slightly hallucinatory human community that always sprang up in the aftermath of a major natural disaster"—comprises a credible future, and this future is a compelling one.

Futures are Sterling's specialty. Faulkner makes up human beings he gets inside of; Sterling does the same with worlds. I like to imagine that on his hard drive he's catalogued dozens of them, each with its own distinct ecological, economic, biotechnical, communications, and, yes, psychological parameters and folkways, all laid out in telling outline and visionary detail. The stories collected in *Crystal Express* and *Globalhead* jump from possibility to possibility, most of them set not in the fantastic 4000 or 8000 A.D. of classic sci-fi but in cyberpunk's near future, or sometimes a recognizable present altered by some invented past event or discovery—or even an altered past, most audaciously in Gibson and Sterling's *The Difference Engine*, which describes an 1855 England changed utterly by the successful development of steamcars and huge primitive computers. The worlds Sterling posits are as likely utopian as dystopian, livable at least. All cyberpunks share what he once called a "boredom with the Apocalypse" (and hence an aversion for "those everpresent space operas in which galactic empires slip conveniently back into barbarism"), but even by comparison he's an optimistic soul—as in the corporate counterculture of 2023's Rizome Industries Group, base locale of the novel that made his reputation, 1988's *Islands in the Net*, which reads like what Steve Jobs had in mind for Apple before he discovered the inexorability of capital.

In *Holy Fire*'s 2095, Earth has righted itself. Its human population cut in half by the plagues of the '30s and '40s, it provides bland, nutritious, force-farmed food and carefully monitored medical care to all, at least in the European cities where most of the action unfolds. True, things have changed a great deal. The Indonesians, buffered against microbes by barriers of ocean, have purchased Indianapolis and rebuilt it as a cultural mecca that rivals Stuttgart itself. Individually concocted "tinctures" have replaced recreational drugs from vitamins to heroin. The world's biggest talk-show host is a dog. And the medical marvels that have always fascinated Sterling are the basis of a world economy whose blue-chip industry is life extension. So Earth's rulers constitute a "gerontocracy" born largely, all you losers out there, between 1980 and 2010—like Sterling's ninety-four-year-old protagonist, Mia Ziemann, a vigorous if endemically cautious medical economist. In this world, caution is a prime virtue: "Careless people had become a declining interest group with a shrinking demographic share." But all goodness is rewarded: "The polity was a plague-panicked allocation society in which the whip hand of coercive power was held by smiling and stout-hearted medical rescue personnel. And by social workers. And by very nice old people."

Since one rap on Sterling is that his prose is utilitarian compared to that of his buddy Gibson, let me emphasize the purely linguistic pleasure generated by this book. Where Gibson's forte is the dreamy, druggy detail of his virtual landscapes and interiors, Sterling's descriptive coup here has Mia accessing a digital "memory palace" on antiquated equipment and watching the image deteriorate. But the social dimension is his bailiwick, and while Sterling has always had a sense of humor, particularly in his stories, he's never written anything with the satirical zing and laff relief of the first seventy or so pages here. Indeed, not many have—this English honors boy will take it over any Nathanael West or Evelyn Waugh he knows. Put aside distracting considerations of aesthetic scale and try to conceive A. A. Milne whimsy crosscut with Swiftian acerbity, except that the tone is democratic—more Twain than Swift. And since *Holy Fire*'s plausible world doesn't exist and never will, the conundrum of exactly what the book is satirizing adds an extra layer of weirdness.

The main answer, I think, is generational culture—including by extension that of today's bulgy ruling caste of boomers, which Sterling and I flank at forty-two and fifty-four. One reason the fun is so delicious is that Sterling doesn't just mock their/our self-righteous self-regard, but the paranoid hostilities and expectations of the young people they/we keep down. Equally crucial is that the satire doesn't preclude "deeper" emotional resonances—epitomized by an unexpectedly touching deja vu in which Mia suddenly remembers looking in on her sleeping five-year-old with the husband she ended up divorcing after some fifty years. Because it calls up emotions she'd thought it best to let atrophy, this image, precipitated in part by the death of an imprudent boyfriend, inspires her to choose a risky mortality upgrade in which all her tissue is cleansed or regenerated. Renamed Maya, she scampers through the rest of the novel as a ninety-five-year-old in a twenty-one-year-old's body. You tell me how the novelist achieves "character" under these circumstances, which the characters themselves designate "posthuman." All I can do is swear that Maya's regrowth is credible and that her confused cocktail of impetuousness and sagacity feels uncannily familiar to this boomer. The exposition, which limns righteous plots against the gerontocracy by disenfranchised younguns dedicated to the "holy fire" of passion and artistic inspiration, isn't as flawless as the setup. But Sterling proves too smart to fall into the outlaw-youth trope that Gibson and the lesser cyberpunks have stretched past its limit—and also too smart not to admire the brilliant kids who fill his tale with incident and analysis.

This is a book about triumph, survival, and life-compromise. It's a book about the charms and cruelties of social stability, about the silly illusions and irreplaceable uses of bohemia. It's exceedingly sharp about aging, which Sterling is the perfect age to see from both sides now. And more effectively if less overtly than *Heavy Weather*, it also delves into human love. In all this it's way too vulgar to be taken seriously by the appointed seriousness-takers of letters and academe, and even among the simpatico I've heard complaints that the rather rapid ending spoils the total effect. But I say the deja vu flash of the structure the ending imposes packs the kind of revelatory power one should expect of significant form.

Village Voice, 1996

YA Poet of the Massa Woods

Sandra Newman's *The Country of Ice Cream Star*

Sandra Newman is a forty-nine-year-old American writer now settled in New York after spending most of her adulthood in England—starting when she was just seventeen, as she recounts in swift, moderately harrowing detail in her 2010 memoir, *Changeling*. She's also lived in Germany, Russia, Malaysia, and elsewhere, and has worked as a prostitute and a professional blackjack player as well as in low-status editorial jobs. Her jumpy, alienated 2003 debut novel, *The Only Good Thing Anyone Has Ever Done*, was shortlisted for a Guardian First Book Award; 2007's *Cake*, replete with drugs, homicide, and pedophilia, garnered less praise but is just as accomplished. Each novel favors postmodern distancing techniques, and each stars two pairs of female-male siblings or near-siblings, none related by blood. Half of these eight bohemian outsiders function as fully autonomous adults long before they turn twenty, the rest not long after.

Although the distancing doesn't impair clarity much, it's a little affected, and there wasn't anybody in the two novels I enjoyed spending time with: these are the kind of self-regarding cynics who are why I've long labeled myself an anti-bohemian bohemian. Yet both are pretty remarkable. Newman doesn't idealize or sugarcoat her characters, leaving prigs like me free to mistrust them. But she accounts for their flaws with palpable compassion, then tops that by plotting a portion of uplift into denouements that could pass for happy endings. This bespeaks considerable moral complexity and a hell of a skill set—but not a skill set also capable of a book that reads like this: "I lead her to our walking highway, private in this nightish hour. Road be like a valley of sky between the forest's detail life. Where we come out, a roadsign lean: SPEED LIMIT 65. In woods across, is horses tethern, and one blackish pony look up to us curiose. Munching sprig hang from his mouth."

Lyrical where the other novels are clipped, epic where the others are microcosmic, PG where the others bend to offend, luxuriously imagined where the others seem translated from life, Newman's five-hundred-page postpandemic tale *The Country of Ice Cream Star* is basically a pop novel—the kind of near-future sci-fi that transmuted what was once dubbed cyberpunk into what is now buzzworded dystopian fiction. But although it's safe to assume that the dystopian minitrend reflects widespread anxiety over the ecological disasters most book buyers can see coming exacerbated by the financial uncertainty only Wall Street hustlers argue is behind us, this says more about novel readers than novel writers. For authors like Newman, dystopian settings provide a narrative opening: an opportunity to reimagine human relations in a smaller world of one's own devising. Nothing in her previous work would seem to presage the new novel's formal and emotional departures.

Ice Cream Star takes place sometime around what we would call 2100. In "the Massa woods," where the first two hundred pages are set, reside just four hundred or so humans. All are of African descent, divided into four tribes: the slaveholding Nat Mass Armies, the pastoral Christings, the tech-savvy urbanist Lowells, and narrator Ice Cream Star's hunting, scavenging, lying, and stealing Sengles. Eighty years before, almost all of North America but especially its white population was wiped out by a disease called WAKS (an extermination rate that Newman reminded an interviewer—Emily St. John Mandel, please note—would never happen "in real life"). There are still skeletons to be found, their musty houses sources of clothing, canned goods ("The person invented Beef-a-Roni, that person be a valuable genius"), liquor, cigarettes, "pharmacies," and, last but not least, reading matter. Amid wondrous names like Dollar Saver Six Fall, Baboucar Seven Grandpa, Keepers Eight Fofana, and Progresso Nine Wilson, my favorite is Redbook Twelve Ba.

If you wonder why the names have numbers in them, it's simple. They're ages that rise every birthday—and seldom reach Twenty. The people of the Massa woods and the rest of the Nighted States may not be subject to WAKS—or may, since no one knows exactly what WAKS was. But every one of them is fated to die, generally at eighteen or nineteen, of a disease they call "posies," which alert readers will eventually identify as Kaposi's sarcoma. So the adult characters are all teenagers, Ice Cream Star herself is fifteen, and Newman's big novel has a foot not just in dystopian science fiction but in YA—a development that's less surprising when you recall the adolescent lives in extremis of her previous books. You could even surmise that one reason *The*

Country of Ice Cream Star got what Newman has called a "healthy" advance, if not the four hundred grand she told an interviewer she was offered if she'd make just one concession, is that it does retain YA elements beyond the ages of its personnel. Its improvement on *Hunger Games*–style notions of heroism is one. But far more impressive is how Newman exploits a dystopian premise to reimagine not just human relations but prose itself.

Both *The Only Good Thing Anyone Has Ever Done* and *Cake* are foul-mouthed and bluntly sexual, and *Changeling* doesn't mince words either. But although sex plays an important role in the new novel, and the words "sex" and, painfully, "rape" arise often, the Anglo-Saxon obscenities librarians still censor have disappeared from a world in which excrement is called "shee." This YA-cosseting effect, however, was not the goal of Newman's diction. In fact, normalizing the novel's language was precisely the concession she wouldn't take four hundred grand for, and she was so right. The conceit of *The Country of Ice Cream Star* is top-drawer sci-fi, and the plot is rich. But the reason I kept reading even before the story was pulling me forward was Ice Cream Star's version of a patois Newman has asserted (and bluenoses have complained) is based on African-American English, albeit laced with historically Senegalese Gallicisms like "bone" (good) and "bell" (physically attractive). The patois is a delight in itself, but the narrator's acuity, sensitivity, wit, and flow are unique to her—a distinct voice that translates readily into a distinguished prose style. Especially when she's describing her beloved woods, that style is intoxicatingly poetic—Wordsworth with ironic asides.

Not strictly in the realm of style but putting considerable meat on it are the heroine's powers of observation and analysis. Like her two lovers, El Mayor of Lowell and Mamadou the NewKing of the Nat Mass Armies, and like her posies-stricken brother Driver, too, Ice Cream Star sees more and understands it better. She's also as bell and brave as *The Hunger Games*' Katniss Everdeen, and much more mature, but that's not the most heroic thing about her: "I ain't know what other children feel, but I swear I feel more. See my Keepers frighten, and it feel like swallowing ice." The same is true, in a truncated way, of the dysfunctional narrators of Newman's bohemian novels. The adopted Rosa Espuelas, a/k/a Chrysalis Moffat, is the only one of the debut's four principals with any semblance of a normal emotional life and ends up drawing one of them into normality after the other two die. And as *Cake* approaches a close, the compulsively promiscuous narrator's nicest shag tells her why he dug her: "If you want to know the real truth, I saw you had a kind heart. It was your gentleness I saw in you, I hope that's not the worst thing to say." So for Newman, this literary sci-fi and/or grown-up YA may be less a departure from her avant-gardist fiction than a fulfillment of it.

As an epic heroine, however, Ice Cream Star is obliged to do more than open a furniture store with her boyfriend. It is her destiny to try to save the world even if she only wanted to save her brother. The plan is to woo and if necessary battle the Panish, who rule Ciudad de las Marias, as New York City is now called, and—after a brief stint as the Virgin Mary—lead her new allies down to Quantico, where she means to defeat invading Russians who've crossed the sea to trade a posies cure for penal servitude and worse. After brilliant victories, terrible defeats, hideous violence, and idealistic acts of kindness, she comes to realize that healing her people will require not just valor and wisdom but personal humiliation and sellout realpolitik—a tangle of compromises and successes the novel indicates without fully describing. So Newman has set herself up for a sequel, and why not? No *Hunger Games* fan myself, I found the rhapsodic beauty of *The Country of Ice Cream Star*'s set-up somewhat more delicious than the action-packed unlikelihoods of its quest, although the two hundred pages in Panish NYC pack serious satirical bite. But I'm dead certain Newman put her all into every page.

In part that's because I've also enjoyed Newman's 2012 *The Western Lit Survival Kit: An Irreverent Guide to the Classics, from Homer to Faulkner*, which is what its title says: a thumbnail history with jokes, cheap ones definitely included. Like: "At one time, the *Iliad* must have combined the joys of an action film with those of a slasher pic. For some readers, it still does. For others, it's uncannily like reading the same paragraph over and over and over and over." Or: "Romantic poets were above mundane concerns like making money. This was lucky, since no one bought their poetry. Some were trust fund kids, some parasites. The fact that they were later recognized as geniuses has been an unhealthy example to slackers for more than a hundred years." Or, concerning Dickens: "It's not too much to say that he helped create the twentieth-century consensus that the poor deserve society's help. (Yes, it seems laughable now. But people did believe this at one time, honest.)"

You could call Newman's critical wisecracks cynical the way I called her bohemian characters cynics. But they're also fair and funny—and often moral as well. As I raced through her literary joke book I became convinced that this longtime margin dweller—who does not, as I knew from *Changeling*, possess anything like a Ph.D.—had downed just about everything she was making mincemeat of. As a highly intelligent and phenomenally well-read person, she had plenty of reservations about this Great Tradition she'd immersed in.

But she also clearly loved and savored it—and despite her pomo bent wanted to be part of it. "Literature is a pleasure," her introduction declares. "It should be emotionally satisfying, intellectually thrilling, and just plain fun." Newman seems self-aware enough to suspect that her first two novels don't quite meet this standard. *The Country of Ice Cream Star* does.

Barnes & Noble Review, 2015

A Darker Shade of Noir: The Indefatigable Walter Mosley

Walter Mosley is a fifty-four-year-old former computer programmer with a BA in political science who must live in fear that he took up writing too late. In just sixteen years he's published a mind-boggling twenty-three books: eight detective novels and one story collection featuring his signature character, the African-American sleuth-janitor-landlord Easy Rawlins; a portrait of Rawlins as a young man in East Texas; two lesser detective novels that pair the brainy Paris Minton with the steely Fearless Jones; two sets of linked stories featuring the do-gooding ex-con Socrates Fortlow; two science-fiction novels and one linked science-fiction collection; a science-fiction-tinged historical novel for teens; two political tracts; and three "serious" novels—*RL's Dream*, about a dying bluesman cared for by a young white secretary in New York City; *The Man in My Basement*, about a white fixer-financier who voluntarily imprisons himself in a black drunk's Sag Harbor home; and the brand-new *Fortunate Son*, about intimately connected, diametrically opposed black and white stepbrothers. The past two years have been especially fruitful. After an eight-year drought that produced one Rawlins detective novel, Mosley has brought forth two excellent new ones, *Little Scarlet* and *Cinnamon Kiss*. He's also produced the slavery-themed young-adult *47* and, this year, the sci-fi fantasy *The Wave* and *Fortunate Son*.

Although the literary novels get respect, Mosley's reputation rests mostly on the Rawlins books, as it should. Starting in 1948 and proceeding by multiyear leaps to 1961, *Devil in a Blue Dress*, *A Red Death*, *White Butterfly*, and *Black Betty* chronicle a Los Angeles in which the artificial boundaries of de facto segregation are transgressed in disastrous secrecy. In four narrowly spaced subsequent novels, that secrecy starts to dissipate. These eight historically evolving books constitute the finest detective oeuvre in American literature, surpassing even that of card-carrying formalist Hammett and dwarfing Chandler and Leonard and Macdonald. Craving Greatness in fiction may be atavistic, but they're pretty Great, applying quick, meaty prose to plots rich in cultural and social detail.

Because Mosley writes to be understood and loves the way the world looks, feels, and tastes, he's always a pleasure to read, but the Easy novels go down easiest. That's the attraction of a genre in which one's hunger to find out what happens next defeats the fatigue of reading as a task. In Mosley, however, the pull isn't the mystery, with denouements that turn on racial ambiguities almost as often as Ross Macdonald's turn on skeletons in the closet, and he doesn't play the puzzler's game of dropping hints about whodunit. The fascination isn't who but how and why—moral drama in page-turner mode. Easy is a genuinely amateur detective who often finds himself questioning neighbors he knows slightly or well, and Mosley is so interested in these people that his hero hangs out a lot more than professional investigators like Sue Grafton's efficient Kinsey Millhone. Whereas Raymond Chandler's Philip Marlowe looks askance at the sleazy, shallow LA he romanticizes, Mosley feels the struggles and screw-ups of all his black characters and many of his white ones. The nearest fictional counterpart to his portrayal of working-class travails compounded by racist pathology is the wartime black LA of Chester Himes's *If He Hollers Let Him Go*—as opposed to the gritty cartoon Harlem Himes later imagined for black cops Coffin Ed Johnson and Grave Digger Jones. Mosley has admitted to Zolaesque ambitions for the Easy series, and he's sometimes Dickensian in his fond eye for how people get by.

But Mosley is more than a social realist in genre disguise. For him, culture is complicated by psychology, especially Easy's. Easy respects everyday lives because he longs for one. He has a highly unsleuthlike domestic side—handy around the house, he loves to prepare simple, tasty food that grows more sophisticated as the series progresses, and he has adopted two children orphaned by early cases. But his love life is troubled by the same inner turmoil and inability to trust that fuels his compulsion to comprehend America's racial maelstrom and morass. With a nod to le Carré's George Smiley, there is no knottier character in pop fiction. Even so, however, Rawlins falls short by the standards of the canonical; he's less complex than Raskolnikov or Hurstwood, Jane Somers or Mr. Biswas. That's one reason he so needs his alter ego, who is my nominee for Mosley's most memorable creation: Raymond Alexander, a/k/a Mouse.

If a character is supposed to have an inner life, Mouse barely qualifies; in the bildungsroman *Gone Fishin'*, Rawlins calls his best friend "the only man I ever knew who didn't have a heart at all." The slight, natty, gray-eyed, light-skinned, sexually irresistible, murderous Mouse is less a character than a force of culture, an amoral and apparently immortal orisha who's always there at the end to save Easy from his own misreadings, insecurities, and equivocations—often by killing people who may not require killing. Mouse doesn't worry about who deserves what because if he did he'd be dead by now. Late in *Devil in a Blue Dress*, he angrily tells Easy to watch out for the white man in him. "You be thinkin' that what's right fo' them is right fo' you. . . . A nigger ain't never gonna be happy 'less he accept what he is."

Like many black artists, Mosley is of two minds about questions of racial identity. As a committed race man, he's worked with PEN and CUNY to foster black writing and publishing and co-edited the 1999 essay collection *Black Genius*. But he's all too aware that categorizing (to choose an example he's cited himself) Toni Morrison as a black writer is to suggest that she should therefore be judged by looser standards than Doris Lessing or Saul Bellow. And for Mosley, the impossible question of identity has an additional dimension, because Mosley is black only by the one-drop rule of a racist culture. Fact is, Mosley is biracial—his father, who died in 1993, was "black," which here in America almost never means 100 percent African, while his mother is white, Jewish with her share of communist relatives. Here in America, however, biracial equals black, and Mosley knows it. Hence, Mouse. If white America defines Easy as black, then Easy had better accept that Mouse's stereotype informs how he, Easy Rawlins, is perceived. Nor is Mouse merely a caricature of how white America sees blackness—Easy loves Mouse, admires Mouse, and identifies with Mouse. And although the memoir material in *What Next* makes clear that Easy is more a projection of the author's father than of the author himself, Mosley clearly shares Easy's feelings.

At around the time Mosley was inventing Mouse, hip-hop cliques nationwide, particularly in LA, were modernizing the Stagger Lee myth through the prism of *Superfly*, *The Mack*, and *Scarface*. Collectively, they created that now ubiquitous cultural figure, the gangsta. Though separated by many decades, Mouse and the gangsta are brothers. Their lawless, apolitical "blackness" mocks the meliorist dreams of the talented tenth and its hardworking, well-churched foot soldiers. It gets them just deserts on terms they define. As Mosley puts it: "Raymond was proof that a black man could live by his own rules in America when everyone else denied it." True, even the most self-aware gangstas—Biggie Smalls, Tupac Shakur, Ghostface Killah—

have proudly claimed the "reality" of the role, whereas Mouse remains a fictional device so lovingly fleshed out you long for him to reappear so you can watch Mosley put him through his paces. But Mouse is so crucial to the Easy books that it's not altogether clear who's in charge—he's like an anima Mosley can't get away from.

In the pivotal *A Little Yellow Dog*, Mouse enters the usual climactic confrontation armed only with a meat cleaver and is fatally shot. Driven to kill off this deus ex machina as spirit of the race, Mosley didn't publish another Easy novel for six years. But although Mouse remains dead in the disoriented *Bad Boy Brawly Brown*, he haunts it—Easy can't stop wondering what Raymond would have done, or lacerating himself for his loss. Easy believes that if he hadn't drawn his friend into the mysteries that are a detective's fate, Mouse would still reign as king of the ghetto—admired by men and adored by women, although mellowing a bit because he killed his father and, blessed with a heart after all, feels bad about it.

The Fearless Jones novels of 2001 and 2003 turn on a safer, simpler version of the Easy-Mouse relationship, a dichotomy that recalls such pairings as Rex Stout's housebound Nero Wolfe and athletic Archie Goodwin. The cowardly bookstore owner Paris Minton is a less obsessive detective, with none of Easy's self-searching or violent undercurrent; the scarily intrepid Fearless Jones is a less avid killer, with a chivalrous code of honor. But Mosley couldn't stay away from his anima. For five installments of the deft *Six Easy Pieces*—six stories that originally baited six 2002 Easy reprints plus a new one to bait the collection—Easy tries to relocate a Mouse he can't believe is dead. In each he finds yet another murder instead, with killers who include a white security thug, the neglected teenage son of a crooked Cajun garage owner, an overprotective black mother, and Mouse's widow. The sixth story begins with a rapping on the door. Mouse is so well named that six-foot-two Easy doesn't realize his friend has returned from the dead till he looks down. How about that? All it took to heal the little man's life-ending injury was the voodoo of Mama Jo, a conjure woman who dates back to *Gone Fishin'*.

Yet the two new Easy books find Mouse in a subdued mood, while Mama Jo emerges as more than a plot device. In *Little Scarlet*, about a redheaded black woman murdered during the Watts uprising, Mouse runs looted goods with a white partner, and Easy survives the big shootout alone; in *Cinnamon Kiss*, about the murder of a radical white lawyer in an Oakland abloom with hippies and interracial love, Mouse fails to lure Easy into an armored-car robbery and instead does the detective a series of favors that require his intelligence and his dangerous reputation but not his deadly force. As ever, Easy needs Mouse alive to feel fully alive. But now he handles the dirty work himself, and in both books Mama Jo, "like an African myth come to life in the New World," heals Easy's battered body with potions that "rivalled the medicines most doctors prescribed." African-American artifacts were major plot elements in *The Man in My Basement* and one Fearless Jones novel, and Mama Jo too embodies Mosley's turn from the survivalist cunning of black street knowledge to the visionary wisdom of black history. But note that her remedies "rival" the white man's rather than supplanting them; the premise of *Cinnamon Kiss* is that Easy needs big money to send his critically ill young daughter to a clinic in Switzerland.

Mosley is anything but a separatist. In *Bad Boy Brawly Brown*, Easy disentangles a friend's son from black-nationalist gangsters who call themselves the First Men, and the integration that comes with the civil rights movement excites Mosley's closest scrutiny. After leapfrogging from 1948, the last four Easy novels take place in 1963, 1964, 1965, and 1966. In *Little Scarlet* Easy hunts down a homeless serial killer whose parents passed for white, but who turned out too dark-skinned to maintain their cover. And though the bad guys in *Cinnamon Kiss* are Nazi collaborators and their enablers, its racial intricacies are unmappable. The murderer is a white public-interest lawyer with eyes for Easy. The title character is an optimistic, ambitious, sexually pragmatic young African-American woman who by the end is preparing to rise to the top of a New York brokerage firm, presaging the coming black capitalism in all its expedient hedonism. A black ex-soldier doing penance for the Vietnamese village he destroyed has adopted the little girl who was its sole survivor. And then there's Robert E. Lee, a mean, rich, shady white private investigator who leaves Easy wondering who's the better man because he can forgive his woman for trying to kill him when Easy can't even live with an infidelity.

Mosley was thirteen when he watched his father fight the urge to go out and join the Negroes trashing Watts's crude joke of an infrastructure, and he was a full-fledged adolescent by Summer of Love time—just old enough to fall into the trap of romanticizing his own hopeful youth and the historical hopes it fed off. So though you could say he has gotten hung up savoring the moment when integration became a reality—one twist of *Little Scarlet* is the credibility Easy has gained with the white cops who've dogged him since his first case—you could also say he can't bear what happened next. The Socrates Fortlow books *Always Outnumbered, Always Outgunned* and *Walking the Dog*, their protagonist a repentant murderer back on the streets after twenty-seven years in stir, present today's black LA as a disaster zone where brave souls still carve out lives worth living. Both are winning and satisfying but, relative to the Rawlins novels, slender. As someone who anticipated Zolaesque Rawlins reaching into the present, I wish Mosley would move on. We need Easy's take on the poverty programs, Maulana Ron Karenga, the integration (and Latinization) of LA politics, the crack epidemic, Bill Cosby and O. J. Simpson and Rodney King and Maxine Waters and Suge Knight. I'd also love to meet the little guys Mosley would devise—the unemployed grifters and middle-class aspirants, the thugs and fiends, maybe finally even a few gays. The '60s were something, but excavate them too obsessively and you idealize them in spite of yourself.

One avenue of escape from this trap has been Mosley's "serious" novels, all set in the present. And although the first two take place in or near New York, where Mosley has resided since 1982, *Fortunate Son* returns to LA, as does the new science fiction novel *The Wave*. Like all of Mosley's ventures into shameless respectability, *Fortunate Son* is too schematic, essentially a fable. It's even more so than *The Man in My Basement*, where Sag Harbor's racial history and narrator Charles Blakey's self-destructive anomie provide welcome content, and *RL's Dream*, a nadir, not least because its romanticized bluesman reflects the same puritanical indifference to contemporary music Mosley deplored in a recent *Nation* essay (apparently somebody forced some hip-hop on him in the meantime). In *Fortunate Son*, Mosley's depiction of the private world the black brother creates in a secluded alley when he's just six, of his homeless years, and even of his job in a barbecue restaurant counteract the novel's penchant for fantasy, which dictates that the crippled black brother is at key junctures incredibly lucky and the hale white brother is so gifted that nothing is denied him except happiness. Detailed and enticing, that alley sticks in the mind. But the plot sits poorly. Even in the detective novels, a villain like the ruthless favor dealer Kronin Stark would be a bit much. It's too bad Mosley needs him here—and that Stark bears a suspicious resemblance to Anniston Bennet, the man in Charles Blakey's basement. It could even be argued that where Mosley gets truly serious is in his critically neglected science fiction.

Extraordinary villainy and supernatural fantasy have long bubbled beneath the surface in Mosley's work. From the start many plots have hinged on evil in high places, and few detective novelists describe so many dreams. The Fearless Jones and Socrates Fortlow books remain outlets for his old realist faith. But in *Cinnamon Kiss*, both the superrich Nazi and Mama Jo ratchet up his wilder tendencies, and in the sci-fi and the related *47* these take over. The slave plantation of *47* has zero room for anything but brutal, endless, unremitting labor, and in the science fiction—1998's *Blue Light*, 2001's *Futureland*, and now *The Wave*—the heroes battle governments whose ruthlessness differs from that of a slave owner only in magnitude and scope. Yet three of the four also encompass extraplanetary energies that feel distinctly religious. In *47* it's a brother from another galaxy called Tall John—John the Conqueroo with fancier technology. In the sci-fi it's variations on a magical wave-force charged with assuring the fate of life throughout the universe. The detective-novel and science-fiction impulses are so antithetical that this notion may alienate Easy fans, and its limitations show in *The Wave*, an ambitious combination of futuristic horror story and mystical fairy tale into which Mosley mixes his recent life project of raising his father from the dead. But *Blue Light* is more substantial. Beginning in the Berkeley of the high '60s, it's an oblique tribute to a hippiedom envisioned as the struggling salvation of a multicultural humankind.

Blue Light's battle between extraterrestrial forces is humanized and politicized in the little-noticed *Futureland*, which while clumsier structurally than *Six Easy Pieces* is packed with the indelible images that are the special province of the best science fiction. Where Mosley's other sci-fi is premised on an optimism in which brave men and women prevail over imminent world-death, *Futureland* is a nightmare—a disturbingly recognizable surveillance dystopia where adults indenture themselves to buy their parents medical care, the jobless are banished to underground warrens, and justice is dispensed by computers. The longest story begins by describing the nine-hour workday of a "labor nervosa" sufferer in a windowless prod station hundreds of stories off the ground—details all too readily projected from the rationalized drudgery of post-union America.

Futureland fills in the outlines of Mosley's increasingly grim and detailed political vision, and however Bushlike its setup may seem, it was completed during the presidency of Bill Clinton, whose public enthusiasm for the first Rawlins books made Mosley's career. Although Mosley detests Bush and his world war (see 2003's *What Next*), here the deepest evil is corporate (see 2000's *Workin' on the Chain Gang*). The plot is demonized B-thriller like *The Formula* or *The Net*, but the imagery is as vivid as that of *Blade Runner* or *Soylent Green*. As in most recent Mosley, the good guys come in many colors. But the finale, "The Nig in Me," goes back to what he knows. An international white-supremacist movement develops a virus that will kill everyone of African heritage, but a black scientist reverses the formula—instead, only those at least 12.5 percent African can survive. Having failed to save his white cubiclemate, the black protagonist encounters "three swarthy-looking white men." "Hey, nig!" they shout before shooting at him, and he escapes into the woods. The book ends with a one-sentence paragraph: "The world had started over."

It's a truism that the American detective novel admits existential doubt where the classic British model snaps shut like a jewel box. But recent history has eroded our greatest detective novelist's tolerance for the provisional. That's why he can't extricate his signature character from the '60s, why he dreams godlike interventions. Amid these stratagems, however, Mosley's attachment to social and physical detail continues to ground him. *Blue Light* gets the '60s; *The Wave* evokes LA quasi-bohemia before diving into its mysteries; *Little Scarlet* and *Cinnamon Kiss* satisfy even an Easy fan like me, who—forget Zola—wants the series to turn into Balzac. My own best hope is that Mosley's science fiction will texture cyberpunk on the William Gibson model while his detective fiction grows old with an Easy Rawlins who settles down with his better half. But I suspect Mosley has more in mind for himself than that.

The Nation, 2006

All selections identified as having originated in *The Village Voice* are reprinted by permission, copyright the year indicated by *Village Voice*, LLC.

Some of the articles in this book originally appeared in *The New York Times* and are reprinted here by permission.

A Darker Shade of Noir: The Indefatigable Walter Mosley appeared in *The Nation*, 2006.

PART VI

BOHEMIA MEETS HEGEMONY

Épatant le Bourgeoisie

Jerrold Seigel's *Bohemian Paris: Culture, Politics, and the Boundaries of Bourgeois Life, 1850–1930* | T. J. Clark's *The Painting of Modern Life: Paris in the Art of Manet and His Followers*

Everybody knows something about bohemia and nobody understands it. As an idea, or image, or catchword, it's a given of modern culture, but conceptually it's nowhere—its prestige is so compromised, even among presumed sympathizers, that almost nobody puts much thought into it. Although romantics who pine for creative freedom outnumber hard-nosed aesthetes who identify art with discipline, they're far less articulate and influential, whereas for most radicals bohemia comes too close for comfort, emblematic of the marginality their opponents regard as the fate of the left in this best of all possible political systems. The young who dominate bohemia demographically are for the most part so ill-informed that only in retrospect, after they've "outgrown" it, can they name their bohemianism as something that subsumed their involvement in Beat, or the counterculture, or rock and roll. With good critics almost as rare in bohemia as they are in academia, and good social scientists rarer, bohemia inspires fewer sharp manifestos and reports from the front than you might think, and almost nothing in the way of aesthetic, sociological, or historical perspective.

I've been aware of this quandary ever since my early days on Avenue B two decades ago, when I began to wonder how what I'd taken for an anomaly of my own path had turned into a movement. Committed to life on the cheap yet employed, unmarried and childless only temporarily I hoped, a sloppy but far from outlandish dresser, I bought the occasional beer at Stanley's but never got the hang of hanging out. In short, I was half bohemian and half nerd. This alienation-once-removed I associated with the side of me that preferred simple, readily available pop pleasures to obscure experimental art distinguished primarily by its grand ambition. But soon I learned that countless cooler scenemakers felt the same way, and before I knew it the rock and roll I'd taken as one token of my distance from bohemia symbolized it instead. This made me curious. Was "mass bohemia," as I later termed it, really "an unprecedented contradiction in terms"? Finding out wasn't easy.

One superb source presented itself almost immediately—*Exile's Return*, Malcolm Cowley's unsurpassed memoir of the American literary expatriates of the '20s, which includes a chapter called "The Greenwich Village Idea" that remains the best essay ever written about bohemia fifty-two years after the book was first published. Other references also surfaced: rogue sociologist Ned Polsky, bits of Walter Benjamin, and another find from the '30s, Albert Parry's *Garrets and Pretenders: A History of Bohemia in America*. But though my knowledge was increasing, my thoughts weren't clearing, because all these analyses took refuge in an irony that was less than conducive to conceptual coherence. Bohemia is in crucial respects reactive, breeding paradox ad infinitum, and as such it is formidably amorphous. Is it place or state of mind? Intrinsic to the creation of art or botched betrayal of the aesthetic life? Fountain of youth or crazed escape from adult responsibility? Hotbed of revolution or last refuge of bourgeois individualism? The only possible answer to these questions is all of the above.

Bohemia's elusiveness as an object of study contributes to its low status in academia, where one would hope useful perspectives might emerge. The subjects of thousands upon thousands of monographs and dissertations have passed through bohemia, and so have many professors. Yet German sociologist Helmut Kreuzer is the sole academic ever to attempt a world-historical overview, and his only competition comes from a yawping freelance everything named Richard Miller, whose *Bohemia: The Protoculture Then and Now* is so fanatical in its San Francisco chauvinism that it relegates Greenwich Village to a four-page aside. A few academics—Joanna Richardson, Malcolm Easton, Cesar Graña—have turned in their best-known books on bohemian Paris, but all three prove too stricken with hauteur to do it justice; the gossipy accounts of American journalists Allen Churchill (about the pre-Depression Village) and Emily Hahn (a 1966 update of Parry) are every bit as informative. Roger Shattuck's *The Banquet Years*—about pre-dada Paris, 1885–1914—deserves its classic status, but it's a work of criticism informed by cultural history rather than vice versa. And then there's the English Marxist art historian T. J. Clark, who in 1973 published two studies of post-1848 Paris. *The Absolute Bourgeois* traces the explicit and implicit political histories of Millet, Daumier, Delacroix, and Baudelaire, glancing off bohemia only in passing. But bohemia is a key to Courbet in the companion volume, *Image of the People*.

By the time I encountered Clark in the late '70s, I was distressed by two lacunae in my investigations: pop and politics. My aim was to make some sense of my own observation and experience, to figure out how two zigzagging cultural trajectories, pop and bohemia, not only commingled but also fed into the imperatives of leftism, as I believed they did (or anyway, had and could). Reading between the lines, it was possible to intuit a rough theory of bohemian pop—you quickly learn that many bohemians have made their living as journalists and entertainers and that bohemians are generally less snobbish in their tastes than more respectable patrons of the arts. But of all the writers I've mentioned, only the wild-eyed Miller regards the connection between bohemia and revolution as more than a pose. So I seized upon the Marxist Clark with high hopes, which he didn't fulfill. Clark is a fecund, original, endlessly stimulating critic and historian, but he's fervently committed to the idea that the proletariat is the engine of history. This doesn't mean he scorns anomalous class formations, or remarkable individuals of whatever politics or objective self-interest. But bohemia only interests him insofar as its opposition to the bourgeoisie is unremitting and its poverty spectacularly involuntary. In practice, this means that he approves of it until 1851, at which point French history turns into farce or tragedy or something, with a brief interruption for Paris 1968. This didn't suit me, or convince me either, and it marked a hiatus in my bohemian studies. Cutting my losses, I stored up what I'd learned and expended it when the need arose.

My leave of absence ended when I read Jerrold Seigel's *Bohemian Paris*, which to put it plainly is the finest book about bohemia ever written. I could make an exception for *Exile's Return*, but Cowley's subject is really a generation, a generation he says wasn't exclusively bohemian, and wasn't defined by its bohemianism when it was. Seigel provides the most detailed and sweeping description extant of what it's fair to think of as bohemia's nativity and then sets an overarching theoretical program on top—he means to explain bohemia as a world-historical phenomenon, and comes close. Well expressed if not stylish, coherently organized for all its sweep, *Bohemian Paris* tackles the pop question, and if its answer to the political question isn't what I'd hope, well, with the '60s two decades behind us politics aren't what I'd hope either. It would be mean-spirited to blame Seigel for his skepticism, especially at the outset.

Writers who hope to understand bohemia combat its amorphousness by framing it with a conceit, a focus, a thesis. Working in the '30s, future Sovietologist Parry sets up his story by recounting Soviet critiques of bohemian classlessness, while Cowley distinguishes sharply (although not without ironic qualifications) between "bohemianism and radicalism." Working in the '60s, Graña concentrates on renowned (and often not very bohemian) writers, while Easton avers that bohemia is quintessentially the domain of the visual artist. Miller thinks bigger, propounding the millenarian notion that if bourgeois capitalism doesn't take the proto-culture road it's doomed to fascism, and who knows, he may be right, but his argument is so slapdash and overstated that it defeats itself. Seigel, a fifty-year-old Princeton history professor whose two previous books are a well-regarded thesis called *Rhetoric and Philosophy in Renaissance Humanism* and a monumentally convincing psychohistory called *Marx's Fate*, is just the opposite: calm and thorough, he examines the same bohemian-versus-bourgeois polarity and sees a continuity. Bohemia, he contends, is an essential adjunct of bourgeois capitalism, a proving ground where the presumed boundaries of bourgeois experience can be tested and extended. The two realms, he says, "imply, require, and attract each other."

If this strikes you as a less than startling thesis, it's because you already assume it—but as a joke, not a thesis. Chances are you're neither a boho lifer like Allen Ginsberg or Richard Miller (these are very rare) nor a cultural reactionary like Hilton Kramer or Jeremiah Denton (these aren't)—that like most settled liberals (and radicals) you think bohemia is interesting and silly in some proportion or other. And chances are you derive a certain comfort from snickering at it now and then. It was ever thus. Bohemians have been figures of fun since they went public in the 1840s; from the once and future provincial deserting his comely grisette to the hippie wedding, their tendency to revert to bourgeois norms has always tickled supposed sympathizers. This joke has gotten very stale, and Seigel's greatest achievement is to insist that it signifies, to suggest that rather than invalidating a social phenomenon that's survived almost as many obituaries as capitalism itself, it explains that phenomenon.

Seigel's explanation is remarkably sane and sensible within the limits he sets, and I can think of no more effective outline of bohemia than a critical summary of what he has to say. If it feels a bit amorphous at times, please be patient—a certain fogginess does seem built into the thing itself. Just to clear the air a little, we'll eventually call in Seigel's acerbic, barely acknowledged adversary, T. J. Clark, but don't worry—a comforting mist of ambiguity is sure to hang over our labors when they're over.

Boasting such precursors as François Villon, early student subcultures, Grub Street, and Rameau's nephew, bohemia had its inception in Paris in the first half of the nineteenth century. Exactly when is less certain, although most would go along with Seigel and set the date at 1830, the year of the July

Monarchy, and (as Miller emphasizes) the battle of *Hernani*, when an "army" of outlandish-looking Latin Quarter youths made a succés de scandale at the opening of Hugo's play. Certainly bohemia was under way by the 1830s, but the term didn't become current until 1849, when an impecunious coffee addict named Henry Murger adapted four years of newspaper sketches into a play that was soon to be a best-selling book called *Scènes de la vie de Bohème*. In the 1890s, it would prove the source of Puccini's *La bohème* as well.

Murger is a crucial figure in the history of bohemia, not least because nobody who isn't a student of bohemia remembers him anymore. A prematurely bald little guy with a chronic skin condition, he grew up in awe of the genteel artists his father served as a concierge and died before he was forty. And from his first success he was ridiculed. Although his archly ironic sentimentality touched a large audience, his stilted prose betrayed his lack of education, and he grew two left feet whenever he went in for a bit of climbing. He longed for a comfortable life, yet the barbs of his old Left Bank allies hurt him, and he found himself unable to write well about anything but the bohemia that writing about bohemia had enabled him to escape. Nevertheless, he deserves better than the condescension he gets from more socially secure writers of smaller historical consequence, such as Graña, who barely mentions him, or Miller, who drags him forward as a tragic cooptee. Clark is actively hostile, on the grounds that Murger conflated student styles with "the reality of Bohemian life" in a deliberate attempt to flatter bourgeois taste. For Seigel, on the other hand, Murger is where bohemia's story must begin. He wasn't "a great writer," Seigel admits, but neither was he "a mere popularizer"; it was Murger (not even Puccini) who gave bohemia "the widespread appeal, and peculiar evocative power, it retained for so long."

This is typical of Seigel. There's no snobbishness and very little arrogance in the man; he's not carrying the torch for modern art, local color, cultural revolution, or the great ideas of western man. He just wants to make sense of this thing. He wants to know how it changed the lives of the millions nobody remembers anymore, the true predecessors of all but a few of us. Murger's vision of bohemia as a way station between penniless artists and fame or the grave may have been appropriated from his onetime roommate Champfleury, a talented opportunist who soon attached himself to Courbet and Baudelaire and was dubbed "king of Bohemia," and certainly had the unacknowledged effect of glamorizing the poverty he hoped to leave behind. But Seigel refuses to reduce him to these circumstances; he sees even Murger's failings and little hypocrisies as exemplary and situates him near the center of bohemia's unchartable tangle of causes, effects, tendencies, tangents, symptoms, coincidences, misdirections, slipped concepts, and acts of God. He understands that even if Murger was flattering bourgeois taste—and given his intense ambivalence and insecurity, it's probably fairer to describe his attitude as half-conscious aspiration—he was also shaping it. His confusion was society's confusion.

If Seigel's story has one overriding theme, it's the inability of capitalism to solidify the social boundaries "harmony and stability" require of the supposedly unfettered individuals the system exists to serve and exploit—even though such boundaries are imposed de facto by the exigencies of daily life, no less real (and often more oppressive) for being so hard to define. Bohemia, then, is "the appropriation of marginal life-styles by young and not so young bourgeois, for the dramatization of ambivalence toward their own social identities and destinies." Its "signs" are "art, youth, the underworld, the gypsy life-style." Yet although Seigel distinguishes between art and bohemia as strenuously as any snob bent on proving that bohemians make lousy artists, it's the first of these "signs," art, that his history of bohemia keeps coming back to. Whatever their connections to "youth, the underworld, the gypsy life-style," his protagonists are artists, especially if you don't define art in a snobbish way—if you grant access to the "itinerant street artists" who make an all-too-fleeting appearance (confused by police with "the underworld") and to such inside journalists as Alexandre Privat d'Anglemont, Jules Vallés, and Paul Bourget. Again and again Seigel's bohemians explore whether they can make their lives meaningful through art, and whether they can make a living as artists. For most of them, art—often bad art, or art that exists only in fantasy and conversation—remains a plausible way of plumbing the hidden potential of one's identity and destiny. But it's of significantly less use in the little matter of keeping body and soul together.

However you explain this sad state of affairs—and I think it's more fruitful to focus on the influx of artists from the low end of the class system than to bewail the maw of the marketplace—its effect among bohemians was to valorize poverty. Already alienated by the contradictions of capitalism, the votaries of self-expression assumed a principled repugnance for its prime mover: money. It would be cynical to reduce bohemian radicalism to this syndrome—political rationalizations grasped at under spiritual duress can take on a life of their own. But because bohemianism is so tied up in dramatization, outsiders are universally suspicious of the sincerity and/or historical necessity of bohemian politics, and Seigel has a more specific point to make as well. He believes bohemia's status as a social entity, a self-conscious subculture, is politically moot; whatever political lessons it's good for, solidarity isn't among them. His chief exhibit is journalist Jules Vallés, who was jailed several times by the Second Empire and escaped to London after the fall of the Paris Commune in 1871. Although Vallés's rhetoric became ever more communistic (and antibohemian) in his later years, Seigel argues that at the root of his politics "he was torn between a sense of membership in the bourgeoisie and a contradictory consciousness of exclusion and hostility that could not be firmly attached to any other class identity." In other words, he was prey to "refractory individualism," the bohemian motive to beat all bohemian motives.

Most chroniclers of bohemia have been nominally liberal aesthetes who've dismissed bohemian leftism in passing. Seigel has an ax to grind—politics rather than the arts is his specialty, and although he can't avoid writing mostly about artists, his overview is political. Seigel stresses that the Bourgeois Monarchy of 1830 was far from hegemonic, quickly giving rise to two opposing factions within the bourgeoisie—the Party of Resistance, which envied and courted the old regime, and the Party of Movement, which kept faith with the peûple in whose name the Revolution of 1789 had been joined. He sees bohemia as aligned willy-nilly with the Party of Movement, functioning "to keep bourgeois society open to new elements and energies." In short, bohemians are functionally liberals. When hopes for imminent social transformation ended with the failed revolution of 1848, bohemia's discrete if undefinable "political and cultural space" became a necessity. Seigel detects two political subtexts in the reviews Murger's breakthrough received two years later: "To some, la Bohème was attractive as an escape from nearly two years of revolutionary agitation and uncertainty, but to others it represented a reservoir of radical sentiments and energies."

Either way, it seems that one of bohemia's prime political functions is to provide a refuge from the tedium and dangers of actual politics. And while their attraction to the visionary, as well as what Seigel calls "their orientation toward the lower parts of society," inclined even the most hidebound bohemian aesthetes to a vague leftism, all but the most ideological bohemians tended to work out their radical sentiments and energies in artistic terms—if not as practitioners, then as critics, comrades, fellow travelers, hangers-on, or fans. Here Seigel finds two tendencies once again. Call one avant-gardism, the other commercialization, and don't believe for a second that they divide up so neatly. Commercializers were rarely hailed as avant-gardists (although some may have deserved it), but avant-gardists were fascinated by commercialization, and politically the two categories were even more mixed up. If anything, the commercializers were further left.

The avant-garde attitude is clearly discernible in the future Parnassian Gautier and the protosymbolist Nerval, veterans of the battle of Hernani who are often cited as the first bohemians. But like most commentators, Seigel takes some pains to separate avant-garde from bohemia. As a term, "avant-garde" apparently originated with an obscure Fourierist pamphleteer who used it to describe art manifesting "the most advanced social tendencies" in 1845. But just as the idea of bohemia gained currency in the wake of the failed revolution of 1848, avant-garde art, which Seigel dates to the onset of impressionism in the 1860s, became a recognizable concept after the fall of the Paris Commune in 1871. Commercialization, on the other hand, is an antecedent of bohemia as old as Grub Street, which Cowley tells us "was already a crowded quarter" in Rome and Alexandria.

So what distinguished the bohemia of the 1960s was its domination by fans, not the pop connection itself. From its inception, bohemia hasn't merely revolted against the commodification of art—it's coped with it. Bohemia grew up right alongside mass culture, and many of its denizens not only earned their pittance from Paris's two dozen daily newspapers and countless lesser periodicals, but became media-savvy while doing so. Ever since *Hernani*, bohemians had been partial to public display, transforming life into performance as a matter of aesthetic principle, and soon they became specialists in self-promotion. That's why the virulently antibohemian reactionary Goncourts complained so bitterly about writers who were, in Seigel's paraphrase, "attuned to the contemporary world of publicity and display and devoid of links to the past and its traditions." By the 1880s, many poets (including a few pioneering singer-songwriters) were making their living in the new Left Bank and Montmartre cabarets, some of which whetted the bourgeois appetite for la vie de bohème by publishing their own newspapers. In the visual arts, where Courbet had demonstrated the commercial potential of negative publicity, Manet's bad reviews combined with his visionary art to make him notorious in the '60s, an investment in the '70s, and independently wealthy in the '80s. And while the avant-gardist Manet kept his (less than absolute) distance from bohemia, such separations proved difficult to maintain during the banquet years.

For Seigel, the pivotal figures here are Erik Satie and his suicidal counterpart Alfred Jarry, seminal avant-gardists who intensify the bohemian confusion between art and the artistic life. Jarry's confusion goes all the way—his ambivalence toward bourgeois boundaries is really a compulsion to overcome the limits of "material existence itself." But Satie is a survivor, and gradually his bohemianism evolves into his avant-gardism—his mastery of both self-advertisement (he even wrote pseudonymous newspaper columns about himself) and the commodity form (from pop tunes to what he dubbed "furniture music"). But his pop bent—part nose-thumbing, part survival tactic, part sheer sensibility—was only one of his and Jarry's many gibes at the valorization of the aesthetic as a category. By undermining the hallowed significance of art itself, Seigel says, the two artists thrust eccentric, marginal, borderline "life on the edge" center stage, preparing the way for dada. There's even a sense in which dada's refusal to make any distinction between art and life is foreshadowed by Satie's retirement to a Paris suburb, where he traded art in for life, abandoning "serious" composing for a dozen years, which didn't stop the locals from regarding him as a weirdo.

Does Satie cease to be a bohemian when he leaves bohemia? Or, to take a rather different example, how about Picasso, who was soon to achieve superstardom with the most effective self-promotion in the history of bohemia—not only was he a great artist, he symbolized the great artist. It's not so easy to say, is it? After all, neither man can be accused of reverting to bourgeois norms. The problem is that bohemia is evolving and expanding almost unrecognizably. To this day it's good sport to tweak bohemians for hypocrisy and foolish to write bohemia's obituary. But Seigel ends his story in 1930 not only because Paris's ascendancy as the locus of bohemia ended about then, but also because bohemia has become ever more unchartable throughout the century.

Seigel emphasizes how bohemian usages now lace through bourgeois fashion, sexual mores, popular culture, and political progressivism, so that "the form of life we call bourgeois today would hardly be recognized by those who defended it a century ago." But he might also have pointed out, as Cowley did long ago, that the bohemian ideal of self-expression was instrumental in popularizing the consumption ethic without which capitalism would have collapsed. Or mentioned all the variants on "youth, the underworld, the gypsy life-style." Bikers, hobos, cultists, sectarians, uncloseted gays and lesbians, proud ethnic minorities, permanent students, crackpot inventors, media workers, drug addicts, new wave fans, ordinary failures pursuing their elusive dreams from town to town and continent to continent—all of them dramatize marginality in a way that often touches bohemia and rarely embraces it. And yet, bohemia remains. As Seigel puts it: "The fact that Bohemia's history has not been ended by these changes suggests that what has declined since the 1920s is only one particular form of it. We may now call it the classic Bohemia, corresponding to the classic phase in the history of modern bourgeois society that extended between the French Revolution and the First World War." Bohemia is everywhere—but it's still somewhere.

If I've made Seigel sound too sweetly reasonable or vaguely all-embracing, that's as it should be. He is. The formal limits he imposes on his subject reflect the philosophical limitations of a man who seems rather uncomfortable with pitched conflict. That's why he stresses the continuities rather than the polarities of bohemian-bourgeois, and never gets too explicit about the polemical subthrust of his putatively descriptive work.

Seigel's distaste for pitched conflict—for struggle—typifies his liberalism and is related to his tendency to fudge questions of class, which while a somewhat clearer concept than bohemia is also notoriously resistant to definition. In fact, one of Seigel's most salient insights is class-related. Early on, he asks why bohemia is associated with both privation and hedonism: the "willingness to renounce gratifications" of the aspiring artist and the "demand for personal liberty that borders on indulgence" of the consciousness-expanding rebel. His solution seems obvious once he's stated it, but it was a new one on me: the bohemian commitment to poverty, he suggests, bespeaks the lower-middle-class discipline inculcated from childhood in the likes of Murger, while the bouts of big spending and appreciation for the finer things originate with refugees from the upper bourgeoisie who have "known bourgeois comfort and even luxury" and "feel they have the right to know it again."

Still, this is one of the few times Seigel's speculations stray far from what one might designate the comfortable bourgeoisie, which I assume to be his own class now and somewhat nervously venture to guess (these things are rarely neat) is the class he came out of. It's one of the few times he describes a disparity in bourgeois culture as a polarity rather than a continuity—a polarity he qualifies immediately by adding that since the goal of lower-middle-class discipline was wealth, bohemians like Murger naturally "felt the appeal of both perspectives." This is strange when you think about it, one reason *Bohemian Paris* ends up feeling amorphous for all its coherent good sense and base-covering attention to analytic detail. Mapping a region of society that has always defined itself in terms of outrage and opposition, Seigel leaves us with the impression that it's also somehow an unbroken field.

We can only conclude that his investment in this unbroken field is why neither working class nor ruling class figure in his bohemia at all. I suspect one reason he doesn't dwell on those "itinerant street artists," say, or describe any of the salons that made room for respectable bohemians, is to avoid various kinds of class mess that neither interest him nor further his thesis. But in fact both bohemia and bourgeoisie are even less hegemonic than it suits him to emphasize. Unaccustomed to manual labor though he may have been, Murger the concierge-tailor's son is more like the farm girl turned seamstress with whom he spent his last years than like his erstwhile roommate, the provincial haute-bourgeois Champfleury, who spent his last years directing the national ceramics museum. Really, now—is a seamstress, or a tailor who can't make ends meet, a true petit-bourgeois? The answer may not be an unequivocal no, but it isn't an unequivocal yes either. It's just a mess. And elsewhere Seigel muddles his class analysis further by coming this close to snickering at the willingness of poorer bohemians to take "whatever jobs they can find" and then half equating their simple need to survive with their sporadic hedonistic indulgences, a very different strain of materialism that he doesn't understand so well either. Sometimes what he calls ambivalence toward bourgeois life might better be described as smart shopping.

I assume Seigel harps on ambivalence because ambivalence is an animating force in his own life. It certainly isn't complacency that drives a respectable liberal academic to devote one admiring tome to bohemia and another to Karl Marx, who, the most powerful passage in *Marx's Fate* suggests, was also a creature of ambivalence—an ambivalence rooted in the kind of class mess Seigel sidesteps. For on the one hand Marx was a practical politician whose decade-plus in the First International was consumed by the issue-bound contingencies of a working-class movement, and on the other he considered it his mission to bestow the "spirit of generalization" on historical actors whose relationship to the means of production never rendered them as philosophical as Marx always predicted it would. You get the feeling that Seigel (who declares himself "frankly ambivalent" about Marxism) is a little disappointed in the working class, however warm his wishes for "the lower parts of society." He has his ambivalence about the bourgeoisie too, goodness knows, but in the end he appreciates its moral complexities as well as enjoying its comforts. After much doubt and pain he's realized it's his home, and a fine home it is.

So Seigel's determination to bind bohemia to bourgeoisie is less than disinterested. He not only has an ax to grind, he also has an adversary to fling it at. But just as in *Marx's Fate* competing biographers are chastised only in the notes, so in *Bohemian Paris* Seigel declines to do battle with T. J. Clark's *Image of the People*, which is called out in a bibliographical afterword.

Purportedly and primarily a study of Courbet, Clark's book is a cranky but far-reaching—sometimes startlingly astute, sometimes wrongheaded, sometimes both at once. Crankily, Clark prefers bohemia to avant-garde, which he brands "a finishing-school, an unabashed form of social climbing." But that's only because in Clark's view the great artists of the nineteenth century—including Rimbaud, Baudelaire, Stendhal, Millet, Daumier, Van Gogh, Cézanne, and Courbet—were those who "bypassed, ignored and rejected" the avant-garde. Bohemia, Clark insists, was "part of working-class Paris"; it comprised "an unassimilated class, wretchedly poor, obdurately anti-bourgeois" that fought on the barricades in 1848; these were "the men of the gutter, the self-made gods, not the students and lovers of the Latin Quarter." In short, bohemians aren't—or rather, weren't—liberals manque, but revolutionaries now long gone. In support he cites Champfleury, whom he both despises and, as Seigel demonstrates, misquotes—where Champfleury wrote "true bohemians," Clark sees (italics added) "*the* true bohemians."

To point out that Clark is eccentric is by no means to minimize his brilliance. Instead his very willfulness exposes once and for all the extent to which bohemia and avant-garde are rhetorical rather than historical concepts. I'm three-quarters won over by his irreverent view of the avant-garde, whose covertly retrograde political tendencies he forces nicely to the surface. When it comes to bohemia, though, I polarize over on the far side of Seigel—I'm inclined to make it more rather than less inclusive. Although Clark feels considerable affinity with fellow oddball-Marxist Walter Benjamin, his political reading of bohemia draws upon the old Marxist idea of the "intellectual proletariat." Marx himself considered bohemians adventurist conspirators if not lumpen trash, but that didn't stop his heirs from enlisting the artistic types who were always coming around anyway in the neat, putatively "economic" "intellectual proletariat" catchall and rationalization. But having added enough flesh and grit to the concept to make Seigel nervous, Clark makes clear in 1984's *The Painting of Modern Life* that his defense of bohemia was somewhat expedient. Though his ideas are provocative enough, he adopted the pose at least partly to shock his elders in academia and on the left. Like so many others, he was only passing through.

Yet *The Painting of Modern Life* aids our inquiries anyway—although it never touches directly on bohemia, it puts both pop and politics in an artistic setting, which is almost as good. With Manet as his focus, Clark examines the Haussmanized Paris that so fascinated Benjamin and finds significant concentrations of class mess. Subjugating formalist truisms about flatness and light to impressionism's boulevardscapes, suburban vistas, and scenes of rationalized leisure as new as the techniques used to depict them, he finds in three celebrated Manets doomed, compromised victims of bourgeois exploitation struggling to make themselves knowable. The courtesan of Olympe, the day tripper of Argenteuil, les canotiers, and the bargirl of *Un bar aux Folies-Bergère* make their way along the edges of the new dominant class with varying degrees of autonomy, aspiration, and dependency; all have, in Seigel's adaptable phrase, "appropriated a marginal life-style." Because they reflect unprecedented class formations, they're highly ambiguous, and no doubt highly ambivalent about their own status and meaning. But Clark holds that artists have no business exacerbating this ambiguity—or indulging whatever ambivalence they might feel about it. If clarity is impossible, then the painter must at least cut into the condescension and mystification that usually greet such confusing figures. Thus he argues that Manet disturbed bourgeois viewers as much as he did by forcing them to really look at what the progressive politician Léon Gambetta was to call les nouvelles couches sociales.

Even though his latest book abandons the special meanings he once assigned "bohemia" and "avant-garde" (both terms come up in more or less normal usage), Clark is still Seigel's adversary. He thinks marginality and ambivalence are overrated orthodoxies and demonstrates that the idea he sums up as "art seeks out the edges of things" was already a modernist truism by the 1880s. His concentration on class mess, on enactments of marginality that have little or nothing to do with bohemia, contrasts strikingly with Seigel's class myopia. When you read Clark, you realize how hegemonic Seigel's view of the bourgeois is—he comes close to implying that the most trustworthy agent of change in bourgeois society isn't Marx's working class but a bohemia he defines as totally bourgeois. He seems incapable of seeing any culture but bourgeois culture—he knows there's other stuff out there, but he can't make it signify for himself.

Clark tries. He speculates knowledgeably and imaginatively about what a Sunday in the grass might have meant to the burgeoning subclass of clerks and shop assistants. And he devotes half a chapter to the great café-concert singer Thérèsa, a nineteenth-century cross between Edith Piaf and Marie Lloyd. Seigel also writes extensively about cafe performers, but he never crosses Clark's path, describing only the overtly arty—yet popular or at least semipopular, and most often political—cabaret singers who flourished in the 1880s. Clark doesn't bother with such secondhand small-timers—like

Manet and Degas, he's attracted to the Real Thing. He believes that the café-concerts of the 1860s signal nothing less than the onset of popular culture as a discrete concept, a development about which he is frankly ambivalent. He sees how Thérèsa and others open pockets of freedom by challenging the strictures of the forces of order, but in the end he thinks they're, well, objectively counterrevolutionary. For Clark, "it's above all collectivity that the popular exists to prevent." The new forms conquer by dividing the wage slaves, turning les nouvelles couches sociales into spectators of the working class as represented by artists like Thérèsa. Content with entertainment and puffed up with connoisseurship, these permanent residents of the bourgeois margin appreciate the popular so they need never feel compelled to identify with the proletarian.

This is the kind of provocation I want from Clark, who clearly believes his analysis remains applicable today, although naturally things have gotten worse—the epidemic of romantic primitivism and the commodification of an indigenous middle-class culture have put the truly proletarian even further out of reach. But it fails to satisfy. Clark is very vague about the who and how of popular culture's creation, and also of its control—his excellent research into police censorship doesn't offer much purchase on the subtler workings of hegemony. Thérèsa's "pugilist's face" and "preposterous song" are described more condescendingly than I expect he intended, and les nouvelles couches sociales, like bohemia before them, retain Clark's sympathy only as long as they resist bourgeois blandishments. This is a writer in thrall to two intellectual passions, class struggle and great art, and while both are obviously rich categories, there's something cripplingly nineteenth-century about their grandeur and certainty. I mistrust modernist irony plenty, but while I'd rather read Clark, whose mind and language give off sparks, I find myself agreeing more with Seigel as he slogs tenaciously through his swamp of ambiguities.

Still, with my own orientation toward the lower parts of society—not only am I a leftist with connections to bohemia's respectable fringe, I'm a scion of les nouvelles couches sociales, which Clark persists in referring to as the petit bourgeoisie but which is known here in the U.S.A. by the more redolent name "service sector"—I'd like to believe some resolution is possible. And I find in Seigel leads I only wish Clark would follow up. What about those radical-bohemian cafe performers of the 1880s, for instance? Clearly they hoped to combat the café-concerts' objectively counterrevolutionary tendencies. How can they be said to have succeeded, failed, or both, aesthetically as well as politically? What parallels can we find in more recent popular and semipopular culture? And what about the audience? With the lower-middle class increasingly indistinguishable from the working class in its access to goods and services, maybe the ambivalence of lower-middle-class bohemians, whose numbers and expectations have risen markedly, has more in common with good old class animosity than anyone yet understands. Maybe the regrets of bohemia's legion of obituarists, forever bemoaning the latest generation's decadence and lost ideals, are really aimed at this horde of cultural interlopers. And maybe the right artists and agitators can teach these interlopers a little collective spirit after all. A long shot, but these days what isn't?

Clearly, Seigel's more generous overview and freedom from arrogance are better spiritual equipment for the job I've proposed, but he just as clearly lacks the requisite political sensibility and will, while if Clark could put great painting on hold and overcome the pessimism hidden beneath his dutiful outbursts of revolutionary hope, he might begin to figure out how the marginality endemic to advanced capitalism could serve the cause of rapid, necessary change. If instead of defining bohemia so stringently that it ends around 1849 he went the other way, using it as a catchall for who knows how many half-assed revolts and protests and expressions and escapes and self-immolations, he might manage to link all that discontent and missed connection to more systematic patterns of economic oppression. If instead of putting students and lovers in one box and men of the gutter in another, if instead of dismissing pop connoisseurship as snobbery he granted its potential in solidarity and educational pleasure, he might write a book that doesn't take place in the lost past—he might become a theorist rather than a historian of revolution, cultural or otherwise. Maybe he'll finally articulate what I hope is his hidden agenda—some new synthesis of the individualism he finds so crucial in art and the solidarity he finds so crucial in politics.

After all, isn't it unnecessarily cranky for a Marxist to find so much historical significance in heroic, faction-transcending geniuses from Courbet to Manet and so little in collectivities like bohemia, avant-garde, and for that matter audience—even granting that such collectivities don't deserve the privileged standing Marxism grants classes? Seigel's commitment to change may be soft on struggle, but his attraction to the less than heroic individual is exemplary. For it's the refractory but unheroic vagaries of bourgeois individualism that make class struggle seem too absolute a category in a world where only the most anal Marxists deny marginal folk their part in radical change.

Previously unpublished, 1987

The Village People

Christine Stansell's *American Moderns: Bohemian New York and the Creation of a New Century*

"Bohemia is, after all, inherently apolitical," opined a designated expert just a few months ago in the section you're reading. This revelation must have surprised Christine Stansell, whose vision of Greenwich Village in the 1910s assumes the opposite. Three of the four figures she follows most closely are remembered for political discourse: anarchist celebrity Emma Goldman, Red journalist John Reed, and progressive-utopian essayist Randolph Bourne. Only Margaret Anderson, her *Little Review* a literary counterpart to *The Masses*, owed her first allegiance to the arts that are supposedly bohemia's raison d'etre. Stansell's choices aren't willful, either. Earlier chroniclers Albert Parry, Allen Churchill, and Emily Hahn also count Reed and Goldman co-equals of such scenemaking aesthetes as Anderson, Mabel Dodge, and Floyd Dell. Barely mentioned by Parry and ignored by the others, Stansell's ringer is Bourne, who first resided near his job when he worked at the Chelsea-based *New Republic*. But money problems soon forced him downtown, where he rubbed elbows, wooed actresses, wore a cape, and died of influenza at thirty-two. If Stansell wants to call him a bohemian, she's got a right. Bohemia is, after all, protean and elastic—so much so, in fact, that you can define it any way you please. So give Stansell credit for making her definitions stick. Her focus is narrow, and though her tales are swift and specific, she's not a stand-out storyteller. But she sure makes everything cohere and signify.

One of the commonest barbs tossed at bohemia is that it talks better art than it produces, and this is certainly true of the early Village—beyond the young Eugene O'Neill, the transitory Georgia O'Keeffe, and the early Ashcan School, none of its principals is remembered for his or her creative output. Stansell's brilliance is to look beyond this embarrassment. She knows Isaac Babel's *Red Cavalry* stands as "a fully modernist narrative of war as unimaginable horror" where Reed's *Insurgent Mexico* merely "reworks late-Victorian conventions into what was to become the reigning left-wing idiom of revolution." But the life achievements of Reed and his cohort seem to Stansell at least as far-reaching—and even, in their ever-dispersing way, enduring—as anything a minor master like Babel ever wrote.

Needless to say, this judgment propels us into the vague realm of sociology. None of the historical phenomena Stansell cites can be strictly or exclusively attributed to bohemia. But as history actually took place, all of them did pass through the early Village, and all were empowered by the contact. Free speech. Birth control. Sexual freedom in all its bravado and hypocrisy (although not for gays, not yet). Human interest journalism. The cross-class nexus of empathy and publicity that established the now assumed bond between artists and the wretched of the earth (although not blacks, not yet). The emergence of the ethnic hero, especially the Jew. The rise of New York as cultural capital and nationwide magnet.

Two concerns predominate, however, one already noted. Tracing her bohemia back to the Lower East Side of the 1890s and unlikely outposts like Davenport, Iowa (hometown of three major Villagers, and later, although Stansell doesn't mention it, Bix Beiderbecke), Stansell insists on what ought to be obvious—that people who defy political convention, people who defy artistic convention, and people who defy social convention gravitate toward each other whatever their deep ultimate differences. She also demonstrates persuasively that the shape progressivism/socialism took in America had its template in bohemia, not least because journalism is a bohemian occupation whether arty know-nothings like it or not. The only factor that looms larger in Stansell's bohemia than politics is one that wasn't yet politicized enough: the influence of women.

It's no surprise that Stansell, author of a history of women in New York and coeditor of the ground-breaking feminist sex anthology *Powers of Desire*, remembers Margaret Sanger, Susan Glaspell, Neith Boyce, and Ida Rauh as well as lecture star Goldman, salon keeper Dodge, and Hollywood-ready Louise Bryant, all of whom provide welcome relief from the nostalgic bonhomie of so many bohemias recollected. What's more impressive is how persuasively Stansell's analysis foregrounds them. She believes that, rather than art, the most important heritage of the early Village is "distinct forms of sociability" that soon spread everywhere, and that these were produced or inspired primarily by women. The associative style of conversation that avoided "glorious fighting and keen arguing" reflected close social and professional relationships between men and women, often the "New Women" who were venturing onto the streets in those years. When such relationships were sexualized, they inevitably took the form of romantic marriages that "assumed unprecedented significance as conduits of mutual understanding"—although Stansell is properly forceful in pointing out that, in a world without servants, housework and child-rearing were harder on women than ever and that, for all but a few self-reliant wives, what free love advocates called "Varietism" wasn't all that different from what disgruntled spouses call fucking around.

Stansell's bohemia didn't survive World War I, which repressed *The Masses* and *The Little Review*, led to the early deaths of Bourne and Reed, and sent Anderson and Goldman into exile, voluntary and involuntary respectively. In a regrettable boho tradition, she's a little waspish describing what came after her great moment, which may have commercialized sex, if that's a bad thing, but also had far more room for African-Americans and popular culture as well as producing better writing. Hart Crane, Edna St. Vincent Millay, E. E. Cummings, and the maturing Eugene O'Neill may not have been much for demos or hanging out, but they left their own enduring heritage—including an ever more protean and elastic bohemia, every era of which deserves a history or three as thoughtful as this one.

Village Voice, 2000

A Slender Hope for Salvation

Charles Reich's *The Greening of America: How the Youth Revolution Is Trying to Make America Livable*

The Greening of America has achieved a success somewhat comparable to that of *The Outsider*. *The Outsider*, since you probably don't recall, was the 1956 debut of a bookish young Englishman named Colin Wilson who identified with every exemplar of alienation in the history of literature. Apparently, he believed that to describe a series of these constituted a theory of modern society. His conclusion: individual Outsiders, inspired by figures as diverse as Nietzsche and Madame Blavatsky, could resolve their dilemma (and by implication the world's) in a prophetic religious reawakening. Writing in *The New Yorker*, Dwight Macdonald described Wilson as "a Philistine, a Babbitt, a backwoods revivalist of blood-chilling consistency." Nevertheless, or consequently, *The Outsider* was popular among campus intellectuals in the late '50s; for some of them, in fact, it was almost holy writ. Nobody reads it any more. Wilson is a successful writer in England.

The striking parallel between these two books accentuates their differences and reminds us if we need reminding how quickly times change. Like Wilson, Reich takes for his theme nothing less than the redemption of the modern world, and like Wilson, he suggests that this can only be attained through individual salvation, a process he dubs "revolution by consciousness." Like Wilson, Reich is a popularizer who candidly borrows ideas from respected authorities. End of parallel. Wilson claimed to be an optimist, but like all good '50s intellectuals he wallowed in anger; the pessimism of Reich's analysis extends far beyond existentialist brinksmanship, yet in the end he is sanguine to the point of fatuousness. Wilson was an individualist who scorned politics and the hoi polloi, while Reich's vision, as befits a forty-two-year-old Yale law prof, is more humane, partaking of none of the ugly elitism of Wilson's arrogant Übermenschlichkeit. Reich is also the superior writer. His style is pedestrian rather than barbarous, and he has taken the time to digest his influences. The resulting cud has a curious bland consistency. This may be why *The New Yorker*, which panned *The Outsider*, devoted most of one issue to a thirty-nine-thousand-word precis of Reich's book.

Another reason is that people are scared. In the '50s, apocalyptic thinking enjoyed a certain modishness but could be dismissed for just that reason as avant-garde chic. Now the daily editorial page reads like the Revelation of St. John the Divine. People are scared about Indochina, about racial strife, about the ecocrisis, but the most visible and consciousness-provoking source of their fear is the very phenomenon that motivates Reich's optimism: the polarization of young people. How neat—the young, that inescapable proof of our dissolution, will save us all. If the world is indeed saved, of course, then the young will save it. No one else will have the chance. But the likelihood that it will be saved as Reich predicts is, unfortunately, small.

Reich believes that states of mind, not social and economic classes, are basic to the politics of change in America: "There is no class struggle; today there is only one class. In Marx's terms, we are all the proletariat, and there is no longer any ruling class except the machine itself." The core of this strange idea is presented in a formula likely to be his one enduring contribution to the way we talk about ourselves: the concepts of Consciousness I, II, and III. Consciousness I is rugged individualism, self-reliant at best and rapacious at worst. Consciousness II is the New Deal, organization-man mentality Reich takes to pervade the corporate state. But Consciousness III, youth consciousness, is the key to our future, simultaneously self-directed and communitarian, adventurous, anti-hierarchical, and above all open to continuous change. It would be otiose to criticize this scheme as crude—it is a convenient popularizing device, nothing more, and Reich acknowledges its drawbacks. And once it is granted that Reich's book is not in itself an epochal work, then the real question of quality concerns its effect: who reads it for what reason and what do they do about it?

Reich's admirers are young (or wish they were) and (vaguely) radical. They especially appreciate its delineation of the development of Consciousness II from Consciousness I and the description of Consciousness III that took up much of *The New Yorker* version. He falters, they feel, in his analysis of how Consciousness II becomes Consciousness III. I think it is just the opposite. Reich's analysis of the corporate state combines the popular sociology of the '50s (Reisman and Whyte, especially) with jeremiads about American imperial power. Not that much of what he says isn't true, although his description of ye olde organization man sometimes seems a little quaint. But it's so familiar that it's lost its information value. Only his presentation of the identity of state/corporation/foundation/union/university contains insights that are at least secondhand. What's the point of disseminating concepts already available in *Time* and *Newsweek*, and even more, what's the point of exulting over one more rehash of the old truisms?

The Consciousness III section—called "The New Generation," naturally—is not so much a description as a celebration, and its major fault is obvious: it's inspired by possibility and rhetoric rather than reality. Reich does warn against hip chauvinism and youth chauvinism, but his rendering of Consciousness I and Consciousness II is flawed by both sorts of condescension. (Since Reich is forty-two, the first predominates.) Even worse, he fails to make explicit the fear, anger, and isolation that lie on the other side of liberation for most of the young. Fear, anger, and isolation are not unreasonable responses to the paradoxes of life in America, but they do mar the reality of Consciousness III, and they do affect the accuracy with which Consciousness III people analyze their homeland. The same syndrome is to some extent responsible for the contradictions of Reich's presentation, all of which boil down to one: like so many dissidents throughout American history, he cannot decide whether he loves this country or hates it.

It's not surprising that Reich's most fundamental ambivalence concerns material things, for of course it is in the realm of objects—the power to reshape the physical environment—that American culture is most specifically itself. The America-is-bad part of the book is full of the usual stuff about technology and materialism—production as pollution, consumption as self-definition, ownership as status, electric toothbrushes as hydrogenated peanut butter. Reich even goes so far as to suggest that if America is to reorder its priorities in a way that is both just and economically sound, liberal shibboleths about military spending will crumble. The military budget, he says, will barely cover the cost of an effective educational system, much less clean up the environment and cure the rest of the social ills he acknowledges. To do all that, a vast decrease in consumer spending will also be necessary.

At the same time, Reich shares with Marx the notion that utopia can only be achieved through technology and offers a rather original suggestion as to the material basis of Consciousness III. The new consciousness, he says, results from a contradiction in advanced corporate capitalism. In order to expand the gross national product, citizens must on the one hand produce and on the other hand consume. The best producer is a self-denying automaton; the best consumer is a healthy hedonist. Inevitably, these two functions collide. Even among Consciousness II people, the authenticity of whose pleasure he somewhat gratuitously challenges, the hedonistic impulse sometimes produces quasi-dropouts like Reich himself. For young people, who consume with gusto before they must take on the realities of production, dropping out is a natural solution.

This way of explaining the children-of-affluence idea is the one instance in which Reich's popularization elevates itself to synthesis, which is really what popularization should do. It is a concise and sane interpretation of ideas implicit in thinkers like McLuhan and Fuller. That it has received scant attention even from Reich's fans indicates how deeply ingrained the Consumer Society cliché, which it contravenes, has become among American naysayers. This in turn suggests the Europeanization of institutionalized dissent, especially within the university system: legitimate criticisms of consumerism are almost invariably inspired by a certain down-the-nose disdain for the nouveau vulgarity consumption usually entails. What Reich understands is that the demeaning lust for still more upward mobility that so often powers conspicuous and compulsive consumption is a transitional phenomenon. The children of affluence show a unique ability to consume selectively, to define their enjoyment rather than allowing it to define them. Since Consciousness III reacts against the common American decision to be spic-and-span even at the cost of fertility—that is, to be sterile—this means in practice that hip young people buy goods that help them contact themselves and their environment. They purchase a stereo, which they program themselves, before a television set, and a motorcycle, which provides cheap and immediate transportation, before an air-conditioned automobile.

Critically, however, this ability depends on the very class system Reich dismisses so peremptorily. In order to react against a pattern of consumption, you must first experience it, and the simple fact is that even among the young, sophisticated, autonomous consumption is deviant behavior common only in the urban well-to-do—upwardly mobile middle-class kids, professional families, and the wealthy. The exceptions are numerous—a remarkable number of young factory workers, for example, tend to save up a bankroll and take off for a while—and the relative flexibility of class barriers in the United States can't be denied, but that doesn't mean they don't exist. Even more important, the class relationship of the United States to the rest of the world is impossible to overlook—unless, like Reich, your vision of the coming world is shaped in the cafeterias of Yale. What kind of conclusions might he have drawn at a Peace Corps project in India, or a ghetto high school, or a community college in Queens?

For Consciousness III does have a material base, and it can't flatten out too far. Abundance and affluence are myths, or anyway, metaphors—there just aren't enough expensive stereos and steamer trips around the world to go around the world. Nor is there any reason to believe that Consciousness III encourages a realistic estimate of one's share. Reich, like many Consciousness III folk, has a rather cavalier attitude toward what more pessimistic thinkers refer to as suffering, or oppression—he doesn't like to dwell on it. But oppression is more than just a drag. The economic well-being of each of us depends on it, and it is built into our psychology. It will never be excised by vague good wishes. Reich ventures no hard-headed projections of what sort of economic reorganization might provide the world with an effective educational system, and his blithe assumption that once America adopts Consciousness III it will simply abandon imperialism ignores fair and serious questions—first suggested by someone named Lenin—about how such a withdrawal might affect our own wealth. Reich throws an occasional compliment towards black people for their heavy contribution to Consciousness III, but seems unaware that many blacks doubt that racism will be expunged by soul-searching. And he never even refers to women as a group with grievances. Feminism hadn't hit the newsmagazines when his book was being written, and you don't pick up that sort of insight at Yale.

The reasons for this gap are obvious: it avoids thorny questions about concerted political action. In fact, I get the crawly feeling that the purpose of this book is just that: to offer a copout on politics. It is Reich's explicit message that you can change the world just by doing your thing. Now, as most leftists admit, politics are a bummer. Yet as long as people are dissatisfied they must be dealt with, and what the best of the left is trying to do—however gross and neurotic its failures—is create a world in which everyone can achieve something like Consciousness III. Affluence has been good for American young people in a spiritual way by enabling them to achieve new kinds of selfhood, and it's good to read a writer who understands that—but only if he also understands the paradoxes of smugness and myopia the new spirituality entails. This Reich refuses to do, maybe because it would be too much like work.

The best way to judge popular art is by its effect on its audience: who reads it for what reason and what do they do about it. Reich's bestseller describes a possibility that may be present—America has always confounded its pessimists—but seems unlikely. He reinforces all of young people's most self-satisfied presumptions and encourages them to eschew politics and any systematic attempt to broaden their own compassion. He has written a bad book.

Los Angeles Times, 1970

The Lumpenhippie Guru

Ed Sanders's *The Family: The Story of Charles Manson's Dune Buggy Attack Battalion*

The Family is the first complete, authoritative account of the career of Charles Manson. A small-time thief, forger, and pimp who was paroled after seven years in prison at the dawn of San Francisco's 1967 Summer of Love, Manson, hirsute and acid-eyed, was charged with the Tate-LaBianca murders less than three years later. In January 1971, he was convicted of these seven murders. He must still stand trial for two others—one of them, according to this book, a hideous torture experiment—and is implicated in many more.

The Family tells how an ambitious petty criminal focused some cunning amateur psychology on particularly vulnerable examples of the mass alienation of California's youth bohemia, and created a "family" of disciples bound together by a macabre synthesis of antisocial pathology and communal ideals. Combining calculated alterations of tenderness and violence with awesome sexual stamina and a line of pseudo-guru babble, he attracted a following of pathetic young women whose sexual favors helped him move his band of lumpenhippies through various crash scenes. He used drugs and sex for blackmail and mind control, developed a doom philosophy influenced by the satanist cults that flourish around Los Angeles, and prepared his disciples for racial Armageddon, which they all believed was imminent, with a battalion of stolen dune buggies equipped with booty acquired on stolen credit cards. The murders that resulted from this runaway obsession with violence seem inevitable in retrospect.

The outline of this story has been known for quite a while—sometimes reliably, sometimes not. Ed Sanders has solidified it, filling in particulars and verifying rumors. Manson's close relationships with hip Hollywooders like record and television producer Terry Melcher and Beach Boy Dennis Wilson, now minimized by the principals, are fully described. His occult connections are detailed. The crimes and their solutions are recounted with care for sequence and consistency. Sanders's research occupied a year and a half of his life; tens of thousands of pages of data were organized into some fifty subject files and dozens of chronological files. All the allegations he reports have been checked against known facts, and for the most part he refused to use any information that didn't come from at least two unrelated individuals. This work was extraordinarily difficult, requiring auxiliary investigators and even disguises. Since most of Manson's associates are partisans of violence, it was also dangerous.

So why did Sanders bother? The money accrued is certain to be matched by the pain, and Sanders is by profession a poet, not a reporter. The answer is that, despite his taste for what he calls "a quiet life of poetry and peace," Sanders has found himself impelled, by aesthetic and ethical commitments that are often indistinguishable, into a series of progressively more public manifestations. In 1961 he was one of the pacifists who attempted to board a nuclear submarine in a seminal act of passive resistance that seemed aberrant at the time. In 1962 he founded "A Magazine of the Arts" whose title could not be reproduced in a newspaper. But he ended up on the cover of one of *Life*'s hippie issues in 1967, the leader of a successful and influential rock group called the Fugs. The Fugs gave way almost imperceptibly to active support of the pop-hip politics of Yippie and Chicago 1968, which Sanders immortalized last year in the mock-heroic novel *Shards of God*.

So it was a natural step for Sanders to turn to Manson, one of the culminations of America's public romance with the hippies. Like Manson, Sanders was into sex, dope, the occult, and the downfall of straight society. Both his Fugs monologues and *Shards of God* were full of references to jelly orgies, titanic mindwarps, and arcane rituals. Of course, many of these references were ironic, overstated metaphors that weren't intended literally. But metaphors have content—Sanders really does believe in expanded sexuality, sacramental and recreational psychedelics, and non-rationalistic modes of knowing—and irony is a sophisticated tool. What could Sanders do when a would-be groupie actually brought a jar of jelly to a Fugs concert—send her back for the Skippy? Such misunderstandings are inevitable when avant-gardism is transformed into a mass movement. This is a liability that long-haired criminals like Charlie Manson and who knows how many other punk charismatics can exploit.

In the age of the new togetherness, it isn't just the good guys who get together. In *The Family*, Sanders states this problem once and never makes the point again: "The flower movement was like a valley of thousands of plump white rabbits surrounded by wounded coyotes. Sure, the 'leaders' were tough, some of them geniuses and great poets. But the acid-dropping middle-class children from Des Moines were rabbits." Sanders doesn't dwell on this idea because his narrative is almost compulsively free of what in a more literal context he refers to as "horse dooky." He refuses to philosophize, psychoanalyze, or make excuses. *The Family* is nothing more than a chronological arrangement of all those facts, apparently written direct from the files, rapidly. True, the diction is characteristic Sanders Americanese—in all his work he has a way of coming up with hyphenated coinages like "bunch-punching," "murder-fated" and "hell-creep," and he is fond of words like "tycoon" and "sleuth"—and he will occasionally add a jarring note of boyish sarcasm to some especially grisly disclosure by ending the paragraph with a brief "far out" or "oo-ee-oo." But the book is determinedly non-written. There is no theorizing, and no new journalism either—no fabricated immediacy, no reconstructed dialogue, no arty pace.

This data-mania is itself an anti-middlebrow avant-garde ploy. Sanders is quite capable of normal prose and fictional technique, and had he deemed the effort worthy he probably could have made *The Family* into something like *In Cold Blood* or even *The Boston Strangler*. But he represents a sensibility that has pretty much rejected such devices, and his book is truer and more exciting for it. His terse notebook style, avoiding comment and ignoring conventional standards of rhetoric, functions as a deliberate artistic choice. Although he may mention in passing that arrests for possessing a harmless euphoriant or for "felonious breast-feeding" can be expected to spark dangerous resentment, he clearly feels that the facts about Manson and his followers speak for themselves, and that they are horrible beyond explanation.

The intensity of this feeling, which reflects Sanders's commitment to nonviolence, is the greatest virtue of an excellent book. The Manson case engendered much confusion in the ranks of hip. A distressing minority—represented at its most extreme by Weatherwoman Bernardine Dohrn (who cited the murders as revolutionary acts before going underground) and, more reasonably, by those who suspect a frame-up—were unwilling to believe that a long-haired minstrel could also be a racist and male supremacist who used dope and orgasm and even some variety of love to perpetuate his own murderous sadism. In his coverage of the trial for the *Los Angeles Free Press*, Sanders did his best to protect Manson's presumption of innocence, and he was severely critical of anti-hippie hysteria among straight journalists. But his own research convinced him who was guilty and ought to convince anybody.

Guilt is definitely the word. Sanders believes that, for whatever reason, the plump white rabbits in Manson's entourage have become "crazed with the willingness to murder" and must be separated from society. His portrayal of Sharon Tate and associates, on the other hand, while tinged with the deep disdain of a genuine psychic voyager for ruling-class dabblers, is temperate. He doesn't conceal their connections with big-time dope and the occult, but he does withhold damaging but irrelevant information "in respect for the memory of the innocent slain."

The murderers are guilty and their victims were innocent—after years of rationalization and hip irony, such a formulation has a refreshing moral directness. Let others fulminate over co-optation by rich straights. Sanders knows that for the most part the co-opters are only contemptible, and he will return to oppose the death-creeps who rule this society some other time. For now, he is horrified by the satanist coyotes who battle the forces of Yippie for the soul of the disaffected young—the sexist bikers, the cults that traffic in animal and (it would appear) human sacrifice. In order to say this, Sanders has done nothing less than risk his own life, for that's how serious he believes the enemy within to be, and who knows enough to gainsay him? It is only fitting that such a risk should produce such a terrifying book.

New York Times Book Review, 1971

Strait Are the Gates

Morris Dickstein's *Gates of Eden: American Culture in the Sixties*

That the '60s are at present discredited should come as no surprise to anyone with a sense of historical rhythm. Even if the accreditation procedure wasn't left up to a social group—intellectuals, in the broad sense that includes statusy journalists as well as academic bigdomes—whose tastes and interests were poorly served by the period, we would be on a reaction cycle right now. (After all, what are people going to think of 1977 in 1984?) But the reaction hasn't been as extreme as some hope and others fear. Misgivings and recriminations about the excesses of the past aren't tantamount to cultural conservatism. It's one thing to blame a philosophical detour or blown year or old love affair or dead friend on the '60s, another to take the position advocated most forcefully by Daniel Bell in *The Cultural Contradictions of Capitalism*—that in its pathological self-indulgence the culture of the '60s exemplified the American malaise rather than countering it.

For most people under forty who care about culture at all, the '60s were fun. Getting through them wasn't so very difficult or unpleasant, and it isn't only diehard hippie nostalgiacs who retain fond memories of the time. What's more, no matter what they may say about the '60s, there are few young culturati who do not continue to take advantage of passe ideas about liberation in their lives, from details of leisure and style to the structure of work and sexual relationships. For anyone honest enough to recognize this, to reject the '60s is to reject oneself.

Morris Dickstein, a Columbia '61 born in 1940 on the Lower East Side who teaches English at Queens College and serves as an editor of *Partisan Review*, voices the judicious retrospective enthusiasm of such beneficiaries in his widely reviewed new *Gates of Eden*. Although the text is not as millenarian as the title implies, Dickstein is happy enough to acknowledge that the counterculture was good for him, opening him up politically—although he is so vehemently anti-anticommunist that I suspect he underwent earlier training elsewhere—and sexually. At the very least, they made it possible for him to mention these personal matters in the course of a book of criticism, which for an academic is liberation aplenty. Given the formalism and presumed "objectivity" that once again dominates serious cultural discussion,

Dickstein's need to bring his own experiences to bear on his analysis is a significantly '60s-ish impulse. Its effect is to bring what he has to say down to human scale. He does not pontificate or claim absolute validity, and that's gratifying.

Because Dickstein candidly accepts his own limitations—that is, acknowledges his own identity—it's possible to dismiss some of his odder critical judgments ad hominem, a method as useful as it is taboo. Thus, his excessive distaste for Leslie Fiedler—a thinker just as valuable, in his flawed way, as the flawed Herbert Marcuse, who Dickstein admires—is probably related to Fiedler's admittedly repugnant anticommunism. And his unmitigated preference for Maileresque, *Voice*-style, "confessional" new journalism over the quasi-fictional Tom Wolfe mode (in an uncharacteristically arrogant moment, Dickstein says of *The Electric Kool-Aid Acid Test*: "stupefyingly boring—I got through only half of it") would seem to reflect his discovery of the personal in his own writing.

The payoff for such critical self-indulgence is several relatively brave and idiosyncratic judgments. It takes some guts for an academic moving in highbrow circles to single out *Catch-22* as "the best novel of the '60s" or to recall that *Cat's Cradle* remains a fine little book even though Vonnegut has since diddled his reputation away. It takes even more to put Dylan, the Beatles, and the Stones in an equivalent context; as Dickstein observes, "many highbrow critics are still unable to acknowledge . . . that the line between high culture and popular culture gave way in the '60s and on some fronts was erased entirely." A final bonus: Dickstein's wonderful analysis of Paul Goodman's prose, which clearly grew out of personal inspiration.

But Dickstein's affable conviction that a critic must remain himself has far more serious consequences than a few judgments up or down—it slants his book so severely as to distort it altogether. For like most English professors, Dickstein is in love with the written word. When Daniel Bell tries to dissect "the sensibility of the '60s," he deals with painting, sculpture, and theater as well as fiction; even though Bell makes it seem as if he never went so far as to experience much of this work firsthand, he knows it would be obtuse to pretend that sensually apprehended culture wasn't a key to his subject. But although Dickstein would deny it, that is an implicit message of *Gates of Eden*. His discussion of the music of "rock," notably halting and imprecise in a treatise rarely distinguished by vivid description, is his only venture into nonverbal aesthetics. By the end of the book, his frank "personal" admission at the outset—"I've slighted cultural phenomena for which I felt little affinity"—seems like nothing more than an easy way to forestall criticism.

Dickstein's admission that he has "chosen to exploit slippery ambiguities of the word culture" is equally suspect, because exploitation is all too unambiguously what has taken place. It's acceptable to treat works of art as paradigms of "the assumptions and mores of a whole society," and laudable (although not as adventurous as Dickstein seems to think) to relate the evolution of (literary) form to more general historical developments. For Dickstein, however, to concentrate on the intersection between art and society—on "culture"—is to submerge in convention; sometimes it's as if he defined culture by remembering what the brightest and most au courant graduate students were reading back then.

So on the one hand, Dickstein's sense of the Important Subject is completely predictable—there's no art for art's sake here, no indigestible weirdness. Is it because he believes off-the-wall tastes lead a narrow cultural life that he offers no surprises, or does he simply enjoy no such tastes? Beyond '40s avatar Delmore Schwartz and the usual roll call of black novelists, he doesn't discuss a single nonstandard author. Whether the specific name turned out to be Grace Paley or Ross MacDonald (who I admire), John Hawkes or Jacqueline Susann (who I don't admire), or someone I'd barely recognize (who I might admire), I would have valued a crotchet or two—crotchets are the mark of an inquisitive critical intelligence. Instead, *Gates of Eden* could double as a text in '60s Lit. And on the other hand, Dickstein dares no real innovations of method. One reason the word "culture" is so slippery is that the concrete connections between a society's art and its people—how artworks actually affect "assumptions and mores"—are very difficult to figure out. But for all his readiness to allude to the goings-on in his own world—which in the '60s centered around Columbia—Dickstein hardly makes a pass at such questions.

This omission glares because the '60s were uniquely, preeminently, and unprecedentedly a time of mass bohemianism—a time when millions of Americans of divergent class backgrounds aspired to a vaguely artistic ("creative," "self-expressive") lifestyle. Popular culture critics have proved best suited to thinking about the problematic intersections this phenomenon created—as in Greil Marcus's struggle with the art/audience nexus in the Randy Newman chapter of *Mystery Train*, or Michael Arlen's evocative analyses of TV news. But avant-gardists and modernists have also contributed—see the theater criticism of Richard Schechner or John Lahr, the dance criticism of Jill Johnston or Kenneth King, or invaluable polemics like Harold Rosenberg's "Politics of Illusion." Up against such writing, Dickstein's modesty looks like timidity.

For finally this is a timid book. By sticking close to fiction, Dickstein neatly avoids all of the decade's more recondite avant-gardisms, and fiction maven though he may be, also fails to mention two quintessentially '60s genres, science fiction and pornography, which is perhaps a clue to one totally incomprehensible omission: William S. Burroughs. Christopher Lasch in the *New York Times Book Review* and Walter Clemons in *Newsweek* may conclude—in miraculously similar language—that Dickstein "distinguishes between good and bad rock music," but in fact he foregoes suggestive challenges—Jimi Hendrix, say, or the Velvet Underground, who once wrote a song for Delmore Schwartz—for an uninspired (if surprisingly adequate) account of the usual triumvirate; what's more, he obviously failed to get what is generally considered (by critics) the Rolling Stones' greatest album, *Exile on Main Street*, which happened to appear in 1972 and which also happens to be by far their most difficult work. Again and again I got the feeling that Dickstein wasn't trying hard enough—that he hoped to make the decade acceptable by presenting it at its neatest and most received. There is no surer way to warm a culture critic's heart than to argue that a decade is summed up by its novels.

My initial judgment wasn't so harsh. There was something about the sweet reason of Dickstein's tone that I found attractive; he even got me to read Donald Barthelme's *City Life* (which I liked, although not as much as Dickstein) and Thomas Pynchon's *The Crying of Lot 49* (Dickstein should delve into Steely Dan, whose music provides a physical correlative that transforms the idea of California into something more than a hackneyed abstraction). The theoretical limitations of the book were offset, I thought, by its propaganda potential—it could begin the re-education of a cultural establishment that has rejected the decade whole. But as a respecter of the '60s I should have known better than to hedge my bets. Cultural philistines like Hilton Kramer, for whom any deprecation of the '50s smacks of Stalinism, fumes at Dickstein as if he were Jerry Rubin, while anti-'60s moderates like Lasch find in Dickstein's "judicious sympathy" more sophisticated and efficient fuel for their own arguments.

Me, I enjoyed the '60s, and profited from them, but that wasn't all: I cherished their promise. That promise included liberating new contexts for art, a political usefulness that did not diminish art's pleasure or its truth, and even a redefinition of the senses. The promise is fainter now, but I haven't forgotten it. Dickstein seems to have given it up with a sigh of relief.

Village Voice, 1977

The Little Counterculture That Could

Carol Brightman's *Sweet Chaos: The Grateful Dead's American Adventure*

In 1965, Carol Brightman helped found a useful little periodical called *Viet-Report*, whose well-researched battles against government disinformation helped fuel the antiwar movement. By 1969 she was organizing the Venceremos Brigade, a grander, riskier, more deluded enterprise that sent American radicals to Cuba for the sugar harvest. She spent the early '70s as part of a typically hypercharged and atomized Berkeley collective, fomenting a revolution that never began. Then, as near as one can determine from *Sweet Chaos*, she disappeared for twenty years, surfacing (the jacket informs us—the book never mentions it) as the author of *Writing Dangerously: Mary McCarthy and Her World*, which won a National Book Critics' Circle Award in 1993.

Since *Sweet Chaos* is ostensibly—and also actually—about the Grateful Dead, you might think it peculiar that it reveals even this much about its author, whose earlier tome, as near as I can tell without actually reading it, only breaches polite standards of "objectivity" in its introduction and postscript. But then, *Sweet Chaos* is a peculiar piece of work. Although much of its story was familiar to me as the reader of several books and countless articles on the Dead, I found Brightman's retelling swift and compelling. And for a literary scholar to describe any species of rock and roll with such clarity, delicacy, and detail is a mitzvah if not a miracle. Yet consider these anomalies.

Thematically, Brightman's prevailing interest is the Deadheads, who in their nomadic pursuit of Dead concerts became a piece of Americana in the '70s, and who remain today the most visible remnant of a counterculture she and her friends believed would spearhead a revolution. Yet she doesn't home in on them until well into the final third of her book. Instead, and despite the fact that she only attended her first Dead concert in 1972, she devotes most of *Sweet Chaos* to the band's mythic early career—acid, Ken Kesey, the Haight, the Warner albums, the fabled '60s. This story she has reconstructed without interviewing Jerry Garcia, who died well after she began her research and who she rightly identifies as the essential genius of the Dead's sprawling collectivity. In fact, despite the entree provided by her sister, Candace Brightman, the Dead's lighting designer for upwards of two decades (and also her roadie brother Chris), she seems barely to have gotten to the band at all—mostly, one infers, because the Dead's PR honcho had his own bio in the works. Instead, her main informants are Garcia's second wife, the formidable Mountain Girl, and his principal lyricist, the paradoxical Robert Hunter. As I said, peculiar.

You can see why Brightman couldn't resist this project. It was redolent, it was commercial, it was a change, and that family access—whoo! She's such a smart cookie that she's come up with a very readable book, too. But there's clearly a sense in which the subject was too much for her. The Dead weren't the problem—they've never gotten the critical respect they deserve, and she might have done a service by focusing more faithfully on their music. No—where she founders, like so many before her, is trying to figure out the fabled '60s. If she didn't go in with that juicy subtext in mind, it soon took over her research and speculations, so that what begins as an exploration of a vast alien world just beyond her field of vision turns into a postmortem on her own life choices that's sometimes an all too thoroughgoing defense of same. Hence the coyly selective autobiographical detail. We never learn where she went to college or what her father did for a living—the sort of angle-of-vision info that's always more useful than vague references to middle-classness in calibrating the reliability of any participant-observer's truth. And of course, we never learn how Brightman-as-paradigmatic-politico occupied her time while the-Dead-as-paradigmatic-freaks built their road show into a mass-bohemian religious enterprise and entertainment empire.

This question looms especially large because Brightman states explicitly that the hippies were "the last hurrah for American bohemianism" and acts as if the New Left vaporized once its revolution did. From my more distant participant-observer vantage, these positions appear patently unfactual. I know many individual radicals who remained politically active—democratic-socialist union steward and Marxist-Leninist tenant organizer and tragic cultist, troublemaking journalists and barely middle-class legal advocates and prophets of a dubious academic "vanguard"—even after concluding that they were doomed to struggle and compromise all their lives, that the "long march" Brightman and her comrades referenced so proudly in 1970 would in fact be endless. As for bohemianism, it would seem a permanent adjunct of and/or alternative to bourgeois society—one whose veterans whine about the good old days as much as any other self-pitying old fart on the cultural landscape. You may not think the posthippie punks of the '70s and the postpunk slackers of the '80s and '90s deserve the tradition of Ada

Clare, Max Eastman, and Gary Snyder, each of whom was very different from his or her predecessors. But they're of it nevertheless.

Why did this particular bohemia fall apart? Common sense tells us that affective and material ties with spouses and especially children are sure to undermine a youth subculture conceived without them, and that revolutionary energy, whether cultural or political, is generally short-lived. Any pop sociologist could mix in an economic double whammy: just as the end of the postwar boom was radically diminishing leisure time, capital was figuring out dozens of new ways to make money off it. But although she's aware of these factors, Brightman—who only started smoking pot in 1968—can't resist another notion. In her best *Viet-Report* mode, she recapitulates the CIA's many experiments with psychedelics, concluding quite credibly that without these experiments the Haight might never have happened. This sort of accidental historical synergy is common enough, however. To believe in addition, as Brightman implies and has Kesey say in so many words, that the government deliberately destroyed '60s bohemia with "counter revolutionary drugs—booze and heroin and coke" is a self-protective if not paranoid if not drug-induced fantasy.

It's hard to pin down where the Dead fit into this schema, in part because there's never been anything remotely like them. The closest analogy I can think of is the Oneida community, which began as a free-love experiment in 1848 and ended up a major industrial corporation. But music isn't silverware, and this music is even less a consumer durable than most, because by mutual agreement it only truly occurs when artists and audience feed off each other in the same physical space. For an intellectual to respond with warm insight to such an evanescent aesthetic is a rare thing. There are moments when Brightman seems naive musically, but her naivete is preferable to the preconceptions of rock critics who measure the Dead by rhythmic and emotive criteria that never address the more associative and unpredictable music they set out to achieve.

Brightman is too dismissive of the band's experimental '60s albums and doesn't realize that two drum sets can't generate much groove unless the bass plays rhythm. But she appreciates how uncommonly open-ended the Dead's vision of folk-rock eclecticism was. She loves the Hunter-Garcia poetry of *Workingman's Dead* and *American Beauty*: "western songs" in which "the frontier seems to have closed," "which sing more sweetly than they read—so sweetly that one can forget one's troubles." She describes in-concert epiphanies so acutely that it's possible to believe something like them actually occurred, though she acknowledges that they got rarer and rarer as the band played on. And she grants Garcia's guitar the awe it generated.

Sociopolitically, Brightman is just as enlightened. She's too good a leftist to fall for the fatalism that attributes the communal virtues of Deadhead culture to the band while blaming its failings—from countless drug horrors to its unwillingness, especially once the '60s were history, to address any concrete political question, much less change society—on karma, human nature, and other such imponderables; she's scathing, for instance, about the band's refusal to protect fans from narcs when the drug wars heated up in the late '80s. But she has the decency to see that the Deadhead culture, for all its infuriating interlock of know-nothing hedonism and mystical jingoism, succeeded where the New Left failed. It stands as a social formation of relatively "ordinary" people—Brightman uses the word to refer to class, which is crucial; I would add that, in my experience, they tend to be a shade dimmer than radicals, or than the early movers and shakers of alternative rock—who within Deaddom try to live by such oft-preached values as tolerance, humankindness, and utopian imagination. These are values that the seekers of the Venceremos Brigade, inspired by their vision of Castro's Cuba, sought to inculcate in themselves. ("You thought we were perfect," one Cuban noted, "and we thought you were revolutionaries.") Though the Venceremos Brigade wanted more—the end of racism, sexism, and capitalism, to be precise—and Deadheads often settle for less, Brightman has reason to worry about how one success reflects on the other failure.

As a leftist since the '60s whose deepest loyalties ended up with rock and roll, I don't think the solution to this puzzle is merely that Deaddom succeeded because it was willing to settle. It's that the Dead understood America better than the New Left did—a lot better. As Brightman observes: "Their politics, loosely speaking, mirrored the laissez-faire libertarianism that most hippies and students lived day to day, whatever the latter's views on the war in Vietnam, or how to end it." And in a lovely sentence at the end, she sums up what Deadheads treasure in their nomadic phase: "An odd kind of security, it's the sweet oblivion of the road, the music, and the friendship of strangers." In the absence of economic disaster—not just a downturn like the one that took hold between the revolutionary illusion's circa-1969 peak and circa-1973 fizzle—the individualism encompassed by "laissez-faire libertarianism" and "the friendship of strangers" is inimical to revolution.

No matter what countervailing tendencies it's possible to discern and righteous to encourage, this individualism is at the heart of both rock and roll and the American ethos. Moreover, it is inimical to most of the communal ideals leftists hold dear—and a starting place from which any American leftist must work. Brightman has been pushed very close to a bedrock truth by prolonged contemplation of the Grateful Dead. It is my sincere hope that now, instead of devoting her impressive intellect to either literature or CIA conspiracies, she will figure out a way to lay out the political options such a truth leaves open.

Los Angeles Times Book Review, 1999

The Pop-Boho Connection, Narrativized

Bernard F. Gendron's *Between Montmartre and the Mudd Club*

For anyone who cares about the history of pop—and also, in a better world, anyone who cares about the history of the avant-garde—*Between Montmartre and the Mudd Club* has a big story to tell. Popular music is generally identified with the rise of song publishing and piano manufacture in the mid-nineteenth century. But starting in the 1880s, artists and other fringe-dwelling weirdos have been active as pop performers, composers, impresarios, and entrepreneurs. Gendron aims to turn all these interrelationships into a single coherent narrative.

His organizing conceit locates the relevant connections first in modernist Paris (section title: "Pop Into Art") and then, at greater length, in postmodernist New York ("Art Into Pop"). He posits five stages: bohemian cabaret, '20s jazz as misapprehended in Paris by Milhaud and Cocteau, then bebop, the canonization of the Beatles, and New York punk/new wave and postpunk/no wave. That bebop is no more "postmodernist" than abstract expressionism isn't the only flaw in the schema—swing was far more aestheticized than Gendron acknowledges, the hippie ballrooms of San Francisco get short shrift, etc. But Gendron doesn't pretend to touch all the bases, and deserves thanks for tackling a topic no one else has ever gotten near. His research has been prodigious; I learned hundreds of things. But I was left in the dark about many others, and in what is always a dismaying pattern, found that the more I knew about any subject, the less I thought Gendron did.

Piquantly, Gendron levels an arsenal of Big Concepts at what the average snob would judge a minor cultural byway. Pierre Bourdieu's notion of "cultural capital," in which status traders valorize works of art and styles of connoisseurship to augment their own social and economic power, underlies Gendron's entire analysis. Andreas Huyssen's essential distinction between the "high modernism" of the '30s and '40s, which was "unrelentingly hostile to mass culture," and "historical avant-gardes" (especially dada) that were friendly to it, is adduced most explicitly in an endnote but fruitfully fleshed out in the text. Primitivism enters in '20s Paris, which inspires a chapter called "Negrophilia" and informs the bebop chapter before petering out into scattered animadversions in the rock section; notions of the folk and the traditional also come into play. Gendron's own useful terminological contribution is the "secondary practice," which encompasses all the public lifestyles, presentational paraphernalia, venue stylings, and promotional ploys that inflect the meaning of the art they touch. Most important of all, however, is the Foucauldian notion of "discourse."

I know a great deal about the histories of bohemia and popular music, and was present at the creation for most of the last half of the book, having personally participated in "The Cultural Accreditation of the Beatles" and, as music editor of *The Village Voice*, overseen a fair portion of the discourse Gendron cites in re postmodernist New York—that is, "downtown," a neighborhood and state of mind I've made my home since 1964. I'm far less intimate with Foucault and the vagaries of discourse studies. But I do know this—although it hasn't disappeared, and shouldn't, discourse studies, in which disparate written materials and cultural artifacts are read and deconstructed as expressions of a hegemonic ideology, has faded as an academic fashion. Gendron, who seems to have conceived this book in the fashion's heyday and then been stuck with it as such indelible fantasias as history and aesthetics staged their comebacks, is unlikely to inspire a revival. Even though some of what little history he does essay is wrong, he would have been better off writing more of it. And while he claims to be down with the aesthetics revival, he's way too cautious to convey much about what specific pieces of music mean, how they sound, or whether they're any good.

Gendron is strongest historically and aesthetically at the very beginning, in two chapters on artistic cabarets, which though rooted in the working-class goguettes outlawed by Louis Napoleon only came into their own in 1881, when Paris's Chat Noir kicked off a complex and colorful tale replete with bitter rivalries, outrageous self-promotions, hype, burnouts, sellouts, turf wars, and flashes in the pan. Gendron even gives some notion of what "the song of Montmartre" might have sounded like, although a few contemporary analogies would have added spice (it's my fancy that Chat Noir pioneer Maurice Rollinat was the Nick Cave of his day), as would a fuller analysis of the scene's great pop crossover, careerist-provocateur Aristide Bruant. Nevertheless, the story remains quite concrete, most likely owing to a dearth of primary discourse—the relatively modest volume of cafe-published newspapers and mainstream commentary, which forced Gendron to rely on memoirs and other people's scholarship. All too soon he won't need them.

It's more than a little odd that Gendron's account of '20s jazz in Paris should peak before jazz was recorded by black Americans, and before the so-called Jazz Age (which was really a Pop Age). Nevertheless, Milhaud's misbegotten ballet score *La création du monde* does have the illustrative virtue of demonstrating how shallow and uncomprehending this prophetic early avant-garde (and French) attraction to (American) pop was. Gendron recounts events as well as rhetoric, and when he details Cocteau's asinine racial pronunciamentos, he names the man rather than pretending he's the zeitgeist. By the time of bebop, however, his interest is not the antithetical twin reactions against the conventions of swing—the mind-bending harmonies and rhythms of bebop versus the body-slamming beats and sounds of r&b. Instead he pits the proudly progressive critical champions of the bop cool cats against the putatively populist champions of a half-imagined New Orleans revival. This is OK as far as it goes—both tensions are pretty rich. But I kept wishing he'd characterize the principals. Shouldn't it be noted that moldy fig Orrin Keepnews turned into a major postbop producer? And Keepnews's critical ally Ernest Borneman seems pretty smart even though he was wrong. Is his writing of, pardon me, lasting value?

Onward to the '60s, where Gendron renders the glorious sprawl that was mid '60s pop as a saga of cultural upward mobility in which the Beatles first won over key middlebrows in 1965, and then, after a media lull Gendron makes too much of, got decisive if fickle highbrow props from Ned Rorem and Richard Poirier while begetting rock criticism, which from the first challenged the genteel presumptions of the Beatles' earlier status providers. Gendron has a right to emphasize the Beatles, especially since he doesn't dismiss Dylan's major pop-into-art role. But he ignores some crucial questions. Didn't something about the '60s as a whole—beyond Gendron's plausible but offhand and unresearched guess that magazines were cosseting a new young-adult market—help inspire these aesthetic developments and reevaluations? Are hindsight-equipped academics the only ones who can perceive such truths? Which reminds me, were the Beatles great artists, or whatever we call them these days? Or is it incorrect even to ask?

Gendron makes a welcome exception to the basic strategy of discourse studies, which is to obviate the agency of the discoursers—his three-page summation does Lester Bangs more justice as a "theoretician" than Jim DeRogatis's entire biography. Other combatants in the punk wars are ID'd—*Creem*'s Dave Marsh, *Who Put the Bomp*'s Greg Shaw, *Punk*'s John Holmstrom and Legs McNeil. But for the very reason that Gendron has read every word of *New York Rocker* and all the relevant *Times*, *Voice*, and *SoHo Weekly News* coverage, his '70s research gets the best of him. Where the best discourse studies deconstruct substantial passages, Gendron's annoying practice of clunking up the workaday rhythms of his exposition with the print equivalent of soundbites—a catchphrase, a clause, if we're lucky a sentence—impinges drastically on his flow toward the end. And by now we're in discourse-land, with authors annotated but rarely named in the text. Only by paging back to the notes will you discover that among these anonymous ideologueurs are many critics of considerably more distinction than Gendron: MacArthur winner Dave Hickey, National Magazine Award winner Tom Carson, and such renowned journalistic toilers as John Rockwell, James Wolcott, and the late Robert Palmer.

Another generally unnamed star is Roy Trakin, a *SoHo Weekly News* and *New York Rocker* stalwart who was the only major byline back then regularly to take up the cudgels for the postpunk avant-noise tendency labeled no wave (although many excellent critics honored parts of it and still do; Palmer was a supporter). Trakin has long since recanted—he did say it was the future of all music, after all—and logged sixteen years at the in-your-face trade magazine *Hits*, to which he lends much irreverent attitude. I didn't remember his quitting *SoHo* for the *Rocker*, a historical detail to which Gendron attaches significance, so I called him up, and double-checked with *Rocker* headman Andy Schwartz. Admittedly, both are acquaintances, but both are also affable guys who would happily have chewed Gendron's ear off—and both were certain no such switch occurred. Then I asked Trakin whether I had really "bloodied" James Chance of the Contortions that night I sat on him at Artists Space (details available upon request), which isn't how I or two other witnesses remember it; he allowed as how a little hyperbole never hurts a description. Gendron has me bloodying Chance, and so in academia it shall ever be. I guess I should be proud. As for that moment when the *Voice* stopped calling pop reviews "Riffs" and subsumed them under the rubric "Music," which Gendron cites as an example of rock's elevation into art's empyreal realms, does it matter that the change was instituted—imposed, in fact—by a design director who declared section heads like "Riffs" guilty of "clutter"?

Hegemonically, ideologically, it's conceivable that the answer is no. But though hegemony and ideology—and discourse too—are powerful concepts that have changed the way anyone reading this understands the world, inconvenient inconsistencies like those I've noted should remind us that these concepts, too, have serious limitations as analytic and explanatory tools. All too often, *Between Montmartre and the Mudd Club* falls victim to such limitations.

Bookforum, 2002

Cursed and Sainted Seekers of the Sexual Century

John Heidenry's *What Wild Ecstasy: The Rise and Fall of the Sexual Revolution*

Some thirty years into the so-called sexual revolution, near the end of what might as well be designated the sexual century as anything else, veterans of its intricate physical skirmishes and pitched rhetorical battles are left with one question: Just how important is sex, anyway?

Of course, to declare this the sexual century—playfully, for argument and fun's sake—is not to anticipate enthusiastic assent. Few would deny that never before did such a vast array of women and men think so much about the concept of sex, or that the era's profusion of sexual representations was unparalleled. Clearly, in no previous epoch of Western culture did so many put so much time and effort into the pursuit and perfection of genital pleasure, its polymorphous correlatives, and the psychodrama that surrounds them. But the commentators who devote more than a condescending glance to these trends are usually dismayed by them. Right, left, or center, they want to tell us that modern sex is at best the opiate of the people, wrecking the family, marriage, romance, love itself. The commercialization of sex suffers special opprobrium, whether in advertising and popular culture, where promises of impossible bliss further cheapen dubious goods and entertainments, or in the sale of sexual products per se—manuals, men's magazines, porn loops, mail-order underwear. As a final blow, some sages top off these animadversions by announcing that the harder sex consumers try, the less fun they end up having. Tsk, tsk—poor buggers don't even come good.

John Heidenry, a former editor at the *Penthouse* spinoff *Forum*, can't resist his own autumnal wistfulness about the diminishing returns of the sexual round. But his engrossing, authoritative survey of modern sex's issues and players offers support to ordinary folks who are so glad they lost their virginity earlier than their parents did, who have concluded that the twentieth-century vogue for fellatio and cunnilingus is good for one's affective relationships, psychological equilibrium, and skin tone. It's not that he advances either argument, but that he writes calmly and knowledgeably from a credible place where they're home truths. Heidenry doesn't mince words about the foolishness and worse to which most of the many sexual seekers described here occasionally succumb. He's scathing about the likes of cocaine-scamming porn star John Holmes and wife-beating sex promoter Chuck Traynor as well as his natural enemies, the money-grubbing moralists of the antisex reaction. But most of his life stories and thumbnail portraits display a human tolerance that reflects well on the sexual tolerance he preaches. Even such oft-ridiculed figures as Andrea Dworkin and Gay Talese get what any neutral observer would adjudge their fair due.

In short, Heidenry's book performs the useful function of naturalizing liberal sexual mores without implying that they're beyond criticism. Just because it's so unfailingly open-minded, it should make anybody with second thoughts about paths not taken think again. From entrepreneurs like self-made porn king Reuben Sturman and self-created playboy Hugh Hefner to adventurers like the prostitute turned performance artist Annie Sprinkle and the late pornographer Marco Vassi, the principals of this subculture of disparate yet like-focused seekers have paid for their treasurehouse of orgasms with strange, perilous, difficult lives. The curse extended to William Masters, who warned that overwork was inimical to a good sex life but didn't take a day off for fifty years. And Johns Hopkins's John Money, a bisexual who helped make the world bearable for transsexuals by exploring such concepts as "paraphilia" and "lovemaps," was himself unable to form the erotic bond he craved after the painful end of an especially passionate relationship. One may be impressed by the Dutch anarchist Willem de Ridder, who has learned to achieve whole-body orgasm at will via a shallow-breathing technique he picked up from his old lover Sprinkle. But only the fanatically sex-positive would want to be de Ridder. There are other things to do with one's elan vital—getting the kids to school, say, or watching television.

Heidenry's regard for John Money reflects two of his thematic concerns. Knowing as much about sex as he does, he understands how uncontrollably it resists stereotype, and thus feels for those on its margins. He devotes a moving chapter to a transsexual from Indiana, is clear on the victimization of *Deep Throat*'s Linda Lovelace, and details gay and lesbian liberation and the s&m scene with unequivocal sympathy (although he also holds that s&m, with its commingling of blood and semen, was a hothouse of HIV, as was female circumcision in Africa). He focuses on Sprinkle and Vassi—the latter of whom he reports, quite credibly, was "cursed, or blessed, with a libido of monstrous proportions and a sexual imagination and spirit of erotic adventure such as befall few men or women in a generation, or maybe a century"—because he regards them, also credibly, as innovative geniuses. But even in their radically atypical voracity Heidenry sees a search not only for pleasure but for love, portraying Vassi's inability to complete that search as tragic, comic, and pathetic all at once. And that is why he honors Money's idea of the "lovemap," which holds that gender identity is determined not by who you can have sex with but who you can fall in love with.

Anyone who glances through Heidenry's notes on sources will be aware that much of his research isn't primary—especially in the later parts of his story, he's content to collate the reporting of others. What's most striking about this method is that it affirms the value of such declasse journals as *Forum*, *Penthouse*, *Hustler*, and *Screw*, without whose uninhibited attention much of this information would have been lost to history. Yet despite what you might conclude from complaints by authors whose work Heidenry relied upon—most vociferously his former *Forum* boss Philip Nobile, whom Heidenry praises almost unstintingly—Heidenry adds something to the work he appropriates. There's a warmth to his book that is rarely apparent in the sex mags, where the tone tends toward a snide knowingness even shallower than the sophistication it pretends to.

It's also worth noting that for Heidenry, the century's "third sexual revolution," from the '60s to now, succeeded insofar as it freed women from millennia of repression and failed insofar as it didn't. Thus, even if "simple aversion to sex" has become a major concern of sex therapy only because "relatively 'easy' problems" like premature ejaculation are now solved at home, he believes that in the end the revolution failed. Many women would look askance at Heidenry's do-her feminism, in which the genitally explicit erotica of filmmaker Candida Royalle is hailed as a relief from a phallic narcissism whose worst sin is that it is "dreary" and "outdated." And his Reichian thesis that "'sexually awakened women . . . would mean the complete collapse of the authoritarian ideology'" seems a tad tautological. Nevertheless, *What Wild Ecstasy* makes an excellent case for the humane notion that sex can and should be exactly as important as you want it to be.

New York Times Book Review, 1997

Bohemias Lost and Found

Ross Wetzsteon's *Republic of Dreams: Greenwich Village: The American Bohemia, 1910–1960* | Richard Kostelanetz's *SoHo: The Rise and Fall of an Artists' Colony* | Richard Lloyd's *Neo-Bohemia: Art and Commerce in the Postindustrial City*

Read a lot about bohemia and soon you notice two things. The first is that bohemians, especially young ones, don't like to call themselves bohemians. Infatuated with the uniqueness of their particular social and formal rebellions, they have less than no need for some fusty old label their unacknowledged forebears didn't like either. The second is that the "real" bohemia, like "Old" England, is always gone—stuck in an irretrievable past just now corrupted or obliterated by modernity and/or commerce. Never has this cliché been more content-free, because never in history have so many neighborhoods and subcultures yoked artistic creation to nonconformist lifestyles. Bohemia isn't gone. But like most things in capitalist modernity, it's always changing.

In recent years the scant literature of bohemia has picked up markedly, from conservative fifth-columnist David Brooks's spottily researched, snottily written 2000 *Bobos in Paradise* (somehow the title neologism, an attempt to do something cute with the old bohemian-bourgeois polarity, didn't catch on) to intellectual historian Mary Gluck's suggestive, frustrating 2008 *Popular Bohemia* (which begins with a bang by grounding Parisian bohemia in early melodrama and ends up in the cultural studies ether with Gauguin's amanuensis—at a time when Montmartre had become an entertainment center whose popularity Gluck declines to unpack). Much better are two histories of Greenwich Village: Princeton historian Christine Stansell's *American Moderns* (2000) and my late *Village Voice* colleague Ross Wetzsteon's

Republic of Dreams (2002). Because Wetzsteon died in 1998, neither book bears any trace of the other, and they're remarkably complementary.

Rooting feminism, the union movement, and many other progressive tendencies in the early Village on her way to an overriding thesis that the neighborhood was the breeding ground of twentieth-century American sociability itself, from romantic marriage to associative as opposed to argumentative conversation, Stansell conceptualizes bohemia as a sociopolitical site. Wetzsteon is more traditional. By organizing *Republic of Dreams* into biographical chapters with titles like "Mabel Dodge's Salon: 'Oh, How We Were All Intertwined!,'" "Thomas Wolfe and Aline Bernstein: 'The Knife of Love,'" and "Delmore Schwartz: Alien in Residence," he keeps his focus on artists and their art.

But Wetzsteon knows that many eminent bohemians have proven more enduring as characters than as creators. So he devotes chapters to impecunious poseurs Maxwell Bodenheim and Joe Gould, folds in a dozen or two briefer sketches, and takes an interest in these adventurers' sex lives that some might call prurient and I say provides an essential gauge of their quality of life. Stansell is good on this stuff too—cutting on "independent women"'s domestic labor and the inequities of free love. But compare Wetzsteon on the same relationships and you'll invariably find more flesh and nuance. Moreover, Wetzsteon was an accomplished critic, and his aesthetic assessments—of O'Neill, Millay, Cummings, Dawn Powell—are as astute as any I've encountered in the literature of bohemia. Lacking the climactic summation he didn't get to before he died and seriously short-changing '30s leftism, *Republic of Dreams* isn't quite Jerrold Seigel's *Bohemian Paris*. But it's a deeply intelligent and entertaining counterpart.

It's also a better book than Richard Kostelanetz's 2003 *SoHo* or Richard Lloyd's 2005 *Neo-Bohemia*. But Kostelanetz and Lloyd have something Wetzsteon and Stansell don't—the psychological distance to concoct a credible portrait of a contemporary bohemia. Not that there haven't been such books in the past; I'm sure there are many more than I'm aware of. But these tend to be either works of advocacy like Lawrence Lipton's 1959 "inside story of the Beat Generation" *The Holy Barbarians*, a resource some academic press should reprint, or quickies like John Gruen's haphazard 1966 *The New Bohemia*, keyed to an attempt to dub mid '60s avant-gardists "the Combine Generation" that went nowhere faster than "Bobos." Kostelanetz and Lloyd are more authoritative, more objective—and like Stansell and Wetzsteon, they're complementary.

Lloyd is an academic outsider, Kostelanetz an anti-academic insider. For an academic, Lloyd writes with easy grace, bogging down only in a methodological overview he gets out of quick; for the author of fifty-plus books, Kostelanetz is a sloppy, puffed-up stylist—adverb-happy, using "bovine blood" for "beef blood" and "the reason why" for "the reason," given to clunkers like "the inordinate attentiveness paid by some to people above themselves in a hierarchy as distinct from those below." An urban studies Ph.D. from the University of Chicago, Lloyd thinks like Stansell, fascinated by the pomo folkways of Chicago's Wicker Park; a proudly uncategorizable literary-musical-visual artist best known for his criticism, Kostelanetz is more like Wetzsteon, chronicling favored avant-gardists in piecemeal chapters while telling the story of the SoHo he's seen. Lloyd first ventured to Wicker Park to see a band in a bar, and the big local success he celebrates is Liz Phair, about whom he's not terribly insightful; the editor of two music journalism collections who sticks in a chapter about Sonic Youth and Suicide, Kostelanetz reserves his heart and most of his pages for the recondite and the esoteric. Finally, Lloyd identifies his object of research as a "bohemia," shoring the term up with a brief, sensible, well-informed history, while Kostelanetz insists that the nabe where he bought a surreally cheap coop in 1974 is, or was, an "artists' colony," like "Fire Island, Provincetown, or Woodstock"—none of which was an artists' colony for long, although Woodstock might still be half a bohemia.

Not that this is totally off the wall. As bohemias that are always changing go, SoHo is more an artists' colony than most, so be glad Kostelanetz is the kind of guy who goes to everything and then takes notes on it. There are memorable chapters on Fluxus founder turned real estate mastermind George Maciunas, on quintessential avant-gardist turned totemic art icon Nam June Paik, on children's book illustrator Hannah Tierney flowering into an experimental puppeteer, on the self-photographing Cindy Sherman and Hannah Wilke, as well as descriptions of shows I'm sorry I missed and performances I'm glad I only read about. In short, he does the art of his bohemia the justice he's convinced it deserves. And he understands it is a place as well.

In SoHo, the decline of small-manufacture zoning laws that for two decades permitted only working artists to live in abandoned factories, few as young as the typical Wicker Park settler. And the north-south length and architectural uniformity of the thirty blocks bordered by Houston, Thompson, Crosby, and Canal are ill-suited to bohemian strolling and hanging out. When the carpetbagging stockbrokers and media execs were allowed in, however, this exclusive community was more vulnerable than a mixed-use one would have been. Not only were many artists displaced or outbid, but their institutions—a few bars, restaurants, and performance spaces, many galleries—were priced out of the neighborhood. The gentrification that follows bohemia leaves similar wreckage everywhere—as Lloyd details, there've been real estate battles in Wicker Park for almost as long as there've been bohemians. But in SoHo the effects were devastating. Quickly, Kostelanetz's postindustrial loft haven was transformed into a ritzy enclave. Soon it was as gone as Greenwich Village—maybe goner. So around the time Kostelanetz finished *SoHo*, he cashed in his coop and moved to Rockaway Beach, where he has even more room for his archives, his artworks, his holograms, his LP collection, and his fifteen thousand books.

All of which is sad, and none of which means SoHo wasn't a bohemia. Kostelanetz's rationalization for this piece of crankitude is some theory about bohemias harboring "political radicals," natural perhaps in a white guy who cites "disadvantageous race and gender" as barriers to the fame he's due. But I suspect the main reason he believes SoHo is an artists' colony is that bohemias don't meet his exacting aesthetic standards. Read almost any historian of bohemia closely and you'll find that inside bohemia as out, artists come in varying shades of ambition. You get Baudelaire, but you also get Henry Murger, whose sentimental newspaper sketches brought bohemia down to a level Puccini and *Rent* could comprehend. You get the night-crawling avant-garde M.D. William Carlos Williams, but you also get the night-crawling sonneteer Edna St. Vincent Millay. You get Philip Rahv's anti–Popular Front *Partisan Review* but you also get Barney Josephson's left-wing cabaret Cafe Society. You get Jackson Pollock and Frank O'Hara but soon also Allen Ginsberg and Andy Warhol. You get thousands of bohemians who excelled as journalists (Gluck plays up l'art-pour-l'art poet Théophile Gautier, Wetzsteon obscurantist novelist Djuna Barnes). By the time Kostelanetz came of age in the mid '60s, popular bohemia was in ascendance, soon to be followed by mass bohemia, a/k/a hippies. No matter what else was happening in bohemia or rock and roll, the two have overlapped ever since.

Because he doesn't self-define as an aesthete, Lloyd takes these multivalences for granted. For him Wicker Park booster John Cusack is an art hero, while it's conceivable Kostelanetz, who disdains Hollywood, doesn't even know who Cusack is. Lloyd attends plays and openings, acts in a friend's film, and loves him some Liz Phair, but in the end his interest is how art functions in life, not what art says about life, much less what art says about art. In interviews more redolent of profile journalism than of sociological fieldwork, he skewers the intolerance of several ignoramuses' claims to cultural capital. He accepts the inevitability and even appropriateness of deviance in a capitalism that is always changing, but he hates the emotional costs the normalization of that deviance exacts from individual seekers, like the South Dakota–born kid who tats up to fit in and is shooting heroin twelve pages later. And he's matter-of-factly appalled by the economics of postmodern bohemia's hedonistic and self-indulgent nonconformity.

Kostelanetz is admirably lucid on the gallery system's winner-take-all social networking scheme and specific about income and wealth among losers and hanging-ons. But he's in it for his interest group. Lloyd surveys the big picture, where the number of Americans who self-defined as artists tripled between 1970 and 1999, where in 2000 more than a third of Chicago artists reported incomes below twenty-five grand and three-quarters earned less than half their living from their art. He calculates the measly wages of art part-timers providing design and content in the online bubble and the information-driven new economy. He turns over an entertainment-district economy descended from Montmartre and finds that the hip, cool, funky, sharp bartenders and waitstaffs of Wicker Park's booming scene tend toward alcoholism and are embroiled in potlatches where they blow their big-night earnings on huge tips for their colleagues in other locales. And he understands what Kostelanetz does from his end—that in rock and roll and design just as in gallery art there are a few geniuses, hustlers, and genius hustlers who win the lottery and a great many exploited young workers who will eventually quit, teach, or, at best, carve out an income-bearing niche that satisfies their creative urges.

One reason it's kooky for Kostelanetz to deny his bohemianism is that he himself has carved out such a niche—stubbornly promoting his dubious claims to greatness, he's an exemplary bohemian eccentric, with a lot more to show for it than Maxwell Bodenheim. Me, I'm a journalist on the bohemian fringe—scruffy around the edges, making my living off the arts, still gaga for a Greenwich Village girl who thirty-seven years ago traded free love for a romantic marriage. I delve into the latest alt-rock rave and blanch, yet continue to derive a major chunk of my musical sustenance from that world. I read Brooks smugly satirizing bobo hegemony and snort even before I've encountered Kostelanetz's forgotten moments or Lloyd's grim statistics. Bohemia isn't gone. But it's more endangered and also more dangerous than the smug think. That's one reason it remains something to care about, and believe in.

Barnes & Noble Review, 2009

Autobiography of a Pain in the Neck

Meredith Maran's *What It's Like to Live Now*

Before picking up this book I'd never heard of Meredith Maran, although I might well have met her and would be surprised if I don't know someone who remembers her all too well. A sometime journalist of low-profile byline, she's not the kind of forty-three-year-old who ordinarily gets seventy-five grand for an autobiography, which may be why she's so gauche as to reveal that handsome if hardly precedent-setting figure. Well, good for her—Maran believes in letting it all hang out, and her unexpectedly compelling book would lose most of its charm if she didn't.

Her commercial angle is that increasingly mystified historical concept referred to by true believers and their equally credulous opposite numbers as "the '60s." Born toward the young end of the baby-boomer generation, Maran was precocious, organizing antiwar marches at the Bronx High School of Science when she was fifteen. Over the next twenty-five years she would hang out on the Lower East Side, help build a commune near Taos, join the Berkeley Women's Health Collective, put in nearly a decade of Marxist union organizing with the October League and a San Jose community group. She would work on an assembly line and in a sex shop, for Banana Republic and Smith & Hawken and Working Assets. She would do considerable pot and acid, try kundalini yoga and Zen and co-counseling and icky-sounding New Age meditation techniques and even the Judaism she was born to, experiment with holistic therapies and turn to vegetarianism, undergo an abortion and a lumpectomy and years of infertility treatment, see dear friends through infertility and cancer and AIDS, and invest thirty-five grand in psychotherapy. She would marry and bear two now-teenaged sons, then discover that she preferred the other half of her avowed bisexuality in a ten-years-and-counting relationship with a woman who shares the mortgage on a house in the black-bohemian Oakland flats but not necessarily the waterbed, not every night—they both still need their own space.

As full as this resume is, it's not off the curve—"the '60s" did indeed produce lives like this, and Maran's warm, breezy, efficient prose makes that life seem quite logical in its way. I only wish I could force '60s-haters incensed by *Heather Has Two Mommies* to read her account of family life, although maybe they'd think she makes it sound too much like fun—the loving enthusiasm with which this unathletic lesbian yogurt eater nurtures the two heterosexual male jocks she conceived so onerously is summed up by the birthday celebration in which one gets to tank up at every fast-food chain he desires between Oakland and their weekend cabin. In fact, it's not as a "'60s" book that *What It's Like to Live Now* wields its strongest appeal—it's as the testament of an autobiographer who is neither famous nor literary. On its eccentric terms Maran's is an ordinary life, and Maran herself a familiar type of the sort that makes most people's alarms go off. It's fascinating, and heartening, to get inside her.

Maran never comes out and says she's hell on wheels, probably because after all that therapy she still hasn't quite figured it out. But she's explicit enough about her moodiness and her neediness, the storm-tossed emotions that are the unquestioned ground of her presumptively logical life, to make clear that she's one of those people who not only needs her own space but takes up more than a fair share of everybody else's. This quality is called charisma in the famous and shrugged off with a what-can-you-do? in the powerful. In ordinary folks like Meredith Maran, however, it's deeply resented outside of a small circle of friends. Unintentionally, I believe, *What It's Like to Live Now* functions as a convincing defense of this character formation. Meredith Maran may be a pain in the neck sometimes. But she's nice! She's funny! She's smart! And she has far more perspective on herself than her self-centered self-righteousness would lead you to think.

And this perhaps is why Maran deserves to represent the decade that would be better off not knowing its name. While she presents her life as one of a million '60s stories, her long involvement with Marxism renders her highly unusual no matter what you hear from that pretentious history teacher turned Speaker of the House. Most habitues of the "counterculture," who never comprised a majority of American youth in any matter that went deeper than hairstyle, were reflexively antiwar, confused if well-meaning about race, and basically individualist in political philosophy. For one of their number to leave the essential qualification "For Me" out of the title *What It's Like to Live Now* is typical self-aggrandizement. It's typical of the left, which wallowed in the delusion that its experience was America's experience, and of Maran's character formation. But it's also typical of the larger "counterculture." Most counterculturists overestimated their own importance, and claimed more than their share of space as a result. And most of them are nicer, funnier, smarter, saner, and righter than their opposite numbers will ever know. How feckless they can be is proved by the noninhaler in the White House, who inspired hopes in Maran that I trust embarrass her now that the history teacher, who is his and her contemporary, is ordering him around. Here's hoping (although not predicting, God knows) that others of them—of us—learn even yet how to realize our kindest impulses in a world where institutionalized callousness is regularly mistaken for wisdom.

New York Times Book Review, 1995

PART VII
CULTURE MEETS CAPITAL

Twentieth Century Limited

Marshall Berman's *All That Is Solid Melts into Air: The Experience of Modernity*

What's most important about Marshall Berman's *All That Is Solid Melts into Air* is that it's a good read. I embrace that cliche first of all to encourage people to buy it and read it, and I hope it helps. No doubt the news that it's not "hard" will make this study of "the experience of modernity" more attractive to young demi-intellectuals, but not necessarily enough to overcome their defenses against old-fashioned academic culture. And its very readability—the apparently effortless lucidity with which it passes back and forth between art ("modernism") and socio-economics ("modernization"), progressing from Rousseau to Goethe to Marx to Baudelaire to a whole bunch of Russians (beginning with Nicholas I and ending with Andrey Biely and Osip Mandelstam) and then to Jane Jacobs and Robert Moses and Richard Serra—will seem suspicious to Berman's peers. Going-on-middle-aged profs who share Berman's humanism might admire the grace of his style in the abstract, but they'll distrust its synthesis of Lionel Trilling's literary tact and Paul Goodman's pancultural radicalism—that dichotomy has come to seem an either-or to many. And across the fence, the structuralists and poststructuralists, virtually the only avowed leftists in America attempting cultural criticism of comparable scope, will continue to explain away their disdain for honest English prose the way Fredric Jameson does. Jameson, as you of course recall, proudly describes Adorno's "bristling mass of abstractions and cross-references" as "a warning to the reader of the price he has to pay for genuine thinking."

The structuralists have a point, of course. Not only is the world complex, it's obdurately conflict-ridden, and canons of clarity often conceal ideology—they intimate that conflict can be resolved by reason alone. But though the idea that straightforward exposition equals brainwashing has its appeal, it's an untestable generalization with its own secrets. Sometimes it merely serves to obscure the fact that among the cabalists now squirreling away their apercus in Academe are many semiskilled writers, or to rationalize a collective snobbishness about the way most "bourgeois" (formerly "middlebrow") readers conduct their discourse and their lives. But often it expresses a resignation that borders on a rather cozy despair—a withdrawal from the vulgar business of propagandistic action on the ground that it's futile, neutralized by the totalitarian information system within which it must function.

Berman makes a similar point about structuralism in his introduction, where he dispatches it as a kind of climax to his outline of the shortcomings of other modernist ideologies: futurism (callous), Bauhaus ("technocratic pastorale"), and McLuhan-Fuller Inc. ("spaced-out"); mass culture theory, hopelessly elitist from Spengler on the right through Weber in the center to Marcuse on the left; ivory-tower aestheticism from Greenberg to Barthes; the counterculture's doomed-by-definition project of escaping contemporaneity; the tradition of the new, which by bearing down on revolt "leaves out the great romance of construction," and the epidemic neoconservatism which holds that the modern edifice might actually stabilize if only modernism didn't always mess it up; pop, which in its adoration of the baby gets stuck with the bathwater; and "postmodernism," which attempts to end the era by nomenclative fiat.

Berman's alternative might be called the tradition of the modern—a tradition that becomes a necessity of life whenever human beings begin to conceive themselves as point men for history, whenever they define the present as the focus of ineluctable flux, whenever they call change their condition. For Berman, the tradition of the modern is inextricable from "the tragedy of development," in which "the affinity between the cultural ideal of self-development and the real social movement toward economic development . . . turn[s] out to exact great human costs." As you a might expect of a book that takes its title from *The Communist Manifesto*, Berman's basic purpose in laying out this tradition is political. And thus the irresistible polemical flow he's worked so hard and so self-effacingly to achieve does more than suggest the contradictory rush of modernity as he conceives it. His readability has a political meaning of its own—it embodies Berman's charity, the root of his faith and his hope.

For surprisingly enough, Berman is glad to be alive. Unlike most '60s veterans, he's always known the difference between the peace you long for and the escape you settle for, because he's always known that the turmoil of the moment was more or less permanent. And he learned to think this way from the tradition of the modern. Always his presentation falls on both sides of the either-or. He begins with Faust, where the modern hero's tragedy stems "precisely from his desire to eliminate tragedy," his desire to create a safe new world "in which the look and feel of the old world have disappeared without a trace." His examination of Marx's "self-critical" side warns that in Marx criticism is "meant to be dynamic, to drive and inspire the person criticized to overcome both his critics and himself," while his take on Baudelaire emphasizes the old flaneur's struggle to bring together the enthusiast who invented "modernolatry" and the skeptic who invented "cultural despair." Berman both extols the city and explores "the modernization of underdevelopment" in a long history of St. Petersburg, where "a politics of enforced backwardness in the midst of forms and symbols of enforced modernization" produced the surreal, self-conscious antigentility of the raznochintsy—sons of clerks and tailors, inventors of nihilism, forerunners of Picasso, Neil Young, and the Latin American novel. The final section is about the author's New York—how in the '50s Robert Moses's pseudo-Faustian vision destroyed the look and feel of Berman's old world, the Bronx; how in the '60s museum artists like Claes Oldenburg and the latterday raznochintsy of Berman's generation brought their own visions into the streets; how in the '70s Berman came to understand that expressway or no expressway he would never have stayed in the Bronx, and that he was determined to define a past for himself regardless.

Of course, those who set about defining their pasts, especially with the sweet ease Berman manages, leave themselves open to charges of sentimentality, charges Berman doesn't foreclose as conclusively as he might. A shameless urban romantic, he revels in the hurly-burly socialization of the street like Red Grooms with a Ph.D. He betrays a lurking idealism when he mentions the "unacknowledged legislators of the world" and a weakness for civics-class corn when he slips into phrases like "the modern world we all share." And some of his readings are on the wishful side. Dostoyevsky becomes an admirer of engineers and Marx's manifesto an "impassioned, enthusiastic, often lyrical celebration of bourgeois works, ideas, and achievements" only if one disregards the Underground Man's sallow sarcasm and Marx's bitter, magisterial irony.

But if Berman seems a little naive, that's mostly because these are cynical times: when John Leonard says that Berman "indulges" Gramsci's "pessimism of the intellect, optimism of the will," it takes a moment to realize that he might better have used the word "exerts." Exertion is what Berman's kind of criticism is all about—he's less an explicator or a commentator than an inspired reinterpreter. This is doing it the hard way. When he devoted 1970's *The Politics of Authenticity* to Montesquieu and Rousseau, whom he claimed as "first seekers" after a "radical liberalism" that prefigured the new left, Berman could almost have been a college student trying to fit all the world's wisdom into a term paper about *Heart of Darkness*, or a post-Marcusian poring over Marx's *Economic and Philosophic Manuscripts* not for insight but for corroboration by holy writ. His second book is entirely more confident, more sweeping, more his own. Like many leftist aesthetes before him, Berman is convinced that the art he loves (a category that includes all the writing he loves) is consistent with the rest of what he knows and feels. "Modernity"—a less nebulous concept than "authenticity," thanks be—is his rubric, but what drives him is a refusal to abandon either pessimistic intellect or optimistic will. In his first book he suggested that "authenticity" synthesized freedom and happiness; now he defines "modernity" as demanding both criticism and celebration. *All That Is Solid Melts into Air* is a report from a passionate reader who has put his passions in order. The softness around the edges of Berman's argument is small price to pay for his passion, and in the end it only affects the edges.

Because he's taken the dialectic to heart, Berman is forever doubling back on himself—again and again I found him filling in the holes I'd poked in what he had to say, often in surprising ways, and though some of my questions stand it's reassuring to know that Berman felt the need to answer them in his own terms. Anyway, the man has been to college. He's quite aware that Marx opposed the bourgeoisie and that Dostoyevsky hated Western European culture, and when he refers to "unacknowledged legislators" he's not so much citing Shelley as updating him, saying that even if artists can't make law they can shape and instigate political action. All he wants to do is identify undercurrents that really are present in these writers, even if they weren't fully conscious. After all, it is these undercurrents that enable most of us to respond to Marx and Dostoyevsky as deeply as we do. Berman is proposing a slight readjustment of this response, so that it jibes with the rest of what we know and feel. And if once in a while he must risk truism or gush to make his proposal clearer, he's willing to lose face.

All That Is Solid Melts into Air is a visionary work that by all rights ought to have the impact of such '60s bibles as *Growing Up Absurd* and *Life Against Death*; very roughly speaking I'd say it combines *Against Interpretation* (Berman makes up in warmth for Sontag's blinding brilliance) and *The Accidental Century* (Harrington is cruder both critically and politically, but he does call his final chapter "A Hope"). I wish I believed he'll get what he deserves, but he probably won't. For one thing, the time for such books may have passed, at least partly because what there is of a young audience for radical literacy is no longer prepared to accept the trickle-down theory of culture.

That's why the closest we came to '70s bibles was such left-field ventures as *Mythologies* and *The Teachings of Don Juan*, both of which commented on the European Tradition primarily by ignoring it. Berman is no art snob, but because his loyalty to his own intellectual roots assures that his passing references to Chaplin, Dylan, Coltrane, Crumb, and others will remain just that, he surrenders some of the accessibility he's striven for. And in any case he's up against something bigger and more ominous—the simple fact that these really are cynical times. Because so many of today's would-be visionaries are arrant fools, most thinking people consider it a sign of bad breeding to "indulge" in visionary work.

This feeling is shared by intellectuals on the left, Berman's natural constituency, and on the right (i.e., "center"), where any hint of new left revanchism is greeted these days with machine-gun fire. On both sides they'll tell you that these ought to be cynical times—because all eras offer less than meets the mind (which is what neo-conservatives believe) or because our contemporary despair is historically determined (the mandarin-Marxist approach). At the same time they'll complain that *All That Is Solid Melts into Air* offers no political program. The fact that Berman climaxes his argument by proposing an immense mural/sculpture on the Cross-Bronx Expressway, which struck me as a properly self-deflating absurdist finale to a book that might otherwise seem overly earnest, has elicited much mockery among the reviewerati. But because poets can't really legislate anything, it's unreasonable to demand that in addition to limning our dilemma Berman tell us how to escape it. Works of art are exemplary, this one included. Berman can't teach any individual, much less an entire culture or an entire world, how to achieve pessimism of the intellect and optimism of the will. But he can demonstrate that it's possible.

Most of my reservations about what Berman has to say connect up with Jean Renoir's "It is practically the only question of the age, this question of primitivism and how it can be sustained in the face of sophistication." It's a question Berman cares about—hence his attention to "the modernism of under-development"—but his kind words for *Roots*-style ethnic neotraditionalism are hardly adequate to it, as the current upsurge of antimodernist (and antiurban) politics in Iran, the US, etc., makes all too clear. There's a sense in which the simple accumulation of time has eroded the patience of twentieth-century men and women; if Goethe had had to live through another 150 years of Sturm und Drang, he might have sent Faust back to Gretchen in Part Three. But that's just why we need this book—a book that traces modernist roots so naturally it seems like you always knew or never forgot they were there. Marx and Baudelaire and lots of others figured out that what human beings had to do was get past the either-or, and maybe it's not our job to be geniuses in their wake. Maybe it's merely to exceed their will.

Village Voice, 1982

Dialectical Cricket

C. L. R. James's *Beyond a Boundary*

In 1963, when C. L. R. James's *Beyond a Boundary* was first published, spectator sports, unlike blood sports, rarely figured in serious fiction, and they were almost never subjected to searching critical-political-historical analysis. There was good sportswriting, sure, but only within journalism's built-in limitations of space, tone, and occasion; even A. J. Liebling's *The Sweet Science*—at the time, *Beyond a Boundary*'s only full-length competition this side of Hemingway's *Death in the Afternoon*—was a collection of *New Yorker* pieces. And although there were valuable essays or chapters from the likes of Brecht, McLuhan, God help us Norman Podhoretz, and the criminally neglected Reuel Denney, not one professional thinker found the games he loved worthy of an entire book.

Of course, if you define "professional thinker" stringently, that holds true to this day; in athletics as in all other popular culture there's still a dearth of major-league books. But at least this US edition of *Beyond a Boundary* takes on all comers in a recognizable arena. And where before the book seemed a sport (a mutant, a freak, a caprice of nature: the word's etymology is far from entirely complimentary), now it has the unmistakable lineaments of a champion. With all respect to Roger Angell and Roger Kahn and Harry Edwards, they don't belong on the same field with C. L. R. James. Nor do they necessarily share the same grounds.

James didn't become a world-class bigdome in academia. Born the son of a Trinidadian schoolteacher in 1901, he was a devotee of town cricket by age six and soon after proved a prodigy in English literature as well—he read *Vanity Fair* every three months, we are told, for most of his boyhood. But though rewarded with a free education at the island's finest government school, he declined to go on to Oxford or some such after graduating at eighteen; instead he worked as a schoolteacher, with plenty of writing and plenty of cricket on the side. During the '20s he gradually became politicized, and when he finally set off for England in 1932 he had just composed a pioneering treatise on West Indian independence. His patron was England's first black professional cricketer and an old Trinidadian opponent, Learie Constantine, by then such a hero that James was imported to assist with his autobiography. Constantine eventually financed the printing of *The Case for West Indian Self-Government* and helped James get a job reporting cricket for the *Manchester Guardian* while he prepared his epochal biography of Toussaint L'Ouverture, *The Black Jacobins*. By the time he resettled in the US, where he was active as a union organizer from 1938 to 1952, James was an associate of Jomo Kenyatta and Leon Trotsky. Many credit him with originating the idea of the third world vanguard.

Most of this information can be gleaned from *Beyond a Boundary*, which like a lot of sportswriting by intellectuals celebrates the game's role in socializing and humanizing the author. But *Beyond a Boundary* is much more than a fond memoir. It has to be, because for James this game is much more than a locus of personal growth—although he never quite comes out and says so, he clearly regards cricket as a human achievement on a par with dialectical materialism itself. Aesthetically, it's a "structurally perfect" enactment of a fundamental "dramatic spectacle" that in addition epitomizes the "movement" and "tactile values" singled out by Bernard Berenson as the prime constituents of significant form in the visual arts. Historically, it preserved essential agrarian values in an era of rampaging industrialization, and continues to do so, although not without the deformities struggle imposes, in the face of a "decline of the West" that James dates to 1929. Politically, it's been instrumental in bringing down racial barriers throughout what was once the British Empire. And on every level its interactions with its audience have expressed the inexorable desire of human beings for genuine democracy.

Even if you judge all this rather eccentric (and who wouldn't?), you have to grant it an impressive audacity. It's easy enough for centrists like Angell and Liebling to wax romantic over the symbolic competitions they treasure, because the rules of the game flatter their presumption that competitiveness is both innate and containable. James, however, almost alone among philosophers of sport, is a leftist, and not only that—he's a leftist historian. His all-encompassing social vision gives this book an emotional sweep and intellectual reach the centrists can't match. But unlike most leftist historians, who are rarely utopian-spirited enough to account gracefully for the unruly distractions of aesthetic pleasure let alone competition or play, James enjoys that sense of connectedness to his own childhood that marks fully functional adults of whatever political persuasion. For him, discovering Marx didn't mean dismissing Thackeray or cricket, it just meant understanding them. Comfortable with such supposedly bourgeois categories as the human condition, he has no trouble accepting a world of winners and losers, and he gets a kick out of heroic individuals even when their exploits don't seem to illustrate noble lessons about sacrifice to history and the common good.

Just as he does in his 1936 novel *Minty Alley*, James takes an almost Dickensian relish in the colorful characters he sketches in *Beyond a Boundary*—from the blacksmith-batsman Cudjoe, the first and only black on his turn-of-the-century team, to W. G. Grace, whom I'd call the Babe Ruth of cricket if I thought the Babe's rough and rowdy ways likely to please James, who credits the moderately well-fixed Englishman Grace with focusing all the creative democratic and anti-capitalist instincts of the Victorian populace. But although there's a sense in which what he values most about both Cudjoe and Grace is their apparent inutility, it would be misleading to leave it at that. For like the post-Freudian, young-Hegelian Marxians/anarchists of the counterculture generation, James believes that the purpose of revolution is to liberate the realm of the apparently useless—which is also the realm of pleasure, beauty, spirit, the meaning of life. What sets him apart from these much younger theorists, not to mention their intellectual progenitors (and James's slightly younger contemporaries) in the Frankfurt School, isn't merely that he was broad-minded enough to find such virtues in popular culture, in cricket and later calypso. It's that he discovered them there. Thackeray and Trotsky helped, no doubt about it. But it was the enjoyment James took in cricket, and the meaning the game's "mass" audience found there, that inspired him to work with the people as well as write about them, that made his politics more than the obsessive rage for justice into which leftism so often devolves.

The prose of *Beyond a Boundary* combines the cultivated lyricism of someone like Hazlitt (whose boxing essays James extols) with the excitable quasi-Victorianism of the more hightone English sportswriting, and nothing else I've seen by James equals it stylistically. But the book isn't as perfect as *The Black Jacobins*, by most accounts James's masterwork. In the usual manner of fully functional adults well connected to the lessons of their childhood, he does tend to overpraise the culture that made him what he is, and while in 1962 the description of the racial integration of West Indian cricket that occupies his last thirty-five pages may have seemed to work structurally, today it clearly suffers from journalism's limitation of occasion. The brief introductory "Note on Cricket" doesn't go far enough toward helping us noncolonials to understand the detailed technical analysis or James's passionate philosophical commitment to "back play," whatever exactly that is. Since James is regarded as a prophet in some circles, it's also worth noting that, as far as I can determine, the "young Romantic" James predicted would soon "extend the boundaries of cricket technique with a classical perfection" has not yet made himself manifest. But I still don't know of a greater sports book. And I don't know all that many works of cultural theory to match it either.

Village Voice, 1984

The Oblique Strategies of a Radical Pluralist

Andrew Ross's *No Respect: Intellectuals & Popular Culture*

With the triumph of "theory" making it harder than ever for leftist intellectuals to debate vernacular culture in the vernacular, Andrew Ross's cannily casual *No Respect* is enough to renew your faith in the future of sanity. Quietly ambitious, unfinished by design, it presents itself as a history of "Intellectuals & Popular Culture"—leaving Ross free to move from secondhand account to secondhand account when concrete works might prove unwieldy. Yet though his reliance on competing authorities can be maddening at times, the lively, wide-ranging practical enthusiasm he conveys definitely makes him sound like a fan. And if his ending, dubbed "Defenders of the Faith and the New Class," is also disappointingly secondhand, intellectuals have by then provided the perfect cover for what he's really trying to bring off—an up-to-date overview of popular culture as theory and practice.

It's foolhardy to try such a thing, especially in 232 pages; even if you could get a handle on the overwhelming volume of subject matter, which you can't, there'd be no way to reduce what you know to words without sinking into abject abstraction. So Ross tries an oblique strategy. Not only does he never come out and admit what he's doing, but he picks and chooses like any other consumer from the incomprehensible welter of information products. *No Respect* has the unassuming look of a collection of linked and rewritten journal articles tracing cultural byways that happen to interest him. There's no way every theme and suggestion that arises is going to be woven neatly into a blanket conclusion, but in general his method serves him well.

The argument per se, for instance, kicks off from an unlikely place. "Reading the Rosenberg Letters" first skewers the aestheticist snobbery of the infamous essays in which Leslie Fiedler demonstrated the supposed A-spies' moral bankruptcy by dissecting their prose styles, then goes on to charge that critics from Harold Rosenberg to Morris Dickstein fall into the same trap when they accuse Fiedler of shallowness or inauthenticity, because those are aestheticist categories. For Ross, what's most significant now about Ethel and Julius's letters is their "continuing capacity . . . to compromise every possible canon of 'legitimate' taste. The problem of petty-bourgeois taste, culture, and expression remains to this day a largely neglected question for cultural studies and a formidable obstacle to a left cultural politics." Very smart. Yet only rarely does Ross address this problem in so many words himself. Instead it reappears in variations on his most crucial assumption, which is the folly of hoping that good art and good politics will always be congruent—or that somebody else's good art (or good politics) will always be yours. If this smacks of liberal pluralism, tough noogs—Ross is a radical pluralist, a spokesperson for what he likes to call the "liberatory imagination." Refusing closure, his episodic book complements this pluralism, reflecting his commitment to "*impure criticism*" (Ross's italics), his refusal of "any high theoretical ground or vantage point from which an entire historical trajectory could be summed up," and his stubborn belief that the art people like tells us something about the life they really need, even if those needs are inconvenient or unjust.

Ross's political orientation leads him irresistibly to the Rosenbergs, the magnificent obsession of American leftists and their feuding cousins for two generations, and informs his choice of stopping places elsewhere. Anybody tackling such a project would feel obliged to trek through '50s mass culture theory, as Ross does in "Containing Culture in the Cold War." But he soon abandons academic obligation for pleasure and polemic, moving on to black music, communications theory, camp, and pornography. While these subjects clearly reflect the author's own interests, they also dovetail with the great targets of post-Marxist activism: racism, imperialism, homophobia, and sexism (though not eco-collapse, proving that other people's good politics aren't always pop intellectuals' own).

It worries me that the only one of these chapters I find seriously wanting deals with music, the subject I know best—among other things, Ross's discussion of funk skips from Stax to rap with no mention of late James Brown or George Clinton, who between them invented the genre even if no one's written a book about it. But by emphasizing "hip" as the key to black-white musical crosstalk, he introduces one of his chief fascinations: intellectuals coming to grips with pop culture by putting it at a distance. His basically antihip conclusion is that "racial integration" would have to "feel its uncharted way . . . not in the best possible world, where ethnic self-respect and self-determination can always be guaranteed a fair hearing, but in the impure setting of the marketplace of cultural exchange." This is his most fundamental and paradoxical perception: that mass media comprise a highly inefficient instrument of social control, and, conversely, that when the media liberate, the political risks can be disturbingly high. Tough noogs again.

Ross recasts the same point in a chapter on cultural imperialism that starts with megabucks quiz shows and Candid Camera, does a job on McLuhan, and ends up refuting Ariel Dorfman–style theories of US global domination—his final observation is that in the real-life frontierland of the Third World, supposedly propagandistic westerns like *Bonanza* have subversive lessons to teach native peoples about their allotted fate. He sums up the convoluted distancing devices of camp and its cousin Pop, and finds his faith in unsafe culture fulfilled by the prosex feminism of the anti-antiporn vanguard. An expert might be able to pick holes in some of his history, but as a half-expert I found all of it solid and stimulating. And I couldn't name a heterosexual man with a warmer or more comprehensive take on gay sensibility, or a more candid, realistic, and just plain acute analysis of pornography.

No doubt the theory crowd will carp that most of what Ross says has been said before. His central idea that popular culture is a force field rather than a hegemony—the site of a "struggle for fun," as Simon Frith put it a decade ago, although Ross (prematurely) cedes the term "fun" to the yuppie postmodernists, opting for the more academically fashionable "pleasure"—has become the working assumption of all but his most Frankfurtized colleagues. Those who've thought seriously about these matters may recognize this or that apercu from their own speculation as well as their own reading. But Ross has a bead on the inescapable truth that the body doesn't much care about political correctness, and especially when he gets down to cases, much of his presentation is original, even brilliant. He's put a large number of sound ideas into a book that's as coherent as right reason demands. Ross believes in culture for use. *No Respect* exemplifies that belief.

Crucial to the book's usefulness, not to mention its coherence, is that it's written to be understood. The ideas can be dense and complex, and when I said Ross was vernacular, I didn't mean he used a lot of slang. But his forceful, declarative prose amounts to a grandstand play in an intellectual environment where sentences, paragraphs, sometimes whole books have been known to disappear in whirlpools of jargon. A Scot who teaches at Princeton, he typifies the affection for common sense and common experience that has always distinguished Britain's cultural studies tradition, yet explicitly resists its localism, anti-Americanism, rigid class analysis, and tendency to break out in splotches at the first whiff of mass production. As he says in his porn chapter: "To refuse to be educated: to refuse to be taught lessons about maturity and adult responsibility, let alone about sexism and racism; to be naughty, even bad, but mostly naughty; to be on your worst behavior—all of this may be a ruse of patriarchy, a ruse of capitalism, but it also has something to do with a resistance to education, institutional or otherwise. It has something to do with a resistance to those whose patronizing power and missionary ardor are the privileges bestowed upon and instilled in them by a legitimate education."

Certainly *No Respect* leaves the two comparable American projects of the '80s sucking dust—Robert Pattison's *The Triumph of Vulgarity*, a pugnaciously slapdash polemic, and Patrick Brantlinger's *Bread and Circuses*, a piece of scholarship so evenhanded it reads like a course summary. Though they're very different books, Brantlinger's a pretty good one, both fail utterly to convey the aesthetic give-and-take that makes Ross so engaging. *No Respect* is more in the spirit of Reuel Denney's *The Astonished Muse*, a 1957 tour of TV, football, science fiction, skyscrapers, and other stuff that caught a sociologist's fancy. Like most of the '50s academics who bothered to pay attention to mass culture before rattling on about it, Denney was no leftist, and three decades later his appeal is undermined somewhat by the complacency of his, well, liberal pluralism. Let's hope Ross's radical pluralism doesn't suffer the same fate. Because we know for sure not all good politics are congruent. And giving the rude demands of popular culture some respect just might help us figure out how to cram all those politics together.

Village Voice, 1990

Inside the Prosex Wars

Nadine Strossen's *Defending Pornography: Free Speech, Sex, and the Fight for Women's Rights* | Joanna Frueh's *Erotic Faculties* | Laura Kipnis's *Bound and Gagged: Pornography and the Politics of Fantasy in America*

For a while there in the '80s the feminist porn/sex debate got pretty scary. Rank-and-filers whose First Amendment principles weren't shored up by a personal attraction to pornography were so reluctant to go against the flow that there seemed a chance women's libbers would exhaust themselves jousting with the sex merchants the way their nineteenth-century sisters veered off into temperance, with Andrea Dworkin our very own Carry Nation. But all that had really happened was that prosex feminists had taken too much for granted. As the likes of Ellen Willis, Carole Vance, Jane Gallop, and Pat Califia, to name just a few, launched their diverse attacks on the Robin Morgans and Catharine MacKinnons, a fundamental fact reasserted itself. Whether sex is an irresistible physical urge or an elaborate social construction, twentieth-century American women are as determined to enjoy it as twentieth-century American men, and no amount of specious prudery is going to stop them.

'Nuff said? Sometimes I wish—after almost two decades, the debate often seems rather ritualistic. Words matter tremendously in sex; anybody who needs Foucault to figure out that moral codes and subtler verbal phenomena profoundly affect how human beings disport their genitals and activate their erogenous zones enjoys a more unimpeded communion with his or her sacred essence than I managed at sixteen, eighteen, twenty-three, twenty-seven, thirty, thirty-two, thirty-eight, forty, forty-three, or forty-nine (although now, of course, I'm beyond all that). But basically, the lines are drawn regarding censorship and pornography as well as the right of women to do what they want with their bodies and fantasy lives. Certainly most *Voice* readers know which side they're on—the right side, the pleasure side, rah rah rah. And although dissections of Camille Paglia and interviews with lap dancers may still mean a lot to young women and men painfully working out their unique sexual identities, the porn controversy and its numerous offshoots often have the aura of a summer-camp color war.

Only a bluenose would want discussion to cease altogether—real human suffering, and also real human ecstasy, are still at stake. No one has gotten near the bottom of such essential concepts as abuse, harassment, or, especially, desire, and in this era of market-driven political volatility it isn't just paranoia to fear that an American fascism might yet put an end to eros as we know it. There are plenty of bad people out there thinking up new ways to say sex is sinful, and a distressing if small proportion of them do so as feminists. The fact remains, however, that few adults are likely to change their minds about this stuff just because some post-Lacanian has reconceptualized the varieties of phallic experience. So when I thumb through Lisa Duggan and Nan Hunter's strong-principled *Sex Wars*, say, I get irritated with Duggan for poking fun at poststructuralist rhetoric without bothering to juice up her own. And as I soak up *Straight Sex*'s useful overview of modern feminism's interface with the erotic, I wish Lynne Segal could render her empathetic intelligence in less utilitarian prose.

It would be snobbery to posit any essential connection between verbal and sexual pleasure. The ability to write well is one thing, the capacity to fuck well another. But there are metaphorical connections. Readers have as much right to be turned on as do sexual subjects (and sex objects), and putting some jam into your style is an excellent way to tone up your ideas. So it's too bad Nadine Strossen's *Defending Pornography* is the kind of book you read fast not because you can't put it down but so you can. As legal director of the New York Civil Liberties Union, Strossen has done as much to make the world safe for sexual speech as any player in the debate. But she writes like a lawyer marshalling evidence rather than a thinker examining nuances, and Oliver Wendell Holmes she's not. Her prose is devoid of grace or wit; recounting a rib-tickler about lesbian pornography, she takes a hundred words to get to the punch line, which she carefully explains before it arrives.

At times, too, Strossen's one-sidedness becomes irritating. Surely there's something to the notion that pinups can be used to harass in the workplace, even if that doesn't mean they should be forbidden, and her preferred vision of porn actresses as imaginative freelance contractors is a good deal rosier than the evidence warrants. Nevertheless, she has produced a sobering book. However boring the old points may seem in a liberal enclave, the sex debate gets scarier than ever when Canada's MacDworkinite porn law is selectively applied to political undesirables—such as feminists (many of them lesbians) with ideas about sex (including Andrea Dworkin herself).

It's easy to forget how big a horror MacKinnon is—a hypocritical powermonger who means to establish her aversion for erectile tissue as the only feminist truth. Taking her on won't be a rhetorical exercise until she is totally defeated.

Not surprisingly, many of the battles Strossen describes occur on college campuses—with their rampaging hormones, their behavior codes and thought police, their theorists working out liberationist abstractions in a hothouse where any piece of horse dookie can have its moment in the sun. Fortunately, both University of Nevada art historian Joanna Frueh and Northwestern University filmmaker Laura Kipnis make a point of opposing all the pieties of this sexualized environment—not just the repressiveness of collegiate antisex leagues, but the intolerance, evasiveness, and elitism of their own prosex allies. Moreover, these university-press books take explicit exception not just to earlier scholarship, which is how scholars earn their livings, but to the specialized lingo all such books are expected to share.

Although it would be possible to pass Frueh off as one more academic hustler, her unutilitarian verbiage is convincing and sexy. *Erotic Faculties* collects not essays but lectures, complete with stage directions. Vain and proud of it, Frueh lovingly describes her outfits, her tone of voice, her bared navel and buffed limbs. "Erotic scholarship is lubricious and undulant, wild, polyvocal, cock- and cuntsure," she proclaims, and whether she's attacking "the Postmodern Mysteries" in "Fuck Theory" and "Pythia," celebrating her marriage in the pornographic "Mouth Piece" and the contentious Louise Bourgeois hommage "Jeez Louise," or gazing upon her own inevitable decay through the eyes of postmenopausal and dying artists, she keeps her word. Frueh may not persuade everyone to seek out the work that inspires her poetic criticism. But she makes the most of the truth that, in the end, art is what the viewer makes of it.

Declaring poststructuralism's "old refrain of revolution" merely "reformist," Frueh posits her subjectivist paradigm-busting as an alternative, but that's just the usual radical one-upspersonship. When Laura Kipnis talks revolution, she has the decency to mean class struggle. As the 1991 essay and videoscript collection *Ecstasy Unlimited* demonstrates, she was one of the earliest theory mavens to come out against theory's avant-gardist pretensions. Claiming popular culture as people's culture rather than an image bank for tenure-grubbing bricoleurs, she climaxed with a half-finished defense of *Hustler*'s antibourgeois grotesquery that grew into *Bound and Gagged*. Assuming that pornography merits "critical exegesis" as much as any other art form, these five connected essays on s&m fantasy, transvestite self-portraiture, soft-core fat mags and flicks, *Hustler*'s unremitting attacks on the rich and famous, and the MacDworkinite reaction deploy the conceptual arsenal of theory and cultural studies in language a disinterested outsider might take for forceful, coherent English prose—educated to be sure, but so full of feeling and ideas it's worth the reasonable effort it requires.

Structurally, Kipnis's only problem is how to follow a magnificent first chapter, an essentially journalistic investigation rooted in many hours of taped evidence and interviews with Daniel DePew, a gay s&m bottom-turned-top now serving thirty-three years for conspiracy to film kiddie porn. Not only does Kipnis establish beyond a reasonable doubt that DePew was entrapped, she makes clear that he regarded the entire police-initiated scheme as a courting ritual, and provides a picture of DePew's actual sex life that can only be called touching. This is as clear a take as one could expect on the intertwining of sexual fantasy and reality, and Kipnis isn't just scoring points when she emphasizes that the cops' gruesome snuff and kidnapping scenarios appealed far more to the law enforcers than to the "perverts" they thought they were bringing to justice.

The rest of the book interprets more and reports less, and Kipnis's failure to find any genital buzz of her own in the analysis leaves her looking a tad detached—somehow the assertion that porn is "not just friction and naked bodies" always rubs me the wrong way. But the material she's found, the playful and sometimes surreal fatty stuff especially, took impressive original research. And throughout she remains true to her class analysis, seeing men as well as women as sexually victimized by their upbringing and material circumstances without pretending that *Hustler* doesn't gross her out. She also tosses choice barbs at Allan Bloom and Jeffrey Masson as well as Masson's inamorata MacKinnon. So rah rah rah. To wonder whether the porn/sex debate has gone on too long isn't to suggest that either subject has lost its intrinsic fascination. Especially when rendered in a language that generates a seductiveness of its own.

Village Voice, 1996

Growing Up Kept Down

William Finnegan's *Cold New World: Growing Up in a Harder Country*

The most remarkable of William Finnegan's many literary gifts is his compassion. Not the fact of it, which we have a right to expect from any personal reporting about the oppressed, but its coolness, its clarity, its ductile strength. Compassion is a solvent, and in its bleeding-heart variants quickly turns writing soggy. That's why Alex Kotlowitz's gripping *There Are No Children Here* seems soft at times, its two Chicago project kids too well-meaning to be fully believed. Paragons can't be paradigms, and although Kotlowitz refrains from airbrushing the brothers he's all but adopted, they exemplify nothing. *Cold New World*'s protagonists are different. In their late teens or early twenties, they're already succumbing to a class war that hasn't abated since Reagan turned it up, and because the author's suspended judgment never flirts with impassivity or outlaw romanticism, they seem ordinary in their failings. As a result, their talents, their aspirations, and their struggles toward selfhood also seem ordinary, in the best way—organic attributes of a shared American humanity.

Finnegan's book is powered emotionally by the impact of "downward mobility" and "the frightening growth in the number of low-wage jobs" on young people, especially young people of color, in a supposedly booming economy that favors not just whites but the elderly. Despite his tendency to demonize "the American religion of liberal consumerism," Finnegan's historical-intellectual grasp exceeds that of Kotlowitz or Gini Sikes, whose frightening report on female gang-bangers, *8 Ball Chicks*, flanks *Cold New World*'s hard side the way *There Are No Children Here* does its soft. And for the most part he submerges his ideas in patient, perfectly paced reporting that first surfaced as four long *New Yorker* pieces dating back to 1990—not one, remarkably, situated in a large city, although the metropolis's cultural lure and capital resources inflect them all.

Starting the sequence is "Terry Jackson," a decent, unmoored African-American teenager who bounces in and out of the New Haven dope trade. From there the story passes to rural East Texas, where black twenty-three-year-old chicken plucker Lanee Mitchell provides the youth angle, although the focus is a white populist sheriff ruined by his disinclination to come down on the hard-working black capitalists who go into drugs when Houston's construction industry collapses. The next section follows Juan Guerrero, the slacker son of two Mexican-born United Farm Workers activists in Washington's Yakima Valley, past the moment when his genius for martial arts gets him run out of town. Finally Finnegan goes home to Southern California, where "the sense of extreme freedom" he recalls from his surfer youth proves "anomalous—an unearned blessing." Before the end of his time in Palmdale, a vast exurb two hours north of L.A., the only African-American among the antiracist skins he's been hanging with has killed a racist bonehead, and Finnegan's white subject, the compulsively flirtatious Mindy Turner, has extended her quest for a father into a correspondence with ex-GI James Burmeister, currently serving consecutive life sentences for the random slayings of two black civilians.

Finnegan acknowledges the distortion built into all high-access reporting—he has to like his subjects enough to spend months with them, and vice versa. So it's no surprise that all are articulate and insightful about themselves no matter how ignorant they are about the world, and also no surprise that toward the edges of their circles Finnegan encounters much uglier and stupider individuals. He roots shamelessly for these kids who have become his friends—and in several cases offers them substantial material support once his *New Yorker*–imposed presumption of journalistic "objectivity" is mooted by publication, even financing Juan's escape to San Francisco and Texas. But just because he's supportive doesn't mean he lets them off the hook. Terry makes promises he can't keep and lands in jail. Juan also does time he could have avoided, and is too shallow or callow to return the love of a woman he probably doesn't deserve. Mindy's vagrant impulses are more reliable than her utterly muddled principles. Even lovely Lanee, who's old enough to have put adolescent self-absorption behind her, smacks her young son around for no reason Finnegan or the reader can credit.

The calm with which Finnegan relates these missteps never registers as acceptance. He respects his subjects too much to deny their responsibility, and himself too much to fall into cultural relativism. But his compassion compels him to emphasize how circumstances constrain the poor. Mindy lost her dad in an industrial accident. Juan is a basically honorable guy whose social disaffections would be marks of hip in an upper-middle-class scion with more time to get himself together. Just as gangsta rappers rationalize, Terry becomes a crack-hawking "work boy" because he wants to make something of himself and help the people he loves—including his mother, whose ability to enjoy drugs engages Finnegan's bemused sympathy, and his grandmother, whose refusal to tolerate them excites his undisguised admiration. And it's heartening Lanee can raise a child at all in a local economy that draconian law enforcement has relentlessly restacked against everybody outside the old white elite.

Finnegan, whose three excellent earlier books are set in Africa, correctly believes he's telling a crucial American story here, and *The New Yorker* deserves credit for underwriting it. If it seems suspect that such a smug venue should launch a substantial attack on the bland lies of Clintonian pseudo-prosperity, thank literature that it isn't, because literature is why it happened. Finnegan writes like a dream. His prose is unfailingly lucid, graceful, and specific, his characterization smooth, and the pull of his narrative pure seduction—he knows just when to move from summary to incident or analysis and back again, and if he's a bulldog when he smells a turning point, he's a pussycat tracing the stray ends of a silly yarn. In this he seems to keep getting better. Not even *Crossing the Line*, which recounts a year spent teaching at an apartheid high school in "coloured" Cape Town, moves with such clarity at such a clip.

Beneath this generous story subsists a rather purse-lipped analysis—Finnegan's consumerism shibboleth, his skimpily explored assertion that boomers make lousy parents, his distaste for *New Jack City* and Smashing Pumpkins. But the tale itself is so rich and open-ended that it leaves each of us free to speculate. Me, I was struck that for all his determination to write about class, Finnegan couldn't escape race, even (especially) in "white" Palmdale. I understood more vividly than ever that the state's "war on drugs" is a vile travesty, another way to render the poor redundant. And however tedious pro forma anticonsumerism may be, I could see how high material expectations messed up Finnegan's kids, who couldn't match the will and spirit palpable in his *A Complicated War*—about Mozambique, the most impoverished nation on the planet. But I also noted that these kids were far braver and more resourceful than the smug assume. And I was grateful that Finnegan had provided the means for any reader to enter deep into their worlds—so irreducibly individual in one way, so historically freighted in another.

Village Voice, 1998

Jesus Plus the Capitalist Order

Jeff Sharlet's *The Family: The Secret Fundamentalism at the Heart of American Power*

Any believer in American democracy is obliged to come to terms with a wing of the citizenry few devout secular humanists have the wherewithal to think about—Christians. Not "mainline" modernists, so useful for validating progressive pieties when we godless need moral ballast, but the seventy-five million Americans whose Christianity takes such modifiers as the respectable evangelical, the unapologetic fundamentalist, the doctrinal Bible-believing, the thoughtful convinced, and the emotional born-again. Especially the white ones, of course—even black churches that oppose abortion and homosexuality are aligned with the social gospel, while Latino Pentecostals and Korean Presbyterians generally gather in their own congregations. Anyway, secular humanists are inclined to cut African-Americans and immigrants some slack. White Middle Americans they have a problem with.

These generalizations are crude, obviously. For one thing, there are plenty of secular humanists in Middle America, where proximity mitigates incomprehension a little. But in New York, my eternal home, folks are less sophisticated. As someone whose atheism proceeds directly from his demographically unlikely childhood in a fundamentalist church in Queens, and whose brother has spent his life ministering to conservative churches in various distant suburbs, I got on this problem back when my *Village Voice* colleagues dismissed Jimmy Carter out of hand because he was a Southern Baptist. I argued back then that the specifics of Carter's religious history suggested levels of honesty and compassion unusual in a politician, which turned out to be true—in 2000, Carter quit the by then explicitly right-wing Southern Baptist Convention after a fruitless struggle to moderate it. Other politically prominent Southern Baptists include Pat Robertson, who founded the Christian Broadcasting Network in 1960, and Jerry Falwell, who founded the Moral Majority in 1979. They do not include famed born-againer George W. Bush—or the most devout Christian currently running for president, Barack Obama. Generalizations are often crude.

Jeff Sharlet's *The Family: The Secret Fundamentalism at the Heart of American Power* examines a group of politically engaged Christians far more secretive than Robertson or Falwell. Sharlet establishes that since the end of World War II, The Family, a/k/a The Fellowship, has exerted its influence in an impressive and frightening array of mostly dire events. Its first coup was the wholesale exoneration of minor Nazis and major Nazi collaborators after the war. The addition of "under God" to the Pledge of Allegiance and "In God We Trust" to US currency were its initiatives. Its first major government operative was Kansas senator Frank Carlson, who persuaded Dwight Eisenhower to run as a Republican, purged progressive bureaucrats from his chair at the obscure Civil Service Employees Committee, and lobbied for such heads of state as Haiti's Duvalier. Other dictators abetted by The Family included Ngo Dinh Diem of Vietnam, Haile Selassie of Ethiopia, Park Chung Hee of South Korea, Artur da Costa e Silva of Brazil, Haiji Suharto of Indonesia, Mohamed Siad Barre of Somalia, and Carlos Eugenio Vides Casanova of El Salvador, which got its first infusion of special aid at the behest of Jimmy Carter, who has called Family leader Doug Coe a "very important person" in his life. Hillary Clinton has also been a Family "friend," and not just via its major public manifestation, the relatively anodyne National Prayer Breakfast. The Family was instrumental in the creation of Chuck Colson's Prison Fellowship, and of the Community Bible Study project through which George W. Bush found Jesus in 1985.

Deeply researched yet fast-paced, moving easily from first person to third person and incident to overview, *The Family* is an exceptional piece of bookcraft. Its revelations are fascinating, especially with political history having propelled Christians deep into polite discourse since 1976. Yet since it came out in May, it has attracted just two major reviews, both censorious; I found out about it only when I was asked to share a panel with Sharlet in June. You could say this reflects the dismal state of book coverage in a journalistic environment where new arts cutbacks come down from on high every month. But when I try to imagine how an unbroken phalanx of individual literary editors decided not to squeeze this book into their pathetic page allotments, I keep remembering how exotic my old co-workers found my hunch that Carter was a smart, sensible, decent guy. Secular humanists know more about Christians now, but not that much more. And The Family doesn't fit their template.

Sharlet is a thirty-six-year-old historian and journalist of religion, the son of a Jewish father and a Pentecostal mother. He's a contributing editor at *Harper's* and *Rolling Stone* and has founded two online journals of religion: the NYU-backed *The Revealer* and *Killing the Buddha*, which is also the title of his first book, written with co-editor Peter Manseau. While clearly a left-leaning skeptic, Sharlet is just as clearly drawn to spiritual quests. *Killing the Buddha* alternates between heretical interpretations of Bible chapters—by such guests as Francine Prose (Exodus) and Rick Moody (Jonah), although most are less prominent and several outshine the stars—and sojourns with cultists nationwide, more than half of them Christian. These tales are both more empathetic than the standard yahoo-bashing expose and less polite than the pained coverage of evangelical activists that became a journalistic staple once Karl Rove transformed churchgoers into margins of victory. Sharlet and Manseau feel the pain of almost everyone they write about, but that doesn't blind them to the foolishness of these suffering seekers and penny-ante ideologues, which they're not above mocking when the joke is good enough.

The world of *The Family* is much different. For its first three quarters, the individuals Sharlet observes and interviews come from more money and wield more power than those who populate *Killing the Buddha*. Yet you won't meet the usual cast of hucksters and theocrats—James Dobson, Tony Perkins, John Hagee, Rick Warren, Tim LaHaye, whoever. A few politicians pass through, notably Sam Brownback, but for the most part you've never heard of these rather colorless people, every one of whom Sharlet engages on a human level. This failure to flatter stereotype couldn't have helped Sharlet get reviewed and typifies his insight into American Christianity, which subdivides endlessly. The most important such grouping, argues Gallup-pollster-turned-Rice-sociologist D. Michael Lindsay in *Faith in the Halls of Power*, a well-researched, widely reviewed 2007 overview of American evangelicals whose "sympathetic perspective" Sharlet notes with some asperity, pits populists against cosmopolitans. The populists have become familiar figures in secular humanist folklore. The Family—which is neither an official organization nor a coherent conspiracy—enlists only cosmopolitans.

Among The Family's members is none other than Jeff Sharlet, who in 2002 was invited by an acquaintance to spend a month at Ivanwald, a Family training facility in Arlington, Virginia, along with a shifting cast of some dozen young men. All of them tended the house and grounds, served occasional meals at a nearby Family mansion, played ball and horsed around, joined a female auxiliary at weekly swing dances, and attended meetings where they learned what it meant to serve Jesus. Everyone knew Sharlet was a half-Jewish journalist who might write about them. After a draft of the first chapter of *The Family* was published in *Harper's* in 2003, he was vetted by Family associates overt and covert, including a sexy blonde; in the end the group's archive in Wheaton, Illinois, where he'd done extensive digging, was closed to the public. But Sharlet's social relations with his Family contacts remain cordial. Why not? He's a smart guy with a future. Someday he might prove useful.

That's how *The Family* operates, and quite often it goes over people's heads, as it is meant to. Take *U.S. News & World Report*'s religion specialist, Jay Tolson, whose faint-praise review indignantly disproves that political fundamentalists get "marching orders from The Fellowship"—which Sharlet never suggests. No wonder they call themselves The Family and The Fellowship—uppercase removed, those are the relevant models. The Family makes connections and encourages behavior based on bonds of friendship, faith, and shared experience. It's networking for Christ, theocracy as hegemony. Sharlet's research establishes (as even Tolson acknowledges) that all the dictators named above received crucial support from the organization begun in Seattle in 1935—with seed money from a local developer—by Norwegian-born clergyman and Goodwill Industries middle executive Abram Vereide. But as with the State Department, some of its projects are benign—orphanages, hospitals, even peace accords. And always the dirtiest details are left to Family-linked power brokers—carefully nurtured local "key men"—in the belief that, ultimately, Christ thrives in a stable capitalist order.

Doug Coe, Vereide's successor for nearly half a century now, has some provocative ideas. He likes to cite the Mafia, Hitler-Goebbels-Himmler, and Communist Party cells as examples of the strong faith of a few changing the world. Sharlet pinpoints one of his favorite slogans as especially fraught: "Jesus plus nothing." You could say this mantra aspires toward Godhead. But in a world of many Jesuses—*Killing the Buddha* touches upon at least a dozen—it can also be seen as undercutting Jesus' reality. Is Jesus still Jesus without his life example, his teachings, his scripture, his churches that Coe says have no biblical basis? For Sharlet, Jesus-plus-zero equals power for its own sake, an abstraction with disastrously concrete consequences. Family members are inculcated with the principle of loyalty—"Loyalty to what? The idea of loyalty." Part of him clearly feels that Coe and his enablers are monsters. But he also conveys that at some level the guys he meets are nice, normal, well-meaning. If Doug Coe is a little strange, he knows how to stay quiet about it. A Family of monsters wouldn't function.

For nearly three hundred pages, including some of the best background on seminal evangelists Jonathan Edwards and Charles Grandison Finney I've ever read, Sharlet says to hell with stereotype and traces this shadowy seam of Christianity. I so admired his formal austerity that at first I was disappointed when he switched up, devoting the book's final quarter to reporting on more familiar fundamentalist types—home-schoolers, abstinence activists, life-tossed devotees of a prelapsarian Ted Haggard, even some Oregon progressives. But there's no resisting Sharlet's empathy, which must have been sorely tested by his several seasons among the evangelical elite—whether they're as nutty as the Colorado Springs insurance agent who fears demons in every urban place or as sharp as the virgin Brooklyn grade-school teacher who'll probably have a ball in bed once he gets married, you can see why these people need Jesus in their lives and hope their spiritual struggles won't ever ease to a complacent halt.

Constructing a single argument from this plethora of activity is a knotty undertaking, and Sharlet doesn't quite put a bow on it. But though the most fluent stylists are rarely as lucid essaying exegesis as writing narrative or history, Sharlet's many philosophical passages go down much better than most. Here he closes with a few progressives, believers who work mostly in the helping professions salving their pain over the shooting of a mentor by renewing their belief in "absolute Truth." Then he visits David Kuo, Bush's Coe-trained "faith-based initiatives" expert, who later wrote a much-praised book exposing how crassly political his supposedly charitable office was. Sharlet, whose research has left him rather pessimistic about combating hegemony, suspects Kuo hasn't really changed his spots. Sure Jimmy Carter and Hillary Clinton are preferable to George W. Bush and Sam Brownback, but in the end, as *The Family* understands, all serve the same order.

Sharlet proffers one shred of hope, a constituency of sorts—"believers and unbelievers alike, all of us who love our neighbors more than we love power or empire or even the solace of certainty." Devout secular humanists can scoff if they like, but I'm here to testify that Sharlet is both more intelligent and better informed than most of them. If he believes that "believers and unbelievers alike" fall into this constituency's sainted host, then I believe him.

Truthdig, 2008

Dark Night of the Quants: Ten Books About the Financial Crisis

Nine months ago, seeking a readable take on the prospects of my retirement savings, I picked up Michael "Moneyball" Lewis's character-driven financial crisis tale *The Big Short*. Soon a word Lewis favors there caught my fancy:

quant. A quant is a math whiz who sells his skills to the banking industry. Quants invented, elaborated, and tailored the collateralized debt obligations (CDOs) and credit default swaps (CDSs) that wrecked the world economy, and like everyone in the banking industry, albeit at a higher level of difficulty, they think more in numbers and less in words than you or me. The term stayed with me because I was given my college scholarship to become a quant but stubbornly trained instead to become a wordsmith. Soon my math aptitudes atrophied, as did any chance I had to internalize the fast-evolving language that would so profoundly affect my material well-being. In this I'm like most civilians—it's not an easy language.

So having already decided that *The Big Short* was too glib to serve as my last word on the defining political issue of our time, I hoped more reading might help me become, if not fluent, at least an informed citizen who knows how to ask directions out of town. Intuitively and associatively, although with an eye to balance, I ended up downing ten books all told, a million-some words' worth, without ever getting to Andrew Ross Sorkin's well-regarded *Too Big to Fail* or anything by a name left-liberal economist like Joseph Stiglitz. Since there's no way to cover them fully, let me begin with a graded list in the order I finished.

- **Michael Lewis, *The Big Short***
  Focuses on the value investors who bet against, that revealing parlance, the mortgage securities market. Too entertaining about greed and irrationality for its deep pessimism to be altogether trustworthy. B+
- **John Lanchester, *I.O.U.***
  Having survived a mortgage of his own, British novelist and banker's son finds a journalistic specialty, which he aces. Explains credit default swaps, dismantles risk models, and actually visits one of the ruined neighborhoods whose fates so many bemoan. A
- **Ha-Joon Chang, *23 Things They Don't Tell You About Capitalism***
  South Korean-born British economist loves Swedish capitalism and hates the free-market kind. Like most liberal economists, not much use on the political implementation of his sane proposals. A-
- **Richard Posner, *A Failure of Capitalism***
  With dispassionate clarity, brainy, union-hating conservative jurist insists the recession is a depression, puts "greed" in quotes, and calls for regulation in due time—because, after all, "no one has a clear sense of the social value of our deregulated financial industry." B+

- **Matt Taibbi, *Griftopia***
  Rolling Stone staffer explains abstruse things lucidly, nails the evil Alan Greenspan, and uncovers heartbreaking stuff on commodities speculators ginning up the 2008 gas shortage and investment bankers gulling Greece and Chicago. But he's so mad he can't resist dumb ad hominems like "dumbasses" and thinks his myriad targets are both stupider and more malevolent than they are. A-

- **Robert Scheer, *The Great American Stickup***
  Lefter-than-thou scold proves efficient and clear on the Glass-Steagall and government-sponsored enterprise fiascos that paved the way for the subprime disaster, only mounting his pulpit at the very end. B+

- **Gretchen Morgenson and Joshua Rosner, *Reckless Endangerment***
  In need of a hook, *Times* reporter and the researcher who noted early that "A Home Without Equity Is Just a Rental with Debt" come down too hard and long on Fannie Mae and Freddie Mac—the profit-mad government-sponsored enterprises the right fallaciously blames for the whole crisis. The many lobbying details, however, are scary and disgusting. B-

- **Danny Schechter, *The Crime of Our Time***
  Documentarian lodges poorly written, abysmally edited, sketchily sourced criminal charges against, well, all of Wall Street. But because he knows these can't stick in court and thus puts some thought into other avenues of public action, his name-calling is more tonic than Taibbi's. C+

- **Bethany McLean and Joe Nocera, *All The Devils Are Here***
  Although the *Vanity Fair* and *New York Times* stars are too understanding about the inner lives of cutthroats, their outrage is palpable as they get the story. From the earliest mortgage-backed securities to Dodd-Frank, they drive their narrative by devoting whole chapters to firms and agencies, whose cultures vary just like characters do. A

- **Henry M. Paulson, Jr., *On the Brink***
  The long-winded treasury secretary who oversaw the bailouts gets credit for working inhuman hours in 2008, and for emphasizing if not quite elucidating the "repo" market in overnight liquidity loans. Wish he'd mentioned his leverage-escalating efforts as Goldman Sachs CEO. Or the $500 million stock sale that would have been $400 million if he'd ponied up capital gains taxes. Or that Fannie Mae mortgage Schechter says he got his mom. These guys don't pay cash for *anything*. C

Let me continue by briefly explaining some of the terms above. What I call the banking industry includes many entities that aren't banks and has been weasel-branded the "financial services industry," a phrase I can't type without scare quotes. Glass-Steagall is the 1933 law that prevented commercial banks, where citizens and small businesses can stockpile and borrow money, from acting like investment banks, which deal speculative, high-stakes instruments and maneuvers affordable only by rich people, large corporations, and such naive collectivities as local governments and pension funds; its Republican-powered 1999 repeal was abetted by gung-ho Democratic Treasury secretaries Robert Rubin and Larry Summers and a complaisant Bill Clinton. A collateralized debt obligation is a bond typically backed by student loans, credit-card debt, and, notoriously, mortgages; even more notoriously, *synthetic* CDOs are backed by other CDOs, and then additional synthetic CDOs are backed by them, pretty much ad infinitum. A credit default swap is an insurance policy on debt you're owed—if your creditor defaults, your insurer has to cough up the cash instead. And if you're "subprime," another weasel brand, many would say you can't afford that mortgage some shyster is talking up. Multiply by X million home buyers—and homeowners transforming their abodes into piggy banks—and many CDOs will go south.

And there you have the makings of what we hope is merely the worst financial crisis since the Great Depression. If you take the Glass-Steagall rout as a metonym for the breakdown of regulation that began with Reagan, speeded up with Clinton, and took off under Bush, all that's missing is the perfidy of the rating agencies and the ugly specifics of the greed Posner doesn't believe in. We all know the crisis is upon us, certainly including the 1 percent, as we've learned to label them. The difference is that few of the 1 percent are morally gifted enough to internalize it, while even the frugal or lucky or relatively well-off among the rest of us feel the contraction: the jobs sped up or pared down or done in, the savings eroded, the investments gone sour, the kids stuck at home, the public services starved, the stores shuttered, the anxiety and fear and ambient rage.

In fact, many understand how it happened well enough to be depressed if not overwhelmed by their own powerlessness. That's one reason most people I talk to have yet to pick up a single book on the crisis. But this seems wrongheaded to me. I won't claim that my reading has allayed my own sense of powerlessness—certainly not as much as the Occupy agitators have. But at least it's familiarized me with the terms of my exploitation. "We are the

99 percent" is a great slogan. I've chanted it myself. But if we're to imagine what we want from the 1 percent, we need a better grasp on how they're screwing us.

For us wordsmiths, one level of this understanding comes easy: seeing through jargon, obfuscation, and weasel words, like calling an insurance policy a "swap" or saying short sellers are (I love this one) "expressing their views." Weasel words traditionally come in the form of the fine print where Moody's declines to verify the information its ratings are based on, or a buried hedge like "the pool may contain underwriting exceptions and these exceptions, at times, may be material." But "collateralized debt obligation" is itself just a weaselly way of saying "consumer debt bond." As Lewis observes, "bond market terminology was designed less to convey meaning than to bewilder outsiders": overpriced bonds weren't "expensive," they were "rich," divided into risk levels dubbed "tranches" rather than "floors," with the high-risk triple-B tranche designated the "mezzanine," "like a highly prized seat in a domed stadium."

Having defined the 1973 invention of the Black-Scholes formula for calculating derivative risk as finance's modernist moment, Lanchester, the most artful writer-qua-writer here, sees the 2008 derivatives crisis as its postmodernist moment, in which value recedes from our comprehension like meaning in Derrida, with the crash its Derridean "aporia." In this he was anticipated by the genius who was wrong about everything, the Ayn Rand–schooled, postobjectivist Fed czar Alan Greenspan. As Taibbi reminds us, that supreme oracle once crowed about the "ever increasing conceptualization of our Gross Domestic Product—the substitution, in effect, of ideas for physical value."

Speaking in 1998, what Greenspan meant by "ideas" was the business plans of internet start-ups that would soon go bust as the mathematicians who designed them failed to achieve monetization. But his pronunciamento applies as well to the triumph of math in the banking industry. The most telling fact I ran across in my million-plus words appears only in Lanchester. In 1986, the financial sector earned 19 percent of US profits; by the '00s, that percentage had doubled to 41 percent. In other words, two-fifths of what Americans made money on wasn't material goods or human services, but money itself, as average pay in banking, which ran parallel to the rest of private industry till 1982, rose to nearly twice par by 2007. No wonder that for Lanchester "there is sometimes a moment talking to [bankers] when you hit a kind of wall"—a wall "based on the primacy of money and the unreality of other schemes of value."

Granted, I just did some weaseling myself, by pretending that math and money are the same thing. My excuse is that, ultimately, the instruments the quants devised were what separated Lanchester from his City pals, because all serve what McLean and Nocera call "the delinking of borrower and lender." Only rapacious mortgage sellers coked up on Red Bull had any concrete knowledge of the default-prone subprime suckers on whom the "real estate boom" was built. For everyone else they were abstractions, and not just as victims—as risks. With overworked grunts at the ratings firms cowed into adjusting the numbers till every CDO got the triple-A rating few whole corporations were awarded, traders who outearned the analysts by factors of ten and a hundred could convince themselves that even if the boom ended, someone else would be holding, in Taibbi's metaphor, the hot potato.

This is partly because they were as rapacious as the mortgage hawkers—just smarter and better educated. And it's partly because they weren't quants themselves. Because if we're talking competing languages, here's a really scary part: as physicist-turned-risk manager John Breit told McLean and Nocera, most traders were "quantitatively illiterate. Executives learned terms like 'standard deviation' and 'normal distribution,' but they didn't really understand the math, so they got lulled into thinking it was magic." This is especially unfortunate because, as Lanchester explains, the quants themselves are terrible at predicting very unlikely events. According to their risk models, the 1998 failure of the Long-Term Capital Management hedge fund—an early warning sign quickly forgotten—was a "seven-sigma event" that, statistically, could only happen once every three billion years. That is, it was impossible. Nearly-as-impossible five- and six-sigma events arose "numerous times." Yet the risk models remained in place. One hopes they seem less magical now; maybe they're even more realistic. But who knows whether the worst financial crisis since the Great Depression is destined to set off disastrous aftershocks even so? Taibbi, Lewis, Scheer, and Morgenson/Rosner are the gloomiest, but no one's sunny about it. Read up on the euro and you won't be either.

As a better-informed citizen, my biggest takeaway from my million-plus words is that, as Posner especially maintains, the Paulson bailouts addressed not illiquidity, in which cash is temporarily unavailable, but insolvency, in which banks have leveraged themselves so irresponsibly that it isn't there at all. As Lanchester says, "nobody knows which banks are solvent." I'm also persuaded that the doubling of consumer debt between 2000 and 2007 was deeply unhealthy even if I see raw survival as well as rank self-indulgence in it. I'm convinced along with economist Chang that the economics profession is bad for most economies. And I also think Chang is right to argue that markets need to become less rather than more "efficient," thus allowing for the development of long-term "patient capital" as well as impeding the rapid-fire computerized trading that turns Wall Street into a rich guys' casino like nothing else. And with no more idea than Chang how to implement this sane idea, I'll resist sharing any more of my inexpert economic insights. Instead I'll conclude with a few thoughts on language, where I can claim some professional authority.

First, I feel enriched if not empowered to have gained minimal fluency in Quantish and Traderese, including a rudimentary grasp of their mathematical underpinnings. Having glanced regularly at the business pages since the crash of 1987, I find that my ease of comprehension has taken a major leap, and recommend an informal course of study to every politically concerned person. One advantage of my fluency is that it buttresses my right to voice my disdain for those who turn human beings into abstractions by making abstractions the substance of their private subcultural argot—who think primarily in numbers. But it also buttresses my admiration for an economist like Chang, who takes care to deploy numbers humanistically.

Second, these books set me thinking about rhetoric. Partial to Lewis and Taibbi on old New Journalistic principle, here I find their approaches inappropriate. Lewis's characters—the most appalling a walk-on junk-CDO dealer who in one year went from bagging 140 grand in life insurance to twenty-six million in the banking industry—are fascinating. By taking on the sociohistorical task of portraying subcultures, however, McLean and Nocera tell a more gripping story more suitable to the crisis's shape and scope. Similarly, as a lifelong partisan of impolite discourse I share Taibbi's anger that "in our media you're just not allowed to kick the rich in the balls and use class-warfare language." But flinging schoolyardese like "dumbasses" or, famously, calling Goldman Sachs a vampire squid leaves the testicles at issue unscathed. Goldman Sachs is too savvy, complex, and powerful to beat in a bar fight. Still, I was heartened to read that a few Occupy agitators took a papier-mache squid to the streets while I was writing this. And in an October blog post called "Hit Bankers Where It Hurts," Taibbi provided one of the more focused and practical of those lists of demands with which thoughtful progressives have showered Occupy Wall Street.

My own wordsmith's contribution to that struggle is briefer. It's a slogan: "Tax and prosecute/We want their loot." Chant it loud. You may be screwed, but you're still proud.

Barnes & Noble Review, 2011

They Bet Your Life: Four Books About Hedge Funds

In 2011, I reviewed ten books on the financial crisis, an endeavor it will surprise no one to learn straightened out our misshapen economy not a whit. But it did improve my comprehension of this life-threatening phenomenon, and made me feel better the way spiritual disciplines supposedly do. Problem is, all such consolations come with an expiration date, hurried along in this case by my nervous habit of scanning the financial pages. So soon I was feeling the need to know more.

My prospective areas of specialization were different in kind. First, I wanted to learn about hedge funds. Hedge funds didn't cause the 2008 crisis—the big banks were the big culprits. But often it was hedge funds within the banks that speculated most recklessly, and it was hedge funds where the kinds of headlong economic behavior that typified the crisis were rampant. Ever since I was amused to encounter the gerund "hedging" in a plan-your-retirement paperback thirty years ago, I'd been trying to get a better grip on what it was, and this was my chance. But in addition I craved human interest—some kind of bead on the hedgers. Who were the bettors in Wall Street's grand casino? Did they have politics? Scruples? Fun? Did they love their wives (pardon me, spouses) and children (if any)? Or were they all the de facto sociopaths I suspected? Three 2013 titles indicate that the amateur speculators who run the book business think there might be money in these questions: Barbara T. Dreyfuss's *Hedge Hogs*, Turney Duff's *The Buy Side*, and Anita Raghavan's *The Billionaire's Apprentice*.

The first hedge fund was A. W. Jones & Co., begun in 1949 by liberal sociologist-turned-journalist Jones with the aim of protecting the investors he was by then advising, most also his friends, by leveraging their money to buy a maximum of promising stocks while also hedging that money—that is, reducing investment risk—by shorting overvalued ones. (Shorting, in case you're not among the Americans well-capitalized enough to know, means "borrowing" stocks you then sell immediately in the belief that you'll be able to buy them cheaper when time comes to return the loan.) Among Jones's early imitators was humanitarian left-liberal George Soros, probably the most successful trader ever. But profit maximization has its own logic, and it's telling that Jones soon had another bright idea—insider trading, which was not then illegal. Soros too sometimes exploited inside dope in those days, although his specialty was currency fluctuation—when the pound was devalued in 1992, partly due to pressure he applied, he made a billion bucks while fifty million Britons sunk into a recession. That's the way the money business is.

But it would soon get a lot worse as hedge funds, emboldened by cabals of quants devising ever more arcane variations on "value at risk," leveraged more and hedged less. Hence the 2008 crash presaged by the 1998 failure of Long Term Capital Management, whose founder had another hedge fund up fifteen months after his earlier firm almost wrecked the world economy by misreading the ruble. Why not? The (first?) tech bubble was up and floating, with two new pieces of deregulation tempting anyone with a few spare million to put skin in the game.

This fast-moving system was ripe for exploitation by headstrong criminals brainy enough to play all the angles at once and invent a few more. The biggest of these that we're sure about is billionaire Sri Lankan–American insider trader Raj Rajaratnam, in whose legal downfall Raghavan discerns an even bigger story: a meaty chronicle of "the rise of the Indian-American elite," with starring roles for Rajaratnam informant-turned-informer Anil Kumar and, especially, tragic hero Rajat Gupta, the highly respectable financial consultant now appealing his 2012 conviction for a single documented tipoff that many regard as the tip of the iceberg.

Raghavan, a Malaysian-born ethnic Indian who worked eighteen years for *The Wall Street Journal*, goes long on some half dozen South Asians, including US attorney Preet Bharara and the SEC's Sanjay Wadhwa, and provides detail on the meritocratic educational network India maintains for its ruling class. But there's also plenty about the evolution of American finance, particularly the McKinsey Group, the enormous but staid consulting firm Gupta broke down racial barriers to head for nine years. Modernizing McKinsey to compete with the likes of Bain Capital, Gupta supported Kumar's seemingly mad notion of outsourcing American paralegal and research work to English-speaking Indians. He courted tech companies. His penchant for philanthropy brought McKinsey into contact with healthcare and pharma magnates. But avarice ruined him anyway.

Because Gupta rather than Rajaratnam is her protagonist, however, Raghavan doesn't say much about hedge funds per se. She just assumes readers understand that scenes like the book's legal linchpin—in which Gupta steps out of a Goldman Sachs board meeting at 3:54 p.m. to tell Rajaratnam that Goldman has brought Warren Buffett aboard and Rajaratnam's Galleon Fund somehow buys 25 million in Goldman stock in the four minutes before closing—are how hedge funds do business. Duff and Dreyfuss provide more detail.

Duff worked at Galleon before moving on to a smaller fund where he was a bigger shot. While at Galleon, he enthusiastically pursued the company policy of two dinners a week on the expense accounts of bank traders whose sales commissions depended on "buy siders" like him, picking up tidbits of info as he partied. But Rajaratnam himself was the master suborner, which is why he's now doing twelve years in stir. Although Duff glimpsed some shady dealings—like the private "admiral's account" where lucrative transactions were booked so they profited only Galleon employees—he avers that he was privy to nothing blatantly criminal. Instead, his tell-all goes for human interest. No math whiz, Duff compares his edge as a trader to a poker player's. He's an affable character who reads people and situations well and is blessed with a courageous calm he attributes to the low-grade depression that probably fed the same cocaine habit that turns the last third of his book into a tedious dysfunction memoir.

Burning no bridges, Duff concludes by praising his "amazing, intelligent, honest, and friendly" co-workers. But although he majored in writing and is facile enough at it, the only amazing figures I noticed, including the beautiful and sensible wife who dumped him, are bad guys like the appalling Rajaratnam, who claims as his motto, it is my sad duty as a rock critic to report, "Remember never grow up—and nothing is so serious as the pursuit of fun!!!" Few successful bankers are unintelligent, and many seem to cherish their families as respites from the alpha-male math and schmoozing competitions of their daily lives. But even the friendliness of Duff's friends seems provisional, and in the banking business honesty only goes so far. Torn and contradictory, Rajat Gupta is something special. Affable is as much as can be said for the overpaid drones and party people who populate Duff's tale.

The principals of Dreyfuss's *Hedge Hogs* are even bigger shots with more vivid profiles, especially Brian Hunter and John Arnold, the energy traders whose high-stakes 2006 battle to corner the natural gas market destroyed Amaranth Advisors, the firm Hunter came to dominate. The same competition imperiled the pension investments of the San Diego Employees Retirement Association as well as grossly inflating energy and heating costs for countless businesses and municipalities that do more concrete good than Centaurus Advisors, which Enron vet Arnold closed holding nearly three billion dollars in 2012.

Forced to choose between these two believers in extreme "value at risk," most would take Arnold. Based in his hometown of Calgary, Alberta, Hunter seems pure cowboy, with paltry philanthropic impulses; Arnold is at least an early Obama supporter whose wife is a trustee of the Houston Fine Arts Museum, and unlike Hunter he's never been fined thirty million bucks for market manipulation. On the contrary, he signed Bill Gates and Warren Buffett's Giving Pledge, and his John and Laura Arnold Foundation put up money for Head Start programs threatened by the 2013 shutdown. But note, as Dreyfuss for some reason does not, that his chief "philanthropic" endeavor is "reform" of public employees' pensions—that is, promoting legal means, such as a California initiative, to slash them, for fiscal reasons worthy of more debate than the wealthy are inclined to countenance.

Two points, then. First is that, at the very least, the financial markets attract natural gamblers. There are exceptions, and some gamblers are more mindful of risk management than others. But there are always going to be addicts and high rollers, just as there are always going to be crooks, and it's in the public interest to constrain all three. Second is that philanthropy will always involve, at the very least, unnecessarily rich men (and a few women) riding their hobbyhorses. Wealthy speculators may indeed underwrite causes that save some real ordinary lives and improve many others. But their careers as championship number pushers limit their insight into—and sympathy for—the duller struggles of their fellow citizens.

Nor does their main economic rationalization hold much water. As Jeff Madrick argues in his 2011 *The Age of Greed*, the hedge fund chapter of which is the best writing I've found on the subject, the liquidity these funds inject into the economy is an unresearched talking point whose benefits are unlikely to justify the multiple millions winning bettors gain moving money around. Note, however, that in a banking business where terminology is nine-tenths camouflage, "hedging" per se isn't the problem. "Hedging" requires the kind of caution that would have prevented the 2008 crisis if traders and their bosses hadn't dismissed their risk managers as wet blankets, which is why risk-reading hedge funds like John Paulson's made billions betting against mortgage derivatives. And as Dreyfuss explains, "hedging" on a smaller scale is an essential budgeting strategy for any enterprise dependent on commodities whose prices will fluctuate due to unforeseeable market and environmental variations. But while the anti-regulation claque isn't just blowing smoke when it claims that demand and scarcity factors also inflate fuel prices, I buy Dreyfuss's argument that the major reason natural gas costs so much more than it used to is that there's so much money to be made messing with its economics.

Having struggled to gain these unremarkable insights, however, I began to feel I was working from a skewed sample. Book speculators invested in *Hedge Hogs* and *The Billionaire's Apprentice* because they aren't so much finance stories as crime stories, and moreover, the insider trading Raghavan so disdains shocks Wall Street more than other fiduciary malfeasances because it involves bankers robbing each other rather than us. So for balance I went to Maneet Ahuja's *The Alpha Masters*, which aims to turn a profit flattering the industry for insiders rather than exposing it to outsiders. Ahuja is a twenty-nine-year-old hedge fund specialist for CNBC who tweets as @ WallStManeet. Her nine interview profiles, including a long one with Pershing Capital's activist William Ackman, were all vetted by their subjects. But it was an accomplishment to get them to speak for the record at all—although a few hedge fund magnates go public on Ackman's scale, often with the hope of lowering a target's stock price, most prefer to "express their views," as the poets of banking put it, by simple short-selling.

So in Ahuja's business plan, Galleon and Amaranth are off the books and John Paulson is her best friend. Her subjects are all guys who bet right. But all of them are also guys who deploy careful research and analysis rather than—or as well as—what Ahuja describes as "the massive, veiny, brass testicles" Appaloosa Management's David Tepper has hanging on a plaque in his office. Indeed, many of their approaches have discernible social utility. Like Konikos's James Chanos with Enron, they ferret out inflated values before they spin further out of control. They take on risks others can't, financing small companies and saving troubled and bankrupt ones, at what cost to the rescued companies' employees Ahuja never thinks to ponder. At their best—which in this crew means Bridgewater's seventy-five-year-old Ray Dalio, also treated to a 2011 profile by *The New Yorker*'s John Cassidy—they provide low-risk "alpha" returns for institutional investors, including pension funds like the one Amaranth bilked. I didn't like all of these people; I didn't like most of them. But I wouldn't call them all sociopaths without doing more research.

No fan of Wall Street, John Cassidy nonetheless admires Dalio, a guru type unbrushed by scandal who lives modestly for a billionaire-times-ten. Yet in the end he returns to the usual unremarkable points. Especially in an environment where lesser greedheads play follow-the-leader, hedge funds encourage disastrous speculative bubbles. They normalize income inequality by setting an extravagant standard of executive compensation. They attract "some of the very brightest science and mathematics graduates" to what Dalio unapologetically identifies as a zero-sum game—that is, a game whose social utility is limited by definition. And then Cassidy transitions to a sentence that leaves us ordinaries pretty much where we started.

"Rather then confronting these issues, Dalio, like all successful predators, is concentrating on the business at hand."

Barnes & Noble Review, 2014

Living in a Material World: Raymond Williams's Long Revolution

When Raymond Williams describes an act of the mind he assumes that both its individual and its social circumstances must be taken into account. Without falling for determinist equations, he never forgets that human works are inextricable from human lives. That's my kind of social theorist, and my kind of socialist intellectual—yours too, I hope. Yet in America Williams remains marginalized beyond his 1958 breakthrough *Culture and Society*, an analysis of the religion of art to which so many self-interested secular humanists have subscribed since the dawn of industrialism—again and again I meet properly left-leaning academics who profess vast respect for the man but have trouble dredging up the title of another book of his they've read. But forget academics—it's the laity I want. If inquiring college graduates (and dropouts) can read Milan Kundera and Roland Barthes and Dick Hebdige and William Gass, they can damn well read Raymond Williams, a richer writer, book by book or all in all, than any of them.

I go to Williams first for information. Working from an ambit of interest that embraces all human aspiration, he's mastered a distinctive and formidable body of knowledge by concentrating on without limiting himself to examples drawn from English literature. Although this method is more professorial than one would like, it's less professorial than would appear. Williams defines his subject so that it extends beyond the details of thousands of books, beyond Jonson's patronage and Gissing's bohemianism and Lawrence's education, beyond even Smith's bookstalls and Northcliffe's newspapers. And he insists on connecting works to lives—the lives of readers and intermediaries as well as creators, all of them understood critically, psychologically, and politically. He loves the literature of the past but resists the highbrow temptation to be put off by the contemporary world. And while I can't claim his style is scintillating, I do find his presentation tonic. One of the pleasures of Kundera and Barthes and Gass is their elegant self-referentiality, the way their books double back on themselves like the self-enclosed systems of signs they're implicitly acknowledged to be. Insofar as it's possible, Williams rejects this formalist gambit. He believes words refer to real things that precede language, and that's the way he writes. He's devoted to content—which in his terms means he's devoted to politics.

Williams is described by New Left Books, the staunchest of his many publishers, as "the most productive and influential socialist writer in England today." Although along with Stuart Hall and E. P. Thompson (as well as Hall's mentor and Williams's fellow left-Leavisite Richard Hoggart) he's credited with laying the theoretical groundwork for Britain's new left, many would grant pride of influence to Thompson, who in recent years has been instrumental in remobilizing the moribund Campaign for Nuclear Disarmament. But unlike Thompson (whose roots are in Quaker radicalism) and like Hall (who is Jamaican and working-class), Williams (who is Welsh and working-class) has managed to keep talking to all sides during sectarian feuds. And in any case no one will deny Williams's astounding productivity—one reason, though there are certainly others, for his almost as astounding sales totals, now up over a million worldwide.

Counting three collaborations but omitting revisions, which in at least three cases have been major, the 1984 collection *Writing in Society* was Williams's twenty-fifth book, ready just months after number twenty-four, *The Year 2000*. Though the first appeared in 1950, when he was twenty-nine, Williams only gained recognition with number five, 1958's *Culture and Society*, and not until the '70s did his output begin to gather critical mass: fourteen of his twenty-five titles have been published since 1971. Nor has Williams confined production to books. Until 1961, when he was invited back to Cambridge to lecture in drama, he made his living teaching workers evening classes, and he has been a busy essayist, reviewer, and even playwright. He's surfaced politically at crucial junctures, and raised three children with his wife of forty-two years. In 1982, he retired from Cambridge to write (as New Left Books rather dauntingly puts it) "full-time." Georges Simenon watch out.

Williams's prolific habits have left me feeling as if I'd better sit down and write full-time myself before the old man laps me again, an indignity I've suffered three times since this essay was conceived as a way of celebrating Columbia University Press's 1983 edition of *Culture and Society*. Especially given Williams's obsessive thoroughness, though, I'm still not sure I feel ready; having read sixteen of his books (not all of which are easy to come by even in what Williams, with uncharacteristic levity, refers to as "the Yookay"), I don't intend to stop. I'm curious about *Preface to Film* (with Michael Orrom, 1954), one of the first attempts by a critic of Williams's loft to analyze popular culture at length, and *The English Novel from Dickens to Lawrence* (1971), constructed from lecture notes and therefore, it is said, somewhat less dense than most of his nonfiction. An enthusiastic admirer of his working-class novels *Border Country* (1960) and *Second Generation* (1964), I'm eager to locate the thriller-influenced *Volunteers* (1978) and the science fiction-influenced *Fight for Manod* (1979). For me, Williams isn't just a fecund and significant and immensely useful writer. He's an enjoyable and even exciting one.

Which is not to suggest that Georges Simenon has anything to worry about. As someone who makes it his business to recognize serious fun when it kicks him in the head, I can guarantee that Williams doesn't qualify. Lumpy, slightly turgid, unabashedly Latinate, he just isn't a writer with much entertainment value. Not only can't he go up against Simenon as beach reading, he can't go up against Thompson. The semipopular novels and broadcast dramas he's essayed suggest that Williams is willing to entertain as best he can when occasion and audience so indicate. But as far as he's concerned, us college graduates (and dropouts) should relish the ideas and information he provides so abundantly and find nothing less than full-fledged aesthetic satisfaction in his profound, subtle, and inventive command of voice and persona, format and shape.

Nevertheless, or hence, Williams remains obscure in America, where tastes in culture theory generally runs to various Big Frankfurters and Big Frogs, some nouvelle cassoulet of Benjamin-Adorno-Marcuse-etc. and Barthes-Foucault-Derrida-etc. As for those who retain a nostalgic yen for ideas formulated in the English language, they probably prefer American-style quasi-structuralists like Fredric Jameson, or leftist art-critic-plus John Berger, or Williams's star student and fond parricide Terry Eagleton. All of whom would have had a much dodgier time reaching their audience if *Culture and Society* hadn't cleared the way.

It's difficult now to comprehend the radical impact of *Culture and Society*, not just because its hard-earned premises have long since been absorbed as commonplaces, but also because from the first its acclaim was so broadly based. In Britain Williams's account of the evolution of the term "culture" in English letters was praised even by Tories who disdained his sentimental attachment to the lower classes, and here the book was reviewed enthusiastically by Irving Howe, Michael Harrington, Harold Rosenberg, and Alfred Kazin—all except Kazin socialist sympathizers to be sure, but every one a big-name highbrow, which was what counted in the status-hungry US intellectual product market. Here, there, and everywhere, Williams was chided for his "over-solemn" style, but his fairness and thoroughness were so palpable that even his natural enemies found it in themselves to forgive his willful originality and steadfast leftism. And at the same time his natural allies were galvanized.

In Britain, the catalyst wasn't just the book's content but the very idea of the thing, and of the man who wrote it. At a time when the nation's remaining left intellectuals were split philosophically between crude Stalinoid economism and mealy-mouthed quasi-Fabian reformism, when the hot young writers were ravening existentialists like Colin Wilson and William Golding or once-angry strivers like Kingsley Amis and John Braine, Williams stood up as an explicitly working-class left socialist whose enormous intellectual ambition would have been deemed arrogant in a showier, less circumspect man. With figures like Hoggart and Thompson and Hall and Berger and Doris Lessing and Arnold Wesker peeping out after the twin shitstorm of Budapest and Suez, the British new left was slowly beginning to recognize itself, and like its American counterpart of a few years later had its own ideas about how leftists should relate to what economism dismisses as the superstructure. Committed in their personal lives to sensibility as well as to justice, these people had no intention of submerging irreducible aesthetic experiences in ideology. But they were nevertheless suspicious of the traditional British reluctance to embark upon grand theoretical projects. With such congenial thinkers as Gramsci, Lukács, Goldmann, and the Big Frogs still all but unknown in the English-speaking world, Williams emerged as both an inspiration and a citable authority. In 1961, *The Long Revolution*, planned from the start as the social-history counterpart of *Culture and Society*, proved at least as influential on the left as its companion volume.

Because it's always been so specific to British needs, however, Williams's charisma has eluded Americans, and though he's well reviewed here, his reputation rests primarily upon *Culture and Society* itself. Now, *Culture and Society* is certainly Williams's most comprehensive and momentous work, and in an odd way it's his most representative as well. There's no more accessible introduction to the style and scope of his thought, to its dogged complexity, its difficult yet dazzlingly commonsensical insights, its contained confidence, its formal canniness, and above all its balance. It epitomizes both his willingness to learn from the other side's struggle to understand its historical predicament and his sharp overriding awareness of whose side he's on—of how the world presents itself to the union loyalists, small farmers, housewives, night-school students, and other set-upon citizens who constitute "the people." But to most of his allies today as well as Williams himself, *Culture and Society* grants too much to such reactionaries as Burke and Carlyle and T. S. Eliot, and soft-pedals his politics, which in any case were at their most conciliatory during the '50s, remembered by Williams as a period of "disgusted withdrawal" for him no matter how much his unflagging commitment impressed his even more disgusted potential comrades.

Yet although Williams says *Culture and Society* now seems "a book written by someone else," he can see that it played a crucial role in redefining the politics of "this strange, unsettling and exciting, world." For while from here it may be regarded as a narrowly literary project that betrays his lingering sense of obligation to F. R. Leavis, who had redefined the study of English at Cambridge by the time Williams returned to his undergraduate scholarship after three years manning a tank in World War II, in fact it goes up against the fundamentals of Leavisism. It's nowhere near as hierarchical, as politely snobbish, as obsessed with "discrimination." More important, the tradition it invents doesn't comprise works of art in all their organic, undidactic glory. It's a tradition of social commentary, mostly by essayists or poets and novelists acting as essayists, occasionally embodied or even (shocking!) formulated as abstract propositions within living works of art. Yet what Williams values as much as the ideas in such writing is its personal stamp, the same kind of ineluctable individual voice fetishized by Leavis, the New Critics, and soon all of cold war aesthetics. As he puts it in a telling passage: "Burke's writing is an articulated experience, and as such it has a validity which can survive even the demolition of its general conclusions."

In the end, one of the deep satisfactions of *Culture and Society* is the way it maintains the same kind of tension between "articulated experience" and "general conclusions," and one of its disappointments is its failure to formulate that tension abstractly. This is not a book with a neatly extractable thesis—for all its analytic reach, its triumph is one of tone and structure and especially method rather than argument. As Williams explained to a convocation of lefter-than-thou colleagues and students in 1967, its conception is oppositional, countering the candid religious-reactionary conservatism of T. S. Eliot, the covert humanist-liberal conservatism of Leavis, and the economist reductionism of Marxists who believe that the "superstructure" of art and ideology exerts no influence on the economic "base," that it merely reflects or mediates or typifies a mode of production. Although in an oft-cited and significant introductory note he promises to trace the evolution of the words "industry," "democracy," "class," "art," and "culture" from 1780 to 1950, that isn't what he does, not in any schematic way. Instead he unravels the "vital strand" of English thought in which old values are recontextualized by (capitalist) material progress, and in doing so demonstrates, politely, that the elitism of Eliot and Leavis (not to mention the Marxists) isn't necessarily shared by the culture theorists who preceded and engendered them. Here, for instance, is Edmund Burke himself. "I have never yet seen any plan which has not been mended by the observations of men who were much inferior in understanding to the person who took the lead in the business."

Of course, like anybody with the stuff to launch an informed and innovative attack on elitism, Williams has earned elite status himself. This oppresses him. Like the protagonist of his novel *Second Generation*, he chose never to complete his doctorate, but the decision hurt, and if *Culture and Society* seems to respond only indirectly to Marxist tradition while tackling academic orthodoxy with inordinate passion, that's one reason why. He couldn't shake his fascination with the citadels of learning—of "culture"—that he'd breached with such effort and rejected with such ambivalence. And this orientation was anything but misdirected. The above from which capitalist ideology is generated is most often located in an ivory tower, which means that academic truisms quickly degenerate into virulent middlebrow cliches. It's clear enough that Leavis and his minions were the target of Williams's comment on Leavis's beloved George Eliot: "It has passed too long for a kind of maturity and depth in experience to argue that politics and political attachments are only possible to superficial minds." But since the '50s this fallacy has become standard among literally millions of real and would-be aesthetes: neo-expressionist painters, progressive rockers, comic-book collectors, balletomanes, regional theater honchos, you name it.

In fact, it's only Williams's kind of scholarship that leaves me free to treat this chronic idealist bromide so scornfully. During a decade of research that began when T. S. Eliot's *Notes Towards the Definition of Culture* got him thinking in 1948, Williams became something of an expert on all the manifestly unsuperficial minds to stray toward the political since the advent of the spinning jenny. He soon found that what the Leavisites encapsulated in a notion of "culture" that signified either hifalutin minority art or unspoiled preindustrial community was invariably connected, by the sharpest on-site observers of the growth and depredations of English industrialism, to "society"—to explicit considerations of class and power. It was by working from the same premises—in the tradition of Samuel Taylor Coleridge and William Cobbett, of George Orwell and Christopher Caudwell—that Williams made his methodological mark.

At the same time, *Culture and Society* developed Williams's own broad basic version of this tradition, one he's pretty much stuck with ever since. Although he grew up in a village near the Welsh-English border and has always honored rural life and the interpersonal day-to-day, he welcomes popular education and refuses to sentimentalize the human relations of the pastoral past, be it Eliot's Middle Ages or Leavis's mid-nineteenth century; in a credo any historian of culture should recite thrice daily, he declares: "If there is one thing certain about 'the organic community,' it is that it has always gone." But at the same time he has little use for romantic alienation, for the bohemian exile who thinks "society as such as totalitarian," emphasizing instead "the relative normality of the artist" as well as the power of art, "by affecting attitudes towards reality, to help or hinder the constant business of changing it." Yet sane and forceful though this formulation may be, ultimately it isn't the source of the book's power, which is more a matter of "articulated experience" than of "general conclusions"—inhering first in its premises and method, and second in its tone and structure.

Maybe Williams is too solemn, but he's certainly convincing, and *Culture and Society* is the prototype. Like all his nonfiction, it's written in the knobby, inelegant voice of a man honestly struggling to figure things out—a little donnish, perhaps, but in a disarmingly sincere and clumsy way. Next to "culture" itself, the author's favorite words are clearly "difficult" and "complex"; the book is replete with phrases like "the difficulties are obvious" and "a very complex system of specialized developments." He's forever doubling back on himself, or harrumphing asides that neither provide needed diversion nor prove what a witty fellow he is. And if the apparent byways of the argument are often stern gibes at class prejudice—at the mean irony of Arnold ("a stock reaction to 'the vulgar' which is surely vulgar in itself") or the cautious irony of Tawney (whose "manner before the high priests is uneasy"), at misconceptions about adult education or mob violence—who'll be tempted to gainsay them? They obviously come from a man who's studied his field and learned his place.

Learned his place like hell. For in effect Williams has mastered the usages of scholarship so he can turn the tables on the dons who taught him so much and undervalued his experience so profoundly. Anyone who doubts it should ponder the "Conclusion" of *Culture and Society*. A forty-four-page essay that bears no chapter number, bursting with only a page break out of Chapter 6 of Part III ("George Orwell"), it's a structurally audacious kicker to what is in form if not content a proper critical history, proceeding unflappably from certified bigdome to certified bigdome. Rather than humbly summing up or grandly expanding upon the wisdom already received, it takes the discussion into enemy territory: mass and working-class culture. In the '50s, of course, up-and-coming bigdomes spouting mass culture theory were as common as dissertations on Henry James, but not like Williams. As you'd expect, he steers well clear of both reactionary and left elitism, and in addition refuses the nostalgic evasions of such well-meaning democrats as Richard Hoggart, who in *The Uses of Literacy* sets up an invidious comparison between mass communications and the homely entertainments of his youth in Leeds. Williams doesn't go this way because he doesn't buy the whole concept of the mass: he's willing to use the term adjectivally, but he's deeply suspicious of its origins in "masses," which he labels "a new word for mob." In the most simply memorable sentences he ever wrote, he puts it bluntly: "To other people, we also are masses. Masses are other people."

Yet although Williams's good sense about modern popular forms has proceeded as one might hope from this beginning—he has never panicked over the supposedly built-in perceptual perversions of new media, always extended his interest in drama to movies and television, and has even said that new communications technologies signaled "a new phase of civilization"—in the end he's more taken with modern popular processes than modern popular products. His assessment of "mass culture"—"the strip newspaper, the beer advertisement, the detective novel"—isn't much more enthusiastic than Hoggart's might be. His analysis of working-class culture, however, is far more radical than Hoggart's praise for club singing and *Peg's Paper*. After all, Williams says, mass-disseminated forms are rarely created by "working people" anyway, and why would we expect them to be? Working people don't create cultural objects, they create cultural institutions. "Culture in the narrower sense" is the special province of bourgeois individualists, leaving the working class with its own project: "The culture which it has produced, and which it is important to recognize, is the collective democratic institution, whether in the trade unions, the cooperative movement or a political party." As Williams observes, a little dryly, this is "a very remarkable creative achievement"—no less so, and perhaps more so, because it's collective, prefiguring the "common culture" he believes human beings must achieve.

Imagine what it might have been like for E. M. W. Tillyard, the Cambridge tutor who before the war dismissed Williams's earnest young Communist Party line on the progressivism of Dickens and Hardy as "a fantasy," to come upon this sharply reasoned attack on the illusions of status Cambridge dons hold so dear. And imagine too how it might have hit Tillyard's student acolytes as they pondered the bomb and the angry young men from their dank, time-honored chambers. By climaxing a respectable scholarly work with a utopian postscript, Williams unleashed an unforeseen blast of cultural energy. It wouldn't be the last time he united formal mastery and political effectiveness, but it might yet prove to have been the best.

That lucky old art-action synthesis has been Williams's abiding goal ever since, and because his appetite for more democracy—for socialism, whatever precisely that turns out to mean—is so tenacious and ingrained, the defeats he's suffered pursuing it have troubled him even more than they do most writers of radical conscience. And then there's a second complication: although politics is the ground of his existence and the soul of his writing, it's writing that possesses and sustains him, both as his work and, to an extent that must concern him, as his subject. No wonder this fervent materialist insists that culture is material—he'd hardly be content devoting his life to some chimerical play of ahistorical signifiers.

Williams's '60s were energetic and involved. His resurgent activism was characteristically unsectarian, his confident creative output characteristically uncategorizable. He fruitlessly mediated the bitter disputes engulfing *New Left Review* when Perry Anderson's group took over from the old-at-thirty-five guard of Thompson and Hall; joined the Labour Party in time to see the Campaign for Nuclear Disarmament vanquished there in 1961 and stayed on till 1966; helped organize Britain's Vietnam Solidarity Campaign in 1965; conceived and assembled two versions of *The May Day Manifesto* in an attempt to rally the Labour left when Harold Wilson's union and monetary policies became too much; and chaired the National Convention of the Left until it dissolved in fractious turmoil after the Conservative victory of 1970. During the same time he published *The Long Revolution* and *Border Country*, both written in the '50s; revised his 1952 *Drama from Ibsen to Eliot* (to end with Brecht); did two plays with the BBC; produced numerous major essays and countless reviews; and completed five books: *Communications*, a Pelican adult-education primer regarded by many reviewers as a dastardly call for the nationalization of culture; *Second Generation*, a working-class novel and an academic novel simultaneously; the iconoclastic *Modern Tragedy*, which not only brought novels into the canon but in 1966 included a chapter comparing "Tragedy and Revolution"; *The May Day Manifesto*, first published privately and then taken by Penguin; and *The English Novel from Dickens to Lawrence*.

The last-named is probably Williams's easiest nonfiction, not for its discursive, semicolon-studded style but for its subject matter, and his novels aren't just more fun to read than his cultural writing, they're richer, in that way fiction has. But Williams's most exciting books of the period are *The Long Revolution* and *Modern Tragedy*. Although chastised by Thompson for vagueness and gradualism, *The Long Revolution*'s leftism scandalized mainstream pundits, and once again structure and method intensified impact. Bracketing a 50,000-word abstract on creativity and society and a 25,000-word forecast of the politics of British culture in the '60s around seven part-critical, part-sociohistorical case studies of topics Williams had taught in night school (among them a devastating dissection of one of his pet peeves, "correct" pronunciation), the book's apparently haphazard structure was as careless of academic propriety as its casually cross-disciplinary reach. And the topics themselves were ground-breaking: the class and educational training of 350 literary eminences, the empty-headed history of "standard" English, the interrelations between what is taken for strictly formal progress in theater and power shifts in society. These unorthodoxies were compounded by *Modern Tragedy*, an all-out attack on the atavistic twentieth-century theory of tragedy, which in its craving for ritual insults ordinary human suffering ("The events which are not seen as tragic are deep in the pattern of our own culture: war, famine, work, traffic, politics"). Having done the deed, it makes an unsuccessful but daring attempt to resolve the great unanswered question of revolutionary thought: why men and women in nonreligious, individualistic cultures should be expected to risk death for a future they'll never see.

It's really *Modern Tragedy* that marks Williams's turn toward Marx and Marxism, which get nine entries in its index and none in *The Long Revolution*'s. Though in a typical nonconformist gesture he's never declared himself a Marxist per se, modern Marxism has long been the primary context of his discourse. Attributable in the first instance to the increasingly ideological tenor of the British new left, this long-range trend also has roots in Williams's CP days at Cambridge. But it often remains invisible to the casual observer. If Stanford University Press could find three blurbs that make *Modern Tragedy* look like an update of Gilbert Murray, Williams probably planned it that way. This is a man for whom publish-or-perish is all but literal, and he has not the slightest hesitation about exploiting his status as a certified bigdome to do subversive work in academic subgenres and invent new subgenres himself.

His genre work includes a monograph, *George Orwell* (1970), which looks behind the plain-talking persona of Britain's consummate class exile; *Television: Technology and Cultural Form* (1974), a communications textbook complete with outlines and flow charts; two survey-course overviews, *Marxism and Literature* (1977) and *The Sociology of Culture* (1982), both of which take on Britain's structuralism/Althusserianism epidemic almost by the by; and two collections, one formidably comprehensive and the other vaguely thematic. Qualifying as innovations would be the historical dictionary, *Keywords* (1976), which finally completes the lexicography promised in the foreword to *Culture and Society*, and a four-hundred-page interview, *Politics and Letters* (1979), where he spars skillfully with a tag team of Marxist interlocutors. And somewhere in between is his greatest book, 1973's *The Country and the City*, a formal triumph on the order of *Culture and Society* taken to a new level of difficulty.

Marxism and Literature, its ideas crushed down into synoptic concision by Oxford University Press's strict sixty-thousand-word limit, is a slower read. But Williams has never written anything harder to get into than *The Country and the City*. After a brief, thoughtful personal memoir and a devastating demonstration of how the organic community has always gone (even for Hesiod in 800 B.C.), he begins his examinations of pastoral with one of those bombshells I love him for: the observation that where Virgil's narrator Meliboeus, "the 'source' of a thousand pretty exercises on an untroubled rural delight and peace," was in fact a dispossessed smallholder remembering the land that had been grabbed out from under him, Horace's equally celebrated second *Epode*, written a few years later, is "the sentimental reflection of a usurer, thinking of turning farmer, calling in his money and then, at the climax of the poem, lending it out again." Great stuff, but it all takes place inside of twenty pages; as Williams explores his double theme—arcadia as real estate, a bountiful land exploited by the rich and worked by the poor—things slow down precipitously, mostly because his source material (especially the country-house poems that were his original topic) is often tedious whatever its documentary value or standing as literature. Tedious for the general reader, that is—Williams obviously doesn't think so.

In part this is because he has such an appetite for knowledge. And in part it's because he's so moved by any literary effort—from Jonson or Hardy, from George Crabbe or John Clare, from Stephen Duck ("still called with a lingering patronage the 'thresher-poet'") or Fred Kitchen (a farm laborer who entitled his 1939 autobiography *Brother to the Ox*). In part, however, it's because unlike the general reader he isn't blindered by the urban provincialism *The Country and the City* means to destroy. This is no anti-urban tract, but it does redress the distortion of rural reality that's been an orthodoxy ever since the landed gentry began to equate sophistication with the town houses where they consolidated their power. As you work your way in you realize that what's making your eyes glaze over isn't just the prose or the endemic artificiality of pastoral as a genre. It's that like all city folk you've been steered away from any systematic interest in what Marx and Engels, in a phrase Williams will never completely forgive, branded "the idiocy of rural life"—even though you live off that idiocy, less opulently than the landed gentry but no less absolutely.

Williams's unimpeded appreciation of both country and city, not just in theory but in felt detail, makes him a rarity among writers in the Marxist tradition—among writers of any kind. Because rural-urban is one of the great governing tensions of his life, right up there alongside politics-art, *The Country and the City* gathers tremendous resonance. Throughout its second half he juxtaposes the "knowable community" of the English village against new urban ideas of collective consciousness—the Jungian mystification in which "the middle terms of actual societies are excluded as ephemeral," the revolutionary emphasis on "altered and altering relationships." The argument gathers momentum until what began as a monograph about country-house poems blooms into a meditation on imperialism, ecology, and the deep need of human beings to both escape and hold on to their childhoods. The way the book moves, building a surprising but irresistible climax from a wearisome accumulation of analysis and observation, reminds me of how submerged metapolitical themes finally rush to cognition in the preadolescent protagonists of Henry Roth's *Call It Sleep* and Christina Stead's *The Man*

Who Loved Children. This is criticism with the emotional power of a great novel—a moving personal document and a prophetic work.

Except for the 1983 monograph *Cobbett*, *The Country and the City* was the last book Williams devoted to specific works of literature. Over the past dozen years he's produced some of his most imaginative essays (on *Hard Times*, Robert Tressell, science fiction) as well as some of his deadliest (*Writing in Society*'s made-in-Cambridge Shakespeare and Racine papers), but he's also drawn a sharper line between literature and analysis, writing novels on the one hand and straight theory on the other. Williams was an enraptured admirer of *Finnegans Wake* when he decided to take up fiction as a vocation in the early '50s, and although he soon embraced conventional narrative technique, he's never stopped chafing at what publishers dictate to be publishable length; like Joyce, he wants his novels to contain whole worlds. He labors hard at them (several have undergone five or more complete rewrites over periods of many years), and they're impressive in several respects—their avoidance of the satiric marginality that afflicts so many academic settings no less than their judicious refusal to turn working-class characters into paragons. But they've never been his most influential or (what hurts) widely read works. So it's in philosophical matters that he's made most of his recent impact.

Because metaphysics has been of the essence for left intellectuals in this time of sectarian impotence, Williams's attention to theory can be seen as strategic, as defensive practical politics within his real ambit of power: the left. *Keywords* and *Marxism and Literature* carry on his lifelong battle against establishment culturati, but more than *Culture and Society* they're also aimed at the pet notions of his presumed political allies, not just vulgar-Marxist base-superstructure dualism but also what he's described as "a mode of idealist literary study claiming the authority of Marxism and the prestige of association with powerful intellectual movements in many fields"—in a word (though one will never do), structuralism.

Williams is accused with some justice of continuing to trundle out the base-superstructure model for ritual dissection long after it's lost its credibility. By now, most left culture theorists subscribe to some version of what Williams calls "cultural materialism," which stresses the symbiotic relationship between the realm of the imagination and determinative economic forces. Nevertheless, his discussion of the crucial base-superstructure concept—in a 1973 essay reprinted in 1980's *Problems in Materialism and Culture* as well as in *Marxism and Literature*—remains essential, if only because all materialist thinkers tend to slip toward its hypostatized categories in moments of philosophical panic. This applies even to those who employ the much subtler Gramscian concept of hegemony. Williams has done some of his most useful work classifying what Gramsci calls counter-hegemonic modes: whether "oppositional" or simply "alternative," they're often also "residual" (consider all the apparent conservatives who've made progressive contributions to culture theory) or "emergent" (and probably destined for absorption into an improved hegemony, as in Williams's exemplary "The Bloomsbury Fraction"). His emphasis is on language and culture as material practices ("meaning is always produced; it is never merely expressed") that address "the lost middle term between the abstract entities, 'subject' and 'object,' on which the propositions of idealism and orthodox materialism are erected."

Another way to designate that lost middle term is "experience," a Leavis keyword that means a lot to Williams's leftist contemporaries, particularly E. P. Thompson, but has been rejected on grounds of epistemological instability by upstart British Francophiles. Typically, Williams hasn't hung on to it with anything like Thompson's schismatic stubbornness; where the historian has devoted a book-length essay (a long book-length essay) to an attack on Althusser and his hellspawn, Williams has made a valiant if self-aggrandizing attempt to turn back what I'll call sign-and-structure theory by co-opting it into his own view of culture—*Marxism and Literature* and *The Sociology of Culture* are the relevant texts. Williams's early theoretical impulses clearly prepared him well for the Big Frogs. His nonspecialist fascination with lexicography immunized him against the silly semiotic tendency to treat words as synchronic givens. And he'd devised the term "structure of feeling" to capture that lost middle term long before structuralism had had its covertly idealist way with the best minds of the next generation. From the beginning he's seen it as his mission to get at the synthesis of subject and object without which humane and effective politics are impossible.

But as leftists learn again and again, it's easier to make politics not impossible than to make them possible, and though Williams's activism has been diligent, his political writing has never been as visionary as his cultural writing. Sympathizers to his right and left feel constrained to point out its manifest inconsistencies: this is a man who was still expressing qualified support for Pol Pot in late 1977, but who also believes that a true bicameral legislature would do Britain a world of good. Such positions are difficult enough to support individually, much less in tandem. But as leftists learn again and again, any wise guy can poke holes in other people's ideas—coming up with just one that holds water itself is the hard part. Williams is torn by the same contradictions that rip at all but his most self-deceived or cold-hearted allies: on the one hand he sees that reform has ended up next to nowhere, and on the other hand he sees where revolution's ended up. Because he'd rather risk making a fool of himself than remain mute, he tries to do right by the tactical matter before him without necessarily piecing it into a totally systematic worldview. And if these shifts don't render him the most convincing strategist, they do no dishonor to his articulated experience. This is also a man who's elevated "difficult" into a byword and spent a whole book proving revolution is tragic. There's nothing glibly armchair-Marxist in his willingness to countenance contradictions. He makes you swallow them lumps and all.

And then he complicates them even further. Of course neither reform nor revolution has achieved enough. But Williams has no use for the armchair shibboleth that they've done nothing for people. As he's learned about the role of physical force in Chartism and before, as he's pondered Russia, China, and the third world, his politics have toughened markedly; it's his considered position that, even in Britain, "the condition for the success of the long revolution in any real terms is decisively a short revolution." The evidence of his own experience has been too overwhelming, however, for him to scoff at the progress his class has made since 1688—a progress Williams perceives not in terms of physical comfort but of culture, especially education and the growth of genuine democratic self-confidence among working people. As Eagleton has complained in *Criticism and Ideology*, this awareness does tend to stymie Williams when he gets into tight political questions. But he would never have articulated his experience without it.

There may be reason to fear that Williams's work has peaked. I'm hampered in this judgment because I don't know his late novels, but nothing leads me to believe that Williams's fiction will ever have the impact of his nonfiction. And since *Marxism and Literature*, his nonfiction has skirted both the eccentric and the perfunctory. *The Sociology of Culture* seems as rehashed as *Communications* without the earlier book's modest instructional aura. *Problems in Materialism and Culture* is only a collection by a writer who's never gravitated toward the born essayist's concision and wit, which goes double for *Writing in Society*. Readable though *Politics and Letters* is, you have to know Williams's oeuvre to feel the fascination of its revisions and commentary and autobiography. And *The Year 2000* takes a typical formal leap and falls flat on its face.

The project at hand is an analysis of the crucial decades to come that doesn't credit utopian/dystopian cliches or cede a specious primacy to any determinative force—economic, cultural, political, religious, what-have-you. Williams begins with a searching little disquisition on futurology as a theoretical practice. Then he volunteers to make himself a guinea pig by reprinting for critical examination "Britain in the Sixties," the 25,000-word conclusion of *The Long Revolution*, which holds up well enough to provide a convenient kicking-off place. But Williams never subjects it to the kind of scrutiny we've been led to expect, a scrutiny that might help us think for ourselves about his continuing biases. Instead of a richly self-referential speculation, we get a predictably depressive, predictably undespairing prognosis that's unlikely to read as well in the year 2000 as "Britain in the Sixties" does now. For Williams's lifelong habit of putting culture before comfort is certainly a bias: in his plausible utopia, citizens attend lots of electronic meetings and relegate crass consumer desires to the unenlightened capitalist past. I agree that Williams's theoretical model, the Club of Rome's limits-to-growth analysis, isn't taken seriously enough by the paper profligates of socialist futurology. But I find calls to self-denial less convincing when they come from prophets who indulge their ascetic tendencies to begin with.

A product of the '50s, an era of expansive material well-being, "Britain in the Sixties" tempers sane skepticism with a sense of burgeoning possibility. For this its author has been called wooly-headed, which even if true misses a crucial point: at some deep temperamental level Williams is so dour that without access to optimism he's in danger of becoming unbalanced. As a reader, I take a certain amusement in his grave, graceless refusal to joke around. But I'm a little suspicious of the experience his worldview articulates. For if there is a category missing from this determinedly comprehensive body of work, a human fundamental that rarely seems to cross Williams's mind, it's pleasure—especially, materialist though he may be, physical pleasure.

Williams almost never theorizes about sex, and he really doesn't like Freud much. Sex does, however, play a major role in his bildungsroman, *Second Generation*, which among other things functions as a tract against "the old bourgeois fantasy" of "the personal break-out, through sex"—a theme that both charges and narrows the book. The climactic epiphany comes when the protagonist and his true love go dancing, apparently to rock and roll of some sort. For Williams, this scene is a striking achievement. Despite dribs and drabs of approbation for the symphony here, jazz there, insurgent pop somewhere else, he rarely evinces any feeling for nonverbal art (his awkwardness around painting and sculpture seriously cramps *The Sociology of Culture*). It's also one of the few places in any of his books that this half-witting champion of popular culture seems to enjoy any. True, in the television columns he wrote for *The Listener* at the turn of the '70s, some glimmers of fun flicker through. But even that casual context occasions remarks like: "There are laughs of so many kinds. Those induced don't usually last."

A key to Williams's anti-hedonism is "Advertising: The Magic System," a circa-1959 essay that in its grimly acerbic way is as visionary a piece of left culture theory as Walter Benjamin's "The Work of Art in the Age of Mechanical Reproduction." Williams acknowledges advertising's news function and its crucial ancillary role in the growth of the democratic press, but he loathes what it's become: not merely the instigator of dysfunctional desire but the chief means whereby capitalism deflects attention from its inability to provide basic social needs. It's a devastating account of consumerism as a pathology. But Williams's hostility to consumption is clearly somewhat pathological too, tied as it is to an obsession of his own: production. His refusal of the passive mode is too unbending; his critique of sensationalism verges on the prissy and puritanical. Not only does he find it hard to respect people's right to be lazy, but he won't understand that the modern need to get done, turned on, zapped, even blitzed isn't always the result of media manipulation. In an information-saturated environment that isn't going to get less volatile under any kind of socialism an anti-authoritarian like Williams wants to see, such needs are also legitimate aesthetic responses, often to works by artists who have as much claim to speak for and to working people as he does.

For if Williams is exceptionally curious and open, he's also rather guarded and chauvinistic. Somewhere within him there's a pass-fail affinity meter. If like Burke or Eliot you edge into the black, he'll give you everything's he got. But if you fall short, beware: Williams can be brazenly small-minded about work he doesn't approve of, especially smash middlebrow succés d'estime in which he detects the cynicism virus—*Smiley's People* ("an owlish confirmation of deep inner betrayals") or *The Threepenny Opera* ("cold-hearted muck about the warm-hearted whores and engaging crooks"). He seems virtually unaware that there's any such thing as American literature except in his academic specialty, drama, where he stops at Miller and Williams. He'd no sooner endorse modernism than formalism and doesn't bother himself much with the twentieth-century avant-garde. His astute comments on social marginality proceed from a fascination compounded of clear-eyed sympathy and dark suspicion—this is not a man inclined to believe that anything enduring can emanate from bohemia.

Both his distrust of simple pleasure and his distrust of arty arcana make Williams look like a cultural conservative, and in important respects that's what he is. But there's another way of putting it, as anyone who's absorbed *Culture and Society* should recognize. Like the backward/forward-looking movers of that saga, Williams refuses extremes of bourgeois individualism—both the easy availability of consumer culture and the recondite self-involvement of minority culture. I think this is a mistake. Whatever the perils of these modern/modernist options, they're so vivid for people that much of the century's best art engages them, and if postmodernism turns out to mean anything it will necessarily achieve some synthesis of the two. Still, I also think it's a mistake to dismiss Williams's pet notion of artistic progress, in which the culturally dispossessed find their own voices, arriving at a kind of homely yet formally innovative realism-plus that bears the same relation to Williams's beloved realism that his cultural materialism does to materialism as ordinarily understood. One might even cite quasi-postmodernist art—the Latin American novel, say, or Yookay semipop—that does both these things at once.

In fact, if you were feeling particularly perverse, you could try to squeeze Williams into quasi-postmodernism himself. I don't mean to slight the practical political value of his work, especially since its unstylish usefulness is intrinsic to its aesthetic effect. But I think there's a clue to Williams's hopes for himself (as distinct from the world) in his 1964 essay on that urbane Scots empiricist David Hume, now reprinted in *Writing in Society*. Eagleton has sniffed that Hume would seem "an unlikely candidate" for Williams's praise, given the "anti-intellectualism" of Hume's reversion to direct sensory experience. But Williams makes clear that he shares this kind of anti-intellectualism. He has peered into the abyss of absolute skepticism and decided that if it comes down to a choice between life and metaphysics, he'll take life, thank you very much. And in any case there's an equally pressing if less noble reason for his interest—Hume's neglected stature as pure writer.

Williams tips his hand with an uncharacteristically elegant opening sentence: "In the republic of letters a man can live as himself, but in the bureaucracy of letters he must continually declare his style and department, and submit to an examination of his purpose and credentials at the frontier of every field." He wonders whether Hume should be classified as "moralist, logician, historian, essayist," and then quotes Boswell, who called him "quite simply, 'the greatest Writer in Britain,'" and Hume himself, who described the "Love of literary Fame" as his "ruling Passion." Williams approves, arguing that "we can read Hume, sensibly and centrally, as a writer, and . . . this literary emphasis not only does not weaken his importance as a philosopher, but is even fundamental to it." By now he's plodding like himself again ("weaken his importance" indeed) and thus set apart from Hume's unrepentant hedonism (enough is enough), but he clearly identifies with the philosopher—with his "curiosity and ambition" and his "subtlety of reference not wholly separable from confusion," with his attachment to society and his conviction that a skeptic must always be skeptical of his own skepticism. And also, one must suspect, with his "Love of literary Fame."

Moralist, historian, essayist, sociologist, reviewer, literary scholar, communications theorist, political thinker, Williams refuses to submit his purposes and credentials to the bureaucracy of letters. He feels he's earned the respect he accords Hume—he wants to be seen simply as a writer. But he's not beyond classification: just as it isn't unreasonable to call what Hume does philosophy, it isn't unreasonable to call what Williams does criticism. Williams will object. He can't stand the Leavisite association of "criticism" with consumption-oriented abstractions like "taste," "cultivation," and especially "judgment," all of which separate "response from its real situation and circumstances," and he thinks "the young Marxist anti-realists" are just as bad: "this culture is rotten with criticism." Yet his best writing does respond to other writing, and naturally enough it shows just the salutary sense of context he prescribes—it both engages historical, sociological, political, and philosophical contingencies and candidly originates with a specific individual.

Something like the great Eric Blair character George Orwell, who (as Williams points out) manipulated language to convince us that content determined what words he used, Williams criticizes criticism as he plays the critic-in-spite-of-himself, and while I don't think his reluctant professor is as self-conscious a persona as Blair's decent Englishman, it's clearly a literary creation. If unlike Hume he isn't running for "greatest Writer in Britain," that's only because his distaste for judgment is real—as real as the socialist principles that inspire it. And of course his socialist principles effectively eliminate him from the competition. His natural enemies continue to regard him with respectful condescension, even more for his loyalty to a Marxist tradition that's now counted passé on top of everything else than for his small interest in what Hume called "Elegance and Neatness," which as Williams notes "is what the literary pursuit was often and is still often understood to be." Meanwhile, those allies who continue to honor the great-man theory—and there are many who are secretly quite slavish about it—disqualify him on doctrinal and/or realpolitikal grounds.

Although I wouldn't think of nominating anybody for greatest Writer anywhere, Williams's non-Marxist affinity with Marxism jibes with the promise and broken promises of that great secular religion. What's more,

I say it's determinative economic forces that have prevented him from pulling off another art-action synthesis on the order of *Culture and Society*—his interventions in the popular leftism of the '60s and the elitist leftism of the '70s are realpolitik enough for me. In a lifetime of deeply imaginative, formally adventurous writing, he's made more sense than anyone about the conjunction between art and society, commenting tellingly on an amazing range of other matters while doing so. I wish he were more fun, but I'm not going to make a federal case out of it. I hope he learns to enjoy the occasional cynical laugh before he dies. And I hope he lives to see the revolution—long or short, I don't care.

Village Voice, 1985

With a God on His Side

Terry Eagleton's *Culture and the Death of God*, *Culture*, and *Materialism*

Richard Rorty, the only American cited in all three of the Terry Eagleton books reviewed here, gets just one mention in *Materialism*, but it's such a tell I'll quote Eagleton's sentence whole, nosegay of quotation marks and all: "'Anti-philosophy,' declares Richard Rorty, 'is more unprofessional, funnier, more allusive, sexier, and above all more "written"' than conventional philosophy." What makes this a tell is how aptly it describes Eagleton himself while ostensibly honoring his heart's delight Wittgenstein. And if you doubt that either Wittgenstein or Eagleton is sexy, you've been sandbagged by its faux-pro-forma comparison. Take heart—compared to conventional philosophy, you're probably pretty sexy too.

Whether you're as funny, allusive, or written as Eagleton or Wittgenstein, however, is another matter, and the same goes for yours truly. Eagleton is a wonder—an English professor gone to heaven. A sickly kid born into a poor Irish working-class family in 1943, he was educated Roman Catholic and still very much identifies Christian, although he knows the wrong pope might not concur. He also identifies Marxist, has since he began graduate studies at Cambridge under my heart's delight Raymond Williams. And, he declared as a polemical anti-postmodernist as of 1996's *The Illusions of Postmodernism*.

Eagleton has taught at Oxford and Cambridge, Manchester and Lancaster, Yale and Duke and Iowa, Brigham Young and Notre Dame and Trinity College, and published some forty-five books, one of which, 1983's *Literary Theory*, is said to have sold the better part of a million copies. That was the only one I'd read through till I began with 2016's *Culture*, moved on to 2017's *Materialism*, realized those two obliged me to backtrack to 2014's *Culture and the Death of God*, and then decided I had to stop (but took six more out of the library just in case).

None of these books is lengthy—*Culture* and *Materialism* are each under forty thousand words, while *Culture and the Death of God* and the encyclopedic *Literary Theory* barely top two hundred pages. Moreover, they're easy to read for what they are—Eagleton remains lucid, succinct, and engaging no matter how fine his philosophical distinctions. Take this passage from *Materialism*, a philosophical faith he characterizes thusly: "In the face of a hubristic humanism, it insists on our solidarity with the commonplace stuff of the world, thus cultivating the virtue of humility. Dismayed by the fantasy that human beings are wholly self-determining, it recalls to us our dependence on our surroundings and on each other." Well-put and enlightening, I'd say as something of a materialist myself. Ponder it if you wonder how someone can be a Marxist and a Christian at the same time. But if you merely wonder why Eagleton qualifies as an anti-philosopher, bask in its felicity and leave it at that.

I read *Culture* because I recalled Eagleton fondly long after I'd lost interest in the literary theories *Literary Theory* explains so succinctly, turning my quasi-academic interests instead to the long history of a "pop" that only began to be called that around 1850—an expansive notion that's bound up in Raymond Williams's signature concept, culture. Williams, who is substantively cited although never explored in all these books, is chided gently in *Culture* for his tendency to expand the term from the narrow "body of artistic and intellectual work" through "a process of spiritual and intellectual development" and then "the values, customs, beliefs and symbolic practices by which men and women live" until it finally signifies "a whole way of life."

I'm in the values and customs camp myself, but agree that as Williams holds and Eagleton warns, the concept is perilously elastic. So for a typically witty and wide-ranging first chapter, Eagleton distinguishes between "Culture and Civilization." Civilization, he observes, both antedates culture and codifies it as an idea, which doesn't mean it's always such a great thing—after all, "Only civilised people can place sticks of gelignite in children's playgrounds." Then gradually he folds in such concepts as modernity, nature, art, and desire on his way to establishing two key ideas. First, "'Superfluous' does not necessarily mean 'worthless.' On the contrary, what makes life worth living is not for the most part biologically indispensable to it." Second, "Culture must preserve the vigor and freshness of the natural while curbing its disruptiveness. A paradigm of this is the work of art."

This chapter is such a tour de force I half expected the rest of the book to array illuminating epigrams into a glorious whole. But it was not to be. Eagleton comes less to praise culture than to bury both culture in the genteel sense and the cultural studies youngbloods who make it their business to torpedo its pretensions, competing strains he packs into a single epigram: "the opium of the intelligentsia." Glossing Burke, Herder, Wilde, and Wittgenstein and adding commentary from Marx and occasionally Nietzsche—all anti-philosophers, all favorites of Eagleton despite the highly un-Marxist politics of Burke, Wittgenstein, and especially Nietzsche—he honors culture-as-art's vigor and freshness as he details just what enlightenment he's taken from such canonical artists as Swift, Blake, Coleridge, Mann, and Lawrence. But he also pinpoints culture-as-art's blind spot: "It is a moral, personal or spiritual affair, aloof for the most part from the material realm of famines and economic slumps, genocide and women's oppression." About cultural studies, "where in some quarters culture has become a way of not talking about capitalism," he's less measured—it "deals in sexuality but not socialism, transgression but not revolution, difference but not justice, identity but not the culture of poverty." Diversity's not an absolute good, he insists (although ecologists disagree, for impeccably materialist reasons). Social change requires solidarity, not difference.

Functionally a long postscript to the heftier *Culture and the Death of God*, *Culture* left me feeling that Eagleton is more peeved by his left-claiming adversaries in academia than is good for the class struggle. In part this obviously reflects all the ways the succor and solidarity I've found in popular music have helped make my life worth living, and thinking about. Although Eagleton allows that "much popular culture is of superb quality," he never tells us what if anything he's learned from it, and I doubt he rooted for the circa-1970 cultural studies tendency in UK academe as hard as I did. I also doubt he's much more put off than I am by the fussy hermeticism that befell it. Yet he clearly isn't inclined to see how invaluable the historico-sociological research cultural studies has engendered remains after you sift out the lefter-than-thou chaff. Which is probably why *Materialism* sat better with me.

After the extraordinary bit about materialism's moral imperative quoted above, *Materialism* sets off once more into the pomo swamps as Eagleton spends nine pages decrying a post-whatever "New Materialism" previously unknown to me in which matter "is rescued from the humiliation of being matter." Then he grumps briefly about Williams's cultural materialism (the sociology of art rebranded), '70s semantic materialism (Wittgenstein is deployed to take care of that one), and Quentin Meillassoux's speculative materialism, which Eagleton goes on about because he has it in for Meillassoux's project of a bulwark against theism—against the possibility that there is a God. Although I struggled hard to achieve my own atheism and remain devout in that faith, I'd say Eagleton smokes him.

Granted, I'd never heard of Meillassoux, and you probably haven't either. Conventional philosophers, a tiny cabal, no doubt have. But as an anti-philosopher, Eagleton isn't writing for them except by the bye. He's writing for curious outsiders like me and probably you. So as in *Culture*, *Materialism* performs the trick of examining the topic at hand through other philosophers' conceptual apparatus: Aquinas, Marx, Nietzsche, and Wittgenstein again. This particular trick is rendered trickier by the unlikelihood of every choice except Marx, whose main commonality with master theologian Aquinas, deranged anti-humanist Nietzsche, and evolved logical positivist Wittgenstein is genius of a magnitude that dwarfs even Burke's, Herder's, and Wilde's—plus, Eagleton wants us to know, their materialism. I don't have the space to outline Eagleton's arguments, which is just as well because I probably don't have the brains either. But I predict that if the idea of *Materialism* intrigues you, so will the real thing. Above all it celebrates the centrality for human beings of the human body in all its vulnerability, impermanence, and ability to connect us to the rest of matter via the sense organs—although not enough, I'd say, in its capacity for the superfluous pleasures that help make life worth living.

The human body is also the intellectual hero of the trilogy's thesis statement, *Culture and the Death of God*. Basically a history of atheism, a word Eagleton reports only entered English in the 1500s and insists took centuries to establish itself as a living mindset, it's typically informative as intellectual history. Enlightenment skeptics, he observes, targeted "priestcraft rather than the Almighty," "a political rather than a theological affair" conceived by ruling-class intellectuals "to oust a barbarous, benighted faith in favour of a rational, civilised one." Although hampered by the "naively rationalist faith that ideas are what men and women live by"—a point, Democrats please note, Eagleton harps on—most of them accepted religion on the grounds that "the scepticism of the educated must learn not to unsettle the superstition of the populace." Bang: "Secular social orders thus have a problem with their moral rationales." Boom: "Liberalism and Utilitarianism do not fare well as symbolic forms."

The Idealists, the Romantics, and their many progeny fail to escape this dilemma, although Lord knows they try. "Reason, Nature, *Geist*, culture, art, the sublime, the nation, the state, science, humanity, Being, Society, the Other, desire, the life force and personal relations: all of these have acted from time to time as forms of displaced divinity," Eagleton declares, and although *Culture and the Death of God* doesn't touch all these bases, it comes close enough on its way to achieving its grand conclusion—that neither culture as a single concept nor a profusion of mutually tolerant subcultures can provide the moral rationale human beings require. As in *Culture*, I was especially struck by his account of the nearly forgotten Johann Herder, an eighteenth-century cleric from a poor family whose early embrace of German nationalism joined with his unprecedented notion of folk culture and his God-given empathy to render him the first multiculturalist. I was struck too by a point Eagleton likes to make—that in the sentence before Marx calls religion "the opium of the people" he also calls it "the heart of a heartless world."

Although I accept Eagleton's conclusion that where modernism experienced the death of God as a tragedy postmodernism doesn't experience it at all, his anti-postmodernist carping gets tired. And in this book especially his provincialism is irksome—crucial Americans from James Madison to Martin Luther King are MIA, which I hope reminds you that people of color have been strangely absent from this review. That's because the only writers of color these books even mention is Salman Rushdie and a philosopher he whales on named Rey Chow (who's also one of the few women cited). There's no James Baldwin, no Henry Louis Gates, no Paul Gilroy, and indeed no Stuart Hall, the Anglo-Jamaican who pretty much invented cultural studies and does get a nice appreciation in the Eagleton collection *Figures of Dissent*. This troubles me because my own inexpert but intense and lifelong pondering of the philosophical conundrums Eagleton addresses has been so deeply inflected by the earned life force of African-American writers and, of course, musicians—as were, I can't not mention, the more expert theorizing of two dead friends and major influences of mine, Marshall Berman and Ellen Willis, both committed Marxians if not Marxists, Berman more scornful than Eagleton of poststructuralist fiddle-faddle and Willis almost as much. I hope he's checked them out.

One reason I'm such a firm atheist is that my belief system was constructed against the headwinds of a Protestant fundamentalism Eagleton regards with unseemly contempt—it's bad all right, foul sometimes, Christianist I like to call it, but with exceptions and qualifications more complex and numerous than most leftists have the agape to imagine. My moral values and particularly my empathy derive in part from my church youth—"faith, hope, and charity, but the greatest of these is charity." But since I share them actively with a wife who was raised agnostic, I've come to believe they redound more to warm and decent parents, fulfilling work and love, and the psychochemistry I was born with, all of which might also be called my luck, and that this kind of luck is the world's best hope.

My guess is that Eagleton enjoyed similar advantages. But in addition he makes use of a God this atheist found inspirational—a God who proves his love for humanity by inhabiting one of those human bodies *Materialism* makes so much of, and dying in it. That body belonged to a "scruffy, plebeian first-century Jew," "a political criminal," "a prophet who was tortured and executed by the imperial powers for speaking up for justice, and whose followers must be prepared to meet the same fate." I don't have much faith in the practical viability of a Christianity that keeps St. Paul and the Book of Revelation on the down-low. But if Christianity so defined helps Terry Eagleton make the most of his luck, that makes his luck ours and renders his faith a compelling enough moral rationale by me.

Barnes & Noble Review, 2017

My Friend Marshall

Marshall Berman's *Modernism in the Streets: A Life and Times in Essays*

A funny thing happened after the *Village Voice* published my *All That Is Solid Melts into Air* rave in 1982. The author called me up, and within months we became such fast friends that three decades later I found myself delivering a eulogy that nabbed me the only *Dissent* byline of my career. Not that it was all that strange Marshall Berman called—he often telephoned people he knew slightly if at all, including me several times before then. And obviously there was nothing humorous about the sudden loss of a seventy-two-year-old polymath whose intellectual fecundity was unimpaired by that dent in his skull, souvenir of the botched 1989 brain abscess operation his second wife browbeat the hospital into fixing. Nor, I should add, did my eulogy close an SRO funeral. That honor went to Marshall's second son, Elijah Tax-Berman, a blunt twenty-nine-year-old I'd known since he left the incubator. His flow leaning Run-D.M.C., Eli nailed it. At the cemetery, he was still shoveling dirt into his father's grave after the rest of us fell back.

Marshall's call came during the crucial turning point of a life that was pretty tumultuous for someone who resided in one West End Avenue apartment and taught at one no longer free public university for all the time I knew him. Professionally, the turning point was a triumph. Although Marshall's masterwork was assigned a supercilious pan in the *New York Times Book Review*, *All That Is Solid* enjoyed a trajectory more in keeping with the fondly skeptical daily *Times* review John Leonard ended with the perfect "I love this book and wish that I believed it." Spurned in France and Germany but translated into many humbler tongues, it made him a hero in Brazil, Norway, and other nations where socialism had a life. Personally, however, the turning point was a catastrophe: the December 1980 murder of Marshall's five-year-old son Marc by his first wife, who threw the child out of their fifth-floor window and then jumped herself, only he died and she didn't. That, Marshall explained on the phone, was why he hadn't called in a while.

This nightmare had been in the news and on the gossip networks, but I'd missed it, and having struggled for years to conceive a child with my wife, I was primed to listen. So after an hour-plus of talk we made a date to meet. Marshall was already on his way to marrying novelist Meredith Tax, who hit it off with my wife, and for several years the four of us enjoyed a wealth of movies, museum shows, and mutually prepared meals together. Culturally, Marshall usually set the agenda, and to reciprocate I made him rap mixtapes and hooked him up at *The Village Voice*, where over the years he wrote about Georg Lukács and Public Enemy, artists' housing and "urbicide." By 1985 Eli's difficult birth and our daughter's overdue adoption had put us into play-date mode, which continued after Meredith's tumultuous side ended the marriage. Soon commenced a romance with not altogether untumultuous English teacher Shellie Sclan, who married Marshall in 1993. Play-date dynamics having evolved, we hung out less after Marshall's third son, Danny Berman, was born in 1994. But whenever the phone rang late, my default surmise was that it was Marshall, tracking down a detail or raring to schmooze.

Emotional, enthusiastic, interested in everything, Marshall Berman had more to give intellectually than anyone I've ever met. His erudition was so vast and his recall so phenomenal that I came to depend on him for background on non-musical subjects; pre-Google, a local call would tell me what I needed to know, and unlike Wikipedia, Marshall was available for questions. As a Marxist humanist he was nominally to my left, but day-to-day our politics were congruent, and we were both committed family men who regularly discussed the pleasures and tsouris of that way of life. But deep though our friendship was, I never entered his world—an almost exclusively Jewish post-'60s left I couldn't triangulate today except to say that it wasn't altogether congruent with the board of *Dissent*, his intellectual home base. In a way, however, this degree of separation cemented our bond. Without Marshall I wouldn't have read Goethe's *Elective Affinities* as I theorized romantic monogamy; without me, he wouldn't have heard *It Takes a Nation of Millions to Hold Us Back* pre-release at the beach. And although he worked with many *Voice* editors, I was the one who assigned the 1995 Times Square piece that in 2006 flowered after much labor into Marshall's third full-length book.

On the Town is a wide-ranging, deep-diving, exhaustively researched meditation on Times Square that kvells about the Broadway theater of Marshall's youth while advocating for "mass culture," his term, in all its bedazzling strut—his praise for a Benetton sign depicting six near-nude young models of cunningly varied racial identity could have been designed to put old lefties off their feed. It also celebrates many fictional and real-life women, most of them physically beautiful and/or materially powerful, while taking down both the vicious sexism of the Deuce and Laura Mulvey's explicitly anhedonic attack on the male gaze with equal vigor. It thinks about sailors and developers, *Sister Carrie* and *The Jazz Singer*, *Fancy Free* and *Taxi Driver*. It has its gaffes, and in no way surpasses *All That Is Solid*—masterworks are by their nature insurpassable. But its conceptual daring deserved much better than it got from the culturati.

Marshall was passionate about teaching, and CUNY too, but he was a writer first—a writer bent on giving pleasure and doing good. With sleep apnea among his many ailments, he wrote all the time—the morning of his death he was working on a book about Jerusalem and Athens, Paris and New York called *The Romance of Public Space*. And because he loved to write, he took on lots of shorter work, crafting essays, reviews, and lectures that consumed much of his literary energy. Eager to follow up *All That Is Solid*, he only came to terms with this compulsion when he dreamed up the rubric "adventures in Marxism," the title under which Verso assembled sixteen of his essays in 1999, proving to him that, to quote the introduction, "a writer could say something, without saying *everything*." It led with a tale he'd longed to tell about his father, a garment-district schlepper turned *Women's Wear Daily* reporter-salesman who suffered a second and fatal heart attack at forty-seven, five years after the one that ensued when a partner absconded with the capital of a rag-trade magazine they'd co-founded. Before too long, Marshall explained, that trauma occasioned his immersion in Marx's humanistic, then-obscure *Economic and Philosophic Manuscripts*. Suspending Isaac Babel and Studs Terkel as well as Walter Benjamin and *To the Finland Station* from its Marx hook, *Adventures in Marxism* is palpably *conceived*—as editors are always imploring, it "works as a book." We're fortunate it exists.

Marshall died fourteen years after *Adventures in Marxism*, which worked as a book by excluding many essays that didn't suit its concept. So it was inevitable that his widow, heir, and literary executor would plan a posthumous collection. But for emotional as well as financial reasons, Shellie Sclan needed to keep teaching; she had a son to get through SUNY Purchase and was working with Columbia to archive her late husband's books and papers. So having devised a tentative table of contents, she enlisted the help of *Dissent* editor David Marcus, who turned out to have his own ideas. Where Sclan's selections began with the autobiographical introduction to *Adventures in Marxism* and included three more of its picks, one too many I'd say, eight of *Modernism in the Streets: A Life and Times in Essays'* twenty-four chapters, a full third of it, also appear in the earlier book.

Modernism in the Streets is nonetheless a thorough, affecting, and intellectually powerful document—the Berman to read after *All That Is Solid* bowls you over. That it wasn't reviewed anywhere near widely enough could reflect the hegemony of the "theory"-driven post-humanism Marshall opposed, which was one excuse. But the fact that the new book wasn't all that new couldn't have helped—nor its implicit assumption that the Marshall Berman whose legacy the posthumous volume was supposed to cement had barely evolved from the proper left intellectual who gave the world *All That Is Solid*, which claims high culture for progressive politics as if buttering up a *Partisan Review* it then leads onto the Cross-Bronx Expressway. Marshall the tie-dyed hippie who wrote the 1974 Faust-meets-Mick-Jagger screed "Sympathy for the Devil" for *New American Review* was altogether absent. And if Sclan hadn't advocated for Al Jolson, Marshall the omnivore who devoted years to *On the Town* would have been too.

That said, however, the previously uncollected two-thirds is choice, including sanely visionary 1965 and 1971 political interventions published in *Dissent* and, yes, *Partisan Review*, a jaw-droppingly evenhanded 1975

Ramparts piece about *All That Is Solid* villain Robert Moses, and daringly down-to-earth ’oos essays about Jewish fabulist Franz Kafka, in his day job “one of the most creative bureaucrats of the century,” and Turkish novelist Orhan Pamuk, in Marshall’s view a fellow battler against “modernist anti-modernism” whose protagonists in *Snow* are a man and woman in love struggling for a life Marshall calls “unheroic, ordinary, ‘normal’”—a life he suggests is typified these days by interracial couples “schlepping their babies around in ultra-modern snugglies” “in all sorts of American places I and Pamuk have never heard of.”

In an introduction that warmly praises Marshall’s “humanist exuberance, his vision of a feeling Left,” editor Marcus judges the Pamuk essay one of Marshall’s “late classics.” But where Marcus applauds Pamuk for holding that “something about modern life seems to stop us from loving,” Marshall argues that the failure of *Snow*’s lovers to escape together to Germany’s promised land is an anomaly—a “last-minute plot intervention by the author” that reflects Pamuk the novelist’s belief that “stories of love crushed are more poignant than stories of love fulfilled.” Then he adds: “But there’s a difference between the logic of a story and the logic of history. At the start of the twenty-first century, our history may be more open than our literature.”

Accounting himself “troubled” by Berman’s failure to see that *Snow* “revealed the deeper sorrow of modern experience—our inability to connect with one another,” is Marcus himself expounding a “modernist anti-modernism”? I say this dead-in-the-water alienation bromide exemplifies it. Yet I do wonder why neither literary leftist mentions that the encompassing preoccupation of *Snow* is the impenetrable yet also poignant complexity of “Islamism.” And were he alive I’d yell at Marshall that that’s not a “plot intervention,” it’s the plot itself, where this particular meditation on the contradictions of Islam has always been going, and then point out to Marcus that this particular “one another” comprises two complex characters, one of them a porn-addicted cosmopolitan litterateur who rejected the Islam of his youth as a student and ended up far more fucked up about sex than the provincial divorcee he adores. But to take my take home I’d also mention that at the end of *Modernism in the Streets*, as Marcus is well aware, Shellie Sclan gets her own brief section, complete with an introduction that gives *On the Town* its props and then explains that Marshall’s summum will end with two selections from *The Romance of Public Space*: the published version of “Emerging from the Ruins,” the 2013 Lewis Mumford Lecture on Urbanism at CUNY that proved his final public address, and “The Bible and Public

Space," which he was still revising a few hours before a heart attack killed him instantly on September 11 of that year.

As someone who grew up on the King James Bible and reread Genesis plus commentary to review Robert Crumb's 2010 version of that quintessentially foundational work, I hereby report that nowhere in my research did I encounter anything as comic or bemused as Marshall's vision of it—certainly not in Crumb himself. Marshall takes every holy word at face value, yet he's devoid of reverence—not to show off or shock, but because for him Genesis stands as one more philosophically redolent literary text ripe for interpretation. Hence Adam, Eve, and a guy named God are all characters in a confusing tale that, if you'll recall, begins with two different versions of the Judeo-Christian creation myth. But it's a love story nonetheless.

In an afterword to the 2010 British edition of *All That Is Solid*, Marshall writes: "One human right that seems to embarrass both academic and political writers, who often leave it out, but that real people know is crucial to living a good life in the modern world, is the *right to love*. I have written about love (see Gretchen and Faust in Chapter One, and see *The Politics of Authenticity*), but not enough; I will write about it now, in my old age." In the Genesis essay he begins to keep that promise. Among other things, Marshall observes that once God has created Eve he knows he's got trouble on his hands, not because Eve is sure to eat that apple but because she's competition—someone else for Adam to talk to. Why do Adam and Eve cover their genitals? Embarrassment? Maybe not. Maybe it's because they've already figured out that the pull of that joystick and whoopee cushion are so powerful the couple could end up loving each other more than they love God. Which given the pickle God's put them in may be all He deserves: "The couple's survival seems to depend on knowledge. But what are they supposed to know? What are they *not* supposed to know? 'Good and evil'? But isn't God also saying that their knowledge itself is evil? How can they know what they shouldn't know if they don't already know it? Adam and Eve have a lot to work out. Can anybody help them? Probably not in any Jewish, Christian, or Islamic establishment."

Writing about *Crime and Punishment* once, I found myself irritated by the way Harold Bloom and ilk dismissed the afterword, in which Raskolnikov is saved by his pure love for the prostitute Sonia. So naturally I called Marshall, and learned that he loved that ending too, at least until Dostoyevsky's sufferer-murderer went all Christlike on him. Soon we were talking about how poorly served romantic love has been in so-called serious discourse, and Marshall told me that he planned someday to write a book about it. And on the day he died, as he redefined the Garden of Eden instead, human beings' propensity to love each other was nonetheless on his capacious mind.

Previously unpublished, 2018

Index